Expanding the Canon

Directly addressing the underrepresentation of Black composers in core music curricula, *Expanding the Canon: Black Composers in the Music Theory Classroom* aims to both demonstrate why diversification is badly needed and help faculty expand their teaching with practical, classroom-oriented lesson plans that focus on teaching music theory with music by Black composers.

This collection of 21 chapters is loosely arranged to resemble a typical music theory curriculum, with topics progressing from basic to advanced and moving from fundamentals, diatonic harmony, and chromatic harmony to form, popular music, and music of the twentieth and twenty-first centuries. Some chapters focus on segments of the traditional music theory sequence, while others consider a single style or composer. Contributors address both methods to incorporate the music of Black composers into familiar topics, and ways to rethink and expand the purview of the music theory curriculum. A foreword by Philip Ewell and an introductory narrative by Teresa L. Reed describing her experiences as an African American student of music set the volume in wider context.

Incorporating a wide range of examples by composers across classical, jazz, and popular genres, this book helps bring the rich and varied body of music by Black composers into the core of music theory pedagogy and offers a vital resource for all faculty teaching music theory and analysis.

Melissa Hoag (she/her/hers) is Associate Professor of music theory at Oakland University in Rochester, Michigan, where she has served as Coordinator of music theory since 2007. She has taught all levels of undergraduate and graduate music theory and aural skills, as well as courses on counterpoint, form, and twentieth- and twenty-first-century music. Her publications on counterpoint, pedagogy, and voice leading in Brahms have appeared in *BACH*, *Music Theory Online*, *Journal of Music Theory Pedagogy*, *Gamut*, *Dutch Journal of Music Theory*, and *The Routledge Companion to Music Theory Pedagogy* (ed. VanHandel). She serves as reviews editor for *Journal of Music Theory Pedagogy* and is a Question Leader for the AP music theory exam. In addition to a PhD in music theory, she also holds a certificate in Diversity and Inclusion through Cornell University.

Expanding the Canon
Black Composers in the Music Theory Classroom

Edited by Melissa Hoag

NEW YORK AND LONDON

Designed cover image: antishock/Shutterstock.com

First published 2023
by Routledge
605 Third Avenue, New York, NY 10158

and by Routledge
4 Park Square, Milton Park, Abingdon, Oxon, OX14 4RN

Routledge is an imprint of the Taylor & Francis Group, an informa business

© 2023 selection and editorial matter, Melissa Hoag; individual chapters, the contributors

The right of Melissa Hoag to be identified as the author of the editorial material, and of the authors for their individual chapters, has been asserted in accordance with sections 77 and 78 of the Copyright, Designs and Patents Act 1988.

All rights reserved. No part of this book may be reprinted or reproduced or utilised in any form or by any electronic, mechanical, or other means, now known or hereafter invented, including photocopying and recording, or in any information storage or retrieval system, without permission in writing from the publishers.

Trademark notice: Product or corporate names may be trademarks or registered trademarks, and are used only for identification and explanation without intent to infringe.

Library of Congress Cataloging-in-Publication Data
Names: Hoag, Melissa E., editor.
Title: Expanding the canon : black composers in the music theory classroom / edited by Melissa Hoag.
Description: New York : Routledge, 2023. | Includes bibliographical references and index.
Identifiers: LCCN 2022033858 (print) | LCCN 2022033859 (ebook) | ISBN 9781032068282 (hardback) | ISBN 9781032068275 (paperback) | ISBN 9781003204053 (ebook)
Subjects: LCSH: Music theory—Instruction and study. | Music by black composers—Analysis, appreciation. | Culturally relevant pedagogy.
Classification: LCC MT6 .E9825 2023 (print) | LCC MT6 (ebook) | DDC 781.071—dc23/eng/20220930
LC record available at https://lccn.loc.gov/2022033858
LC ebook record available at https://lccn.loc.gov/2022033859

ISBN: 978-1-032-06828-2 (hbk)
ISBN: 978-1-032-06827-5 (pbk)
ISBN: 978-1-003-20405-3 (ebk)

DOI: 10.4324/9781003204053

Typeset in Sabon LT Pro
by Apex CoVantage, LLC

Access the companion website: www.routledge.com/cw/hoag

For my son, Atticus, who inspires me to dream big.

Contents

Acknowledgments	x
List of Contributors	xi
Foreword	xv
PHILIP EWELL	
Introduction	1
MELISSA HOAG	
1 Our Field at Its Best	7
TERESA L. REED	

PART ONE
Fundamentals and Diatonic Harmony 13

2 Rethinking Music Fundamentals: Centering the Contributions of Black Musicians	15
UZEE BROWN JR.	
3 Change from the Middle, Right from the Beginning: Strategies for Incorporating Black Composers in a Music Fundamentals Course	22
ROBIN ATTAS	
4 Rhiannon Giddens and Francis "Frank" Johnson in the First-Year Theory Classroom	28
JAN MIYAKE	
5 From Counterpoint to Small Forms: A Cross-Stylistic Approach to Centering Black Artists in the Theory Core	40
KRISTINA L. KNOWLES AND NICHOLAS J. SHEA	

PART TWO
Chromaticism and Other Advanced Topics — 55

6 Modal Mixture — 57
MITCHELL OHRINER

7 "Elite Syncopations" and "Euphonic Sounds": Scott Joplin in the Aural Skills Classroom — 72
AMY FLEMING

8 Modulation — 81
ALAN REESE

PART THREE
Form — 97

9 A Jazz-Specific Lens: Methodological Diversity in the Music Theory Core — 99
BEN GEYER

10 Of Simple Forms and Firsts: On Francis Johnson and Harry Burleigh — 109
HORACE J. MAXILE, JR.

11 A Trio of Art Songs on Texts by Langston Hughes — 119
MELISSA HOAG

12 Teaching Sonatas Beyond "Mostly Mozart" — 129
AARON GRANT AND CATRINA KIM

PART FOUR
Popular Music — 147

13 Expanding the Scope of Analysis in the Popular Music Classroom — 149
ZACHARY ZINSER

14 Formal Structures and Narrative Design in Janelle Monáe's *The ArchAndroid* — 163
CORA S. PALFY

15 Diving Deeper into Rhythm and Meter Through Drum Parts in Twenty-First-Century Pop — 178
DAVID GEARY

16 Developing Contemporary Rhythm Skills Through
    Contemporary R&B   190
    TREVOR DE CLERCQ

17 Structural Shifts and Identity in Music by Ester Rada   201
    ROSA ABRAHAMS

PART FIVE
Twentieth-Century Music   213

18 Inclusivity and the "Perfect Teaching Piece"
    in the Undergraduate Post-Tonal Classroom   215
    CARA STROUD

19 Dream Variations: An Analytical Exploration of Florence
    Price's "My Dream"   226
    LEIGH VANHANDEL

20 Teaching Twentieth-Century Stylistic Pluralism Through
    the Music of George Walker   239
    OWEN BELCHER

21 Teaching Julia Perry's *Homunculus C.F.*   256
    KENDRA PRESTON LEONARD

    Index   265

Acknowledgments

I am grateful to so many people for their help and guidance throughout this project. First, I must thank my family. My husband Bret and my son Atticus gave me space to work, despite the fact that all of us were at home due to the pandemic for a large chunk of the process, and provided lots of encouragement, humor, and needed distractions. I wish to thank my valued colleagues, Sarah Komer and Stephen Komer, for completing the book's indexing, as well as Deborah Vanderlinde, interim Director of the School of Music, Theatre and Dance, for facilitating generous monetary support through the SMTD. I also wish to thank several close friends, who served as sounding boards and offered moral support and encouragement – you know who you are.

To Mitchell Ohriner: thank you for being incredibly generous with your time, wisdom, and feedback.

To Philip Ewell: thank you for agreeing to write a foreword to this book. I am immensely grateful for, and humbled by, your collegiality and willingness to lend your time and scholarly energies to this project.

To my friend, the amazing Teresa Reed: thank you for sharing your story in this collection.

This book would not have happened without the support of Routledge editor Genevieve Aoki, whose enthusiasm and calm responses to my many emails enabled me to bring this project to fruition in a reasonable timeframe.

Finally, to the brilliant contributors to this volume: I have learned so much from your thoughtful and inspiring chapters, and for those of you whom I've never met, I hope we can meet in person soon.

Contributors

Rosa Abrahams (she/her/hers) is Assistant Professor of music at Ursinus College, where she coordinates the music theory curriculum. Her research is interdisciplinary, centering on analytical approaches to oral tradition musics and the integration of music analysis and ethnographic methods. She works primarily with embodied musical experiences in Jewish and Greek Orthodox liturgical settings, as well as studying embodiment in music theory pedagogy, music cognition, and music philosophy. She holds a PhD and MMus in music theory and cognition from Northwestern University, and a BMus in music theory from the Eastman School of Music.

Robin Attas (she/her/hers) is a White settler music theorist living and working in Treaty 1 territory at the Centre for the Advancement of Teaching and Learning of the University of Manitoba. As an educational developer with a focus on equity, diversity, and inclusion, Robin supports inclusive teaching and learning practices among faculty, staff, and students across campus. Robin remains active as a music theory researcher, presenting and publishing on various topics intersecting with music theory pedagogy, including popular music analysis, social justice, and decolonizing and indigenizing music theory teaching and research.

Owen Belcher is Assistant Professor of Music Theory at the University of Missouri–Kansas City Conservatory. Prior to his appointment at UMKC, he was Lecturer of music theory at the University of Massachusetts–Amherst. In addition to music theory pedagogy, his research interests include the history of theory, the music of J. S. Bach, and the music of Caroline Shaw.

Uzee Brown Jr. is Chair of the Division of Creative and Performing Arts at Morehouse College, former Chair of Music at Clark Atlanta University, and former Director of Atlanta's historic Ebenezer Baptist Church Choir. His diverse career as educator, performer, composer/arranger, and choral director has taken him to 27 countries. Brown holds a BA degree from Morehouse College, an MM degree from Bowling Green State University, and MM and DMA degrees from the University of Michigan. As a veteran educator and composer, he has works that have been performed internationally and at important music centers in the United States, including in Alice Tully and Avery Fisher Halls, the National Cathedral, Severance Hall, and Carnegie Hall.

Trevor de Clercq is Associate Professor in the Department of Recording Industry at Middle Tennessee State University, where he coordinates the musicianship curriculum and teaches coursework in audio theory and sound recording. His research centers on ways that contemporary popular music departs from traditional music theory frameworks, often as shown through empirical methods. His *Nashville Number System Fake Book*, which includes charts for 200 acclaimed country songs, was published in 2015. He holds a PhD in music theory from the Eastman School of Music, as well as degrees in music technology and electronics engineering technology.

Philip Ewell is Professor of music theory at Hunter College, where he serves as Director of graduate studies in the Music Department. His specialties include Russian music theory, Russian opera, modal theory, and race studies in music. His work has been featured in news outlets such as the BBC, *Die Zeit*, NPR, the *New York Times*, the *New Yorker*, and WQXR's Aria Code. He recently finished a monograph, *On Music Theory, And Making Music More Welcoming for Everyone*, which will appear with the University of Michigan Press in early 2023. He is also under contract at W.W. Norton to coauthor a new music theory textbook, *The Engaged Musician: Theory and Analysis for the Twenty-First Century*, which will be a modernized, reframed, and inclusive work based on recent developments in music theory pedagogy.

Amy Fleming is Lecturer in music theory at Baylor University. Her research interests lie primarily in the music of the twentieth and twenty-first centuries, as well as theory pedagogy. She has published her pedagogical research in the *Journal of Music Theory Pedagogy* and presented at the *Pedagogy Into Practice* conference. Her recent research focuses on George Crumb, post-tonal pedagogy, the science of learning, and error detection in the aural skills curriculum. She earned a PhD in theory from the Eastman School of Music.

David Geary is Assistant Professor of music at Wake Forest University, where he teaches undergraduate courses in music theory and music history. He earned his PhD from Indiana University and previously taught at Oberlin College and Conservatory. David's research interests include popular music, rhythm and meter, and music theory pedagogy. His published work appears in the *Journal of Music Theory Pedagogy* and *The Routledge Companion to Music Theory Pedagogy*. He has also served as editor of the *Indiana Theory Review*.

Ben Geyer is Associate Professor of music theory and Director of jazz studies at the University of West Georgia. He has taught at the University of Kentucky, where he earned his PhD in music theory, as well as the Oberlin College Conservatory. Geyer's article "Maria Schneider's Forms: Norms and Deviations in a Contemporary Jazz Corpus" won the David Kraehenbuehl Prize from the *Journal of Music Theory*. He has released two jazz albums as a pianist and bandleader.

Aaron Grant (PhD Eastman, 2018) is currently Assistant Professor of music theory at Missouri Western State University. His research engages issues of form, narrative, and meaning in nineteenth-century music as well as music theory pedagogy. Aaron is currently working on a forthcoming textbook under contract with W.W. Norton tentatively titled "The Engaged Musician: Theory and Analysis for the 21st Century," co-authored with Rosa Abrahams, Philip Ewell, and Cora S. Palfy. His work can be seen in *Music Theory Spectrum*, the *Journal of Music Theory Pedagogy*, *Nineteenth-Century Music Review*, and *Engaging Students*.

Melissa Hoag (she/her/hers) is Associate Professor of music theory at Oakland University in Rochester, Michigan, where she has served as coordinator of music theory since 2007. She has taught all levels of undergraduate and graduate music theory and aural skills, as well as courses on counterpoint, form, and twentieth- and twenty-first-century music. Her publications on counterpoint, pedagogy, and voice leading in Brahms have appeared in *BACH*, *Music Theory Online*, *Journal of Music Theory Pedagogy*, *Gamut*, *Dutch Journal of Music Theory*, and *The Routledge Companion to Music Theory Pedagogy* (ed. VanHandel). She serves as reviews editor for *Journal of Music Theory Pedagogy* and is Question Leader for the AP music theory exam. In addition to a PhD in music theory, she also holds a certificate in Diversity and Inclusion through Cornell University.

Catrina Kim is Assistant Professor of music theory at the University of North Carolina at Greensboro and completed her PhD in music theory at the Eastman School of Music. Her research interests include form in early romantic music – in particular the music of Fanny Hensel – feminist and queer theories, and issues in labor, diversity, and equity in music theory teaching. Her work on these issues appears in *Music Theory Spectrum* and *Theory and Practice* (forthcoming).

Kristina L. Knowles is Assistant Professor of music theory at Arizona State University, where she teaches undergraduate and graduate courses on music theory and cognition. An interdisciplinary scholar, she has work that combines research in music theory, philosophy, and psychology around questions of rhythm and meter in twentieth-century music, perception, and the relationship between time and music.

Kendra Preston Leonard is a musicologist and theorist whose work focuses on women and music in the twentieth and twenty-first centuries and music and screen history. She is the founder of the Julia Perry Working Group and the founder and executive director of the Silent Film Sound and Music Archive. Leonard is the author of numerous scholarly books and articles, including those on composer Louise Talma and music for silent film.

Horace J. Maxile, Jr. is Associate Professor of music theory at Baylor University. His primary research interests center on concert music by African American composers and musical signification. These interests and others are explored in articles in *Journal of the Society for American Music, Annual Review of Jazz Studies*, and *Perspectives of New Music* (among other venues). He has served as Editor of the *Black Music Research Journal*, Chair of the Society for Music Theory Committee on Diversity, Member of the American Musicological Society Council, and Member of the Society for American Music Board of Trustees.

Jan Miyake is Associate Professor of music theory at Oberlin College Conservatory, where she chairs the music theory division and leads the curriculum and pedagogy subcommittee of the presidential initiative on racial equity and diversity. She publishes on the topics of corpus studies, Haydn's instrumental works, *Formenlehre*, linear analysis, and inclusive pedagogy. After being elected Treasurer of the Society for Music Theory (2015–19), Miyake was recently appointed Chair of its Committee on the Status of Women (2021–23). She is a founding member of the Composers of Color Resource Project, which uses Humanities Commons to store, organize, and publicize its resources.

Mitchell Ohriner is Associate Professor of music theory at the University of Denver. There he teaches core music theory courses, seminars on modal counterpoint, pedagogy, rhythm and meter, and popular music analysis and nonmajor courses on hip-hop and the psychology of music preference. His research on computational music analysis and rap music is detailed in the monograph *Flow: The Rhythmic Voice in Rap Music*, available from Oxford University Press. Other writings can be found in *Music Theory Online, Empirical Musicology Review, The Journal of New Music Research*, and in edited volumes. Since 2021, he has served as Editor in Chief of *Music Theory Online*.

Cora S. Palfy is Associate Professor at Elon University, where she researches a blend of music cognition and music theory. Palfy's research examines how music expresses and engages human behaviors and traits and the way these phenomena encourage listeners to form relationships with music or the performers playing it. She is the author of numerous journal articles, the book *Musical Agency and the Social Listener* (Routledge Press), and is publishing a textbook with W.W. Norton that embraces an innovative, inclusive pedagogical framework for music theory. Dr. Palfy is also a singer with a background in opera and jazz performance.

Teresa L. Reed served on the faculty of the University of Tulsa for 25 years, where she taught all levels of music theory and aural skills, was Director of the African American Studies Certificate, Director of the School of Music, and Associate Dean of the College of Arts and Sciences. She has authored four books and is former Chief Reader for the AP Exam in Music Theory. She currently serves as Dean of the School of Music at the University of Louisville.

Alan Reese teaches music theory at the Cleveland Institute of Music and received a PhD in music theory from the Eastman School of Music. Alan's research interests include post-tonal analysis, the music of Karol Szymanowski and Grażyna Bacewicz, and antiracist and anti-oppressive music theory pedagogy. He has presented on these topics at regional and national conferences, and his work on Szymanowski's keyboard techniques has appeared in *Music Theory Spectrum*.

Nicholas J. Shea is Assistant Professor of music theory at Arizona State University, where he teaches undergraduate and graduate courses on music theory, cognition, and computational music analysis. He studies how popular music artists perform, understand, and convey the various components of musical organization through physical gesture. Through his work, he aims to draw music theory closer to inclusive models of analysis, challenging what qualifies as music theory by affirming the perceptual-experiential validity of popular music's practitioners, who often have alternative but complementary perspectives on musical organization.

Cara Stroud is Assistant Professor at Michigan State University, where she teaches courses in undergraduate music theory as well as graduate courses in popular music, music after 1900, and musical narrative. Her work on a range of twentieth-century music topics, including narrativity, intertextuality, the tarantella, nostalgia, form in top 40 pop music, and revising the music theory curriculum has been presented at regional, national, and international conferences. Her writing appears in *20th- and 21st-Century Song Cycles: Analytical Pathways Toward Performance*, edited by Gordon Sly and Michael Callahan, and in journals such as *Engaging Students*, *Music Theory Online*, and *Music Theory Spectrum*.

Leigh VanHandel is Associate Professor of music theory at the University of British Columbia. Her primary research areas are music theory pedagogy, music cognition, the relationship between language and music, and computer-assisted research. Her cognition research focuses on tempo perception, and her music theory pedagogy research focuses on adapting recent research on the cognition of teaching and learning into the music theory classroom. She edited and contributed to the *Routledge Companion to Music Theory Pedagogy* (2020) and has published in journals such as *Music Perception*, *Journal of New Music Research*, *Empirical Musicology Review*, and *Journal of Music Theory Pedagogy*.

Zachary Zinser received his PhD in music theory from Indiana University Jacobs School of Music in 2020. His primary research focuses on popular music analysis, particularly the cognitive processing of recorded sound and the experiential implications of those processes to expand and enrich traditional music-theoretic concepts (e.g., texture). He has presented his work at multiple conferences, including the Annual Meeting for the Society of Music Theory. He currently teaches at Butler University.

Foreword

Philip Ewell

In "Jazz and the White Critic," Amiri Baraka tells the story of how, by the mid-twentieth century, when jazz was emerging as one of the most important American musical art forms, Black music was increasingly appropriated by White America in order to present the music as more than just "Negro." This music was a secret to White America, in the same way that the lives of Blacks were secretive to Whites, and the first musical critics of jazz were often White men who sought to uncover some of these secrets for mainstream White America. But key to the entire endeavor was appropriation. Baraka writes, "The success of this 'appropriation' signaled the existence of an American music, where before there was a Negro music" ([1968] 2010, 17). Thus, in order for a Black musical genre – or, simply, Black American composers of classical and concert music, for that matter – to be presented to mainstream White America, it needed to be stripped of its Blackness, a notion that, for so long, too long, represented a subhuman form to be avoided at all costs. And from this sanitized version of the music emerged an *American* musical art form, now ready for the main stage and the world at large.

Against all odds, over centuries, Black Americans created all forms of music, yet the erasure of this music, especially with respect to classical and concert music, had been nearly complete until relatively recently. This erasure has created an American music academy, and an American music theory curriculum, largely devoid of materials – scores, textbooks, monographs, analyses, recordings, collections, among others – to work with regarding Blackness and Black composers. The present volume goes a long way in filling that void.

Expanding the Canon: Black Composers in the Music Theory Classroom represents a dearly needed source for music theory. Practical yet grand in scope, *Expanding the Canon* is loosely formatted, something like an undergraduate music theory sequence, with five parts: "Fundamentals and Diatonic Harmony," "Chromaticism and Other Advanced Topics," "Form," "Popular Music," and "Twentieth and Twenty-First Century Art Music." From this point of view, it is quite practical – the theory pedagogue can go straight to that part of the volume that corresponds to where they might be in the theory sequence and cull materials accordingly. Yet digging deeper into the text, one understands that it is more than just practical. *Expanding the Canon* challenges the racial order of music theory, which, sadly, has heretofore simply mirrored the racial hierarchy of our country since the field's inception in the mid-twentieth century, a hierarchy in which Whiteness reigns supreme while all other races are segregated out of the most important structures of society. In an instance of what I call "colorasure," the erasure of non-Whiteness from White structures, American music theory has generally removed the names, the humanity, of Black music and relegated it to genres: ragtime, jazz, blues, rap, funk, R&B, among others (Ewell 2021). Significantly, *Expanding the Canon* reinstates Blackness's humanity and gives numerous names and faces within the many genres represented, including classical and concert music.

But I'm most struck by the volume's practicality. Whether one needs something for a fundamentals class (contributions by Attas, Miyake), chromaticism (Reese), ear training (Fleming), or form (Grant/Kim, Maxile), the reader will find materials. Popular music pedagogy is skillfully represented in the musical works of contemporary Black women artists such as Ester Rada (Abrahams) and Janelle Monáe (Palfy), as well as through a focus on rhythm (Geary, de Clercq). And traditional post-tonal topics are expanded through compositions by George Walker (Belcher) and Julia Perry (Preston Leonard). It's heartwarming to see so many songs by Black composers analyzed and offered in the volume (Abrahams, de Clercq, Hoag, Ohriner, Palfy, Reese, VanHandel), since for too long songs in the music theory classroom only occurred in their "western art" form, as German Lied or certain other European versions.

Occasionally, the contributors invite us to think profoundly about the pieces being examined, through new concepts such as "protonotation" (Knowles/Shea), in topical classes already taught, in one case "Sound, Syntax, and Space in Popular Music" (Zinser), or with how post-tonal topics have been taught in the United States historically and how that undergirds White male supremacy (Stroud). And sometimes they deal with broad topics in the field, like "modulation" (Reese) or "modal mixture" (Ohriner). Still other authors seek to foreground traditionally Black genres, such as ragtime (Fleming) and jazz (Geyer), while others give a perspective of teaching music theory at a historically Black college (Brown, Jr.). Overall, the great wealth of material is a testament not only to the richness of the music of Black composers but also to the many talents and broad knowledge of the contributors themselves.

With this said, it's worth noting the many identities of those contributors. Men and women (I don't know if any of the authors would identify as gender nonconforming, so I ask for the reader's indulgence here), both White and Black and of other races and ethnicities as well. Further, this diversity is matched in rank and institution as well, with junior scholars appearing alongside senior colleagues, and with those who teach at large institutions and small, public and private, all of which point to the successful and expansive nature of the project.

I'd be remiss if I didn't comment on the contribution in *Expanding the Canon* of my friend and colleague Teresa L. Reed. With her as one of only a handful of African American women in our field, her voice is so sorely needed. She writes beautifully of how we Black music theorists have had to wall off our love of Black music, knowing that the field never really considered Black music worthy of consideration in the past for any number of reasons – I myself did exactly that with my love of blues, jazz, and rap in the 1980s and 1990s. Not long ago, Teresa emailed me to ask what I knew of the history of African American women in music theory, and I responded with the four or five names I could think of. I mentioned that my much-loved colleague at Hunter College, Jewel Thompson, was likely the first Black woman to graduate with a PhD in music theory in 1982, from the Eastman School of Music, and whose dissertation on Samuel Coleridge-Taylor was likely the first in American music theory to focus solely on a Black composer (Thompson 1982).[1] The simple fact that there are virtually no Black women in American music theory speaks volumes about the field, and not at all positively. *Expanding the Canon* allows for us all to begin to right this injustice.

I've been working extensively with African American music and musical genres over the past several years, and when I asked two senior White male colleagues, friends, in music theory whether they might be interested in collaborating on something, they both said "yes," but that they don't really know anything about "this music." But in fact, they do – they just don't realize it. In the atonal sounds of Olly Wilson, the sparse minimalism of Julius Eastman, the quasi post-tonality of Zenobia Powell Perry, the neoclassicism of Ulysses Kay, or the 12-tone serialism of Hale Smith. That is, classical and concert music written by African Americans is also Black music, as American classical music is also indebted to African American music and musical genres. This musical story, so strongly outlined in *Expanding the Canon*, closely mirrors the story of our country, and it's great to see so many scholars coming together to tell this story.

In "Here I Stand," something of a mini manifesto that he wrote for Eileen Southern's *Readings in Black American Music*, Hale Smith laments the difficulties of the Black composer in how they are never allowed to be judged outside of their Blackness, adding:

> Are we to be expected to sit back while white America takes the fertile seeds of our imaginations and benefits from their fruition again? What else is to be expected as long as our work can be seen, heard, and absorbed, while at the same time being considered too inferior to the work of our white contemporaries and forbears to stand in direct competition with them.
>
> (1983, 324)

With *Expanding the Canon*, the contributors and main editor, Melissa Hoag, are not "sitting back" but, rather, standing up together and presenting compositions by Black composers as they should have always been, as exemplars of great American music, neither superior nor inferior to European or other models, replete with all the elements so crucial to the study of music theory in the United States. I'm honored to have been one of the first to read its contents, and to offer this brief foreword to what will surely be a key text in the field for many years to come.

Note

1. The first African American man to receive the PhD in music theory was likely Horace Boyer (1973). I cite and thank here my go-to guy for such historical information about African American figures inside and outside of music theory, Horace Maxile, another contributor to the present volume.

Works Cited

Baraka, Amiri. (1968) 2010. "Jazz and the White Critic." In *Black Music*, edited by Leroi Jones. Akashic Books.

Boyer, Horace. 1973. "An Analysis of Black Church Music with Examples Drawn from Services in Rochester, New York." PhD diss, Eastman School of Music.

Ewell, Philip. March 25, 2021. "Erasing Colorasure in American Music Theory, and Confronting Demons From Our Past." *Bibliolore: The RILM Blog*.

Smith, Hale. 1983. "Here I Stand." In *Readings in Black American Music*, edited by Eileen Southern, 2nd edition. W.W. Norton & Company.

Thompson, Jewel. 1982. "Samuel Coleridge-Taylor: The Development of His Compositional Style." PhD diss., Eastman School of Music.

Introduction

Melissa Hoag

I am sure I am not alone when, looking back on my 12 years (1996–2008) as a music student in higher education institutions, I can recall studying almost no music by Black composers. Those I did encounter were notable precisely because they were such outliers: Scott Joplin, William Grant Still, and Duke Ellington were mentioned in undergraduate music history; a colleague wrote a paper about Nathaniel Dett in music history; and I chose Mary Lou Williams's *Mary Lou's Mass* as a paper topic in a graduate course. These tokens were the entirety of my exposure to Black composers.

Indeed, I learned more about the music of relatively distant White cultures, for example, through Bartók's ethnomusicology of Eastern and Southern Europe, than I did about music of non-White composers from my own country. Lost on me and my peers was the work of Black scholars and composers – those like Harry Burleigh, Nathaniel Dett, Margaret Bonds, and many others – who did similar work on the rich heritage of Black folk music in the history of music in the United States. At the same time, Black experiences and culture were silenced in our curriculum. The borrowing practices of Charles Ives with regards to Protestant hymnody were taught, but not his practice of borrowing from minstrelsy with its attendant racial insults.[1] More broadly, the composers we studied most closely, the "Bach to Brahms" canon written between roughly 1725 and 1890, coincide precisely with the height of American slavery and Reconstruction. Scholarship on the musical culture that resulted from that history, for example, Eileen Southern's *The Music of Black Americans: A History* (1997), was a visible yet unexplored path.

The Whiteness of the field was, of course, not limited to classroom content. Of the dozens of students in my cohorts across three programs, only one was Black. According to demographic data collected by the Society for Music Theory, my experience is still a common one, as the Society remains less than 1% Black in its membership.[2] In its curricula, student enrollment, and faculty, the field of music theory, now as then, presents Whiteness as a default, regardless of the positionality or efforts of any individual faculty members.[3] But this Whiteness was also invisible to me as a White undergraduate and graduate student. My sole focus in those years was on finishing my degree and getting a job as quickly as possible; my privilege allowed me to pursue these goals without considering the role my race played in that pursuit. I had not considered the experience of students of color in these spaces, and I hope readers of Teresa L. Reed's essay, which appears as Chapter 1 of this volume, will find themselves as moved as I was by her account.

In the first decade of my career, I continued the default Whiteness of the field by teaching as I had been taught. There are many complex reasons for this, and I have too little space to fully unpack them, but a few of these reasons include the desire to maintain collegiality within my department, pre-tenure precarity, and the fact that revising a curriculum in this way is difficult and often extracurricular labor. I had already begun increasing the number of marginalized composers represented in my courses, especially music by women

DOI: 10.4324/9781003204053-1

composers, and I had always used examples from jazz, popular music, and musical theater. But a dam burst when, in the wake of the murder of George Floyd in 2020 and several local precipitating events, our department held a series of discussions with students about issues of diversity. Students of color in my department reported feeling ignored and invisible. I knew then that I had to make more drastic changes, so I began educating myself on issues of diversity and inclusion in a serious, systematic way. In reading Philip Ewell's "Music Theory and the White Racial Frame" (2020), work like *Becoming a White Antiracist*, and most recently, pursuing a certificate in Diversity, Equity and Inclusion through Cornell University, I was encouraged, for the first time in a sustained way, to consider the role of race in my classroom approach.[4] Why did I propagate the idea of the "master" composer, despite its obvious racial (and gendered) coding? Why did I adhere to the idea that students must know well a certain catalog of pieces (all by White male composers)? I began studying and then teaching music by composers who have been, in Ewell's nomenclature, "colorased" (2021). I now see these composers – Harry Burleigh, Florence Price, Margaret Bonds, Howard Swanson, George Walker, Julia Perry, and others – as indispensable.

Learning a large amount of new music well into my career also raised doubts about my own competency as a teacher. I am not an expert in the music of these composers. While I can teach the music of Brahms, Bartók, and Ives, I am more likely to learn alongside students when bringing the music of Black composers into the classroom. But at this stage of my career, I'm letting go of the need to be an expert on a piece of music or on a composer before teaching it or discussing it with my students – something Cara Stroud discusses in Chapter 18 of this book. This insistence on expertise serves to maintain the status quo and prevents faculty from branching out into lesser-known repertoire.

As a 2008 PhD graduate, myself and my cohort are, as of this writing, in the primes of our careers. Many faculty who are my generation and older have assumed leadership roles and are being awarded higher ranks. Many of us now have power and influence. It is important for all of us, regardless of our training, to resist the complacency afforded by White privilege (and, in many cases, tenured privilege) and to teach what is right, rather than allowing our training to determine what we teach. Unless we critically examine what we were taught and continuously re-examine what should be taught, what we teach is often a matter of intellectual inheritance, compounded by inertia brought on by the day-to-day demands of academic life – teaching, research, and service – all of which are required for continued employment in an academic career. I thus view this book as an invitation for practitioners to make more room for music by Black composers, and composers of other marginalized populations. I hope others will join me in continuing to interrogate the structures influencing what we teach in music theory courses, and to foster discussions in our courses about these issues.

Common Threads

Organized in a way that roughly parallels a typical music theory sequence, *Expanding the Canon: Black Composers in the Music Theory Classroom* offers 21 chapters intended to help music theory faculty inject their teaching with a substantial dose of diversity and inclusion. The Supplemental Materials website comprises a rich compendium of additional examples, assignments, appendices, and lesson plans that accompany each chapter. I have been fortunate to try out quite a bit of the material presented in these chapters over the 2021–22 academic year and can attest to their effectiveness and accessibility. I have already mentioned Teresa L. Reed's introductory account of growing up in the Black Pentecostal church, where nothing was notated and everything was improvised, and then gaining all her credentials in White, European-focused schools of music, where almost nothing was improvised and everything was notated. I believe that this chapter should be required reading for anyone who teaches music theory.

Part 1 includes four chapters on teaching the introductory topics of fundamentals and diatonic harmony. Chapters 2 and 3 both focus on teaching music fundamentals; first, Uzee Brown Jr. enumerates six best practices he has gleaned as a 40-year veteran professor and department chair at Morehouse College, a historically Black college. He also offers several examples of music he uses in his fundamentals course, including one of his own compositions. Robin Attas's essay on teaching fundamentals critically examines all that the term "fundamentals" can imply for students, and offers strategies that range from simple diversification of examples to a complete rethinking of how one might approach music fundamentals from an antiracist perspective.

Chapters 4 and 5 offer insights into teaching first-year music theory. Jan Miyake offers myriad activities to support teaching intervals, embellishing tones, basic harmonic analysis, cadences, and form through deep engagement with two compositions by Black composers of contrasting styles and time periods: Francis "Frank" Johnson (1972–1844) and Rhiannon Giddens (1977–). Rounding out Part 1, Kristina L. Knowles and Nicholas J. Shea examine how instructors can describe differences between popular music and classical music styles without imposing the "rules" of the latter onto the former. Knowles and Shea also advocate for a sound-first approach that enables students with varying levels of notational fluency to approach a variety of styles. I would be remiss if I did not also point the reader toward Rosa Abrahams's chapter in Part 4 of this volume, which contains numerous resources for teaching first-year music theory using the music of Ester Rada.

Part 2 of the volume offers three chapters focusing on chromatic topics and aural skills. Mitchell Ohriner's chapter on modal mixture not only offers numerous examples of the technique from a variety of repertoires but also reflects upon and critiques the topic as it is usually taught, particularly in his discussion of Stevie Wonder's "Livin' in the City." Amy Fleming's chapter on teaching aural skills using Joplin's ragtime compositions offers a broad range of topics that can be taught, and skills that can be honed, through this important repertoire; the supplemental materials for this chapter are particularly useful and not to be missed. Part 2 closes with Alan Reese's capacious chapter on teaching modulation, which includes an eclectic array of examples and assignments, with even more available on the Supplemental Materials website.

The central part of the volume, Part 3, takes up issues of form. Ben Geyer critiques the teaching of jazz using established pedagogical lenses, advocating that one should use alternative analytical methods when studying and teaching this music. Horace Maxile's chapter on binary and ternary form focuses on several compositions by two important nineteenth-century composers: Francis "Frank" Johnson (also discussed in Miyake's Chapter 4) and Harry Burleigh, who was one of the first composer-scholars to catalog Black folk music and incorporate it into his compositions. My own chapter presents analyses of three art songs by Margaret Bonds, Florence Price, and Howard Swanson, each of which sets a poem by Langston Hughes. While each song does display a different form, the most meaningful feature of this chapter comes in its examination of the text–music relationship in each setting. Finally, Aaron Grant and Catrina Kim offer a scaffolded pathway through the teaching of sonata form using sonatas composed by three Black composers – Joseph Bologne, Samuel Coleridge-Taylor, and Florence Price – instead of the typical Haydn-Mozart-Beethoven model. Grant and Kim argue that teaching sonata form using only three White male composers further solidifies Ewell's concept of the "White racial frame" (2020). Finally, readers should note that the teaching of form – specifically on the smaller scale of sentence, phrase, and period – also features in several other chapters (Miyake, Knowles/Shea, Fleming, and Palfy).

The five chapters in Part 4 have been written to make teaching popular music approachable to nonexperts. These chapters focus substantially on non-pitch elements, like texture, narrative, and rhythm. Zachary Zinser recounts a recently taught course on popular music in which students were allowed to choose the repertoire (with encouragement to explore Black and other underrepresented musical artists). This empowerment resulted not only in increased student engagement but also in an eclectic repertoire list that enabled students to apply newly learned concepts and frameworks, such as virtual spaces, spatial impressions, agency, and musical texture. Cora Palfy's chapter focuses on two songs by Janelle Monáe that feature straightforward formal designs, which Palfy uses to highlight strategies of narrative storytelling and audience engagement.

Two chapters specifically emphasize rhythm. David Geary's chapter on drum parts in twenty-first-century pop songs provides two lesson modules that demonstrate how drum parts often create different expressions of meter, articulate form, and fulfill expressive and other functions, rather than just providing a simplistic and repetitive grid, as is often assumed. Trevor de Clercq argues that rhythm training in classically focused aural skills courses and ensembles does not prepare musicians to perform or teach rhythms typical of the R&B genre; central to this chapter is the use of drum charts, which help students understand form, hypermeter, and phrase organization. Part 4 closes with Rosa Abrahams's compelling chapter on Ethiopian Israeli jazz and soul artist Ester Rada, which not only focuses on building basic analysis skills for first-year music theory students but also engages aspects of narrative and Ethiopian Israeli culture and identity. Finally, though Part 4 is solely dedicated to popular music, readers should be aware that many other chapters also incorporate popular music (Brown, Attas, Miyake, Knowles/Shea, Ohriner, and Reese).

Part 5 offers a set of four chapters on twentieth-century music by Black composers. Cara Stroud's chapter discusses roadblocks that might keep faculty from incorporating a wider variety of music into the post-tonal classroom and includes analysis of and supplemental assignments on music by Julius Eastman, Dorothy Rudd Moore, Zenobia Powell Perry, and Tania Léon. Leigh VanHandel offers a flexible lesson plan on, and detailed analysis of, Florence Price's art song "My Dream" that engages text-music relationships, neo-Riemannian analysis, and octatonicism. Owen Belcher's chapter offers several weeks' worth of teaching material from George Walker's eclectic output. Lastly, Kendra Preston Leonard makes teaching the music of Julia Perry more accessible through her analysis of *Homunculus C.F.*, a work that demonstrates serialist minimalism.

My Hopes for This Book

First, from a practical perspective, I hope this book will mitigate barriers for faculty who want to broaden the scope of their teaching but simply lack the resources – time, energy, intellectual bandwidth – to do so. Among the many calls for revising curricula toward diversity, equity, and inclusion, it is rarely acknowledged that, while some instructors are compensated for such work and evaluated and promoted on that basis, many more are not. Contingent instructors, as well as permanent instructors whose primary area is not music theory, are on the one hand held accountable for their curricula by students, colleagues, and administrators, while on the other hand not provided with time or compensation for effecting curricular change. My hope, and that of the authors in this collection, is that these chapters present classroom activities, readings, and assessments that can be quickly incorporated into existing courses.

I also hope students will be inspired when they encounter these pieces in their theory classes – that they will perform these pieces, arrange them for their own ensembles, and teach them to their future students. I have already seen this happen over the past several years: One student is arranging a piece by Harry Burleigh for her brass quartet. Another programmed three songs by Florence Price on her senior recital. Still others have expressed interest in doing these things as they progress through their degree programs.

Most importantly, I hope that by expanding the diversity of music we choose to address in our music theory courses as a first step, students of color will begin to feel seen and heard and sense that there is a place for them, particularly at predominantly White institutions. At the very least, taking the first step of addressing music by non-White composers might demonstrate an acknowledgment of Black culture and history, a recognition that Black composers exist and have existed for a long time, and a belief that music by Black composers is worthy of our time and attention, so that our students of color can be spared at least some measure of the invisibility and isolation that Teresa L. Reed describes in her opening chapter of this book. At best, we will continue to expand our vision of diversity until we may describe what we do as antiracist pedagogy (as described by Robin Attas in Chapter 3). I hope that, eventually, these changes might lead to more colleagues of color in music theory and related fields.

Purview and Emphasis: What This Book Is, and What It Is Not

This book focuses on music by Black composers, which should not be taken to imply that I (or any of the contributors) discount other kinds of diversity. Music theory also needs to incorporate and appropriately address music composed by people of Asian descent, Latinx descent, and indigenous ancestry, and to continue to increase its representation of music by women composers, composers with other gender identities, and composers with disabilities. Also, the book's title specifies Black *composers* – and while nearly all musicians mentioned in the book literally composed the works discussed, the term *composer* may be understood to be more broadly construed to encompass performance and production as part of what it means to "compose" a work, particularly in chapters that address popular music.

Also, I do not wish to speak for all the contributors in the first section of this introduction. That section, of course, represents my own lived experience and serves as one example among many. Every contributor to this volume, as well as every reader of this volume, has their own lived experience with the lack of diversity in music theory curricula, and we have all found different ways to work toward greater diversity. By extension, I truly believe that there is no one-size-fits-all music theory curriculum. Rather than preaching that there is a single way to structure a curriculum with regard to diversity and inclusion, I hope that this book can be viewed as a unified call for us all to do better, and its contents understood as a set of tools to help us all grow toward that common goal. Not every chapter will work for every learning environment, and that is not the intended purpose of this book.

Finally, this book makes no claim that it is a solution to music theory's White racial frame, as laid out by Philip Ewell (2020). Music theory has a lot of work to do, and a textbook for lower-level music theory is really the most needed resource of all at this point.[5] A book of essays focusing on teaching music by Black composers is just one resource, and a sorely overdue one at that. It is one resource among what I hope will soon be many resources that will become available as we move toward a broader reimagining of how we can continue to grow as a field.[6]

Notes

1. Ives borrowed the occasional minstrel tune (such as "Dem Golden Slippers" in the often-taught song *General William Booth Enters into Heaven*) and wrote several rags. However, the implications

of a White composer using Black musical genres are complex. This is especially the case with Ives, since his racial politics were also complex (see, for example, Garrett 2008, 17–47).
2. Scholars who identify as Black or African American still make up a vanishingly small percentage of the overall membership of the Society for Music Theory, with 72.28% of the membership self-reporting as White, and only 0.97% of the membership self-reporting as Black or African American. (There are many other racial categories and other identities represented in this report, which may be viewed at https://societymusictheory.org/sites/default/files/demographics/2021-report.pdf.)
3. Leigh VanHandel's survey of recent graduates from music theory PhD programs determined that the curricula of music theory PhD programs do not expose students to musical traditions outside of the western canon, making it difficult for them to research or teach in those subject areas (2021). Rather, the survey concluded that degree requirements for PhD degrees in music theory were based more on tradition and existing areas of faculty specialization than anything else.
4. Of course, I do not have space in the introduction of this collection to fully describe all that the authors have to say; I will just entreat the reader to study this book if they wish to work toward dismantling the White framework of their curricula. Particularly compelling is this sentence from Chapter 1: "This book invites you into . . . thinking through what it means to lose an unconscious, unwitting [W]hite supremacist [W]hite identity and embrace a new one, a proudly antiracist [W]hite identity" (Brookfield and Hess 2021, 12). The authors emphasize that those who are White must understand their own racial identities as a first step. Specifically, what the authors frame as the "three core elements of White identity" are as follows: (1) insisting that one has a color-blind view of the world; (2) a belief that being White is not a racial identity – only people of color have race; and (3) being able to opt into and out of engaging with race (48).
5. Phil Ewell is working with three other contributors to this volume (Rosa Abrahams, Aaron Grant, and Cora S. Palfy) on a new textbook, titled *The Engaged Musician: Theory and Analysis for the Twenty-First Century*, that will reimagine how the theory core is taught. I eagerly await the publication of this text!
6. One such resource is the Composers of Color Resource project (https://composersofcolor.hcommons.org), which offers an ever-expanding catalog of examples by composers of color, cross-listed with musical techniques that are commonly taught in music theory courses.

Works Cited

Bisciglia, Sebastiano. 2021. "Annual Report on Membership Demographics." *Society for Music Theory Website.* https://societymusictheory.org/sites/default/files/demographics/2021-report.pdf. Last accessed April 2, 2021.
Brookfield, Stephen D., and Mary E. Hess. 2021. *Becoming a White Antiracist: A Practical Guide for Educators, Leaders, and Activists.* Stylus Publishing.
"Composers of Color Resource Project." Accessed April 10, 2022. https://composersofcolor.hcommons.org
Ewell, Philip. 2020. "Music Theory's White Racial Frame." *Music Theory Online* 26/2. https://doi.org/10.30535/mto.26.2.4
_____. March 25, 2021. "Erasing Colorasure in American Music Theory, and Confronting Demons from Our Past." *Bibliolore: The RILM Blog.*
Garrett, Charles Hiroshi. 2008. *Struggling to Define a Nation.* University of California Press.
Southern, Eileen. 1997. *The Music of Black Americans: A History*, 3rd edition. W.W. Norton.
VanHandel, Leigh. 2021. "The 21st-Century Graduate Student." Presentation at Society for Music Theory Conference.

1 Our Field at Its Best

Teresa L. Reed

I'm seated in the concert hall, program in hand, poised to surrender to the joy of listening. The downbeat comes, and I lean in and focus. And then it happens. Some gorgeous melody, some inventive harmonic sequence, some exquisite phrase, floods me with embarrassing emotion as the music reaches a tender place in my heart. A lump forms in my throat, and salty pools collect in the corners of my eyes. The levee breaks. I succumb to the gratitude I feel for sounds that surprise me with their beauty.

Although music sometimes moves me to tears, my encounters with music theory treatises have never elicited emotional responses of this intensity. At best, I am intrigued, or perhaps excited, by scholarly discourses that spark new conversations and yield new insights. This particular volume, however, instantly touches some tender place in my heart. At my first perusal of the table of contents, I was flooded with emotion from a very personal place. A lump formed in my throat, followed by the salty pools in the corners of my eyes. *Expanding the Canon: Black Composers in the Music Theory Classroom* is a triggering encounter for me, forcing me to reflect, as an African American woman, on my relationship with the discipline of music theory.

It's 1974. I am a 10-year-old trying my first tunes on the newly acquired piano in our living room. All the musicians that I know, admire, and want to emulate are at Open Door Church of God in Christ. There is Cynthia Turner, whose fingers on the keyboard dance in tandem with the nimble movement of her feet on the pedals. While her fingers and feet join in the dance, she constantly manipulates the buttons and knobs on the Hammond B-3 organ to achieve just the timbre she wants. There is Larry Barbour, the bass player, whose lines create their own thumping counterpoints to Cynthia's dancing feet. Walter Jackson's lead guitar interjects with licks and countermelodies that seem to sing. Ronny Perry, only slightly older than me, plays drums like he has extra hands. These and other artists in my church – all self-taught – relied entirely on their ears, their collaborative skill, and their creative instinct. At Open Door Church, singing could erupt from any voice at any time, and those who held forth were not necessarily tethered to a single tonal center for the duration of the tune. It was the musicians' job to follow, to instantly adjust to any modulatory detour, and to support that singer – vocal embellishments and all – as expertly in the key of new arrival as in the key of departure. The musicians were also adept at instantaneous adjustments to tempo and meter, where solo or congregational singing that started in an unmetered rubato could suddenly morph (the Spirit dictating) into hand-clapping, breakneck speed.

This was the world of my formative musical experience – hands-on, dynamic, with more experienced musicians and hundreds of congregants as my teachers, with Deity as the instructor of record. There, no one read music; everyone played by ear. There were no age-related restrictions at my church, nor were there any prerequisites. Anyone who wanted to participate in the musical life of the church was welcomed to do so, provided

DOI: 10.4324/9781003204053-2

they were willing to learn from the more experienced musicians and face a congregation whose expectations were high and whose feedback was instant, open, and brutally honest. I first accompanied the children's choir there when I was 10 years old, and I first played saxophone there as a 12-year-old, making my share of blunders early on, but eventually coming to hold my own. The skill set that I developed in this way was a skill set that everyone at Open Door Church (and numerous, similar Black churches around the United States, in the Caribbean, and other parts of the world) took for granted.

Performing at church convinced me to make music my life's work. To do this, however, I knew that playing by ear wasn't enough. I would need to learn to read music, go to college, and earn a degree. In high school, I began that slow, painstaking process. In my community, private lessons were nonexistent on wind, brass, and percussion instruments, so I enrolled in beginning band. As a saxophonist, I was one of many emerging band kids who learned to read music in a primarily unguided, self-taught way, many of us layering music literacy on top of years of listening and improvisation in neighborhood garage bands and at Black churches very similar to mine. With a fingering chart and lines-and-spaces cheat sheet nearby, I taught myself to produce on my saxophone the pitches notated on the page before me. Seemingly in slow motion, I mentally synthesized the placement of my fingers, to the name that note was called, to the notehead on the staff, to its rhythmic duration, and then produced the resulting sound. And I did this tedious and methodical mental "stitching together" thousands upon thousands of times, with well-placed doses of encouragement from my overworked band teacher, until the synthesis became more fluid and, eventually, sufficiently second nature for me to sight-read passages and pieces and to work up the repertoire for a college audition.

Meanwhile, the vibrant and dynamic musical scene of my church remained an extremely vital part of my artistic life and development. Throughout childhood and as a teenager, I performed there on a regular basis, completely by ear, in a setting where listening, collaboration, spontaneity, and the instant, sometimes-humbling feedback of a God-inspired congregation was the norm.

By the time I started college in 1983, two almost diametrically opposed spaces were forming in my musical consciousness. There was a striking division between the musical customs of my African American heritage and the notated music that paved the way to the credentials I hoped to someday earn. I erected a firewall separating the space where I spoke with fluency the language of what I will call my "native" music, my "born" music, from the space where I acquired fluency in notated repertoire. The energetic, spirited, and improvisatory world of listening, responding, creating, experimenting, and collaborating was enmeshed with all the expressive depth of gospel, blues, rhythm & blues, soul, and amalgamations of all the aforementioned. It was music driven by heart, soul, and in-the-moment, spirit responses to feeling and intuition, music whose best practitioners could literally lift you from wherever you were and transport you to another emotional and experiential space. In this world, the aesthetic yardstick, the measurement of effectiveness, is the degree to which the musical experience alters your space and leaves you inspired, energized, and at least for the moment, transformed. And the aesthetic choices – the florid melismas, the bent notes, the call-and-response, the speech-song, the timbral inflections, the poetic liberty, the rhythmic and metric creativity – are all in service to that end.

In the highly contrasting and developing "notated space" of my musical life, I relished, indulged in, and began to speak with acquired fluency the language captured in the graphics on the staves, notation and directions indicative of melodic, harmonic, rhythmic, formal, timbral, and textural decisions made, not in the moment, but often decades or centuries in advance by composers whose legacies formed a Eurocentric canon. In the mid-1980s, when I completed undergrad, this canon was exclusively male, and exclusively White, and theirs was the language that was the pathway to the degree that I sought.

I was the only African American student among the music majors who started at Valparaiso University in fall 1983. I cherished both my Black musical heritage and the Eurocentric repertoire that I was beginning to understand and master. Every encounter with a piece of music outside of my known world expanded my cognitive and expressive palette as a saxophonist and broadened my understanding of stylistic traditions. Josquin, Palestrina, Bach, Haydn, Mozart, Beethoven, Chopin, Schubert, and Brahms were every bit as welcomed and valued in my life as were Andraé Crouch, Shirley Caesar, the Clark Sisters, James Cleveland, Sara Jordan Powell, the Thompson Community Singers, the Mississippi Mass Choir, Stevie Wonder, Patti LaBelle, and Earth, Wind & Fire. But this utopian, motley crew of musical voices lived harmoniously only inside of my own head. It was not the reality of my academic life.

As an undergraduate, I quickly discovered that the world of my college experience had little to no positive regard for music that could not be captured in and performed from notation. In the mid-1980s, the improvisatory customs of jazz were about as far as the academy was willing to go to acknowledge the value of sounds difficult or impossible to capture on the page. Both as an undergraduate and years later as a graduate student and a scholar, I encountered attempted transcriptions into notation of Black vocal stylings or improvisatory passages. To me, those transcriptions frequently seemed anemic, truncated, hollow, and misguided – well-intended displays of profound ignorance. These types of transcriptions, in my view, tend to lose most everything of importance in translation. You see the notes, but detached from its cultural/experiential context, this music's most salient elements are lost.

My professors, textbooks, and White peers asserted, both directly and indirectly, that music transmitted orally and created and performed by ear was crude, underdeveloped, primitive, poorly crafted, wrong, harmful, and (to some) not real music at all. They conflated the ability to read music with musical proficiency, assuming them to be one and the same; having witnessed the musical excellence of my Black Pentecostal upbringing, I knew that this conflation was untenable, but I kept silent. My music theory professors taught that in all proper tonal music, the rules of good voice leading prevailed, parallel octaves and fifths did not occur (and those that seemed to occur could be justified by some other voice leading loophole), the leading tone and chordal seventh are never doubled and always resolved in accordance with their prescribed tendencies, the dominant is only followed cadentially by the tonic (or sometimes the submediant), and so on and so forth. In the music of my own Black experience, a distinctive set of norms prevailed, favoring coloristic and extended harmonies, tones, intervals, and chords with tendencies in many potential directions, and florid improvisations in both fixed and unfixed keys. My professors and textbooks asserted that the natural metric accents in tonal music are on beats 1 and 3, although in the tonal music of my church, we typically clapped on beats 2 and 4, placing the accents opposite beats 1 and 3. The occasional White visitor to my church who clapped on beats 1 and 3 drew both chuckles and pity and, if he stayed long enough, got a quick tutorial on our metric tradition. Professors and peers who knew really nothing at all about the music of my background asserted with confidence that singing in the Black gospel style would ruin your voice, without producing any evidence of this claim. I harbored unspoken opposition to these and myriad other inaccurate assertions. My "born" music, a synthesis of energy, skill, and instinct, was also grounded in its own set of cultural norms related to African American memory, space, and community. Removed from this context, my native musical tongue seemed impossible to explain to people ensconced in their own superiority. Therefore, I found it safest to silence my perspective and hide this part of my musical identity from those who were certain to misunderstand it, and even more certain to condemn and/or dismiss it.

As I silenced my perspective and concealed my native musical identity, I wondered about the curriculum that led to the degree I was earning. The more experimental tonal and harmonic developments of the later nineteenth and twentieth centuries were taught as expansions of tonality, the next logical evolutionary phases in music ever guided into the future by the great White men accorded this glorious mission. I distinctly remember in my senior year encounters with Schoenberg's *Pierrot Lunaire*, John Cage's *4'33"*, and Penderecki's *Threnody to the Victims of Hiroshima*, and then having a sad epiphany: I was completing a curriculum in which I'd been taught, both implicitly and explicitly, that unwritten music and music performed by ear was simply done the wrong way. Yet White males breaking every rule of tonality and harmony were still guaranteed mention in the music history and music theory textbooks that I was required to read. I wondered about the women and people of color, long faded into obscurity, who were the contemporaries and, quite possibly, the musical peers of Bach, Haydn, Mozart, Beethoven, and Brahms. I wondered why no Black artists or composers were ever mentioned in my music theory classes, since most every tonal concept covered was familiar to me from what I heard and played at church, or that I heard on the local R&B station. And I reasoned that there must be African American composers who loved the music of the Eurocentric canon just as I did, composers whose string quartets, sonatas, symphonies, and concertos were waiting to be heard. I was earning a degree by completing a curriculum that excluded me.

As an African American undergraduate music major, I was both silent and invisible. It was unsafe for me to tell the story of my unique musical skill set, how I acquired it, and how that experience informed my perspective. And it was impossible to find anyone who looked like me in the repertoire or among the artists or composers that I was required to know. My undergraduate experience was nearly 40 years ago. Yet I remember well the experience of being silent and invisible, and the energy it took to maintain the protective firewall between my two musical lives. I remember the fear of ridicule, should anyone discover me singing and playing the gospel music that I dearly loved in the wee hours of the morning in the practice room. I remember the burden of carrying a truth that I could not safely share. I remember what it was like to be African American and female in a space where I simply did not matter.

Thankfully, the world has changed a great deal since the mid-1980s. After undergrad, I seemed to be on a continuous quest to locate my own identity and culture in the academy, to answer the internal questions raised by my own conspicuous absence in the curriculum that I completed for my undergraduate degree. Graduate work in the 1990s afforded me exposure to the field of ethnomusicology and amazing resources like Eileen Southern's *The Music of Black Americans*, the Center for Black Music Research, the Center for Popular Music, and other scholarly resources and venues for treatments of jazz, gospel, rhythm & blues, and hip-hop. My dissertation was a semiotic analysis of a piano sonata by Florence Price, and once on the faculty at the University of Tulsa, I had the great joy of teaching several courses in African American music, including a survey course in the history of Black music, as well as courses on Black American gospel music, Blacks in classical music, and the history of rhythm & blues. Teaching those courses afforded me space to tell the story of my "born" music, imparting to my students all the rich contextualization necessary for proper understanding of and respect for its culture and tradition.

More recent years have seen sincere efforts to reckon with matters of race and racial difference in our field, and to foster more diverse, equitable, and inclusive music-educational experiences for all students. Recent events also remind us, however, that less-informed mindsets persist and that hard work remains. Nonetheless, I am encouraged to see important changes in the field of music theory, changes that bespeak an emerging curiosity and a bold and exciting openness to discovery.

At its best, music theory teaches *how* to think about music – how to wonder, question, investigate, analyze, explore, speculate, discover, and wonder again. In my experience, the best evidence of successful teaching is not the student who produces elegant, figured-bass realizations or the most beautifully crafted counterpoint. The best evidence of successful teaching is the student who acquires and masters all those concepts and skills and then takes the next step to ask, "What if?"

At its worst, music theory teaches *what* to think about music. It indoctrinates. It infuses value judgment with content, leading students to believe that some music is good, other music bad. It equates music notation with musical worth, thereby implying that music of oral tradition is unworthy of attention. It teaches allegiance and culturally biased assumptions. The worst of music theory teaching produces a cycle of narrowly focused self-affirmation, ignoring that there are countless culturally based "right" ways of doing music. The worst of music theory teaching assumes that the analytical tools that we know and love best are the litmus test of musical quality for all people and all time. It teaches the "either-or" false dichotomy that to love Bach is to despise B. B. King. It teaches analysis as a way to prove a point that has already been decided, rather than to discover what might go unnoticed. At its worst, music theory erases and silences students, forcing them to feign cultural and artistic self-deprecation and hide who they really are just to make it to graduation.

And so, it is with a lump in my throat and tearful gratitude that I imagine the impact of *Expanding the Canon: Black Composers in the Music Theory Classroom*. For many teachers and students, it will serve as a resource for engaging with new repertoire, and new pathways for exploring important concepts. More significantly, perhaps, this volume will serve as a beacon, signaling that it is safe for students of color to be heard and seen, and safe for all students to think expansively and embrace curiosity, holding space for one's "born" music as well as for the discovery and appreciation of musical identities, perspectives, styles, and traditions previously unknown.

Part One
Fundamentals and Diatonic Harmony

2 Rethinking Music Fundamentals
Centering the Contributions of Black Musicians

Uzee Brown Jr.

Introduction

I have been a faculty member at Morehouse College, a historically Black college in Atlanta, Georgia, for more than 40 years. While primarily trained as a composer, I have also taught music theory at some level almost every year. This chapter will unfold in two parts. Part One describes some of the best practices I have gleaned as a veteran teacher at Morehouse. Part Two provides some specific examples of the ways in which I use music by African American composers and arrangers in my classroom.

Part One: Best Practices

Consider the "What" and "Why" of Music Theory Fundamentals

In most higher education music programs, the primary focus of a music theory fundamentals course is to introduce the beginning student to basic terminology and concepts necessary to foment a foundational understanding of how music materials work. The music theory sequence tends to be one of the most rigorous tracks within the music major core in an undergraduate music degree program, because learning the rudiments and terminology in music are similar to learning a new foreign language, containing symbols like words, representing auditory responses with which the student might already be familiar but possess no tangible means of processing. This track should begin with theory fundamentals presented unambiguously and in such a way that synergy is established between the practical artistic application of music materials and the more abstract awareness of the physio-acoustical processes taking place in the production of musical sound.

A central objective of music fundamentals should be to equip the student with the basic skills required to implement the rudimentary tools of music as creators, as well as observers capable of synthesizing that which has already been created. This objective should lead to the following student learning outcomes:

- Know the meaning and use of critical terminology in the fundamental theory of music.
- Recognize and demonstrate rudimentary components of music: rhythms, meter signatures, key signatures, major and minor scales, intervals, and triads.
- Write music using rudimentary skills of musical construction listed previously.

Get to Know Your Students

The specifics of any music theory fundamentals course will depend on the population of students taking the course and their reasons for taking the course. At Morehouse, theory

DOI: 10.4324/9781003204053-4

fundamentals classes often include a combination of prospective music majors who will become teachers or performers, alongside music minors and nonmajors who just want to gain a better understanding of the basics of music. Except as a preparatory theory course for majors and minors, music fundamentals may be taken as an elective course toward graduation and is not required in the general education core for the nonmajor. Music fundamentals is the first level of introduction for the beginning student to the basic concepts and foundational building blocks in what is commonly called music of the western world. Traditionally, this would encompass elements of music from the common-practice era (roughly spanning from the early seventeenth century through the late nineteenth century and stemming from western European musical practices).

However, those teaching music fundamentals should consider expanding the paradigm of tonal musical concepts beyond the confines of western tonal common-practice music to include music from diverse cultural backgrounds – in particular, that music which grows out of diasporal culture classes reflective of African influences. Though inclusion of this music is of profound value to all students of theory fundamentals, regardless of racial or ethnic background, the musical contributions of Black musicians are especially important when teaching African and African American students. For students who come from backgrounds where very little classical western European music has been a part of their listening and music-making, it is particularly important that the instructor pay careful attention to what those students listen to, as well as how and why they make specific listening choices. Ideally, one should discern what venues and styles of musical exposition are most common among students and glean some sense of the previous auditory, visual, existential, and even subliminal listening experiences they may have had that could become a connective point of student engagement and enthusiasm in class. Using classroom surveys and pretests to examine various music types from the students' own backgrounds will yield some general understanding of the knowledge base and pulse of students' interests in a fundamentals class. The Supplemental Materials website contains a sample of possible classroom survey questions.

Begin at Ground Zero

Music fundamentals instruction should make few assumptions about a student's previous formal study of music. In other words, it should begin at ground zero. Failing to observe this grassroots approach can be intimidating for a beginning student without a formal orientation in music and may result in losing students who are compelled to ask, "What are they talking about?" A "ground zero" approach creates a path to increased enrollment among students in general studies who just want a basic understanding of musical elements.

Engage with Deeper Questions

Before a student can fully appreciate how to apply theoretical concepts to the practical manifestation of music, they should be guided toward an enthusiastic appreciation for what music really is and the reasons that music fundamentals might even be relevant. In order to truly appreciate music, the student must both understand what it is and what it is not. What is their working definition of music, and how is it distinguished from random noise? Sadly, I have encountered too many students who study music as their major but who do not even have the most basic working definition of music. If one begins with a simple and neutral definition of music, such as *organized sound in time*, no aesthetic presumptions are implied as to its style or its genre, or the outcome of its impact on the listener. This concedes that, within the context of the same definition, music may be provocative, enchanting, haunting, sensual, beautiful, severe; music may be classical, pop, R&B, country, rap, gospel, hip-hop, or a mixture of all these. A beneficial classroom measure may also be to engage students in probing the relevance of "functional music" in everyday life and throughout the ages on the human psyche, inclusive of music used for work or war; music used in movie soundtracks, advertising jingles, or worship; music listened to during socializing, romance, study, etc. When the objective is to provide an exposition of music fundamentals to a wide variety of learners, a practical, accessible definition and methodology might be implemented that ultimately impacts how the instructor conceives, plans, and delivers materials.

Engage Sound First

Music fundamentals students will be more likely to realize the cross-pollination of creative ideas in the arts when they can correlate an integrated understanding of visual and auditory stimuli. If a student cannot *hear* what a major scale sounds like, it will do little good for them to *visualize* the scale, either by letter name or on the musical staff. If an audio-to-visual concept of music is applied, then all musical materials might be visually represented as either vertical or horizontal (melodic, harmonic, etc.), with the awareness that music occurs within a spatial dimension that demands time and can generally be viewed within the context of some form of organization.

Equally important should be the student's formal introduction to both traditional orchestral instruments and nontraditional instruments. If the student receives this brief but necessary exposition to instruments with the goal of fostering an understanding and appreciation of the uniqueness of musical sounds, then the distinct capabilities and qualities of construction and design that contribute to the way instruments vibrate and resonate sound become, in part, a significant factor in understanding both the mathematical and the acoustical principles that define fundamental theory. A beginning student's understanding of these correlations is often eye-opening, especially for the student who already plays an instrument or sings. It is likely that students have never been asked to make associations between the instrument and its capabilities, and the fundamental principles behind the musical sounds it produces, or how those sounds may be captured on a musical score.

Music and Other Arts

African American students, and other students from regions of the Caribbean who are descendants of African diasporal experiences, may appreciate understanding the power of music as it relates to other disciplines within the arts, especially those that include analogous characteristics found in the music of their own culture. Establishing associations with other arts disciplines, such as dance, drama, visual arts, costumes, and pageantry, is relevant to an Afrocentric experience, where characteristics commonly found in indigenous West African culture classes are simply viewed as parts of a complete collective creative experience. Some context is then added to the value of the arts as expressions of life and manifestations of the human experience. It likewise addresses questions posed by some skeptics as to the relevance of music and other art forms to human existence.

Cultural Considerations

Much has been discussed among professional music contemporaries and educators with respect to the pedagogical "free spirit" or natural-learning approach to music, such as the ideas set forth in Randall Everett Allsup's *Remixing the Classroom: Toward an Open Philosophy of Music Education*. These ideas have special implications regarding education among people of color and those who are descendants of the African diasporal experience. The tenets of an "open philosophy of music education" compel one to consider the particular implications of culturally relevant methods used in rudimentary music learning, ultimately resulting in minimizing the attention given to more rigorously structured techniques used in common-practice music. To an extent, there are valid reasons for this position, because in the western paradigms of formal music study, sadly, the historical and theoretical omission of almost any musical examples that are not of western European origin is all too clear. For this reason, alternative thinking should be part of a new learning paradigm when trying to effectively connect with, and tap into, the creativity and enjoyment of music for students from vastly diverse sociocultural demographics.

Parallel with the previous statement, it must be understood that music is the language of sound, and that this language, like any, must be learned in order to appreciate its power to communicate. One must not go too far away from learning the basics. A fundamental understanding of music and the sounds and symbols that make it up cannot be overlooked. Learning these elements is as basic as learning the letters of the alphabet, learning to type, or learning to ride a bicycle, and these requirements have little to do with ethnic or racial demographics. Few shortcuts should be taken in understanding and applying these processes. Engaging in the learning activities previously cited will eventually, with practice, become reflectively inculcated into the musician's visual and auditory behaviors such that the trigger stimuli are automatic, regardless of student background. These include recognizing pitches on the grand staff and learning letter names, scale degrees, and key signatures. It also necessitates the requirement that the beginning music student glean a rudimentary familiarity with the musical keyboard and understand how rhythms contribute to the organization (time) of sound materials in music.

With consideration of the previous statements, however, there are no clear justifications why these rudiments cannot be gained by using examples from African American music, as well as music of other non-western cultures. The examples that follow are all from works by African American composers/arrangers and may be used to address certain specific elements of music fundamentals in a clear and concise way. Whenever possible, a careful and thoughtful economy of resources should be implemented when choosing musical examples so that several important aspects of fundamentals may be addressed within the same examples. Doing so will mean that students learn these examples very well after studying them from different perspectives across the span of a semester. This concept of the "spiral curriculum," where the instructor finds multiple levels of use for the same body of teaching materials, not only better familiarizes the student with specific literature used for analysis but also addresses the discovery of newer and higher levels of musical construction within a single work by looking at the varied layers of materials used to ultimately bring a whole composition into fruition.

Part Two: Musical Examples

A discussion about musical works by Black composers and arrangers that may be used as resources for music theory fundamentals courses can be beneficial and revelatory for both students and teachers. I have included several musical examples that fall within the category of African American songs; the first is one of my own compositions, an art song in a contemporary inspirational style ("This River"). The second is a Negro spiritual arranged by Margaret Bonds ("Hold On!"), and the third is an African American art song by John W. Work Jr. ("Soliloquy"). I have carefully selected each of these works because

Rethinking Music Fundamentals 19

each shows the application of some basic concept of theory fundamentals that should be facile for the fundamentals student: "This River" (C major), "Hold On" (C minor), "Soliloquy" (A minor).

"**This River**," though included in a set of spirituals titled *O Redeemed!*, is an original song, deliberately crafted in a contemporary inspirational song style, because it was intended to capture the essence of a theologian's contemplations through the text by Ja Jahannes (Figure 2.1a). I include this example because the melody demonstrates a C major scale without chromaticism that is nonetheless powerful. The colorful use of chromaticism is captured in the accompaniment only. This excerpt is the refrain of the song, which, though dramatically more intense, retains a certain musical balance and calm by implementing a conjunct C diatonic melody. The melody begins on a dominant anacrusis (G), then descends through the upper tetrachord of C major (C–B–A–G), only

Figure 2.1a Uzee Brown Jr., "This River," mm. 1–11.

stepping upward once to the supertonic D at the dramatic high point of the phrase. Tranquility returns with the lower tetrachord of C major (C–D–E–F), by descending from the dominant of C (G) to a point of repose on C at the cadence. The student should glean from studying this example that musical intensity and profundity can be derived from a simple diatonic melody.

"**Hold On!**" is a Negro spiritual arranged by prolific African American composer/arranger Margaret Bonds (1913–72) (Figure 2.1b). It is extensive in its treatment of several stylistic and idiomatic elements found in African American music. The introduction alone is a wonderful study of each of the three minor scale forms, as well as the minor pentatonic scale. The introduction begins with a minor pentatonic melody (C–E♭–F–G–B♭) that descends from the anacrusis on C_4 to the G_3. It immediately introduces a B♮ (m. 2, beat 3), implying harmonic minor. In measure 3, an F major triad emerges below the sustained C_4 and introduces the A♮, which is derived from the ascending melodic minor scale. Once the solo voice is introduced, the harmonies in the accompaniment immediately shift to the upper tetrachord of the C natural minor scale (G–A♭–B♭–C).

"**Soliloquy**" is an art song composed by African American composer John W. Work (1901–67), set to poetry of Myrtle Vorst Sheppard (Figure 2.1c). This example demonstrates natural minor and captures the rich color of parallel diatonic harmonies on the tonic and lowered seventh scale degrees (i and VII). A pedal tone on F_3 undergirds the harmonies. The sustained E_5 in measure 5 initiates a descent that effectively paints the text "I will not fear" as the melody moves toward a posture of calm in its downward resolution to the tonic note. The piece slowly ascends from A minor to its relative major, C. The entire piece is a powerful example of effective text painting. Consider the text, and if possible, listen to the transition of musical materials that occur as the song moves

Figure 2.1b Margaret Bonds, "Hold On," mm. 1–7. Courtesy of the Theodore Presser Company. Used with permission.

Figure 2.1c John W. Work, "Soliloquy," mm. 1–8. Courtesy of the Edward B. Marks Music Company. Used with permission.

through this text: "If death be only half as sweet as life, I will not fear, I'll shed no tear; nor will I ask my friends to weep; but quietly go, like melting snow upon a mountains steep great height."

Other examples that might be considered for study in a music theory fundamentals class are:

BILL WITHERS, "LEAN ON ME": conjunct melody, diatonic harmonies
SCOTT JOPLIN, "ELITE SYNCOPATIONS": diatonic pentatonic scale, various ascending and descending chromatic passages
DUKE ELLINGTON, "IN A SENTIMENTAL MOOD": demonstrates each of the basic triads

Works Cited

Allsup, Randall Everett. 2016. *Remixing the Classroom: Toward an Open Philosophy of Music Education*. Indiana University Press.

3 Change from the Middle, Right from the Beginning
Strategies for Incorporating Black Composers in a Music Fundamentals Course

Robin Attas

Introduction

A music fundamentals course presents the opportunity to shape students' understanding of what music theory, and music, could be from the first days of their programs. The course's very title indicates what is truly considered "fundamental" for music theory students, instructors, and the discipline itself: a clear, if often implicit, statement of what it really means to study music at a particular institution. Further, since the music fundamentals course is often a remedial or required course that is a prerequisite for further study in music, it serves as a gatekeeper that, along with audition requirements and entrance exams, determines who is permitted to study music at the postsecondary level (Douglas 2010). Those without "fundamental" skills in a particular culturally situated understanding of music theory are not permitted to advance within the degree.

The fundamentals course thus presents a significant opportunity to either reinforce or reimagine the values, norms, and standards of postsecondary musical study. If a music fundamentals course provides the first glimpse for many students into what music theory is and what it isn't, then instructors have a lot of power to change those views. The fundamentals course could allow both students and instructors to uncover, expose, and challenge music theory's "White racial frame" (Ewell 2020) by questioning together what constitutes the core elements of music. It could also introduce foundational elements of critical reflection that encourage students to question received norms and truths about music theory that are in fact rooted in White western European thought and culture. Finally, opening up the music fundamentals course to a wider range of music cultures and values could result in different, and possibly more diverse, student demographics in subsequent courses and degrees, and in music careers beyond graduation.

Revising a music fundamentals course to incorporate music and musical ideas by Black musicians, composers, and theorists would go a long way toward enhancing diversity in the undergraduate music theory curriculum, but it is also important to move beyond gestures of inclusion in order to truly enact antiracist pedagogies.[1] Curricular change is a process, and instructors have different levels of willingness and ability to modify their approaches, but continuous modifications and personal development are required if these modifications are to be meaningful rather than tokenistic.

This chapter describes possible revisions to music theory fundamentals that explore a middle ground between total revision and minor changes. It describes strategies for two core topics in most fundamentals courses (pitch and meter) and addresses a third (texture) that offers an example of how reconceiving the typical topics discussed in music fundamentals can lead to new approaches to the music of Black composers and others. It includes a variety of examples and lesson plans that could be used in multiple

DOI: 10.4324/9781003204053-5

ways: as simple inclusion exercises that add music of Black composers and performers without changing analytical techniques or core values (what I have previously called the "plug and play" option [Attas 2019]), as part of revisions to sections of the fundamentals curriculum, or as motivation for a complete overhaul of the curriculum to reject current White western European common-practice art music norms.[2] Instructors can choose strategies that match their own personal readiness and self-education as well as program outcomes and institutional contexts and goals. Finally, it is worth noting that while Black composers are the focus of this chapter and this volume, the underlying philosophy of course design presented here could be adapted to address the music of other underrepresented groups and music cultures.

Pitch

Teaching pitch is one area where a balance of approaches in a music fundamentals course is vital. In a typical fundamentals course, developing learners' facility with pitch reading in the western European notation system is a core learning objective and is critical for student success in later music theory courses, particularly those focused on common-practice diatonic harmony and voice leading. Eliminating an emphasis on pitch reading would do a disservice to students in western-focused music programs. Yet a disservice is also done if students are not challenged to understand pitch as culturally situated: that is, if instructors never expose five-line staff notation, the twelve-note chromatic collection, Latin letter names, and solfège as products of particular White European cultures, adopted and adapted by other cultures around the world. The activities proposed in the following passages strike a balance between these two important goals.

To begin the conversation around the culturally situated nature of pitch, I recommend asking students to discuss their own differing conceptions of pitch and pitch notation, uncovering their own biases and allowing instructors to add new information to existing understanding. Attas Supplemental Material 3.1 provides a lesson plan for doing so; each activity could also be separated out for a 15-minute discussion, an online discussion board post, or an individual assignment, perhaps integrated with more typical fundamentals discussions of western European pitch notation. Some instructors might even wish to expand further, for instance, by discussing the effect of having some of the definitions of pitch mediated through reporters from other cultures (as in the Chinese bells definition), while others come directly from a member of the culture (as in the blues definition).

Fundamentals courses commonly ask students to complete pitch identification exercises and drills. Using scores written by Black composers for these drills is an easy way to challenge White supremacist norms in the fundamentals classroom. An abundance of options, including scores in the public domain, is available through the Composers of Color Resource Project (https://composersofcolor.hcommons.org). This activity could also be used to reinforce other complementary skills. For instance, R. Nathaniel Dett's "Music in the Mine" (1916) is a four-part vocal score that would allow students to practice sight singing along with pitch reading. The first 16 measures are included as Attas Supplemental Material 3.2. Instructors can consider diversifying genre as well as composer identity: the melodies of Black popular musicians and songwriters such as Yola, Prince, Nina Simone, Missy Elliot, and the numerous songwriters associated with Motown Records are among many, many wonderful possibilities, and transcriptions are easily purchased or created.

To reinforce and deepen these discussions, Attas Supplemental Material 3.3 presents a short assignment question where Black jazz musician Etta James's 1960 recording of "At Last" serves as inspiration for connecting musical sounds with theoretical definitions and concepts. (Answer keys for this and all other assignment questions are also available on the Supplemental Materials website.) In this assignment, listening skills are developed alongside further critical appraisal of the definitions of pitch discussed in class.

Meter

Rhythm and meter are common topics taught in music fundamentals courses, although usually the focus is on duration and time signature notation rather than metric theories and the impact of particular metric and rhythmic choices on the listener. In this section, I present options for teaching rhythm and meter that expand musical examples to include consideration of music by Black composers and that incorporate theoretical frameworks for meter and rhythm that move beyond taxonomic identification of durations and time signatures. This allows instructors to lay a foundation for students to pursue more advanced metrical topics later while also diversifying the curriculum.

I recommend teaching the concept of musical accent before a discussion of time signatures and rhythmic notation, as this theoretical concept feeds into these fundamentals-level discussions but also relates to other musical parameters typically covered later in the course, such as pitch, melody, and harmony. Attas Supplemental Material 3.4 provides a 30-minute lesson plan and follow-up assignment discussing various types of accent using Pamela Z's *Bone Music*. This might be combined with standard fundamentals topics on notation (e.g., dynamic markings, articulation, and accent markings) or with other topics.

Once students are familiar with western European art music duration notation (half notes, quarter notes, dots, ties, etc.), fundamentals texts commonly move to a discussion of meter rooted in time signatures. Correct notation within diverse time signatures is an important foundational skill, but I also suggest discussing the difference between rhythm and meter as well as introducing a basic metric theory to provide a deeper context for learners. In core theory courses at various levels, I have successfully used adaptations of Christopher Hasty's (1997) meter-as-process approach; however, in a fundamentals class, a simpler analytical system deriving from grid-based (Lerdahl and Jackendoff 1983; Temperley 2001) and pulse-stream (Krebs 1999) approaches is likely more appropriate.

Attas Supplemental Material 3.5 outlines a 50-minute lesson plan using a transcribed excerpt from pop musician Janelle Monaé's song "Dance or Die" from her 2010 album *The ArchAndroid* (a class handout and answer key are also included). Attas Supplemental Material 3.6 provides the opening eight measures of Henry F. Williams's Parisian Waltz no. 3 if instructors wish to develop a supplemental assignment or quiz. The lesson plan assumes that students have learned about the difference between rhythm and meter, metric types (simple vs. compound; duple/triple/quadruple, etc.), and time signatures. These topics are described in the lesson plan as review, but instructors could either omit the review or use the review materials to develop preceding lessons as needed.

Attas Supplemental Material 3.7 provides an assignment that gives learners an opportunity to synthesize knowledge of accents, meter and rhythm, and durational notation. In this assignment, students are asked to analyze a stanza from Maya Angelou's poem "These Yet to Be United States," exploring possible accent patterns that would lead to rhythmic settings in various time signatures.[3] The end goal is for students to compose a rhythmic setting for a single stanza of the poem that considers accents in the text alone.

Texture

Topics in pitch and meter tend to dominate music fundamentals courses; in most textbooks, any topic beyond these two areas is rare or nonexistent.[4] Expanding the topics discussed in a fundamentals class to encompass more than the approaches to pitch and

Change from the Middle, Right from the Beginning 25

meter that typically characterize analysis of White western European art music would go a long way toward diversifying the music theory curriculum not just in terms of *whose* music is discussed but on *how* music is discussed. It would prepare music students to engage meaningfully with music where pitch and meter may be less important than other aspects, including, but not limited to, much music by Black composers and musicians.[5] Even a single class period on a topic such as groove, flow, form, text-music connections, music-body connections, timbre, or repetition would go a long way toward breaking down the dominance of White western European approaches to music and music theory.

Texture is another possible area for discussion within a fundamentals course, and one that lends itself well to engaging with music of diverse cultures, including Black cultures. Given the middleground changes this chapter is exploring, discussion of texture might take up just a single class period. However, this single class period might serve as the foundation for deeper engagement in future courses.

As an introduction to the topic of texture, instructors might consider assigning a reflective writing exercise as simple as "What is texture?" This could be done in advance of a class period or at the beginning of a class discussion. Not only does this exercise get ideas flowing and allow students to think prior to discussing, but the open-ended nature of the question also allows for students to bring their own ideas and experiences from their diverse backgrounds and opens western European definitions to critique (or, at least, discussion) rather than presenting them as universal truths. Attas Supplemental Material 3.8 offers that opening question with a few possible definitions drawn from music theory literature.

Taxonomic definitions are a common theoretical approach to the study of texture in undergraduate textbooks. Attas Supplemental Material 3.9 collects a group of definitions of different texture types. This may be sufficient for instructors who want to maintain a tight focus on the music of western Europe and would be particularly easy to integrate into a course sequence that includes the study of species counterpoint. Those with more time, curricular flexibility, and motivation to challenge current Eurocentric norms might consider presenting more diverse definitions of texture, such as those found in ethnomusicological textbooks introducing the study of world or global music.[6]

Whatever the starting place for definitions, instructors have additional agency when it comes to the music they choose as exemplars of those definitions. In the final column of the chart in Attas Supplemental Material 3.9, I have provided a few possibilities for each of the standard textural types, all of which are music by Black composers and which expand repertoire selections beyond western European art music. Many of the examples feature different textures at different moments and could also serve as rich sources for assignments or tests.

Another approach to texture is to focus less on taxonomy and more on process, drawing on the work of Wallace Berry (1987) and Mark Butler (2006). Berry's theory focuses on western European art music and describes two important elements for the study of texture as process: the density of components (how many lines there are; how they are spaced in terms of register, pitch, sound; etc.)[7] and the interactions or relationships among them (how coordinated the parts are; if they work together, independently, in opposition; etc.).[8] These definitions might be enough to spark a general class discussion on textural processes in a specific piece by a Black composer/musician.

Butler's theory is rooted in the study of electronic dance music (EDM) and uses two forms of transcription to explore texture in that repertoire: the textural graph and the sound palette (Butler 2006, 179–81). The textural graph shows how the texture and instrumentation of a track changes from moment to moment, using graphic notation (rectangles, lines, patterns, etc.) to indicate pattern lengths and distinct repetitive elements. The sound palette works in conjunction with the textural graph, cataloguing all the sounds heard in a track in a chart that uses western European music notation to transcribe each loop. Butler proposes three categories of sound for the sound palette: rhythmic, articulative, and atmospheric. Rhythmic sounds are repetitive and generally short, with a function more rhythmic than melodic (i.e., the sounds are not a melody unfolding over a longer span of time but instead part of the repetitive texture of short loops that make up the track). Articulative sounds are brief and intermittent, usually appearing at or near structural boundaries, such as the beginning of a section. Atmospheric sounds are hazy and dynamically soft and generally lack a clear rhythm or pitch profile. They are meant to fill in the texture and contribute to the mood of the track but do not have a pattern of repetition or pitch that is easily identifiable or transcribable.

Attas Supplemental Material 3.10 uses both of these theorists' work to provide discussion questions and transcriptions of excerpts from the track "Despite the Weather" by Haitian Canadian producer and DJ Kaytranada. This information could be used to teach texture as a process, either in class or on an assignment. As with other materials in this chapter, sections of this longer resource could also be used and adapted if instructors have only limited time for a topic that may seem beyond the scope of most music fundamentals courses.

Conclusion

The monumental nature of the changes required in music theory pedagogy may feel overwhelming, and even if instructors adopt all the suggestions here, there is still a long way to go toward equity for Black composers and musicians in the core curriculum. Music fundamentals courses are challenging places to enact change, but the impact of changes in these foundational courses is significant. And it may be that change comes not in content but in an instructor's outlook and approach. If the only thing this chapter provokes is greater self-reflection on the parts of music fundamentals instructors in terms of what is taught and how it is taught, I will be pleased to know that readers are taking the first steps toward antiracist pedagogical strategies and curricular change. But I hope that this chapter also provides support for more significant steps along a path that is long overdue: dismantling the White supremacist approaches to music theory and analysis that should not be the fundamental characteristics of fundamentals courses.

Notes

1. For starting points relating to antiracist pedagogies, see Kendi (2019), Kishimoto (2018), and the Wheaton College Center for Collaborative Teaching and Learning.
2. Some of my inspiration for these curricular revisions comes from advocates for the incorporation of ethnomusicological approaches into introductory music theory courses; see, for example, Moore (2017).
3. This poem, written in 1990, is available in Angelou (2015).
4. Textbooks demonstrating this point include Root (2013), Shaffer and Wharton (2014), Straus (2012), Takesue (2018), Clendinning et al. (2018).
5. For a detailed discussion of the role of pitch and rhythm in European- and African-derived musical styles, see Rose (1994, particularly chapter 3), "Soul Sonic Forces: Technology, Orality, and Black Cultural Practice in Rap Music."
6. See, for example, Bakan (2019), Miller and Shahriari (2017), Titon (2017).
7. Berry's more formal definition of density is "that textural parameter, quantitative and measurable, conditioned by the number of simultaneous or concurrent components and by the extent of vertical 'space' encompassing them." Berry (1987, 191, fn.6).
8. Berry describes this as "the degree and nature of interlinear concordance (agreement, lack of conflict) or coincident factors of relative intensity and variance (counterpoint)" and also includes consideration of "changes in relative *independence and interdependence* among concurrent components in a given musical texture." Berry (1987, 185).

Works Cited

Angelou, Maya. 2015. *Maya Angelou: The Complete Poetry*. Random House.
Attas, Robin. 2019. "Music Theory as Social Justice: Pedagogical Applications of Kendrick Lamar's *To Pimp A Butterfly*." *Music Theory Online* 25/1. https://doi.org/10.30535/mto.25.1.8
Bakan, Michael. 2019. *World Music: Traditions and Transformations*, 3rd edition. McGraw Hill.
Bean, John. 2011. *Engaging Ideas*, 2nd edition. Jossey-Bass.
Berry, Wallace. 1987. *Structural Functions in Music*. Dover.
Butler, Mark. 2006. *Unlocking the Groove*. Indiana University Press.
Clendinning, Jane Piper, Elizabeth West Marvin, and Joel Phillips. 2018. *The Musician's Guide to Fundamentals*, 3rd edition. W.W. Norton.
Cooke, Peter. "Pitch" (II, 1). In *Grove Music Online*, edited by Deane Root. Accessed 16 July 2021. www.oxfordmusiconline.com.
Cooper, Grosvenor, and Leonard Meyer. 1960. *The Rhythmic Structure of Music*. University of Chicago Press.
Douglas, Gavin. 2010. "Decolonizing Music Theory: Some Thoughts from Outside the Field." Paper delivered at the Committee on Diversity special session, "Addressing Ethnic and Racial Diversity in Music Theory." Society for Music Theory Annual Meeting.
Ewell, Philip. 2020. "Music Theory and the White Racial Frame." *Music Theory Online* 26/2. https://doi.org/10.30535/mto.26.2.4
Hasty, Christopher. 1997. *Meter as Rhythm*. Oxford University Press.
Haynes, Bruce. "Pitch (I, introduction)." In *Grove Music Online*, edited by Deane Root. Accessed 16 July 2021. www.oxfordmusiconline.com.
Kendi, Ibram X. 2019. *How to Be An Antiracist*. One World.
King, B.B. 1973. *Blues Guitar: A Method by B.B. King*. Compiled and edited by Jerry Snyder. Charles Hansen.
Kishimoto, Kyoko. 2018. "Anti-Racist Pedagogy: From Faculty's Self-Reflection to Organizing Within and Beyond the Classroom." *Race Ethnicity and Education* 2/4: 540–54.
Krebs, Harald. 1999. *Fantasy Pieces: Metrical Dissonance in the Music of Robert Schumann*. Oxford University Press.
Lerdahl, Fred, and Ray Jackendoff. 1983. *A Generative Theory of Tonal Music*. The MIT Press.
Miller, Terry E., and Andrew Shahriari. 2017. *World Music: A Global Journey*. Routledge.
Moore, Robin D., ed. 2017. *College Music Curricula for a New Century*. Oxford University Press.
Pearsall, Edward. 2012. *Twentieth-Century Music Theory and Practice*. Routledge.
Roig-Francolí, Miguel A. 2020. *Harmony in Context*, 3rd edition. McGraw-Hill.
Root, Jena. 2013. *Applied Music Fundamentals: Writing, Singing, and Listening*. Oxford University Press.
Rose, Tricia. 1994. *Black Noise: Rap Music and Black Culture in Contemporary America*. Wesleyan University Press.
Shaffer, Kris, and Robin Wharton, eds. 2014. *Open Music Theory*. Hybrid Pedagogy Publishing. http://hybrid.pub/
Straus, Joseph. 2012. *Elements of Music*, 3rd edition. Pearson Prentice Hall.
Takesue, Sumy. 2018. *Music Fundamentals: A Balanced Approach*, 3rd edition. Routledge.
Temperley, David. 2001. *The Cognition of Basic Musical Structures*. The MIT Press.
Titon, Jeff Todd, ed. 2017. *Worlds of Music: An Introduction to the Music of the World's Peoples*, 6th edition. Cengage Learning.
Wheaton College Center for Collaborative Teaching and Learning. "Becoming an Anti-Racist Educator." Last modified 2020. https://wheatoncollege.edu/academics/special-projects-initiatives/center-for-collaborative-teaching-and-learning/anti-racist-educator/
Z, Pamela. 2004. "Bone Music." *A Delay Is Better*, 213. Starkland.

4 Rhiannon Giddens and Francis "Frank" Johnson in the First-Year Theory Classroom

Jan Miyake

Introduction

This chapter supports the teaching of intervals, non-chord tones, closure and cadences, form, basic harmony (I, IV, V^7, V$^6_5$), and analysis by engaging deeply with Rhiannon Giddens's (1977–) "Ten Thousand Voices," from her 2019 album *There Is No Other*, and Francis Johnson's (1792–1844) "Victoria Galop," published in 1839.

Giddens is a multi-instrumentalist, singer, and composer who "uses her art to excavate the past and reveal bold truths about our present." Her "lifelong mission is to lift up people whose contributions to American musical history have previously been erased, and to work toward a more accurate understanding of the country's musical origins" (Giddens, n.d.). Giddens found inspiration for "Ten Thousand Voices" while reading the opening chapters of a book about the history of Cuban music. The book began with the history of the trans-Saharan Arabic slave trade, and Giddens came across a description of enslaved women who were talented musicians. These musicians presented their repertoire in books, which allowed a potential owner to see which songs they knew. The lore is that these women knew ten thousand verses.[1]

"Ten Thousand Voices" uses a cello banjo and double bass to drone on the tonal center, D.[2] Giddens's collaborator, fellow multi-instrumentalist Francesco Turrisi, plays the cello banjo and improvises an introduction and three interludes in an Arabic-influenced improvisation, in reflection of the Arab presence in the story. The use of a drone sets this song up well for teaching harmonic intervals. Studying the structure of the song reveals how the resting points gravitate toward members of tonic triad and how multiple musical parameters affect the finality of the strongest resting points. These unharmonized cadences are an excellent starting point for teaching about closure without invoking harmony. Finally, the simple texture – especially the unmetered presentation and unharmonized melody – allows a clear introduction to non-chord tones.

Francis "Frank" Johnson was a famous Black bandleader in Philadelphia. A trip to England with his band in late 1837 divides Johnson's career into two parts. Prior to this trip, he arranged music from abroad for American bands and played the bugle for balls and parades. In England, he gave public concerts, private concerts, and even a command performance for Queen Victoria, who had just ascended to the throne in June of 1837. His public concert programs included music by Bellini, Rossini, de Bériot, and many others, all of which Johnson arranged for his band. In London, he was surrounded by music, where, in addition to performances of Handel's *Messiah* and Haydn's *Creation*, there were promenade concerts (Southern 1977). This trendy concert practice originated in Paris and used a large band to play dance programs of "overtures, quadrilles, galops, waltzes, and arrangements of operatic arias" (Southern 1977, 10). On his return to the United States in the summer of 1838, Johnson's band went on an extended concert tour,

DOI: 10.4324/9781003204053-6

returning to Philadelphia in December of 1838. That Christmas, he gave promenade concerts that were attended by thousands. His final years adopted this schedule: playing in Saratoga Springs, Cape May, or White Sulphur Springs in the summer, touring in the North and Canada in the fall and spring, and wintering in Philadelphia. Every winter, he continued this new tradition of a promenade concert, and during the 1843–44 winter, he joined with vocal artists in Philadelphia to offer the first integrated concert in the United States. Sadly, his death the following April ended the tradition of performing integrated concerts before it could take hold (Southern 1997, 113).

Johnson's "Victoria Galop," published in 1839, stands in stark contrast to "Ten Thousand Voices." It is lighthearted, fully harmonized, untexted, in the major mode, and 180 years older. Originally composed during his London visit, "Victoria Galop" was written in honor of Queen Victoria. A *galop* is a dance form in a fast $\frac{2}{4}$ time that was a forerunner of the polka. It is an example of fashionable dance music played at social functions in 1820–40s Philadelphia and a good teaching piece for parallel periods, basic harmony, cadences, and sectional forms. As a pair of pieces, "Ten Thousand Voices" and "Victoria Galop" provide students with contrasting soundscapes and windows into two moments of time in Black histories.

Intervals

Both "Ten Thousand Voices" and "Victoria Galop" provide examples for interval identification. Worksheet 1 relies on these two songs to teach students that the diatonic intervals formed with $\hat{1}$ and $\hat{5}$ create the major- or minor-mode soundscape of a piece. Additionally, if students know their minor and major scales, they can quickly identify whether thirds, sixths, or sevenths are major or minor. This latter takeaway would need additional reinforcement with classroom examples and standard worksheets.

The worksheet starts with "Ten Thousand Voices" because it offers a musical setting unencumbered by harmony to explore intervals above the tonic pitch. In this piece, a strong drone in the double bass and tenor banjo provides an ever-present bass note over which to hear intervals. Turrisi and Giddens take turns presenting melodies. Giddens's melodies set the text of her poem, while Turrisi's melodies are improvised. The background scale of the piece is unclear, because the first half avoids $\hat{6}$, while the second uses two versions of $\hat{6}$: B♭ and B♮.

Worksheet 1 assumes that students already know how to identify intervals within an octave. Its purpose is to show that thirds, sixths, and sevenths over tonic in a minor scale are minor, and over tonic in a major scale are major. Worksheet 1 first has students measure the intervals each note of a D major scale makes with tonic. This work leads to the observation (in 4a) that $\hat{2}$, $\hat{3}$, $\hat{6}$, and $\hat{7}$ create major intervals with the tonic pitch. It then asks students to listen to "Ten Thousand Songs," paying attention to the presence of a drone, as well as how the given notation (shown in Figure 4.1) models what they hear. After describing the pitch content of the piece, students then measure the intervals each note makes with tonic. This work leads to the observation (in 4b) that $\hat{2}$, $\hat{3}$, $\hat{6}$, and $\hat{7}$ from the natural minor scale create *mostly* minor intervals with its tonic. The worksheet closes

Figure 4.1 Giddens, "Ten Thousand Voices," lines 1 and 2.

its use of "Ten Thousand Voices" with an open question about Giddens's use of both B♭ and B♮ and the impact of these pitches on the moods, meanings, or feel of the piece.

This portion of the worksheet leads well into drilling major and minor thirds, sixths, and sevenths by using major and minor scales. If the second note belongs to the major scale of the first note, it is a perfect or major interval. If the second note does not belong to the major scale of the first note, it is minor, diminished, or augmented. The second is major for both major and minor scales, but by measuring against the major scale first, students will not mistake it for a minor second. For example, if you ask students to identify the interval from B to D♯, they can play a B major scale on their instrument and notice that D♯ belongs to the major scale and is therefore a major third.

After exploring intervals above tonic, the worksheet then transfers that knowledge to intervals above the dominant, $\hat{5}$. Scale-degree 5 is the second most important member of a major or minor scale, and the intervals formed between it and other members of the scale are almost the same as the intervals formed with tonic. All or almost all non-perfect intervals match the modality of the key. For example, in F major, all but one of the intervals above the dominant C are perfect or major, while all the intervals above the dominant C in F (natural) minor are perfect or minor. The combination of these two sets of intervals above tonic and dominant helps explain why pieces built on major scales sound major and pieces built on minor scales sound minor.

Some in-class options for setting up Worksheet 1 could include listening to the first two lines of "Ten Thousand Voices" to tease out the pitch collection (Figure 4.1) by ear. After identifying the tonic pitch, the scale degrees of each line can be recognized. Phrase 1 introduces $\hat{5}$, $\hat{4}$, and $\hat{7}$ (A, G, and C). Phrase 2 adds $\hat{1}$ and $\hat{3}$ (D and F) to the collection, phrase 3 adds $\hat{2}$, and phrase 4 introduces no new pitches. Reordering these pitches to reflect the tonal center of D results in an incomplete scale (D, E, F, G, A, C) because there is no $\hat{6}$. Point out that this is *almost* a scale, and let them know that before the song ends, it fills in the missing pitch in interesting ways. Another important setup idea is to introduce these two composers. Since interval identification is the most basic topic covered in this chapter, students have not yet been introduced to these musicians. Providing pictures, birth and death dates, a short biography, and a sense of what was happening in the United States during these composers' lifetimes will promote diversity and inclusion in the music theory classroom.[3]

Non-Chord Tones

To prepare for the worksheet, students need to know the terms *chord tone* and *non-chord tone*, as well as the types of non-chord tones. Table 4.1 lays out typical non-chord tones by focusing on contour and metric placement. The table is intended to account for common, clear examples. It does not account for more nuanced situations, such as non-chord tones that decorate non-chord tones, and filling in a leap of a fourth with a single passing tone (resulting in a step and a leap of a third). To use this table, first identify and circle the non-chord tone on a score. There are three contours: mountain, valley, and straight line. The way you visualize the contour is by "looking left, looking right." I ask students to center the non-chord tone and then create a three-pitch contour by looking to its left and looking to its right. The three pitches (left, center, right) create a contour that dips like a valley, rises and falls like a mountain, or proceeds in a straight line. Table 4.1 also emphasizes metric placement, which is context-sensitive. Students need to figure out the largest level of meter that contains the non-chord tone. This metric level could be at any level – the sixteenth, the half note, everything in between, and everything beyond. I use Table 4.1 during class by pairing it with simple examples over a C major chord. After I demonstrate

Table 4.1 Important Information for Identifying Non-Chord Tones

Type of Non-Chord Tone	Abbreviation	Contour (Look Left, Look Right)	Metric Placement
Upper Neighbor	UN	Mountain, by step on both sides	Unaccented
Accented Upper Neighbor	AUN	Mountain, by step on both sides	Accented
Lower Neighbor	LUN	Valley, by step on both sides	Unaccented
Accented Lower Neighbor	LUN	Valley, by step on both sides	Accented
Incomplete Upper Neighbor	IUN	Mountain, by leap on the left, by step on the right	Unaccented
Appoggiatura (*this is an accented Incomplete Upper Neighbor*)	App	Mountain, by leap on the left, by step on the right	Accented
Incomplete Lower Neighbor	ILN	Valley, by leap on the left, by step on the right	Unaccented
Appoggiatura (*this is an accented Incomplete Lower Neighbor*)	App	Valley, by leap on the left, by step on the right	Accented
Escape tone, also known as échapée	Esc	Mountain or valley (mountain much more common), by step on the left, by third on the right	Unaccented
Passing Tone	PT, or just P	Straight line by step, ascending or descending	Unaccented
Accented Passing Tone	APT	Straight line by step, ascending or descending	Accented

a few examples, I ask students to come up with examples of the other non-chord tones. We sing them while conducting to pay attention to metric placement.

Worksheet 2 starts with the first eight measures of "Victoria Galop," given here as Figure 4.2a. Students could complete this worksheet in small groups or as homework. The first two steps are complete: (1) identify the chord(s) in each bar, and (2) circle the notes that do not belong to the chord. This simple texture uses only two chords: F major and C^7. In measures 3, 4, and 7, the C^7 is over E in the bass. The left hand needs to be considered as a broken chord – only bars 7 and 8 have two bass notes; all the rest have one bass note. There are four non-chord tones in this excerpt. Measures 2, 4, and 6 are chromatic lower neighbors, because looking to the left and to the right of the non-chord tone results in a valley shape (neighbor), the circled note is less accented than the notes to its left and right (unaccented), and the circled note is not on the F major scale (chromatic). The non-chord tone in measure 8 is an escape tone because it is less accented than the notes to its left and right, approached by step and left by skip, and has a mountain shape.

The worksheet continues with measures 17–28 (measures 9–16 are a *forte* repeat of measures 1 through 8). For this passage, students will need to label the chords (one or two chords per bar) and circle the non-chord tones. One judgment call in measures 17–21, given as Figure 4.2b, can be discussed ahead of time, or the instructor can see what students choose to do and use the variety of decisions to initiate classroom discussion. The question concerns how many chords there are in each bar. While the bass note implies one chord per bar, when combined with the upper voices, there is a different chord over each C. This analytical decision means that measure 17 is an F chord over C, and measure 18 alternates between C^7 and F♯ diminished triads over C. The chord-by-chord reading is more literal and will locate non-chord tones only in measure 20. Reading these four bars as an expanded C^7

Figure 4.2 (a) Johnson, "Victoria Galop," mm. 1–8; (b) Johnson, "Victoria Galop," mm. 17–20; (c, d, and e) four-note melisma in Giddens, "Ten Thousand Voices": (c) uninterpreted, (d) UN reading, (e) decorated IUN reading.

chord will locate non-chord tones on the weak beats of measures 17 and 18 (passing tones), as well as on the weak eighth notes of measure 19 (chromatic lower neighbors). Discussion could touch on how you hear the passage (lots of chord changes or one decorated chord) and/or introduce advanced topics, such as harmonic syntax and common-tone diminished chords. If the instructor would like all students to reasonably arrive at the same answer, they should tell students ahead of time one of two things: measures 17–20 are all a C^7 chord, or every bass note in measures 17–20 has its own chord.

Worksheet 2 closes with identifying non-chord tones in "Ten Thousand Voices." In the non-harmonized texture, we rely on the melismata (multiple melismas) to identify non-chord tones. The melismata in this piece are two, three, or four notes long. Two-note melismata are chordal skips and, by definition, have only chord tones. Three-note melismata can be identified using the "look left, look right" strategy. Four-note melismata are more complicated in this song because they have multiple readings. Figures 4.2c, d, and e present the four-note melisma, which occurs as the second phrase of stanzas 3 and 4.

In Worksheet 2, students are asked to choose between (d) and (e) and explain their choice. They can rely on how Giddens performs it, on how a reading meshes with the rest of the piece, or anything else they can support with evidence.

Closure and Cadence

Cadence is a theoretical concept well-defined by textbooks. For example, a perfect authentic cadence (PAC) has root position $\hat{5}$–$\hat{1}$ motion in the bass, dominant to tonic harmonic movement, and stepwise motion to $\hat{1}$ in the upper voice. Once we leave the textbooks for "real" music, however, those clear definitions are sometimes less helpful. "Ten Thousand Voices" and "Victoria Galop" benefit from broadening the discussion of closure beyond cadence. In addition to evaluating moments of closure as "open" or "closed," weighing their importance along a continuum of local, intermediate, and global impact helps clarify that moments of closure have varying degrees of significance.[4] Students have strong instincts about cadential strength, and working toward identifying musical factors that support or contradict their instincts helps develop their analytical skills.

"Ten Thousand Voices" has no harmony but clearly has moments of closure. Each stanza of Giddens's text has an ABAB rhyme scheme and ends on D_4. Within each stanza, Giddens's breathing and phrasing choices imply four phrases. Table 4.2 provides two different ways to hear closure in the piece, which are reprinted as part of Worksheet 3. Some ideas for how to use Table 4.2 in class include offering a free-write question about which interpretation a student prefers, asking students to prepare performances on their own instruments that communicate each reading, or setting up a debate for students that argues that one reading is "better" than another.

One particularly important discussion point involves the following question: "What musical factors create global closure?" Encourage students to move beyond the text and look at musical factors such as timbre, register, tonality, scale step, orchestration, contour, and any other musical factor they can draw upon. Some of their observations might include the fact that the strongest moments of closure (the end of each line) rest on D_4, on the lowest point of the phrase, and with a descending contour. These factors contrast with the mid-line points of closure, which are all on $\hat{5}$, a relatively high pitch in this song that leaves an open-ended feel to that moment.

Table 4.2 Two Readings of Closure in Rhiannon Giddens's "Ten Thousand Voices"

Stanza	Line 1	Line 2	Line 3	Line 4
1	"stories" local	"songs" intermediate	"worries" local	"wrongs" global
2	"faces" local	"words" intermediate	"graces" local	"birds" global
3	"kisses" local	"tears" intermediate	"wishes" local	"years" global
4	"choices" local	"strong" intermediate	"voices" local	"song" global

Stanza	Line 1	Line 2	Line 3	Line 4
1	"stories" none	"songs" local	"worries" none	"wrongs" intermediate
2	"faces" none	"words" local	"graces" none	"birds" intermediate
3	"kisses" none	"tears" local	"wishes" none	"years" intermediate
4	"choices" none	"strong" local	"voices" none	"song" global

Moving to "Victoria Galop," the same discussion could be had for measures 1–8, with the same closure patterns offered for one stanza in Table 4.2. In this case, each "line" is two bars long. Worksheet 3 provides the A section so that the patterns of Table 4.2 can be transferred to it. It then provides two contrasting excerpts from the Galop (the B and C sections) that will allow students to engage with nuances of differing strengths of closing.

After students complete this worksheet, class discussion can return to teasing out what creates the strongest moments of closure. In the Johnson, there are new musical factors to consider: metric placement, bass motion, and harmony. An instructor will be able to guide students to a definition of a perfect authentic cadence and to show them PACs in F major (mm. 8, 16, 28) and in B♭ major (mm. 32 and 36). Discussion can focus on measure 24, an imperfect authentic cadence complicated by the way the music rhythmically blows right through the resting point of A_4, and how the two PACs in B♭ major are unequal in strength. These discussion questions encourage students to articulate what musical factors create or work against a sense of rest or closure.

Form

This pairing of songs works well for discussing form. At an introductory level, the texted song "Ten Thousand Voices" allows analysts to investigate the impact of lyrics on the form. "Victoria Galop" follows the tradition of popular dance forms by linking sections together and including a da Capo. At a more advanced level, parallel periods exist in both "Ten Thousand Voices" and "Victoria Galop." Many of the examples, however, require nuance and conversation that take students beyond an introductory level. Rather than providing a worksheet on form, this section is organized around potential discussion questions.

"Ten Thousand Voices"

Giddens's lyrics for "Ten Thousand Voices" have a consistent rhyme scheme; each stanza has an alternating rhyme pattern (ABAB). Since none of the rhymes carry over into later stanzas, the song's rhyme scheme is ABAB CDCD EFEF GHGH.

How do the form and pitch organization reflect the rhyme scheme of "Ten Thousand Voices"? How does Giddens use variation to enhance the story's narrative arc? In stanzas 1 and 2, Giddens sets the first and third lines with the same music, a compositional choice that reflects the alternating rhyme scheme. In other words, odd-numbered lines share the same pitch organization and rhyme scheme. This observation does not describe the even-numbered lines, which have contrasting contours; line 2 rises to A_4 ($\hat{5}$), while line 4 falls to D_4 ($\hat{1}$).

The third stanza introduces variation to the setting of its first line and offers new inner lines (lines 2 and 3). The varied line 1 uses the same pitch content as previous first lines but changes the contour so that the overall motion is upwards (A_4 to C_5) rather than downwards (A_4 to G_4). The new line 2 now pairs strongly with the preserved line 4 because

Table 4.3 Rhyme Scheme in Rhiannon Giddens, "Ten Thousand Voices"

Stanza	Line 1	Line 2	Line 3	Line 4
1	"stories"	"songs"	"worries"	"wrongs"
2	"faces"	"words"	"graces"	"birds"
3	"kisses"	"tears"	"wishes"	"years"
4	"choices"	"strong"	"voices"	"song"

of their shared contour of a falling minor third. The new third line introduces the pitch B♭, which feels particularly dark and painful in this context. Finally, an important characteristic connects it with the previous third lines: it has a sense of restart on the pitch A₄.

Stanza 4 continues to break away from the patterns initiated by the first two stanzas. It couples well with stanza 3 because the inner second and third lines – the lines containing B♮ and B♭ – are shared. Lines 1 and 4 are new. Most notably, line 1 introduces the highest pitch of the song, D₅, and falls a fourth from D₅ to A₄. Even though the final line has been the common thread through the first three stanzas, changing it for the final stanza makes sense. Not only is it the end of the song, but it is also the only place where Giddens breaks the pattern of her lyrics, which have started every line with the words "ten thousand." The musical setting of this line is also the only one to start and end on the same pitch – in this case, the tonal center of D₄. Providing different music for the final line creates the song's strongest sense of closure.

To what extent is each stanza of "Ten Thousand Voices" a parallel period? Stanzas 1 and 2 are well described by the term "parallel period." Each could be read as two phrases of two lines each. These two phrases start similarly, and the first phrase, which ends on $\hat{5}$, has a weaker sense of closure than the second, which ends on $\hat{1}$. As the song progresses, the latter stanzas can still be heard as two phrases of two lines each, but the parallelism is loosened to the point where it could be challenging to hear a parallel period. The pattern of closure is maintained, with the first phrase ending on a more open resting point ($\hat{5}$) than the second ($\hat{1}$). It might be more accurate to describe the latter stanzas as contrasting periods.

"Victoria Galop"

In "Victoria Galop," students learn about sectional form. Sectional form is a large form created by stitching together multiple small sections that could have stood alone as miniature pieces, because each section begins and ends in the same key and closes with a strong cadence (PAC). Table 4.4 lays out the form of this dance. Because it is a dance, the four-bar unit reigns supreme. Four-bar units are paired into eight-bar units, which are then repeated. It might be helpful to show a video of the Galop and have students count the bars as they watch the dance (Powers 2016).

Could all the sections truly "stand alone"? The A and C sections make sense on their own. The B section does, too, but an analyst could argue that its four-bar introduction weakens its ability to be an independent piece – that it makes more sense as a middle section, occurring after the key has been established. The four-bar introduction was likely used to allow dancers time to set up for the next section of music. The B section's opening four bars (mm. 17–20) also stand apart because they are the only four-bar unit unpaired with another four-bar unit.

Each section could be described as a parallel period. What are the weaknesses of that description for each section? The sections are built of eight-bar units, each of which are

Table 4.4 Form of Johnson, "Victoria Galop"

Section	Measures	Description
A	1–16	Divided into two halves, where mm. 9–16 are a written-out repeat of mm. 1–8
B	17–28	Four-bar introduction leads into an eight-bar parallel period
C	29–36	Eight-bar quasi-parallel period in B♭, the subdominant
A	37–44	Half as long as the previous A section
B	45–56	Verbatim repeat of previous B section

36 *Jan Miyake*

divided into two four-bar units. Each pair's four-bar units start the same way, which means that the adjective "parallel" fits the eight-bar phrases of the A, B, and C sections. The adjective "period" is more problematic. In general, it applies to a pair of related phrases where the second phrase has a stronger ending than the first. As we look at each pair of phrases, this issue of relative strength opens into a nuanced discussion about cadences.

In the A section, the final two beats of the first four bars have $\hat{5}$–$\hat{5}$ in the melody counterpointed by $\hat{7}$–$\hat{7}$ in the bass (Figure 4.3a). The lack of motion and the absence of $\hat{1}$ leave these four bars open, but does this count as a cadence? Traditional harmony textbooks would not consider measure 4 a cadence, for two reasons: the harmony (V$^6_5$) is not in root position and includes a chordal seventh, which works against a sense of rest. The latter four bars end with a textbook-worthy perfect authentic cadence, where the melody moves $\hat{2}$–$\hat{1}$, while the bass moves $\hat{5}$–$\hat{1}$. Of particular note is the way Johnson parallels the bass line of measures 5–8 with that of measures 1–4, until he changes to a root-position C^7 chord on the weak beat of measure 7. Johnson could have maintained E in the bass but went out of his way to create $\hat{5}$–$\hat{1}$ motion in the bass for the A section's close. Some interesting discussion questions could include: *To what extent do you feel a sense of closure in measure 4? How would a sense of closure in measure 4 be impacted if we change the final harmony to root-position C^7? Or a root-position C chord? How would the sense of closure in measures 7–8 be impacted by using V$^6_5$ instead of V^7?*

In the B section (mm. 21–28), the second cadence is a textbook-worthy example of a perfect authentic cadence. And again, describing and recognizing the close of the first four bars is tricky. Students will be able to feel the restart in measure 25 that parallels measure 21, but a sense of closure in measure 24 is complicated by the melody writing, which does not come to rest (Figure 4.3b). The B section's melody is a decorated descending line: G$_5$–F$_5$ in measure 21, E$_5$–D$_5$ in measure 22, C$_5$–B♭$_4$ in measure 23, and A$_4$ in measure 24. The arrival at A$_4$ ($\hat{3}$) is obfuscated by the running sixteenth-note texture, which first turns around A$_4$, and then in rises by steps and a small skip to regain the G$_5$ from measure 25 as the first pitch of the second four-bar phrase. The overall melodic motion in measures 23–24 of B♭–A ($\hat{4}$–$\hat{3}$), counterpointed with the bass motion of C–F ($\hat{5}$–$\hat{1}$), points to an imperfect authentic cadence. It is difficult to hear that cadence because of the rhythmic texture. *To what extent does the rhythmic texture weaken the sense of a parallel period?*

In the C section, both the internal cadence (m. 32) and the final cadence (m. 36) are excellent examples of perfect authentic cadences (Figure 4.3c). *Can a case be made for a parallel period?* It would be an excellent exercise for students to make a case for and against a reading of a parallel period. Metric placement of the harmonies is key to a case for a parallel period reading. In measure 32, the final tonic occurs on the weak beat, while in measure 36, the final tonic lands on the strong beat. The sense of finality is stronger in the latter cadence because metric accent aligns with the arrival of the final tonic. The earlier arrival of tonic in measure 36 allows for that tonic to be further emphasized with octave leaps that broaden the overall register. An argument against a parallel period reading can draw on the cadence structure: if both cadences are PACs, then the latter four bars are simply a variation of the first four bars.

* * * * *

These pieces are fruitful for teaching at least two additional topics, but not as a pair.

Harmony in Johnson

"Victoria Galop" has clear examples of I, V$^6_5$, V^7, and IV chords. The C section also has an example of an accented neighboring $^6_4$ chord. Worksheet 4 provides a chordal reduction of "Victoria Galop" in traditional keyboard style. Students can analyze these chords on

Figure 4.3 (a) Johnson, "Victoria Galop," mm. 1–8; (b) Johnson, "Victoria Galop," mm. 21–24; (c) Johnson, "Victoria Galop," mm. 29–36.

38 Jan Miyake

the worksheet, and follow-up discussion can go over the function of V$^6_5$ and IV, as well as cadential progressions and aural analysis. V$^6_5$ functions two ways in "Victoria Galop": contrapuntally as a lower neighbor to $\hat{1}$ in the bass line (mm. 1–5) and harmonically as an inversion of a C^7 chord (m. 7). IV can support $\hat{6}$ in the upper voice and participate in an overarching harmonic progression of I–IV–V^7–I. The completed worksheet also shows that there are two standard cadential patterns in this piece: I–IV–V^7–I and I–V–I. Finally, the harmonic texture is simple enough that, with practice, students will be able to do harmonic analysis in real time and build fluency with aural analysis.

Further Analysis of Giddens

Rhiannon Giddens's "Ten Thousand Songs" is saturated with nuance and can serve as a focus of an analytical writing assignment. There are three musical parameters that work together to create an emotional arc for the song: pitch collection, melismata, and range. In the earlier discussion of form, I noted that the first two stanzas held the same music, while the second pair of stanzas shared the use of B♭ and B♮. Therefore, the form of the four-stanza song could be described as AABB. The pitch content supports an AABB form. The first two stanzas draw on a D minor pentatonic collection (D, F, G, A, C), because there are no Bs, and the two Es receive non-chord-tone treatment as middle notes of three-note melismata. In the latter two stanzas, the second and third lines have the same melodies. Line 2 prominently features B♮, while line 3 prominently features B♭. Overall, I hear these lines as D Dorian, because the Dorian scale is commonly used in folk music, and the B♭, as Giddens performs it, feels like a pitch altered for expressive purposes. The addition of B♭ and B♮ in the latter stanzas contributes to the dramatic arc of the song by adding intensity.

The melismata are a productive and unusual nuance to track. With such a sparse palette for creating nuance, these melismata are more important than they would be in a thicker setting. Table 4.5 summarizes how Giddens builds intensity with melismata. Every stanza has 18 syllables, but an unequal number of notes. In the first two stanzas, there are two melismata: the end of line 3 and the middle of line 4. The line 3 melisma is on the final syllable of the line and encloses the final tone $\hat{3}$ by its upper and lower neighbors, $\hat{4}$ and $\hat{2}$. The line 4 melisma is on the accented syllable of ten-THOU-sand. It smooths out the leap from the starting pitch $\hat{3}$ to the final pitch $\hat{1}$ with passing notes. Stanzas 3 and 4 have four melismata each, one per line. After the first two stanzas, which had the same melody, the third stanza breaks the pattern with the melisma from $\hat{5}$ to $\hat{7}$. Since this melisma anticipates the pitch for the final syllable, $\hat{7}$, it might seem redundant. What it adds, however, is intensity. Singing that line without the melisma demonstrates how its loss impacts the intensity. The line 2 melisma in stanza 3 is a clear example of text painting, because it draws attention to the word "tears." Overall, the emotional level is rising in this stanza, both in terms of the text and in terms of the musical setting. The line 3 melisma emphasizes the accented syllable of "ten thousand," which is also the moment that B♭ is introduced. The final melisma of the stanza is in the same place (with the same pitches) as stanzas 1 and

Table 4.5 Count of Notes in Each Stanza of "Ten Thousand Voices"

Stanza	Syllables	Melismata	Notes
1	18	2	22
2	18	2	22
3	18	4	26
4	18	5	27

2. The final stanza adds a fifth melisma, which matches its status as the most emotionally intense stanza.

Range is the final musical parameter that contributes to the narrative arc of the song. With two exceptions, the first two stanzas explore the perfect fifth between D_4 and A_4. The two exceptions are leaps to C_5, always as part of the perfect fourth with G_4. This high point of the opening stanzas sets the noun in the first and third lines: "ten thousand STO-ries" and "ten thousand WOR-ries." Stanza 3 incorporates C_5 into the stepwise melody, instead of only reaching it by leap. This incorporation starts with line 1, which ends on the high C. Line 2 then explores the minor third from C_5 to A_4 (using B♮ as a passing tone). In fact, line 2 initiates a slow descent back to D_4 from C_5. After line 2's exploration of C_5–A_4, line 3 moves from A_4 to G_4, while the final line moves, like the previous stanzas, from F_4 to D_4. The final stanza is the only one to provide the complete octave. It breaks the pattern of starting on A_4 and begins on the highest note of the song: D_5. This pitch is the climax of the piece, and Giddens performs it as the most fraught note of the piece. Lines 1 and 2 of the final stanza explore the top tetrachord of the scale (D–C–B♮/♭–A), while lines 3 and 4 make their way back to D_4.

A possible assignment for students could be to summarize this analysis by using a given thesis statement, such as "Rhiannon Giddens's 'Ten Thousand Voices' uses multiple musical parameters to support the emotional arc suggested by the lyrics." Alternatively, students could answer open-ended questions about melismata, range, and the pitch collection in preparation for class discussion.

* * * * *

In closing, I have offered ideas that draw on Rhiannon Giddens's "Ten Thousand Voices" and Francis Johnson's "Victoria Galop" for teaching concepts of intervals, non-chord tones, closure, form, harmony, and close reading. These pieces could be used as touchstones throughout a semester, or just for a single assignment. The supplemental materials provide scores, transcriptions, and four worksheets that can be edited to suit an instructor's needs. I hope students enjoy and learn from these pieces and the stories of the composers.

Notes

1. The book Giddens references is Sublette (2007).
2. Not all recordings use the double bass.
3. Both of the cited Eileen Southern resources include a picture of Frank Johnson.
4. For a survey of approaches to closure, see Anson-Cartwright (2007).

Works Cited

Anson-Cartwright, Mark. 2007. "Concepts of Closure in Tonal Music: A Critical Study." *Theory and Practice* 32: 1–17.
Giddens, Rhiannon. 2019. "Ten Thousand Voices." track 1 on *There is no Other*, Nonesuch, CD.
_____. "About Rhiannon Giddens." Accessed July 14, 2021. www.rhiannongiddens.com/about
MetLiveArts. May 16, 2020. "Rhiannon Giddens with Francesco Turrisi: There Is no Other," YouTube video, 1:20:52. www.youtube.com/watch?v=Ignhso0iv9U&feature=youtu.be&t=654
Powers, Richard. November 18, 2016. "Canon Galop Quadrille Performance." YouTube video, 2:15. www.youtube.com/watch?v=NZaeTPXlKAg
Southern, Eileen. 1977. "Frank Johnson of Philadelphia and His Promenade Concerts." *The Black Perspective in Music*, 5/1: 3–29.
_____. 1997. *The Music of Black Americans: A History*, 3rd edition. W.W. Norton & Company, Inc.
Sublette, Ned. 2007. *Cuba and Its Music: From the First Drums to the Mambo*. Chicago Review Press, Inc.

5 From Counterpoint to Small Forms
A Cross-Stylistic Approach to Centering Black Artists in the Theory Core

Kristina L. Knowles and Nicholas J. Shea

Introduction

Current music theory pedagogy has been increasingly focused on the need to diversify and expand the repertoire discussed in the core curriculum. A majority of the mainstream pedagogical resources, namely, textbooks, focus almost exclusively on White male–composed western European art music. Evidence from Ewell (2020) is clear: in a survey of seven of the most popular music theory textbooks, 98.3% of examples are by White composers (3.1). Moreover, Ewell argues that the inclusion of the same few Black composers in the pursuit of "diversity," such as William Grant Still and Scott Joplin, tokenizes these artists.[1]

Many instructors may thus turn to popular music examples to supplement the comparative lacuna of analyzed western classical works by Black artists (de Clercq 2020). However, with this change in focus comes at least three pressing pedagogical issues: (1) how to approach musical organization in popular music, (2) how to discuss the similarities and differences between popular and classical music styles without imposing the "rules" of the latter onto the former, and (3) how to create a meaningful progression toward more advanced topics when works by Black artists are currently under-theorized and thus less accessible to instructors.

Beyond these pedagogical issues, instructors also face several practical problems when trying to incorporate popular music into the theory classroom. First, instructors are largely on their own in developing relevant curricular materials, due in part to the lack of theory textbooks that focus exclusively (or even largely) on popular music. Second, there is a problematic assumption that popular music is often considered de facto diverse. While this is undoubtedly true when compared with classical music, a remarkable overrepresentation of all-White ensembles in existing popular music scholarship still persists (Shea 2022, 10–11). Assuming that these publications are ones from which instructors might pull excerpts and concepts, there is still a very real danger of underrepresenting or tokenizing Black artists.[2] Consequently, popular music potentially faces many of the same issues of canonization as classical music. Cora S. Palfy and Eric Gilson capture this issue well, reporting that "the proportion of repertoire and composers drawn from non-canonical works is smaller and, thus, communicates lesser canonical importance due to that proportional skew" (Palfy and Gilson 2018, fn. 16). The tendency to default to canonical works undermines antiracist pedagogy and serves to further reinforce what Ewell (2020) defines as music theory's *White racial frame* (3.4).[3]

In this chapter, we address the racial diversity aspect of Ewell's call by focusing on a variety of popular and classical music examples by Black artists. Some of the examples used in this chapter are explored in depth, while others are revisited repeatedly as part of our spiral approach, allowing students to gain a deeper familiarity with the music as

DOI: 10.4324/9781003204053-7

they learn progressively more complex topics (Clendenning and Marvin 2016). We also provide several lists of examples by Black artists across both styles for various topics that we address in this chapter. We are intentional about the excerpts we sample, particularly with regard to popular music examples, focusing on ensembles led by Black artists and acknowledging Black pioneers often overlooked in the development of popular music styles (Redd 1985).

The methodological aspects of Ewell's call are more complicated to address. Our sound-first model attempts to disrupt the overt focus on notation and harmony typical of theory curricula, primarily because these features may be foundational to classical music pedagogy but do not always generalize to other styles, including popular music, where notation is not a given and harmonic practice is more diffuse. Instead of beginning with notation, we focus on developing aural skills associated with protonotation, including meter inference, tonic inference, motivic repetition, and identification of closure. While we do not ignore staff notation entirely, protonotation allows us to prioritize listening first before moving into any score study. Similarly, rather than emphasizing harmony, we focus on melodies, rhythms, meter, and texture as alternative parameters influencing musical organization. The topics addressed in this chapter primarily encompass the first and second semesters of a typical theory core curriculum, beginning with contrapuntal reduction and moving through cadences to phrase forms before ending with some short recommendations for an introduction to small formal types. We recognize that the pedagogical approaches introduced in this chapter merely attempt to disrupt some of the assumptions Ewell notes as problematic (2020, 3.5). These strategies should be considered an initial step toward answering Ewell's call to dismantle the White racial frame.

A Sound-First Approach

One of the challenges of incorporating popular music and classical music into the same curriculum is balancing score analysis and listening skills, particularly when most curriculums begin with an emphasis on traditional (western) score notation. The sequence is typical. First, introduce fundamentals such as rhythms and pitches using notes on a staff, then show students how to build chords from stacked notes on a page, building into the identification of cadences by looking for leaps in the bass and characteristic melodic patterns. From there, students and instructors are increasingly locked into scores. As Michael Rogers (2004, 103) notes, the ear develops more slowly than the eye, and so both students and instructors are prone to relying on the score for the introduction and comprehension of concepts, particularly as they become more complex. By the second semester, students have almost exclusively been focusing on notes on the page, as contextualized by recordings. It is easy to default to using examples for which there is a score or transcript, and this in turn limits both the genres and artists utilized in the classroom. This pressure for scores is why teams of music theorists have recently devoted their free time to uncovering, encoding, and transcribing works written by Black composers through the Composers of Color resource page.[4]

Implementing popular music only compounds the previous issues. Not only does an overwhelming amount of popular music theory research already focus on White and male artists, but so do score-based transcriptions that may serve as teaching tools, such as those for the Beatles (2011) or Led Zeppelin (2017). Songs by Black artists, who are less "popular" by measures of commercial success or critical acclaim, remain out of reach.

We argue that a paradigm shift is needed. Specifically, we propose centering the curriculum on fundamental listening strategies that can apply to both popular and classical music. By introducing these listening strategies at the start of the curriculum and progressively building upon them in successive semesters, we are able to incorporate a broader range of repertoire into the core curriculum, while also developing the aural skills necessary to support an increasingly diverse range of musical careers. To be clear, we are not advocating for the removal of score-reading skills from the curriculum. Rather, we are proposing a sound-first approach.

We propose introducing protonotation prior to staff notation in both written theory and aural skills.[5] The use of protonotation from the beginning of the curriculum enables instructors to explore fundamental topics without a reliance on the score and can be continued through subsequent semesters for topics such as diatonic harmony, contrapuntal reductions of melodic and bass lines, and cadences. Critically, protonotation levels the playing field for students who may not have had access to musical training and score-reading prior to college. They are therefore able to engage with theoretical concepts while learning score-reading skills, rather than having to develop fluency with the western notation system first. This is increasingly important as schools continue to expand music majors to encompass popular music, music technology, music production, and music therapy.

Figures 5.1a–c shows a typical progression of protonotation using the guitar part in "Hold On" by Alabama Shakes.[6] The guitar part provides an accessible entry for popular music protonotation skills, as it loops throughout the song and is mostly rhythmically isochronous. Following Karpinski, we start with meter. Students conduct to determine the grouping (duple or quadruple) and then listen and count to determine the length, or number of "measures," for the repeating cycle (e.g., two measures).[7] Students then block out the measures on a piece of paper to form the metric framework for the protonotation (see Figure 5.1a). Next, the focus turns to rhythm. This is a good opportunity to talk about pickups (i.e., anacruses), as the bass line uses a repeating rhythmic pattern of a pickup leading into the strong beats 1 and 3. Students might begin by first identifying where the longer notes fall within the metric framework, and then adding in the quicker upbeats. Rhythms and their durations are indicated in protonotation using horizontal lines that connect or intersect with the vertical lines that indicate metric beats (see Figure 5.1b). As with most real-world musical examples, "Hold On" contains elements that may be too advanced for students at this stage. While the majority of the loop utilizes a simple repeating rhythm, it ends with an autotelic rhythmic gesture (Hughes 2003).[8] Instructors can choose to either let students muddle their way through and do the best they can or tell them to ignore the rhythm at the end of the loop for now, with the option to return to it later.

Moving onto pitch requires students to situate themselves within the tonality. There are a few ways to approach this task. A common strategy is to ask students to simply sing the note they hear as "most stable" or "feels like home." However, an instructor is likely to receive a smattering of responses, especially if students are just beginning to wrestle with pitch. A sounder strategy is to aim for specific pitches from the recording, then use what we refer to as the "sing-down method" to determine the relationship of this pitch to the tonic (Karpinski 2007, 12). In this excerpt, focusing on the longer notes is easiest. Have students sing the first non-pickup note on a neutral syllable like "loo," then sing down by step while counting the number of pitches required before they land on the note they feel is most stable. Students will mostly likely report traversing three pitches, meaning, the first long note on beat 1 is *mi* or $\hat{3}$. Another advantage of this method is that students then have *do* or $\hat{1}$ in their ears for the pitches on beat 3. The final long note, on beat 1 of measure 2, is *sol* or $\hat{5}$. Because this pitch is a fourth below tonic, getting students to relate this pitch to tonic requires either flipping the sing-down strategy (i.e., singing up by step, *sol la ti do*) or singing the note up the octave.[9] As students identify pitches, they can be added into the protonotation, eventually resulting in the completed musical sketch of the bass line, seen in Figure 5.1c.

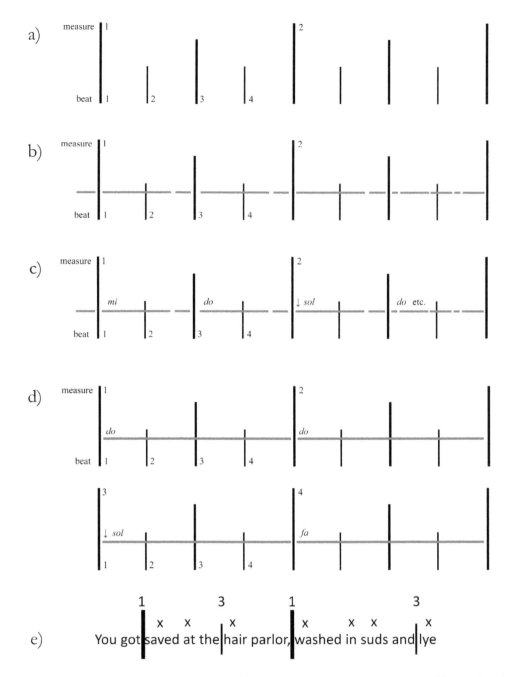

Figure 5.1 (a) Protonotation metric framework for the looping guitar part in "Hold On" by Alabama Shakes (0:20–0:49); (b) protonotation with rhythms for the looping guitar part in "Hold On" by Alabama Shakes (0:20–0:49); (c) protonotation with rhythms and pitches (movable-do solfège) for the looping guitar part in "Hold On" by Alabama Shakes (0:20–0:49); (d) protonotation with rhythms and pitches (movable-do solfège) for the double bass part in "Heavenly Track" by Kaia Kater (0:00–0:10); (e) lyrics with meter lines and pitch-repetition annotations in the first phrase of "Heavenly Track" by Kaia Kater (0:00–0:04).

The remainder of this chapter demonstrates how to build on a sound-first approach using protonotation, beginning with contrapuntal reductions.

Applying the Sound-First Approach from Contrapuntal Reductions to Small Forms

Contrapuntal Reductions

A contrapuntal reduction teaches students to recognize structurally important melodic and bass notes. Contrapuntal reductions highlight how various musical parameters – such as rhythm, meter, dynamics, and register – work together to create emphasis on some pitches over others. Students will need to know scales, keys, intervals, solfège, and the basics of rhythm and meter before starting contrapuntal reductions. Contrapuntal reductions can intersect and lead into a variety of topics, including counterpoint, diatonic harmony, cadences, and melodic harmonization. They can also be revisited as students move into more advanced topics, like phrase forms and formal analysis. Finally, students can create contrapuntal reductions of both popular and classical music utilizing a sound-first approach, as both employ melody and bass lines that can be elaborated or embellished. Creating contrapuntal reductions for both genres allows students to draw comparisons and can set the stage for later discussions on stylistic similarities and differences.

In teaching contrapuntal reduction, we loosely adopt Dimitri Tymoczko's seven parameters for pitch stability (Tymoczko 2011, 179). These are listed in the following text, along with an added parameter noting the tendency for stable pitches (particularly bass pitches) to occur on relatively stable metric positions (Lerdahl and Jackendoff 1983, 88; Mirka 2009, 59–60). While instructors can provide this list of parameters to students when teaching contrapuntal reduction and have them apply it in practice, we prefer to use the discovery method, letting students uncover these parameters through class discussions and activities (Fowler 1970, 25–30; London 1998, 105–10). In what follows, we describe sample activities for contrapuntal reductions using both popular and classical excerpts from Black artists.

Tymoczko's seven parameters for pitch stability:

1. Appearing more frequently.
2. Being held for longer durations.
3. Being accented dynamically.
4. Being accented rhythmically.
5. Being accented registrally.
6. Being the target of stepwise melodic motion, particularly stepwise contrary motion converging on a particular pitch class.
7. Being doubled at the octave, or paired with the note a fifth above.
8. Occurring on a relatively metrically strong beat.

Following our sound-first approach, we start with a popular music example. Kaia Kater is a Black female Canada-based banjoist and singer-songwriter whose album *Grenades* (2018) blends bluegrass and contemporary pop styles. The album's second song, "Heavenly Track," features a more traditional bluegrass texture of banjo, bass, slide guitar, and vocals. Combined with its rhythmic regularity, slow harmonic rhythm, and relatively unembellished melody, the track's first phrase (0:00–0:10) offers students an accessible starting point for contrapuntal reduction.

From Counterpoint to Small Forms 45

As before, we encourage students to follow the protonotation sequence – meter, rhythms, then pitch – starting with the bass line. Students will likely hear a total of four measures in quadruple meter after conducting along with the recording, with the bass pitches sustaining throughout each measure. Figure 5.1d maps the bass line in protonotation. The initial task of determining which notes are more stable or prominent in the bass line is relatively straightforward. That being said, some students may struggle to identify the bass line pitches. In such situations, we encourage students to briefly reference the melody, use the sing-down method to determine *do*, and then sing that pitch aloud throughout the excerpt, paying special attention to where the sung *do* matches the *do* in the bass (i.e., the first two measures).[10]

With meter and pitch from the bass line in place, students should turn their attention to the melody. We like to begin this part of the activity with a discussion that builds on previous concepts from the species counterpoint unit: how might we simplify the melody so that its most consonant, prominent, and stable pitches are made clear? Instructors can point out that there are practical implications to this question. For example, if one wanted to accompany "Heavenly Track" at a bluegrass jam session and they are a vocalist or violinist, it might be helpful to know the main melody notes so they could craft a counterpoint that accompanies, but not overshadows, the main line.[11] Accomplishing this requires students to do a bit of melodic reduction by following the parameters outlined previously.

It is easiest to focus on just three parameters if students seem overwhelmed – pitches that occur more frequently, are held for longer durations, and/or fall on strong metric beats. Students will likely observe that pitches/words at the beginning of the measure meet these criteria. We encourage instructors to sing back the first phrase as a group, multiple times, while focusing on one parameter at a time. Lyrics can also help students visualize the melody. As shown in Figure 5.1e, instructors can mark which syllables feature the same pitch (we use an "x") and fall on metrically strong beats (i.e., 1 and 3) with vertical lines. With this information in place and a little coaching, students can reasonably intuit that the pitch coordinated with the marked syllables might be more prominent. All that is left is to use the sing-down method to determine the scale degree or solfège for these pitches (in this case, *mi* or $\hat{3}$).

The final step is to arrive at some sort of reduction. One option is to begin by focusing only on the first half of the phrase. Assuming students have their metric framework in place, it can be enough to tell students to merely "simplify the rhythms" based on the more stable pitches. If you have spent a great deal of time discussing pulse levels, as we do in our own fundamentals unit, you might encourage them to avoid rhythmic values that are faster than the counting pulse (i.e., the tactus) but slower than the downbeat pulse (i.e., the pulse level for each measure, Cohn 2019). Most often, students will produce something to the effect of Figure 5.2a (Line A, more reductive; Line B, less reductive), even without guidance.[12]

To conclude, we recommend splitting the class and singing volunteered reductions. Discuss the merits of each. Are there rhythms that could be more clear or straightforward? Did anyone else choose a different syllable? This is also an opportunity to make sure everyone is on the same page. For example, if the students are struggling to hear the consonances on downbeats, have them sing along with the melody on a neutral syllable such as "loo," then instruct them to sing only the first word of each measure, followed by each strong beat (i.e., 1 and 3). Raising these questions and practicing these strategies will help students prepare for the subsequent classical music reduction, which is shorter but presents a slightly different set of challenges.

The opening of Joseph Bologne's String Quartet (op. 1, no. 4, mm. 1–3) provides another good example for a contrapuntal reduction[13] and features a typical opening gambit in the form of a *do–re–mi* schemata (Gjerdingen 2007). While shorter than the Kaia Kater

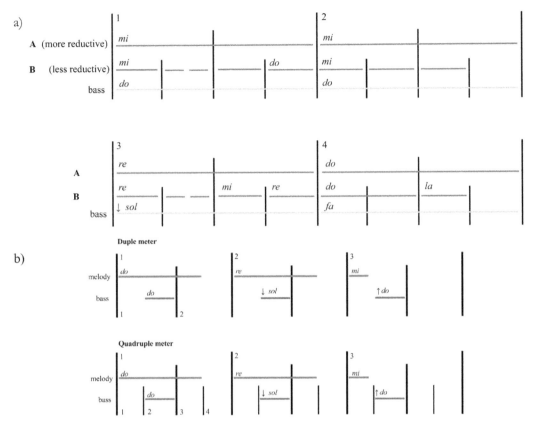

Figure 5.2 (a) Two possible student reductions for the first phrase (melody) of "Heavenly Track" by Kaia Kater (0:00–0:10) in context of the bass line. Line A is more reductive, while Line B is less so. (b) Two possible metric interpretations (duple or quadruple) of the melody and bass line of Bologne, String Quartet op. 1, no. 4 (mm. 1–3).

example, this passage provides several challenges. The excerpt begins with a pickup, and the slow rhythm of the melodic line can cause confusion as to whether the excerpt is in duple or quadruple meter. Finally, the bass line is more challenging to hear, as prominent bass notes are introduced on the offbeats. Consequently, students should be encouraged to listen first for the melody and then focus on the bass line.

Following the established progression, students will likely hear a total of three measures but may disagree on the measure-level grouping, as the excerpt is in *alla breve*. If needed, instructors can play past the opening excerpt to give students more time to settle on the meter. Instructors can either let students choose between duple or quadruple meter for this excerpt, encourage them toward one over the other, or work with students to create a version of protonotation for each. We believe the lattermost option allows for fruitful conversations regarding rhythm and meter, but instructors may choose to focus on one metric interpretation and save these conversations for later in the semester. For ease of reference, we have provided a protonotation example for this excerpt in both duple and quadruple meters (Figure 5.2b).

With the meter in place, students can move onto the melody and bass line. We suggest letting students choose which part to focus on first. Likely, students will want to begin with the melody, due to its slower rhythms and greater prominence in the recording. Starting with the first two measures produces a long-short rhythmic pattern, with the third measure introducing more complex rhythms. Students should be reminded at this point that the goal is to identify the most stable and significant pitches in the melody and bass. Using the rhythmic pattern of the first two measures, students will typically infer that the downbeat of measure 3 is likely the most significant. Following the progression for identifying pitches previously described, students should be able to identify the pitches *do–re–mi* occurring on the downbeats. We recommend letting students sing along with the recording and then discussing other parameters that may confirm the melodic reduction (duration of pitches in mm. 1–2, and repetition of pitches in m. 3). Students can then work on the bass line in small groups or together as a class. Singing along with the recording several times will make it easier to isolate the bass notes. Students will likely settle on *do–sol–do* for the bass line after repeated hearings but may disagree on the metric location of the bass for the first measure. While all bass notes enter on beat 2, the upper-octave *do* in the cello can be hard to hear.

To wrap up the activity, we suggest a discussion regarding the challenges with this excerpt, followed by a comparison between the two reductions. This may start with singing through both reductions before engaging the following questions: What shared strategies were used to emphasize stable pitches between the two excerpts? What was different? What was the greatest challenge for each excerpt? Which strategies were the most helpful? Answering these questions allows students to share strategies and develop a framework for approaching contrapuntal reductions on their own (see Sample Assignment 1 on the Supplemental Materials website).

Cadences

The emphasis on outer voices, pitch stability, and pitch and metric interaction introduced with contrapuntal reductions sets up a later discussion about cadences and varying degrees of closure. While the activities described in teaching contrapuntal reductions draw attention to different ways of articulating pitch stability across genres, cadences afford an opportunity to discuss similarities and differences between classical and popular music.

Kaia Kater's "Heavenly Track," discussed in the previous passages, provides one such example of stylistic differences. As students discover in their contrapuntal reduction, the repeating four-measure phrase ends with *do* in the melody and *fa* in the bass, implying a subdominant harmony. Melodically, both phrases end on $\hat{1}$. Popular music scholars continue to debate what terminological currency is best to classify such an event. Instructors may therefore have their own preferences for cadence labels involving the subdominant. We elect to use "blues cadence" or "blues progression" in popular music contexts, as we find that references to "plagal harmonic patterns" come with unnecessary stylistic baggage, even though we acknowledge that students with experience in AP theory courses may be more familiar with the latter term. Similarly, scholars also disagree about parameters for melodic scale-degree closure at popular music cadences. For instance, Temperley (2011) notes that ending a phrase on $\hat{1}$ is "not a requirement for strong closure" in popular music, although it is a common strategy for achieving closure in other stylistic contexts. Regardless, students will inevitably hear closure in popular music phrases that involve subdominant harmonies.[14]

Given the flexibility of harmonic and melodic closural patterns in popular music cadences, we recommend a nuanced approach. That is, we prefer to approach cadences as existing along a continuum rather than categorizing cadences into the simplified binary of open or closed. This opens the door to discussions of other parameters outside of harmony and melody – such as rhythm, meter, texture, and dynamics – that can strengthen or undermine a sense of closure beyond labels, such as blues cadence, PAC, or HC. Doing so enables a more stylistically nuanced approach to the discussion of closure and encourages students to attend to a wider range of musical parameters.

To help students attend to these nuances, we utilize a gamified listening activity in which students vote on whether a cadence is open or closed, discuss and debate the features that contribute to the given label, and then compare and contrast the degree of closure with previous examples. This activity accomplishes a number of objectives. First, it encourages students to listen critically to musical examples in order to make an initial judgment. Second, requiring students to list reasons that they consider a cadence to be open or closed helps them practice articulating their instincts using a shared terminology and draws their attention to common signifiers for open and closed cadences. Finally, having students compare the degree of closure across excerpts encourages them to attend to parameters beyond pitch to consider how multiple musical parameters interact at cadences to produce varying levels of closure. As an additional activity, students can be asked to identify where the cadence is located in the recording as a first step. This can be accomplished by asking students to raise their hands or shout *stop* when they hear a cadence. A list of potential examples from both popular and classical music that could be used for this activity has been provided in Table 5.1. A follow-up assignment allows students to apply these concepts to a pair of self-chosen excerpts (see Sample Assignment 2, available on the Supplemental Materials website).

Phrase Forms

A solid understanding of cadences is integral when introducing phrase forms. However, as before, the melodic and harmonic flexibility of popular music means that non-pitch parameters are at least as critical as pitch when hearing motives as the building blocks of sentences and periods in these stylistic contexts.[15] More importantly, features such as rhythm, meter, register, and texture are more accessible, especially for first- or second-semester theory students. Popular and classical examples can therefore stand on equal ground by adopting this focus. We discuss two excerpts whose motives are easy to parse, and features easy to hear, and which also raise interesting considerations regarding phrase-form organization. A more substantial list of potential examples by Black artists for both styles can be found in Table 5.2.

Nearly all songs by Sister Rosetta Tharpe offer an accessible entry point into phrase forms. Tharpe, often referred to as the "Godmother of Rock n' Roll," was an American gospel artist who gained popularity playing in churches and clubs alike during the 1930s and 1940s (Jackson 1995, 185–200). Her pioneering guitar techniques (Lewis 2018) and high-energy vocal performances make her a critical figure in the stylistic development of rock music (Maxile 2011, 593–608). Her lyrics are likewise steeped in the gospel tradition of group singing and therefore often feature accessible melodies and clear-cut examples of motivic transformations common to both periods and sentences. The song "My Man and I" follows nicely from our previous discussion of cadences, where Tharpe's use of segmented melodies and end-of-phrase guitar licks clearly demarcate phrase boundaries.

The first vocal phrase of "My Man and I" is a contrasting interrupted period (Laitz 2016, 386) that segments cleanly into an antecedent (0:08–0:22) and consequent (0:22–0:36). To warm up, we recommend an initial hearing to introduce students to the song. Instructors can then guide students to listen for the most conclusive cadence on the second playthrough. While doing so, students can map out the meter in protonotation to determine the number of heard measures or mark bar lines on the song's lyrics. This may require subsequent hearings, but if done correctly, students will observe four breaks in the vocals. Here the instructor has two options – discuss cadences or focus on motives. We prefer to start with the former, using the sing-down method to determine the melodic scale degrees at the consequent then the antecedent. This reveals a balanced 16-measure phrase structure, where the antecedent ends on *re* or $\hat{2}$ and the consequent on *do* or $\hat{1}$.[16]

Table 5.1 Cadence Types, Outer-Voice Schemata, and Associated Parameters for "Open or Closed?" Listening Activity

Piece	Artist	Location	Type	Scale Degrees	Additional Parameters
String Quartet op. 1, no. 2	Joseph Bologne	m. 4	PAC (cad. 64)	M: *do–ti–do* B: *sol–sol–do*	• Occurs on downbeat • Eighth notes in inner voices weakens sense of closure
"Cymbals" from *Cotillions*	Francis Johnson	m. 8	PAC (weak)	M: *re–do* B: *do*	• Bass arrives on downbeat • Melody arrives on weak beat • Use of suspension • Decrease in rhythmic density
"Polka" from *Méphisto Masqué*	Edmond Dédé	mm. 46	HC	M: *sol* B: *(re)–sol*	• Melody arrives on downbeat but is emphasized on beat 2 • Bass moves through *re* to *sol*, and then on beat 2 descends from *sol* to *do* on next downbeat • Rhythm slows down and "arrives" on beat 2 for melody
		mm. 54	PAC	M: *do* B: *do*	• Bass and melody arrive beat 1 • Bass continues moving (arpeggiated tonic) before resting on beat 2
"My Man and I"	Sister Rosetta Tharpe	00:22	HC	M: *re* B: *sol*	• Melody arrives on offbeat (melodic suspension) • Lower register • Bass arrives on downbeat • Bass rhythm speeds up immediately after cadence arrival
		00:36	PAC	M: *re–(mi) do* B: *sol–do*	• Melody arrives on downbeat • Lower register • Bass arrives on downbeat • Bass rhythm speeds up immediately after cadence arrival
"I Will Survive"	Gloria Gaynor	00:22	elided	M: *ti–do* B: *sol–do*	• Fast rhythmic gesture in guitar at point of cadence • Immediately followed by an increase in rhythm, texture (added drum)
"Heavenly Track"	Kaia Kater	00:11 00:23	debatable	M: *do* B: *fa*	• Bass arrives on downbeat • Melody arrives on *do* on beat 1 but continues to *la* on beat 3 • Lower register

Table 5.2 Sample Works for Period, Sentence, and *SRDC* Phrase Forms

Periods	Sister Rosetta Tharpe, "My Man and I," 00:08–00:36 (contrasting period)
	Sister Rosetta Tharpe, "Rock Me," 00:07–00:34 (parallel period)
	Nina Simone, "Chilly Winds Don't Blow," 00:08–00:41 (parallel period)
	Joseph Bologne, String Quartet op. 1, no. 4, ii, mm. 1–8 (parallel period)
	Edmond Dédé, *Méphisto Masqué*, "Polka," mm. 39–54 (parallel period)
Sentences	Joseph Bologne, String Quartet op. 1, no. 2, i, mm. 1–4
	Edmond Dédé, *Méphisto Masqué*, "Polka," m. 39–46
	Enrique Iglesias, "Escape," 00:14–00:22
	Rihanna, "Umbrella," 00:54–01:06
srdc	Stevie Wonder, "Signed Sealed Delivered (I'm Yours)," 00:10–00:23
	Jon Batiste, "Freedom," 00:54–1:17
	Tracy Chapman, "Give Me One Reason," 00:32–00:58

Sentences provide an excellent opportunity to focus on the role of motives, rhythms, and textures in communicating phrase forms. An example of a sentence can be found in the opening phrase of the "Polka" from Edmond Dédé's *Méphisto Masqué*. A Creole composer, Dédé moved from the United States to France in 1885, where he studied at the Paris Conservatoire before becoming an assistant conductor at the Grand Théâtre. The piece itself is reminiscent of New Orleans, where Dédé grew up.[17] The first four measures of the sentence (mm. 39–42) feature a two-measure basic idea that is repeated with minor variation in the second measure. The first measure of the basic idea is memorable, and so it should be easy for students to hear the repetition. The fragmentation that begins the continuation (m. 43–46) focuses on the rhythmic pattern used for the first measure of the basic idea, repeating the rhythm in one-measure increments while changing the contour. Directing students to list similar features between the first and second half of the phrase should help them recognize the rhythmic similarity. The phrase itself ends on a half cadence in measure 46 with *sol* in the melody and the bass.[18]

Periods and sentences appear in both classical and popular music. However, we feel it is also important to draw attention to the *srdc – statement, restatement/response, departure, conclusion –* as a sentence phrase type specific to popular music (Everett 1999; Summach 2011). Its four components are mostly analogous to the classical sentence's 2 + 2 + 4 repetition scheme (e.g., basic idea, basic idea repeated, continuation + cadence). But there are often subtle differences between classical music sentences and *srdc* phrases that, through direct comparison, allow students to focus on features like acceleration and fragmentation, which they sometimes struggle to recognize (Caplin 2013, 55). For example, in "Freedom," written by Autumn Rowe, Andrae Alexander, Jon Batiste, and Kizzo and performed by Jon Batiste, the latter half of the second phrase (0:53–1:17) is more easily parsed into discrete metric units due to melodic fragmentation. This, in turn, contributes to a less convincing continuation function. Such differences are made all the clearer to students when comparing *d* and *c* to their formal analogues in classical sentences. Comparing the phrase forms also encourages students to recognize repetition schemes at different levels of metric hierarchy. It is common for *srdc* phrases, such as those in "Give Me One Reason" by Tracy Chapman, to span 15 seconds or more, while instructors will be hard-pressed to find sentences of similar length in classical music contexts. Finally, we recognize that some instructors may be reluctant to introduce a new phrase form in the *srdc*, as it potentially opens the door for conflation, and so we view the phrase form as completely optional. Nevertheless, we offer a few *srdc* examples in the following table for those looking for more opportunities to practice multi-parameter and cross-stylistic listening strategies.

Overall, some instructors may desire a more robust discussion of harmony in phrase forms than we offer here. We encourage instructors to dive more deeply into harmonic aspects of our examples if they find it relevant to their own curricular needs. In our case, the diverse types of music majors in our theory sequence mean we prefer to put harmony on the back burner, at least at the start. This approach facilitates introducing students to a wider range of phrase paradigms across styles, including those that may or may not conform to more traditional harmonic perspectives on formal and melodic analysis.

Small Formal Types

Our sound-first approach and emphasis on motives, rhythms, and textures can be extended into small forms. Here, instructors may want to begin by listening for cadences and phrase types before moving into score study to identify specific features, such as harmony, modulation, and repetition of formal sections. Francis Johnson's "Maria Caroline" from *Cotillions* is a short, 16-measure balanced binary that introduces elements of small forms, such as rhyming cadence schemes, contrasts between sections, and the use of sequences at the beginning of the B section of small binaries. For a short and readily accessible example of a simple binary where the A section ends tonally open, either Minuet no. 2 (modulation to the dominant) or Minuet no. 3 (ends with a HC) from Ignatius Sancho's second book of minuets would work nicely. Sancho's Minuet no. 5 from the same collection provides an example of a longer and more substantial rounded binary. While the previous examples are all 16 measures long and consequently could be studied predominantly through the sound-first model and the creation of formal sketches and contrapuntal reductions, Minuet no. 5 is significantly longer. We still suggest instructors have students listen first to see if they notice any repetition of melodic material before studying the score. The popular music form AABA pairs nicely with discussions of small forms in classical music. Etta James's 1960 hit "At Last" is an excellent example of AABA form, and a lead sheet can be readily acquired from any number of fake books for instructors who would prefer to have a score readily available.

Conclusion

As we have demonstrated here, our sound-first approach allows us to put classical and popular music on a level playing field while also highlighting stylistic similarities and differences between these two genres. We believe the methods outlined in this chapter move pedagogy one step closer to a more equitable perspective on musical organization, specifically by avoiding the imposition of classical music paradigms onto other styles. Instead, by encouraging students to listen first and engage with theoretical concepts outside of the restrictions of western notation, students learn to attend to and engage with a variety of musical parameters that can be found in both classical and popular music genres. The sound-first approach has the added advantage of leveling the playing field for institutions such as ours, whose students enter the curriculum with different backgrounds and knowledge of music and notation. Finally, we have shown that it is possible to do this using exclusively Black artists for both genres. While it may not be feasible for all instructors to only use music by Black artists for the entire theory sequence, we have shown that there are several options available for a range of topics in the theory core. Incorporating more Black artists requires not only locating potential pieces and examples but also rethinking how we approach topics and skills within the classroom. We hope the sound-first approach discussed in this chapter, along with the activities and materials shared, gives instructors ideas for how to broaden the genres taught and diversify the artists discussed in the theory core curriculum.

Notes

1. Our use of the word "artist" is intended to reflect the cross-stylistic nature of this chapter. Specifically, we survey works by both Black western art music composers and Black popular music artists. The majority of the popular music artists included in this chapter are composers, in that they are the primary songwriter for the materials we examine. We use the term "artist" here, as it encompasses other aspects of musicianship, such as production and performance, which are not necessarily covered by the word "composer."
2. Temperley (2018) provides an excellent framework for teaching popular music to undergraduate and graduate students, despite its intended function as a research study on rock. But of its numerous excerpts, those by primarily Black ensembles and solo artists are significantly overshadowed by all-White groups. It would therefore take considerable effort on the behalf of the instructor to substitute Temperley's examples for those by Black artists. This is work many of us are willing to do but nevertheless highlights the acute need for popular music texts that deprioritize White and male artists, whose success in rock is largely predicated on the R&B traditions established by Black musicians. For more on this topic, see Redd (1985).
3. To summarize Ewell's five components, the frame treats music by White persons, and therefore research by White persons, as the "pinnacle of music-theoretical thought" (2.4), thus enacting systematic barriers that continue to marginalize non-White scholars and scholarship.
4. Interested readers can access this resource at the following website: https://composersofcolor.hcommons.org.
5. Karpinski (2000) provides an in-depth discussion of protonotation in Chapters 2 and 3. Our chapter provides a brief explanation of the process.
6. A recording of the piece can be found here: www.youtube.com/watch?v=Le-3MIBxQTw. The guitar part referenced in our discussion begins at 0:20 and repeats throughout.
7. Discussing "measures" in the context of popular music can be challenging due to the sometimes-murky distinction between meter and hypermeter in the context of a backbeat. de Clercq (2016) explores this issue at length.
8. The term "autotelic gesture" describes typically rhythmic anacrustic gestures found at the end of repeating loops or grooves in popular music. An autotelic gesture directs attention forward toward the beginning of the next iteration of a repeating musical pattern.
9. For an added challenge, students can try to determine the pickup note (*la* or $\hat{6}$).
10. If students struggle to hear the bass line, we recommend having students with lower voices sing more loudly, to help those with higher voices recognize *do* in the double bass part.
11. We also frequently use the bonfire party example: you and your friends are at a bonfire and someone wants to play along to some songs. What is the quickest way to get a sense of how the song goes?
12. Some students may be overwhelmed by the potential open-endedness of the task. For these students, we try to remind them of the practical goals of reduction, that is, what is the clearest protonotation we could offer a performer, for example, that still sounds mostly consonant with the recording? Reductive dogmatism is not the objective of this exercise. We encourage instructors to be gracious when assessing reductions and to only raise concerns when student work starts to look more like transcriptions.
13. Several recordings of this string quartet are available on various streaming services. We recommend this performance on YouTube (www.youtube.com/watch?v=zK2CLTmWczc) as it has a more audible bass line (0:16–0:22).
14. For example, the phrase endings in "Heavenly Track" align most closely with what Temperley (2011, sect. 4) defines as a "plagal stop cadence"; specifically, because the subdominant falls on a downbeat, the following phrase starts on a tonic harmony, thus implying "sectional overlap," and the texture decays slightly before the phrase repeats.
15. For more on the components of sentences and periods, we recommend Chapters 2 and 3 from Caplin (2013).
16. For those interested in harmonic analysis, instructors can take the time to work out the supporting dominant and tonic chords at each cadence; however, the relatively poor recording quality from this era in history can make this extremely difficult for first-year students without the help of an instrument. Instead, we recommend discussing other songs listed in the following table, such as Nina Simone's "Chilly Winds Don't Blow." There, the harmonies are clearer, and more importantly, the song features the subdominant and dominant as cadential chords in the antecedent and consequent, respectively.

17. There is both an orchestral arrangement and a piano arrangement, so instructors have the choice of which version to use.
18. Instructors seeking to teach students about nested phrase structures can return to this example at a later point, as the opening eight measures repeat to form a 16-measure parallel period to end the first section of the polka.

Works Cited

Caplin, William E. 2013. *Analyzing Classical Form: An Approach for the Classroom*. Oxford University Press.

Clendinning, Jane Piper, and Elizabeth West Marvin. 2016. *The Musician's Guide to Theory and Analysis*. W.W. Norton & Company.

Cohn, Richard. 2019. "Meter." In *The Oxford Handbook of Critical Concepts in Music Theory*, edited by Alexander Rehding and Steven Rings. Oxford University Press.

de Clercq, Trevor. 2016. "Measuring a Measure: Absolute Time as a Factor for Determining Bar Lengths and Meter in Pop/Rock Music." *Music Theory Online* 22/3. https://mtosmt.org/issues/mto.16.22.3/mto.16.22.3.declercq.html

——. 2020. "A Music Theory Curriculum for the 99%." *Engaging Students: Essays in Music Pedagogy* 7. https://doi.org/10.18061/es.v7i0.7359

Everett, Walter. 1999. *The Beatles as Musicians: Revolver through the Anthology*. Oxford University Press.

Ewell, Philip A. 2020. "Music Theory and the White Racial Frame." *Music Theory Online* 26/2. https://mtosmt.org/issues/mto.20.26.2/mto.20.26.2.ewell.html

Fowler, Charles B. 1970. "Discovery: One of the Best Ways to Teach a Musical Concept." *Music Educators Journal* 57/2: 25–30. https://doi.org/10.2307/3392841

Gjerdingen, Robert. 2007. *Music in the Galant Style*. Oxford University Press.

Hughes, Timothy. 2003. "Groove and Flow: Six Analytical Essays on the Music of Stevie Wonder." Ph.D. Dissertation, University of Washington.

Jackson, Joyce Marie. 1995. "The Changing Nature of Gospel Music: A Southern Case Study." *African American Review* 29/2: 185–200.

Karpinski, Gary Steven. 2000. *Aural Skills Acquisition: The Development of Listening, Reading, and Performing Skills in College-Level Musicians*. Oxford University Press.

——. 2007. *Manual for Ear Training and Sight Singing*, 1st edition. W.W. Norton.

Laitz, Steven G. 2016. *The Complete Musician: An Integrated Approach to Tonal Theory, Analysis, and Listening*, 4th edition. Oxford University Press.

Lerdahl, Fred, and Ray Jackendoff. 1983. *A Generative Theory of Tonal Music*. The MIT Press.

Lewis, Kate. 2018. "Mothers and Sisters: Instrument and Idiom in the Music of Maybelle Carter, Memphis Minnie and Sister Rosetta Tharpe," Ph.D. Dissertation, University of Surrey.

London, Justin. 1998. "A Different Species of Counterpoint." *Journal of Music Theory Pedagogy* 12: 105–10.

Maxile, Horace J. 2011. "Extensions on a Black Musical Tropology: From Trains to the Mothership (and Beyond)." *Journal of Black Studies* 42/4: 593–608.

Mirka, Danuta. 2009. *Metric Manipulations in Haydn and Mozart: Chamber Music for Strings*. Oxford University Press.

Palfy, Cora, and Eric Gilson. 2018. "The Hidden Curriculum in the Music Theory Classroom." *Journal of Music Theory Pedagogy* 32: 1–32.

Redd, Lawrence. 1985. "Rock! It's Still Rhythm and Blues." *The Black Perspective in Music* 13/1: 31–47.

Rogers, Michael. 2004. *Teaching Approaches in Music Theory: An Overview of Pedagogical Philosophies*, 2nd edition. Southern Illinois University Press.

Shea, Nicholas. Forthcoming. "A Demographic Sampling Model and Database for Addressing Racial, Ethnic, and Gender Bias in Popular-music Empirical Research." *Empirical Musicology Review*.

——. 2019. "Ecological Models of Musical Structure in Pop-Rock, 1950–2019." Ph.D. Dissertation, Ohio State University.

Summach, Jay. 2011. "The Structure, Function, and Genesis of the Prechorus." *Music Theory Online* 17/3. www.mtosmt.org/issues/mto.11.17.3/mto.11.17.3.summach.html

Temperley, David. 2011. "The Cadential IV in Rock." *Music Theory Online* 17/1. www.mtosmt.org/issues/mto.11.17.1/mto.11.17.1.temperley.html

———. 2018. *The Musical Language of Rock*. Oxford University Press.

Tymoczko, Dmitri. 2011. *A Geometry of Music: Harmony and Counterpoint in the Extended Common Practice*. Oxford University Press.

Part Two

Chromaticism and Other Advanced Topics

6 Modal Mixture

Mitchell Ohriner

Modal Mixture: Definitions and Ideology

In the context of notated, Enlightenment-era European music (which I abbreviate as "NEEM" and many would call "classical music"), "modal mixture" occurs when scale degrees from one mode (major or minor) appear in passages written in the other mode and sharing a tonic.[1] These scale-degrees include *le* in place of *la* (i.e., ♭6̂ in place of ♮6̂), *me* in place of *mi* (i.e., ♭3̂ in place of ♮3̂), and *te* in place of *ti* (i.e., ♭7̂, the subtonic, in place of ♮7̂, the leading tone). In this chapter, I begin by detailing NEEM practices of modal mixture, some pedagogical challenges the topic entails, and some latent ideological issues. I then give pedagogical examples from music by Black composers writing in the NEEM tradition in the early- to mid-twentieth century, followed by Black songwriters writing in commercial genres since the late twentieth century. (These are further supported with two analysis assignments and a prompt for a short position paper, hosted by the online supplement to this volume.)

There are three key details in understanding NEEM practices of modal mixture. The first is that the importation of minor-mode sonorities into major-mode passages is much more common than the reverse.[2] This is partly because the major mode is already much more common in NEEM, but also because the minor mode in NEEM often already includes the major-mode scale degrees of *la* and *ti* through the ascending melodic minor scale. Furthermore, when a minor-mode passage employs the most emblematic major-mode scale degree, *mi*, it usually acts as a tonicizing leading tone to *fa*, harmonized by an applied chord like V⁷/iv (Burstein and Straus 2016, 392). The second detail is that because many mixture chords contain *le*, and because *le* has a tendency to descend to *sol*, many have a pre-dominant function. The third detail is that once a minor-mode scale degree (such as *le*) is introduced, it is usually retained – and its major-mode complement is usually avoided – until the music reaches a cadence (Aldwell and Schachter 2002, 392).

Figures 6.1a–c show three ways of conceptualizing sonorities arising from modal mixture. Figure 6.1a shows which sonorities result depending on pairings of scale degree and chord member. (I list the scale degrees in order of frequency in which they're encountered in NEEM repertoire.) Figure 6.1b demonstrates which sonorities contain which (combination of) scale degrees; Figure 6.1c shows the origins of the sonorities in the different "versions" of the minor scale. This, admittedly, is a lot for students to take in, and I include it for reference.

What attracts composers and songwriters to modal mixture? Each of the borrowed scale degrees offers specific advantages. Substituting *le* in place of *la* in the major mode creates a half step above *sol* rather than a whole step. Steve Larson, among others, argued that gravity and magnetism are productive metaphors in music, and both account for why NEEM composers of the nineteenth century considered *le* going to *sol* as more convincing than *la* going to *sol* (Larson 2012). Substituting *me* in place of *mi* in the major mode can

DOI: 10.4324/9781003204053-9

58 Mitchell Ohriner

a.

	as root	as third	as fifth	as seventh
♭$\hat{6}$	♭VI$^{(7)}$	iv$^{(7)}$	ii$^{(ø7)}$	vii^{o7}
♭$\hat{3}$	♭III$^{(7)}$	i$^{(7)}$	♭VI$^{(7)}$	iv^7
♭$\hat{7}$	♭VII$^{(7)}$	v$^{(7)}$	♭III$^{(7)}$	i^7

b.

♭$\hat{6}$	←(both)→	♭$\hat{3}$	←(both)→	♭$\hat{7}$
iv, vii^{o7}, ii$^{ø(ø7)}$	♭VI$^{(7)}$, iv^7	i	♭III$^{(7)}$	♭VII$^{(7)}$, v$^{(7)}$

c.

harmonic minor	natural minor	both
vii^{o7}	♭III$^{(7)}$, ♭VII$^{(7)}$, v$^{(7)}$	iv$^{(7)}$, ii$^{(ø7)}$, ♭VI$^{(7)}$, i

Figure 6.1 Conceptualizations of modal mixture sonorities: (a) mixture sonorities as a pairing of scale degree and chord member; (b) scale degree inclusion relationships of mixture sonorities; (c) scale inclusion relationships of mixture sonorities.

be quite arresting: the tonic triad, the sonority thought to be the most predictable of all, has changed quality. And substituting *te* in place of *ti* is somewhat the inverse of the *le/la* substitution, as now the magnetism that *do* exerts on $\hat{7}$ is minimized, since *te* to *do* is a whole step, not a half step. Due to this decreased magnetism, *te* can often sound weightier than *ti*, its motion to *do* not as obligatory and therefore more impactful.

Because the minor mode is associated with sadness, poignancy, or the tragic, modal mixture is often understood as an incursion of something negative – especially unrequited love in texted music – into the musical narrative. For example, in Robert Schumann's musical setting of Heinrich Heine's "Ich grolle nicht" (*Dichterliebe*, op. 48, no. 7, 1840) – which can be found in chapters on modal mixture in roughly half of available textbooks – the protagonist sings "I bear no grudge, and yet my heart breaks!" The word "heart" ("Herz") is pitched as *le*. Modal mixture also carries associations of evil and cruelty. In "Madamina" from Wolfgang Mozart's opera *Don Giovanni*, the title character's servant delivers a lighthearted aria describing Giovanni's behavior: "He seduces older women for the pleasure of adding them to the list." When the wicked purpose of seduction becomes evident with "list," *le* makes its appearance (Aldwell and Schachter 2002, 396).[3]

Modal mixture is a somewhat difficult topic to teach. First, there is the challenge of terminology. One can encounter "borrowed chords," "altered chords," "chromatic mediants," "secondary mixture," "double mixture," and more. At a close level of description, these terms all have distinct meanings but limited differences. Second, as shown in the preceding text, each of the three imported scale degrees might serve as a root, third, fifth, or seventh of a sonority; thus, modal mixture brings with it a rather large number of new harmonies that students must learn. Third, since most textbooks introduce modal mixture after applied chords and modulation, students must be able to distinguish applied chords and mixture chords.[4] Finally, modal mixture "sticks out" in the typical sequence of topics. For many textbooks and instructors, second-year theory is mainly a story of form, of building on ideas of cadence and phrase structure to encompass increasingly larger formal types (e.g., sonata form). While one can design a sequence that gets to large-scale form without teaching modal mixture, its prevalence in NEEM repertoire makes it unavoidable, though often disconnected. These are daunting challenges for the pedagogue, but I find naming them and relaying them to students makes them more manageable.

Before turning to uses of mixture in NEEM and beyond, there are three issues of ideology that arise with this topic. By "ideology," I mean the beliefs held about the world and its history. Ideology is often invisible in the music theory classroom, where one might argue that the harmonies are ideologically inert. Were that the case, there might be no need for a volume like this one. Considering the ideological framing of modal mixture is especially important for instructors who wish to bring more Black composers and songwriters into the classroom. This move, while laudable, carries a substantial risk of tokenism. One can only partly minimize this risk by teaching more pieces written by Black people. To promote a real engagement in the classroom, one must also interrogate the impact of the systems of thought that organized our slaveholding culture, as these ideologies informed both musical and economic systems.

Consider modal mixture's role in NEEM's "development" and the implications of that development for other music. Modal mixture is increasingly prominent in nineteenth-century music. As such, it was pivotal in Arnold Schoenberg's theoretical project in the early twentieth century. Schoenberg saw the history of NEEM as moving step-by-step toward the atonality he and many twentieth-century composers practiced. Modal mixture aids in this progression by collapsing the 24 major and minor keys into 12 chromatic keys. For Schoenberg (1978, 389), the 12 modally mixed keys were the final weigh station *en route* to "the polytonal chromatic scale." This project is teleological in the sense that it sees history as a directed motion toward some end. But where does this teleology leave, say, hip-hop or country music or Latin jazz? If one isn't careful, a celebration of modal mixture's "complexity" or "chromaticism" can impact how one views more contemporary music.

A second issue concerns the connection between modal mixture and "color." Steven Laitz (2012, 418), for example, characterizes modal mixture as "nonfunctional – a mere coloring of the melodic and harmonic surface of the music." Similar language, including the word "color," occurs in roughly a third of current textbooks (e.g., Kostka et al. 2013, 346; Benward and Saker 2009, 72; Clendenning and Marvin 2016, 882). To say that modal mixture is a "coloring" of the music is to say that the outward appearance of the music, but not its "inner structure," has changed. These authors are trying to maintain a focus in the music-theory sequence on tonal hierarchy. The priority of learning about tonal hierarchy is still widely advanced in music theory pedagogy, but it has also had its detractors for several decades now (Fink 1999; Scherzinger 2004; Kielian-Gilbert 2003). The emphasis on tonal hierarchy is especially pronounced in the writings of Heinrich Schenker, who remains a strong influence on many textbook authors and theorists. Recently, Philip Ewell (2020) has reminded the discipline that Schenker's views on the hierarchy of tones and the hierarchy of races of people were deeply intertwined. It is worth discussing in class what it means to say a chord "provides color" to a passage.

A third ideological issue is the allure and damage binary modes of thinking entail. In most textbooks, modal mixture is presented as the importation of chords usually associated with "the minor mode" into passages of music otherwise containing "the major mode." Note that this definition relies on precisely two nominally fixed collections of pitches. As such, it presents a stark binarism and simultaneously enforces the boundaries of that binarism: the chord imported from the minor mode retains its minor mode identity, even in the major mode context. Daniel Harrison (1994, 19), for example, writes that "major-minor permeation results, not in an integrated chromatic tonality, but in a major-minor tonality in which the two modes remain perceptually separable while compositionally squeezed together in unprecedented density." A priority on binary organization and on the essentialism of labels, of course, can also be seen in prevailing structures of race, gender, sexuality,

60 *Mitchell Ohriner*

and ability. I'm sure some will scoff at linking modal mixture to other identity binarisms. But highlighting modal mixture's insistence on binary labels is also an opportunity to point out just how common such structures are and the ideological work they continue to do.

Mixture in the NEEM Tradition

Betty Jackson King, "Spring Intermezzo"

I begin with a brief example from a composer working in the NEEM tradition, one that neatly introduces modally altered scale degrees one at a time. Figure 6.2 shows the first nine measures of "Spring Intermezzo" from *Four Seasonal Sketches* by Betty Jackson King.[5] The first nine measures of "Spring Intermezzo" constitute a parallel period with quite unequal phrase lengths. What elongates the second phrase is the thrice-repeated descent from A_5 on the downbeats of measures 6, 7, and 8. Modal mixture accrues in each measure. Measure 6 presents a diatonic descent from A_5 to E_5 through G♯$_5$ and F♯$_5$. Measures 7 and 8 alter this descent to include G♮$_5$ and F♮$_5$, first by shifting the D major sonority (IV) to D minor (iv), and then by harmonizing each step of the descent with a different mixture chord that includes F major (♭VI), G major (♭VII), and finally, C major (♭III). The presentation of C major will raise questions about cadence: can this be said to be an authentic cadence if there is no dominant (E major) anywhere to be heard? This is a pivotal question in identifying the nine measures as a period if *period* is defined as "the combination of a phrase with a more conclusive cadence following a phrase with a less conclusive one." Answering the question provides an opportunity to consider what constitutes "dominant," and if a compositional idiom can establish its own tendencies for harmonic progression that exert the same force as traditional "rules."

Samuel Coleridge-Taylor, "The Bamboula," for Orchestra, op. 75

Jackson King's "Spring Intermezzo" is a good starting point because all the accidentals in the passage are instances of modal mixture. But this is rarely the case. Figure 6.3a shows the incipit of Samuel Coleridge-Taylor's "The Bamboula," from *Twenty-Four Negro Melodies*, op. 59, no. 8 for piano (1905), which forms the basis of an orchestral dance I'll discuss next. These pieces take their name from that of a drum brought by enslaved Africans first to the Caribbean and later to New Orleans, as well as a style of dance that traveled with the drumming.[6] The drum and dance were associated with Haiti and the Haitian Revolution, the most successful revolt by enslaved people in the Western Hemisphere. Chenzira Kahina, who teaches the dance and other aspects of Caribbean culture at the University of the Virgin Islands, describes the sound and movements as ones that "used to make enslavers nervous" (Morris 2006). The rhythm heard at the beginning of Coleridge-Taylor's *bamboula*, especially the subdivided second beat, can be heard in a recording from the Virgin Islands released by Folkway Records in 1954.

Figure 6.3b shows the slow passage of Coleridge-Taylor's orchestral "The Bamboula," featuring typical late-nineteenth-century modal mixture in the NEEM tradition. There are several predominants that arise from the presence of F♭ (*le*) and C♭ (*me*) that prepare quasi-plagal cadences on the downbeats of measures 270 and 272. The excerpt is also instructive because Coleridge-Taylor introduces chromatically altered scale degrees in a number of different ways, and analysts are left to sort out which are the result of modal mixture. For example, G♭ (i.e., *te*) occurs three times: in the tenor of the accompaniment in measures 261–2 (as the seventh of an A°7, vii°7/ii), the soprano of the accompaniment in

Modal Mixture 61

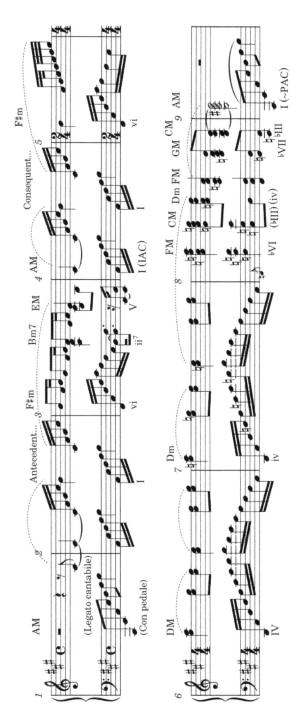

Figure 6.2 Betty Jackson King, "Spring Intermezzo," from Four Seasonal Sketches (Chicago: Jacksonian Press, 1973), mm. 1–9.

62   *Mitchell Ohriner*

Figure 6.3 (a) Samuel Coleridge-Taylor, incipit to "The Bamboula," from Twenty-Four Negro Melodies, op. 59, no. 8 (Boston: Ditson, 1905); (b) Samuel Coleridge-Taylor, "The Bamboula" (Rhapsodic Dance) for orchestra, op. 78, mm. 260–76 (London: Hawkes & Son, 1911).

measure 264 (as part of an augmented sixth sonority), and the clarinet of measure 271 (as an appoggiatura to F♭, the fifth of B♭°$^6_5$, i.e., ii°$^6_5$). Only the last of these is modal mixture.[7]

L. Viola Kinney, "Mother's Sacrifice" (1909)

A final example from the NEEM tradition again shows typical usage but raises broader questions about style and race. Figure 6.4a shows the beginning of L. Viola Kinney's "Mother's Sacrifice" for piano, written in 1909. Kinney was born, raised, and lived in Sedalia, Missouri. Her only times away from Sedalia were her college years at Western University of Kansas, a Black college established in 1865 and closed in 1943. Upon graduation, she served as head of the music department at the segregated Lincoln High School in Sedalia. "Mother's Sacrifice" is her only published work and dates from her student days. There are registered copyrights for two other much later works, but manuscripts do not survive. The university published the piece as the result of a composition competition among their students. All contestants were asked to state why their pieces should be published. Ms. Kinney responded, in part, "Because it shows the Negro in his great Musical Metamorphosis from the rag-time to the nobler, higher tones."[8] The winner, William Lane, responded, "Because it shows the necessity of musical culture in this race, which will cause

Modal Mixture 63

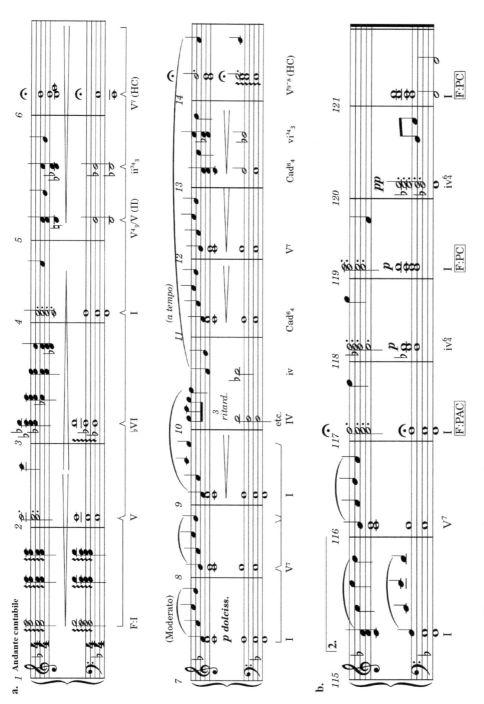

Figure 6.4 L. Viola Kinney, "Mother's Sacrifice" (Quindaro, KS: Twentieth-Century Commercial Society of Western University, 1909: (a) mm. 1–14; (b) mm. 115–21.

someone else to realize their ability and produce something equally as good." Fannie Toles, who received a Special Mention, responded, "Because it shows to the world our appreciation of classical Music in preference to trashy rag-time music, [and] because it creates in the heart of the youth of the Race a love and taste for classical Music" (Kinney 1909).

If one wants their students to be conversant in NEEM practices of modal mixture, "Mother's Sacrifice" is, as Lane noted, "well enough composed to be played anywhere in the world." The altered scale degrees include *le* (D♭) in measures 3, 5, and 10 (as well as m. 18, which repeats m. 10) and *me* (A♭) in measures 3 and 13. These alterations create lowered submediants (the ♭VI chord of m. 3), diminished or minor predominants through passing motion (i.e., the ii°$^4_3$ of m. 5 and the iv of m. 10), and the unusual vi°$^4_3$ of measure 13, also created through passing motion that changes *mi* at the beginning of the measure to *la* at the end of the measure.[9] Modal mixture ends the piece as well as begins it. Figure 6.4b shows the final four measures that follow a perfect authentic cadence ending the main theme. Here, *le* creates a cadence that could be heard as a borrowed iv$^6_4$ in the major, or as a minor-mode cadence with a Picardy third. Frank Lehman (2013, para. 1.4) writes of

> the nineteenth-century harmonic proclivity for modal inflection of the subdominant in order to suggest sentiment or sublimity. It is an inclination that courses through the works of [Robert] Schumann, [Frederic] Chopin, and [Felix] Mendelssohn and reaches its peak with the act-concluding plagal sighs of [Richard] Wagner.

This cadence lasted well into the twentieth century through film music – and even later through Alfred Newman's "Twentieth Century Fox Theme" – in which it "harkens back to an imagined earlier experience . . . [of] a heroic era of film going." Kinney's use of mixture is heard as similarly nostalgic, a suggestion of "Mother's Sacrifice" as something remembered.[10]

Following my earlier comments on modal mixture and ideology, I find it useful in class to discuss how this piece sounds Kinney's race. The idea that music contains sounds with racialized meanings is commonplace in popular music studies but less so in the music theory classroom (Burdick 2013; Nunn 2015; Kajikawa 2015). Kinney's publication came just half a decade after W. E. B. Du Bois's essay "The Talented Tenth" (Du Bois 1903), which argues that freedom, prosperity, and security of the recently enslaved and their descendants rested on the access of the most talented Black Americans to higher education. Ms. Kinney and her colleagues are certainly among Du Bois's "talented tenth," and their attendance at Western University was a progressive act. Their musical politics are more subtle. In both their compositions and what they say in the pamphlet, they uphold the supremacy of NEEM – which is to say, White supremacy – and they are keen to demonstrate their expertise in its procedures. These compositional choices can raise difficult and profound questions about the history of race, music, and genre. Is this music a kind of advocacy, and if so, for what? What is its relation to Whiteness and White supremacy? What, if any, are the obligations of musicians to comment on structures of race? In my experience, these are discussions many students want to have and want to know how to have better.

Mixture in US Popular Music

Beyoncé, "Single Ladies (Put a Ring on It)"

In this section, I'll describe two tracks that facilitate discussion of broader ideological considerations described previously. I begin with Beyoncé's "Single Ladies (Put a Ring on It)," from the album *I Am . . . Sasha Fierce* of 2008, not least because of its impact on early-morning music theory students. Beyoncé's track has a straightforward message about expectations in long-term relationships. This message is paired with straightforward musical choices. The melody is contained almost entirely within the first five notes of an E major scale, from E_4 to B_4 – a very small register, given what we know of her range. The rhythm of the chorus and especially the verses is decidedly square for an artist who ranges through R&B and hip-hop. And there is practically no pitched accompaniment. In the first verse, a synthesizer occasionally sounds E_4, but this is eclipsed by the vocals. In the first chorus and the first "oh-oh-oh" postchorus, longer and lower Es sound. (The form of the track in essence is a verse-chorus-verse-chorus-bridge-chorus form. The distinguishing feature is the presence of a four-bar postchorus – the "oh, oh, oh" part – which in the last chorus falls before the chorus proper. Further, the intro of the song comes back before the last chorus.)

Commentators on "Single Ladies" have noted the "robotic" sound of the opening, which accentuates the robotic features of the choreography and costuming of the music video. These features all connect Beyoncé to what Tom Breihan (2007) describes as "robo-diva" R&B. Robin James (2008) argues these robo-divas (which also include Rihanna, Ciara, and others) "critique [W]hite patriarchal anxieties about the supposedly passivizing effects of both [B]lack female sexuality and technology." That might be a lot to unpack at 8:00 a.m., but it is an answer to questions one should ask about this song: Why does Beyoncé pair predominantly electronic sounds with her anthem of independence and autonomy? Students will likely offer several answers – including, probably, "for no reason" – but one to consider is that female sexuality, and especially Black female sexuality, can be understood as a threat to male control in intimate contexts, a corollary to the threat technology poses in industrial contexts.

The first sign of the technological slant of the song is heard at the very beginning in a synthesized flourish, something you might hear in an 8-bit video game. The sound recurs throughout the song on beats 2, 3, and the "and" of 4 in nearly every measure. Isolate the sound in software, use source-separation algorithms to remove the claps, slow it down, play slices of it at a time, and it is definitely in E minor. I transcribe it in Figure 6.5a. This fragment, which lasts about half a second, can give you a truly astounding duration-to-analytical-significance ratio. Is this sound musical? Is it modal mixture? Is it sad or tragic or evil? If it is supposed to signal the incursion of technology into music making, why use modal mixture here? What musical meaning can anything so brief impart?

The tone of the song changes from teasing to downright menacing with the return of the four-bar chorus at 0:51 (just after the first postchorus from 0:41–0:51), when the synthesizers – who, again, have not yet left E – sound the third from C♮ to A, introducing *le* to the tonality. The model mixture goes beyond this by sounding G♮ (*me*) in the synthesizers as well, against the persistent G♯s of the vocals.[11] How should this introduction of mixture be interpreted in reference to the expressive meanings of mixture identified previously? It isn't sadness or melancholy – Beyoncé is well past sadness at the ending of this relationship. In my hearing, it's closer to the supernatural sometimes ascribed to modal mixture in the nineteenth century. Up to this point of the song, it seems as though Beyoncé is the only sound present, along with perhaps the clapping of her crew. This sparsity makes the suddenly forward synthesizers appear to emanate *from her* through supernatural means. She is *Sasha Fierce*, indeed.

Modal mixture goes further still in the bridge, transcribed in Figure 6.5b. Beyoncé reaches her highest pitch yet, D♮$_5$ (*te*), and presents a melody that is largely focused on the third from F♯$_4$ (*re*) to A$_4$ (*fa*), with G♮$_4$ (*me*, not *mi*) as a persistent passing tone. As in the rest of the song, harmony is highly underdetermined. The bass oscillates between *fa* and *do*, changing pitch each measure before reaching C♮ (*le*) in measure 50. In contrast to what

66 Mitchell Ohriner

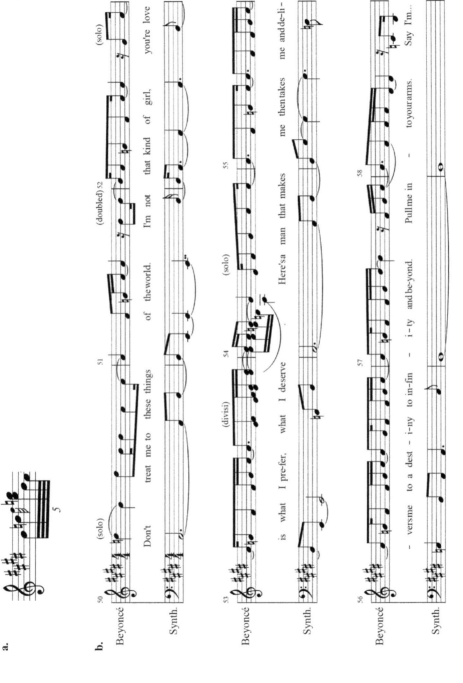

Figure 6.5 Beyoncé, "Single Ladies (Put a Ring on It)," released on *I am . . . Sasha Fierce*, written by Beyoncé Knowles, Christopher Stewart, Terius Nash, and Thaddis Harrell. (a) synth flourish first heard at 0:00; (b) transcription of vocals and synth bass at bridge (2:01–2:23, transcription mine).

we see in NEEM, *le* here is the last modally altered scale degree to arrive in the voice, not until measure 58 (and several more times in the measures that follow). One reason for this is that this idiom relies heavily on pentatonic scales. The minor pentatonic contains no $\hat{6}$; thus, there is little reason to emphasize *le* in modal mixture.[12] When *le* does arrive in measure 50, it can be heard as a kind of text painting – the process by which the man "makes," "takes," and "delivers" arrives at *le*.

This bridge makes available one more discussion that doesn't exactly pertain to modal mixture but one I've found students enjoy all the same. Ask students to analyze the harmonic functions of the bass and voice independently. Both are strange requests. The bass, of course, doesn't have harmonies, but one can treat the longer notes as chord roots, and thus it mainly alternates between predominant and tonic. The vocals seem also to alternate between two harmonic functions: there are spans focused on the third from G_4 to B_4, suggesting tonic function, and there are spans focused on the third from $F\sharp_4$ to A_4, suggesting dominant function. But except for the ending of the bridge, these functions are non-aligned much of the time. This is clearest in measures 51, 53, and 55, where Beyoncé emphasizes A vocally over an E in the bass. Moments like this have sprouted a rich scholarly literature around the term "melodic-harmonic divorce," a term especially resonant with Beyoncé's message. Is she asserting independence not only from her former partner but also from her musical accompaniment? Is harmonic function in this music not what we think it is because of our NEEM-based perspective? Should we take a more descriptive approach and label the chord of measure 51 a 1^{11} chord so that the As are chord tones? While my focus in this chapter is on modal mixture, once you adopt the perspective that theories and repertoires are inextricable, other conversations become available as well.

Stevie Wonder, "Livin' for the City"

In "Single Ladies," the introduction of minor-mode scale degrees has the effect of an incursion, perhaps of the supernatural, into a major-mode context. But as Kevin Holm-Hudson (2017, 384) argues, "[s]ometimes borrowed chords in popular music are not the result of mixing major and minor modes per se, but of the consistent use of modes other than major or minor." This assertion goes against the binarism discussed previously and can be exemplified by Figure 6.6a–b, a transcription of the verse and refrain of Stevie Wonder's "Livin' for the City" (*Innervisions*, 1973), sung in F♯ major. I include a transcription of the two-measure loop played by the bass and keyboard (both played, along with the drums, by Wonder himself) as well as the vocals of the verse and refrain. The accompanimental parts exhibit what the NEEM tradition would call modal mixture with the A♮s (*me*) and C♮s (*le*) in the chord at the beginning of even-numbered measures. In a sense, these measures mix *me* and *mi*. This is a mixture in *pitch-class space* (yes, there are both A♮ and A♯) but not in *pitch space* (there are no A♮s below middle C, and there are no A♯s above middle C). The registral isolation of A♮ and A♯ suggests not a mixture of major and minor but instead a single mode that does not repeat at the octave. There is precedent for such a mode in other musical cultures, including the *maqam saba* in Arabic music, as well as in various experimental approaches in Anglo-European music. It is not my suggestion that Wonder is channeling either of those; the blues is an obvious place to look for the origin of this kind of *mi/me* interaction. But I would suggest that our preoccupation with major and minor modes, as well as with octave equivalence, impoverishes our understanding of this accompaniment.

What of mixture in Wonder's vocals? His singing in the verses, especially the beginning ones, is tonally underdetermined. About half the notes, including most of the nouns and verbs, are sung on F♯ (*do*), which is usually approached from E♮ (*te*) and sometimes from

68 Mitchell Ohriner

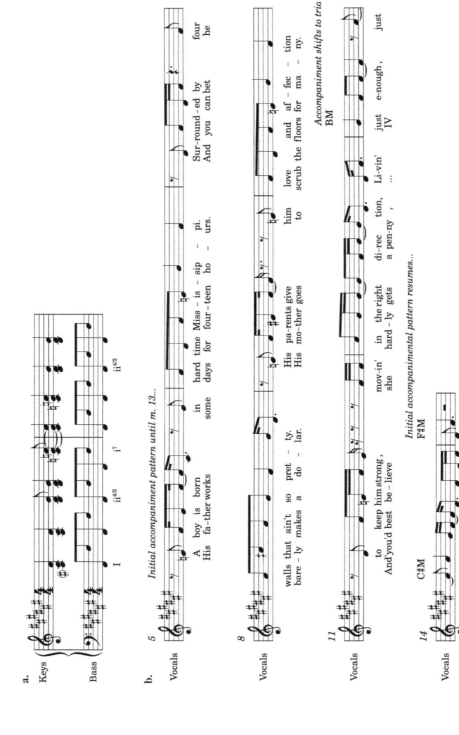

Figure 6.6 Stevie Wonder, "Livin' for the City," released on Innervisions, written by Stevie Wonder. Transcription mine. (a) Electric piano at opening. These measures repeat until the refrain. (b) Vocals of first two verses.

D♯ (*la*). There are no Bs at all, and the only Cs are the quite low C♯ of "that" in measure 4 and the swallowed C♯ of "born" in measure 1. Perhaps this is a mixture of major and minor: the "major" accounts for F♯, G♯, A♯, C♯, and D♯, while the minor accounts for E♮. But this term in the NEEM tradition suggests the use of *le* first and foremost, and Wonder uses *la*. Describing Wonder's vocals as in the mixolydian mode asserts them as a thing with their own identity, not a composite identity of things that don't quite add up. Yet that still implies a presence of the absent B. Describing it as "F♯ pentatonic" rightly conveys that B is avoided but also does not convey the presence of E♮.

Bringing an example like this into the classroom does hazard increasing confusion about the topic. Instructors might rightly be asked – by students with their minds on upcoming exams – whether "Livin' for the City" *does* or *does not* contain modal mixture and how the chords should be labeled. But the music theory classroom is both a place for learning analytical techniques and a place for honing critical thinking. Considering "Livin' for the City" through the prism of a NEEM-based conception of major/minor modal mixture is very pertinent to the latter.

Conclusion

In this chapter I've identified my own challenges in teaching modal mixture – it's a somewhat unwieldy topic that is disconnected from the thread of much of the standard second-year theory curriculum. At the same time, it is laden with NEEM-era ideological preferences for the chromatic over the diatonic, the structural over the surface, and the major/minor dichotomy over a more nuanced categorization. I hope the examples I've presented here help instructors unpack some of that ideology in the classroom, as well as listen to and study some wonderful music with their students.

Notes

1. My term "NEEM" is admittedly quirky. I prefer it because it doesn't carry the value judgments of "classical music" or "art music" or Richard Taruskin's "literate music." To say that eighteenth- and early nineteenth-century composers are working in the era of the Enlightenment is uncontroversial. To say the Enlightenment is relevant to composers like Scott Joplin or Florence Price is open for debate. To me, that debate is preferable to debating whether Beethoven or Beyoncé has a stronger claim to the cultural value that inheres to the word "classical."
2. For this reason, I'll only discuss instances of minor-mode scale degrees in major-mode passages in my NEEM examples in this chapter.
3. Aldwell and Schachter also describe the associations between modal mixture and the supernatural (2002, 390).
4. One additional complication is that a sonority can be both an applied chord and a modal mixture chord. The second chord of Charlie Parker's "Ornithology" – which is in the major mode – is a i^7 (Gauldin 2004, 508). It is followed by V^7/VII and VII. This i^7 chord is simultaneously modal mixture, borrowing *me* and *te* from the minor mode, and also an applied chord, as ii^7 of VII.
5. This score, and many others, is included in Walker-Hill (1992), an indispensable collection.
6. "Bamboula" has taken on derogatory and offensive denotations in modern French, akin to the n-word.
7. Typically, students will not yet be familiar with augmented sixth sonorities when they learn modal mixture, and the sonority of m. 264 may have to be cordoned off for now. But if one makes a brief introduction, one can point out that the sonority has aspects of modal mixture (via *le*) but also aspects of applied chords (via *fi*).
8. Kinney's dig at ragtime is quite a personal one, as her hometown of Sedalia, Missouri, also hosted Scott Joplin from 1894 to 1901, when Kinney was aged 4–11.

9. In the accelerated harmonic rhythm of the consequent phrase, this chord is omitted in m. 19, a point that can be useful for documenting practices of period construction in NEEM.
10. Although beyond the scope of this chapter, "Mother's Sacrifice" can support instruction on several other topics besides modal mixture, including a passage in the minor mode consisting nearly entirely of dominant and tonic, a chromatic sequence where V–I motion is iteratively transposed up by half step, and a clear-cut rondo form that runs throughout.
11. This G♮ is very faint, and I did not find it through casual listening. In the audio from the music video, in which the downbeat of the measure with the return of the chorus is at 0:51.55, select 0:53.5–0:53.8 and you'll hear it clearly.
12. I have not worded this quite right: there is no $\hat{6}$ in the minor pentatonic because, as the name implies, there are only five scale degrees in the pentatonic scale. But whereas the fifth degree of the major pentatonic scale corresponds to the sixth degree of the major (heptatonic) scale (i.e., *la*), the fifth degree of the minor pentatonic scale corresponds to the seventh degree of the (natural) minor (heptatonic) scale (i.e., *te*).

Works Cited

Aldwell, Edward, and Carl Schachter. 2002. *Harmony & Voice Leading*, 3rd edition. Thompson Schirmer.

Benward, Bruce, and Marilyn Saker. 2009. *Music in Theory and Practice*, 8th edition. McGraw Hill.

Breihan, Tom. June 15, 2007. "Rihanna: Good Girl Gone Bad." *Pitchfork Media*. https://pitchfork.com/reviews/albums/10320-good-girl-gone-bad/

Burdick, John. 2013. *The Color of Sound: Race, Religion, and Music in Brazil*. New York University Press.

Burstein, L. Poundie, and Joseph N. Straus. 2016. *Concise Introduction to Tonal Harmony*. W.W. Norton & Company.

Clendinning, Jane Piper, and Elizabeth West Marvin. 2016. *The Musician's Guide to Theory and Analysis*, 3rd edition. W.W. Norton & Company.

Courlander, Harold, ed. 1954. *African and Afro-American Drums*. Folkway Records and Service Corp., FW04502, 33½ rpm.

Du Bois, W.E. Burghardt. 1903. "The Talented Tenth." In *The Negro Problem: A Collection of Articles by Representative American Negroes of To-Day*. James Pott & Company.

Ewell, Philip. 2020. "Music Theory and the White Racial Frame." *Music Theory Online* 26/2.

Fink, Robert. 1999. "Going Flat: Post-Hierarchical Music Theory and the Musical Surface." In *Rethinking Music*, edited by Nicholas Cook and Mark Everist, 102–37. Oxford University Press.

Gauldin, Robert. 2004. *Harmonic Practice in Tonal Music*. W.W. Norton & Company.

Harrison, Daniel. 1994. *Harmonic Function in Chromatic Music: A Renewed Dualist Theory and an Account of Its Precedents*. University of Chicago Press.

Holm-Hudson, Kevin. 2017. *Music Theory Remixed: A Blended Approach for the Practicing Musician*. Oxford University Press.

James, Robin. 2008. "'Robo-Diva R&B': Aesthetics, Politics, and Black Female Robots in Contemporary Popular Music." *Journal of Popular Music Studies* 20/4: 402–03.

Kajikawa, Loren. 2015. *Sounding Race in Rap Songs*. University of California Press.

Kielian-Gilbert, Marianne. 2003. "Interpreting Schenkerian Prolongation." *Music Analysis* 22/1–2: 51–104.

Kinney, L. Viola. 1909. "Mother's Sacrifice." Twentieth Century Commercial Society of Western University.

Kostka, Stefan, Dorothy Payne, and Byron Almén. 2013. *Tonal Harmony with an Introduction to Twentieth-Century Music*, 7th edition. McGraw-Hill.

Laitz, Steven G. 2012. *The Complete Musician: An Integrated Approach to Tonal Theory, Analysis, and Listening*, 3rd edition. Oxford University Press.

Larson, Steve. 2012. *Musical Forces: Motion, Metaphor, and Meaning in Music*. Indiana University Press.

Lehman, Frank. 2013. "Hollywood Cadences: Music and the Structure of Cinematic Expectation." *Music Theory Online* 19/4.

Morris, Ayesha. February 25, 2006. "The Power of Dance: Bamboula has Deep and Strong Ties to African Heritage, Island History, and Freedom Fight." *Virgin Islands Daily News*.
Nunn, Erica. 2015. *Sounding the Color Line*. University of Georgia Press.
Scherzinger, Martin. 2004. "The Return of the Aesthetic: Musical Formalism and Its Place in Political Critique." In *Beyond Structural Hearing*, edited by Andrew Dell'Antonio, 252–79. University of California Press.
Schoenberg, Arnold. 1978. *Theory of Harmony*. University of California Press.
Walker-Hill, Helen, ed. 1992. *Black Women Composers: A Century of Piano Music (1893–1990)*. Hildegard Publishing Company.

7 "Elite Syncopations" and "Euphonic Sounds"
Scott Joplin in the Aural Skills Classroom[1]

Amy Fleming

Introduction

Philip Ewell's plenary address at the 2019 meeting of the Society for Music Theory and his subsequent *Music Theory Online* article have been hailed by many theorists as a call to action, inspiring efforts to challenge the "White racial frame" that has long existed in the discipline (Ewell 2019, 2020). One of Ewell's many compelling critiques of the field was that a mere 1.67% of musical examples in seven of the top theory textbooks were written by non-White composers. In response, many theorists are now seeking to diversify the undergraduate curriculum by increasing the representation of minority composers in their theory courses.[2] While that will not solve the systemic problems within the discipline, it is nonetheless an important step.

Ewell did not provide similar statistics for aural skills texts, but a quick survey through several of the commonly used sight-singing and dictation books reveals that the problem certainly extends to this portion of our discipline as well. Yet it is crucial that the efforts to diversify the undergraduate curriculum include the aural skills core, not just written theory courses. Incorporating underrepresented composers in aural skills classes provides students with the opportunity to engage on an even deeper and more personal level with the works of minority composers through in-depth listening, performing, and dictating of these works.

In this chapter, I offer suggestions for incorporating the music of Scott Joplin into the aural skills curriculum. I have chosen to focus on Joplin for several reasons. First, students are usually familiar with Joplin's style and music, as most have, at the very least, heard "The Entertainer" and "Maple Leaf Rag." Additionally, the texture of the ragtime accompaniment can be helpful to students because of the way the bass line and chords are staggered. Moreover, Joplin's blending of classical harmonies and forms with ragtime and blues elements makes his music approachable to students yet also useful for expanding their musical horizons beyond the narrow confines of the White, European, common-practice canon. Indeed, Joplin's music can be used throughout diatonic and chromatic aural skills courses and is useful for teaching many of the typical aural skills activities. Furthermore, with the use of ragtime music throughout the curriculum, the genre and its norms – such as the typical bass-chord alternation of its accompaniment – become a foundation upon which students can build newer, more complex material as they move from basic diatonic harmony to advanced chromatic topics.

This chapter will proceed in six sections, which correspond to six common aural skills activities: singing, rhythm, dictation/transcription, contextual listening, improvisation, and error detection. In each section, I offer a number of ways in which Joplin's music can be used to teach that activity throughout the undergraduate aural skills curriculum, from introductory courses on diatonic harmony through upper-level courses on advanced chromatic topics.

DOI: 10.4324/9781003204053-10

Singing

Although pianistic in texture, Joplin's rags feature a wealth of singable melodies. Beyond that, Joplin's *oeuvre* includes several songs and one ragtime opera. As we will see in later sections on dictation and contextual listening, Joplin's music offers wide-ranging difficulty levels and thus can be relevant through several semesters. This also means it is crucial to choose exercises of an appropriate difficulty level for specific courses; hence, I will suggest both diatonic and chromatic examples throughout. The rest of this section will focus on two types of singing, which are both invaluable for learning about ragtime and for developing aural skills: melodic singing and bass singing.

First, we will explore Joplin melodies that are useful for singing at different stages of the aural skills curriculum. In early musicianship training, I suggest focusing on diatonic excerpts from Joplin's vocal works, such as the chorus of "Please Say You Will" (Figure 7.1). However, many piano works also contain singable diatonic melodies. Figure 7.2 excerpts the C.1 section of "Original Rags."[3] This melody allows students to practice arpeggiating through not only a tonic triad but also a leading-tone seventh chord. It also requires students to master a hallmark of ragtime style – syncopated rhythms.

As students advance in the curriculum and learn about chromatic solfège and harmonies, they will be adequately equipped to sing more complex melodies from Joplin's *oeuvre*. Consider Figure 7.3, which excerpts the B.1 section of "Leola" and contains several chromatic non-chord tones.[4] The melody in the B.1 section of "Rag-Time Dance," on the other hand (presented in Figure 7.4), features both chromatic non-chord tones and a chromatic pitch that is part of a secondary dominant harmony.

Beyond the four examples – two diatonic and two chromatic – presented so far, Joplin's output provides myriad additional melodies that are appropriate for singing at different stages of the aural skills curriculum. Table 7.1 presents suggestions for both diatonic (left two columns) and chromatic (right two columns) melodies.

As a final word on singing Joplin's melodies, I focus on a challenging melody from the C.1 section of "Palm Leaf Rag." When using an excerpt like this, I recommend walking students through the process of removing the more complicated aspects of the melody at first, in order to get familiar with the framework of the melody, before dealing with complications like chromatic pitches, large leaps, and even syncopations. Consider the C.1 section of "Palm Leaf Rag" as a case study (Figure 7.5). This challenging melody may intimidate students at first, but by removing some of the difficult elements, like the large leaps in measures 2 and 4, the wide range, and the chromatic pitches, students can familiarize themselves with a simplified version of the melody, as in Figure 7.6. Once comfortable with the simplified version, students can gradually add in the more complex elements of the original.

Students will also benefit from singing Joplin's bass lines. Elizabeth Sayrs (2019) has convincingly argued that singing bass lines is crucial to aural development, and I will take that one step further and say that ragtime basses are ideal for this task. Because the characteristic "boom-chick" ragtime bass includes a bass note (often doubled at the octave) on the beat, followed by a chord off the beat, ragtime basses are helpful for teaching students what bass lines do.[5] By presenting students – who often struggle to hear and sing bass lines – with a texture that separates the bass from the rest of the chord, we can help them learn to hear, sing, and understand the unique movement of bass lines, which can also improve their dictation skills. Having students sing along with ragtime bass lines can also help them understand that the same principles of voice leading they are accustomed to in chorale-style writing are typically also present in ragtime.

74 *Amy Fleming*

In the D section of "Rag-Time Dance," for example (Figure 7.7), the bass resolves in expected ways: in the V$_2^4$/IV, it resolves down by step to IV^6; in the German augmented sixth chord, ♭$\hat{6}$ resolves to $\hat{5}$; and the temporary leading tone of the vii°^{7}/V resolves upward.

Activities involving bass singing can be done solo (with students singing the bass line alone), with the teacher playing the accompanying chords and/or melody, or with students singing along to a recording so that they can hear how their part functions within the fuller texture. Alternatively, other students could sing the offbeat chord tones, thus creating the accompanimental harmonies as a class.

Rhythm

Syncopation is a quintessential feature of the ragtime genre and thus a key component to including ragtime in the aural skills curriculum. Obviously, syncopated rhythms will be included in most of the activities in this chapter: in singing Joplin's melodies, performing syncopated rhythms will be required; in dictating Joplin's melodies, hearing the syncopation will be necessary; even in improvising along with a ragtime accompaniment, the addition of syncopation will enliven the improvised material and make it sound more realistically rag-like. However, focusing on the use of syncopation in a purely rhythmic context first can help prepare students to deal with syncopation in these other activities. In order to do this, one can take excerpts from Joplin compositions and have students focus on performing just the rhythms.

In the following paragraphs, I will suggest activities that an instructor could use in the classroom to teach and practice syncopation, beginning with rhythmic performance, then turning to rhythmic dictation. Joplin's rags are filled with syncopations; thus, each activity I suggest could be applied to any Joplin rag. As an example, Figure 7.8 excerpts the melody from the A.1 section of "Elite Syncopations."

The rhythm of this melody can be used to practice rhythmic performance in one of several ways, the most basic of which is to have students speak the rhythm on whatever rhythmic syllables (or neutral syllable) the institution uses. For example, students could speak the syllables presented beneath the melody in Figure 7.9. These rhythmic syllables could also be spoken along with the instructor playing the melody on the piano, the instructor playing the accompanimental harmonies on the piano, or even along with a recording of the full piano texture. The latter two options help students hear more clearly how the syncopated rhythms interact with the metrical framework.

After students are able to articulate the rhythm as a solo, an instructor might ask students to hear and perform both the syncopated rhythm of the melody and the eighth notes of the "boom-chick" ragtime accompaniment. Before having students perform both parts simultaneously, a few intermediate steps might be helpful: working in pairs, one student could perform the melody's syncopated rhythm while the other performs the accompaniment's eighth notes (with directions to listen for the composite rhythm); alternately, students could perform the melody's rhythm (speaking or tapping) while conducting along to the duple meter.

Once students are prepared, they can perform both parts of the rhythm simultaneously, using one of the following methods: (1) students speak the melody's rhythm while tapping the accompanimental rhythm with their hands or stomping it with their feet; (2) students speak the accompanimental rhythm while tapping the melody's rhythm; (3) students tap the melody's rhythm in one hand and the accompanimental rhythm with the other; or (4) students speak the melody's rhythm while walking in place on the accompaniment's eighth notes.

The goal in each iteration is to have students produce both the regularity of the metrical grid and the syncopation of the melody simultaneously. Having the metrical grid in the body somewhere – tapping the foot, walking in place on eighth notes, or conducting

– while also performing the syncopated melody helps ensure students actually engage with the misaligned nature of Joplin's syncopated rhythms. And having students begin by practicing these rhythms as *just* rhythms will give them the skills to incorporate pitch when they sing Joplin's melodies and to more readily recognize when syncopation is happening in dictation exercises.

Indeed, the same principle can be applied to dictation: rather than jumping right into dictating Joplin's melodies, an instructor might start by having students focus just on the rhythm, giving them time to get accustomed to the types of rhythms they will likely encounter in Joplin's music. Most of Joplin's piano works involve rhythms that divide no further than the sixteenth-note level. Joplin's music thus presents a great opportunity to discuss the limited number of possible ways to divide a quarter note. I suggest presenting students with something like Figure 7.10, which presents divisions of a quarter note up to the sixteenth-note level.

By presenting the information in this way first, students begin to conceive of each rhythmic cell as a unit – and of larger phrases as combinations of units, rather than a series of unrelated attacks. After spending some time on practice exercises in which students identify which rhythmic cell they hear for individual beats, instructors can string multiple beats together and have students figure out which cells are being combined. Next, instructors might consider adding ties across beats, helping students see that syncopations do not fundamentally change the possibilities. When using these rhythmic exercises, instructors can speak them on a neutral syllable, tap or clap them, or even play or sing them as a melody. In Figure 7.11, I present a rhythm that combines cells from Figure 7.10 along with a few ties across beats. In fact, this rhythm is from the D.1 section of Joplin's "Something Doing," presented in its original melodic form in Figure 7.12.

As an intermediate step toward getting comfortable with dictating syncopated rhythms, I suggest having the class tap along with the eighth-note pulse. Not only will this connect to the rhythm performance activities suggested previously (in which students perform both the syncopated melody and the accompanimental eighth notes), but it will also instill the importance of hearing the syncopated melody against the underlying metrical grid.

Dictation/Transcription

In this section, I present melodic and harmonic dictation exercises from Joplin works that are appropriate for students studying either diatonic or chromatic harmony. We will begin with melodic dictation. The excerpts in the chart in Table 7.1, which suggested melodies for singing, are also appropriate for melodic dictation. The A section of "Weeping Willow" (Figure 7.13) provides the opportunity to practice chromatic non-chord tones and an implied secondary dominant chord, as well as to encounter melodic parallelisms and repetitions.

I have also used Joplin's music (including the song "Please Say You Will") for take-home transcription projects, in which students can listen as many times as they want, sing the excerpt, and use a piano or other instrument as they work. All the dictation examples discussed here are suitable for transcription projects as well. These projects give students a chance to develop their ears and discover efficient transcription strategies without the limited hearings and silent conditions typical of in-class dictation tests and exercises.

For harmonic dictation, "boom-chick" ragtime accompaniments present both benefits and challenges. On one hand, having the bass note presented separately from the rest of the harmony (and often doubled at the octave) can help students – especially those struggling with bass lines – hear the foundational bass note more easily. On the other hand, the staggered bass note and chord could make it more difficult to discern chord qualities.

76 *Amy Fleming*

To alleviate these challenges, I recommend presenting excerpts in several different ways during the dictation process.

Consider Figure 7.14, the A.2 section of "The Strenuous Life." When using this excerpt for dictation, one could present it in several different ways: (1) just the rhythm of the melody, (2) the melody on its own, (3) the left hand on its own, (4) the entire excerpt as written, (5) the accompanimental harmonies blocked as chords rather than separated into the "boom-chick" ragtime accompaniment, and more. Which stage one chooses to utilize depends on the specific class goals. For example, I might devote part of a Tuesday class to dictating the melody alone; on Thursday, we could return to that melody and make predictions about the harmonies. Once we had spent some time discussing what harmonies the melody implies, we would listen again – this time with the full texture – and figure out the bass line and Roman numerals.

Beyond the example from "The Strenuous Life" (Figure 7.14), I recommend the Joplin excerpts in Table 7.2 for dictation and transcription activities. As in Table 7.1, the chart is organized by diatonic and chromatic excerpts.

Contextual Listening

One crucial step in the process of gaining fluency with the harmonic language of ragtime music is contextual listening. In this section, I will suggest several activities that help students learn to develop what Gary Karpinski calls Gestalt hearing (2000, 119). The goal is to learn to hear and recognize chords more holistically, rather than treating harmonic dictation as multiple melodic dictations that are then analyzed. In the following paragraphs, I will outline several suggestions of ways to use Joplin's music (and the ragtime style in general) to help students develop their Gestalt hearing skills – in other words, to focus on the big picture and understand what is happening in the music without having to notate it.

One contextual listening activity that the ragtime style can be used for is hearing harmonic function. An instructor can play a ragtime accompaniment (either from Joplin or another ragtime composer, newly composed, or improvised) and have students identify certain elements of the harmony. Early in the first semester of aural skills, the instructor might limit the chords to tonic and dominant harmonies. Figure 7.15 presents a brief example of one such exercise.[6] As the instructor plays the accompaniment, students identify whether each chord has tonic or dominant function.[7] Some instructors may also opt to have the class sing back the bass line on a neutral syllable or solfège to help students focus on the interaction between the harmonic progression and the bass line. As students gain fluency at discerning between tonic and dominant harmonies, the instructor might choose to ask for more specifics – for example, is each chord in root position or inversion? As the semester progresses, predominant harmonies could be added as well, as illustrated in Figure 7.16. By removing notation from the activity, students are freed to listen for the forest (i.e., the Gestalt of the chord), not just the trees (i.e., the individual notes of the chord).

In later semesters, students could do the same activity with more advanced harmonies, like second inversion chords, secondary dominants, mode mixture, and more. A course on chromatic harmony could begin with a simplified version of the activity, in which students simply identify whether each chord they hear in a progression (such as the one in Figure 7.17) is diatonic or chromatic. Students could also be asked to identify the harmonic function of each chord in Figure 7.17 – tonics, predominants, dominants, and secondary dominants. In that case, students face the added challenge of several chromatic chords. In particular, they must be careful to distinguish between the dominant-to-tonic sound of the secondary dominants (e.g., the V^6_5/V–V progression in measure 2) and the actual $V^{(7)}$–I progressions. In a unit introducing secondary functions, I recommend using this type of activity to help students learn to recognize when the dominant-to-tonic sound they are hearing is the V–I of the key and when it is a local, secondary V^7 (or vii^{o7})–I.

Once students acclimate to working with these acontextual, instructor-composed or instructor-improvised examples, I recommend returning to Joplin. Instructors could choose sections of Joplin works to listen to as a class and ask students the same questions – about harmonic function, diatonic vs. chromatic chords, and so on. Obviously, the addition of the melody complicates the activity, but by beginning with simple, acontextual examples and working up to Joplin's music, students will be prepared to face the challenge.

Beyond hearing harmonic function, ragtime music can also be used to help students practice hearing phrase-level forms and cadences. Figures 7.18–21 present four eight-measure excerpts – the first from Joplin's "Great Crush Collision," the last three with recomposed endings. Each begins with the same material, yet they all end with different cadence types. Instructors can play these phrases (or other recomposed ones) and ask students to identify which cadence types they hear. This activity could begin with basic questions, like whether the phrase ends with a closed or open cadence, then progress to identification of cadence types.

Once students gain fluency identifying cadence types, instructors can combine two or more phrases into periods, three-phrase periods, or double periods and ask students to identify both cadences and small-level forms. After practicing with recomposed phrases (Figures 7.18–21), instructors can move back to full sections of works by Joplin or other ragtime composers. When listening to entire formal sections, students should discern where cadences are, which cadence types they hear, whether melodic material returns, whether the excerpt modulates, and so on. Other activities could include listening for large-scale formal structures of entire Joplin compositions.

Improvisation

In the category of improvisation, inspiration can be taken from Joplin's ragtime style, and the typical ragtime accompaniment can be used as a framework within which to improvise melodies. It is crucial that these improvisation activities be scaffolded throughout the semester or curriculum so that students can build gradually from simple exercises to more complex ones. By providing clear guidelines for improvisational parameters and incrementally increasing the activity's complexity, those new to improvisation can acclimate gradually.

In the activities I suggest here, an accompaniment from a Joplin composition can be used as the improvisatory framework. Alternatively, Joplin's music can be the inspiration for a newly composed or improvised accompaniment at an appropriate level of difficulty. The instructor can play the accompaniment or make an audio file using music notation software. Students can improvise vocally or instrumentally, depending on the instructor's preferences and objectives.

To demonstrate the type of improvisation that could be performed using Joplin as inspiration, see the C.1 section of "A Breeze from Alabama," which is excerpted in Figure 7.22. This harmonic progression – a simple one by Joplin's standards – provides an ideal framework for improvisation and can be used across multiple semesters.[8] When using this activity in class, I would show students Figure 7.23. In an early semester, the improvisatory task could simply be to sing a single pitch belonging to each of the given harmonies (choosing from pitches on the figure's upper staff) along with the accompaniment. For example, a student might sing the melody in Figure 7.24 on solfège. By providing Figure 7.23, students can see all their options. Their improvisatory task is to choose a path through the chord tones. As students grow more comfortable with available harmonies, solfège, and improvisation, they might not need the written framework.

Guidelines in later iterations of the improvisation activity could include arpeggiating among different chord tones, with two pitches sung or played per harmony, as exemplified in Figure 7.25. As students learn about non-chord tones, the possibilities for improvisation expand – students can still think about finding a path among chord tones, but they can also plan that path with the possibility of passing tones, neighboring tones, and other non-chord tones in mind. At this point, the rhythm will also begin to increase in complexity. With the addition of non-chord tones, a student's improvisation could look like Figure 7.26. With practice, students may even choose to include some of the characteristic syncopations of Joplin's ragtime melodies.

As students learn chromatic solfège and harmonies, the guidelines for improvisation can be adjusted to include chromatic non-chord tones. Chromatic chords can also be included in the accompanimental framework. By starting early with simple path-choosing activities and gradually building as more advanced topics are introduced, students – even those who are new to improvisation – will have sufficient time and practice to acclimate. Using the ragtime accompaniment as a framework for improvisation, and scaffolding a series of improvisatory tasks of growing complexity around that framework, allows students to develop their own sense of creativity and freedom within the constraints of each new stage of the improvisatory exercise.

Error Detection

Mentioned by Karpinski as one of the most important skills for musicians to develop, error detection is unfortunately often an afterthought in aural skills curricula.[9] In this section, I will give a few suggestions for how to create error detection activities using Joplin's music.

Figure 7.27 shows the melody from the B.1 section of "The Easy Winners." When creating error detection exercises, I intentionally include errors of the types I notice students making in dictation and singing activities. As a result, students' focus is drawn toward new or challenging concepts, and students are given the opportunity to approach difficult topics from perspectives other than dictation or singing. Thus, in Figure 7.28, I have made several alterations to the original Joplin melody, including replacing a chromatic neighbor tone with a diatonic one, resizing several leaps, turning diatonic stepwise motion into chromatic, and changing the rhythm. When doing error detection activities like this in the classroom, I suggest giving students a printed version of the original, correct version of Joplin's melody (Figure 7.27) and directing students to study it, thinking about what they expect to hear. After a minute or two of study, the instructor plays the recomposed, error-filled version of the melody (Figure 7.28) and asks students both where the errors occurred and what they were.

Error-filled versions of other Joplin melodies could easily be created by making strategic choices about pitch and rhythmic changes. Error detection activities, however, do not need to be limited to purely melodic examples. Figure 7.29 presents the C.1 section of Joplin's "A Breeze from Alabama" in its original form. Figure 7.30 shows a version of the same section with five key differences: (1) the dominant-to-tonic progression (mm. 5–6) has been replaced by a deceptive resolution; (2) the tonic chord beginning in measure 2 is in inversion instead of root position, changing the bass contour; (3) the diatonic ii chord (measure 7) has been replaced by a chromatic V^7/V chord; (4) the rhythm of the melody (mm. 4–5) has been altered; and (5) the melody in the first two notes of measure 7 does not leap high enough.

In this example, the changes are clearly more complex and varied than in Figure 7.28, due to the full piano texture and the variety of error types. Yet the same sort of approach can be used when presenting this excerpt for error detection – students are given time to think about (or even sing through) what the example should sound like, then they listen to and identify both where and what the errors are. An alternate way to approach the exercise would be to have students prepare the excerpt ahead of class by listening to it, playing it at the keyboard or other instrument, singing through different lines, and so on – whatever they think will help prepare them to know how it is supposed to sound, then come to class and hear the error-filled version of it and compare it to the original, correct version they prepared. Approaching the activity in this way has the added benefit of reflecting how students might need to detect errors as future educators, conductors, performers, and composers, since advance preparation helps them know what the excerpt should sound like ahead of time. Following that preparation, when they hear errors (as they might in a future rehearsal), they can detect them based on their familiarity with how the piece should sound. Presenting error detection in this way gives students the opportunity to learn how to effectively and efficiently prepare scores in ways that will help them in their future music careers.

Conclusion

The examples presented here represent only a small portion of Joplin's output, but my hope is that they demonstrate the types of activities that Joplin's works – especially his ragtime piano works – could be useful for in the undergraduate aural skills curriculum. Beyond Joplin's music, compositions by other ragtime composers like Eubie Blake, James Scott, and Louis Chauvin could be incorporated. The ragtime style offers many benefits and challenges for undergraduate students. Joplin's music in particular works well throughout the diatonic and chromatic aural skills sequence, and (as this chapter has illustrated) can be presented in numerous contexts and through a wide variety of activities that give students the opportunity to practice with typical undergraduate theory topics while also learning about the ragtime genre. Intentionally incorporating Joplin's music in the aural skills curriculum centers both a style and a composer who were crucial in the development of American music in the early twentieth century.

Notes

1. All figures and tables referenced in this chapter, as well as supplemental materials, can be found on the Supplemental Materials website.
2. One such effort is the Composers of Color Resource Project (https://composersofcolor.hcommons.org). A similar effort that seeks to increase representation of female composers is Music Theory Examples by Women (https://musictheoryexamplesbywomen.com).
3. For Joplin's piano works, I will use letters to label sections (e.g., A, B, C). When I refer to subsections, I will use 1 to refer to the first half of a section and 2 to refer to the second half (e.g., C.1 indicates the first half of section C).
4. Instructors and students may choose to adapt some of Joplin's melodies to fit their range by adjusting them up or down octaves as necessary.
5. The topic of ragtime basses being ideal for early aural development will be revisited in the later section on dictation.
6. Even if students are not yet working with all inversions or chordal sevenths, they can still be used in this activity at the instructor's discretion, since the goal is to hear the big picture of the chord, *not* identify it more specifically.
7. There are numerous ways students could identify the harmony as tonic or dominant, including calling out their response, holding up differently colored cards for tonic and dominant, or performing an action or hand sign for each harmonic function (e.g., raise your hand when you hear dominants, lower it when you hear tonics, or hold up your pointer finger for tonic and all five fingers for dominant).

8. While I have intentionally chosen an excerpt with simple harmonies to demonstrate this activity's relevance across several semesters, instructors could easily use more complex Joplin accompaniments or compose their own.
9. Karpinski (2000). For more on the importance of error detection in the aural skills curriculum, see Fleming and Taylor (2019).

Bibliography

Berlin, Edward A. 2016. *King of Ragtime: Scott Joplin and His Era*, 2nd edition. Oxford University Press.

"Composers of Color Resource Project." Accessed December 10, 2020. https://composersofcolor.hcommons.org

Curtis, Susan. 1994. *Dancing to a Black Man's Tune: A Life of Scott Joplin*. University of Missouri Press.

"Engaged Music Theory." Accessed December 10, 2020. https://engagedmusictheory.com

Ewell, Philip A. 2019. "Music Theory's White Racial Frame." Paper presented at the Annual Meeting of the Society for Music Theory, Columbus, OH.

———. 2020. "Music Theory and the White Racial Frame." *Music Theory Online* 26/2. https://doi.org/10.30535/mto.26.2.4

Fleming, Amy, and Edward Taylor. 2019. "Correcting the Error of Our Ways: Rethinking Error Detection in the Aural Skills Curriculum." Presentation at Pedagogy into Practice, Santa Barbara, CA.

Gammond, Peter. 1975. *Scott Joplin and the Ragtime Era*. St. Martin's Press.

Karpinski, Gary S. 2000. *Aural Skills Acquisition*. Oxford University Press.

"Music Theory Examples by Women." Accessed December 10, 2020. https://musictheoryexamplesbywomen.com

Reed, Addison Walker. 1973. "The Life and Works of Scott Joplin." Ph.D. diss., University of North Carolina at Chapel Hill.

Sayrs, Elizabeth. 2019. "The Case for More Bass in the Aural Skills Curriculum." Presentation at Pedagogy into Practice, Santa Barbara, CA.

Schafter, William J., and Johannes Riedel. 1977. *The Art of Ragtime: For and Meaning of an Original Black American Art*. Louisiana State University Press, 1973. Reprint, Da Capo Press.

8 Modulation

Alan Reese

In order to address American music theory's historical exclusion of Black composers, pedagogues have sought to diversify the music theory classroom and thus challenge what Philip Ewell (2020), borrowing a term from Joe Feagin (2013), calls the field's "White racial frame" [1.3]. A natural response is to simply swap in analytical examples by Black composers. While authors have shown the limitations of this approach,[1] such substitutions remain a positive first step, especially for those instructors who are not in a position to fundamentally revamp their curricula. And yet even exchanging examples can prove challenging to implement, as instructors too often lack the time and resources to find appropriate excerpts written by Black composers. As a result, they depend on textbooks and anthologies dominated by White men. These material limitations, irrespective of a teacher's ideological commitments, preserve music theory's White frame.

As a step toward addressing this problem, the following chapter demonstrates how instructors can use the common-practice music of Black composers to teach diatonic and chromatic modulatory techniques. After a short introductory section outlining the scope of the chapter and relevant terminology, Part 1 focuses on modulation to closely related keys, with excerpts featuring diatonic pivot chords, sequential techniques, and phrase modulation. Part 2 examines a variety of chromatic modulatory techniques, including chromatic pivot chords, enharmonic reinterpretation, and common-tone modulation. In both of these sections, I offer analytical vignettes theory instructors can use for lectures or in-class analytical activities, with sample homework assignments and aural skills exercises available on the Supplemental Materials website. Part 3 provides an analysis of Samuel Coleridge-Taylor's (1875–1912) "Tears" from his *Southern Love Songs* (op. 12) that shows how both the key scheme and diverse modulatory techniques express the text and foreshadow the song's tragic turn. Finally, the Supplemental Materials website contains all supplemental figures along with an appendix listing roughly 250 examples by Black composers featuring the modulatory techniques described in this chapter. Examples are organized by modulation type and technique, and additional details, such as key areas and (if appropriate) an excerpt's pivot chord, are provided. This catalog of examples, nearly all of which are found on IMSLP, will prove helpful to the teacher in need of a pedagogically appropriate (and easily accessible) example and will hopefully be a model for future anthological lists devoted to other theoretical concepts.

Preliminaries: Scope and Terminology

My corpus is limited to common-practice compositions, although "common practice" is construed broadly to include the turn-of-the-twentieth-century popular songs of Will Marion Cook (1869–1944) and J. Rosamond Johnson (1873–1954), the piano rags of Scott Joplin (1868–1917), and the spiritual arrangements of Harry Burleigh (1866–1945).

DOI: 10.4324/9781003204053-11

82   *Alan Reese*

While more recent popular music may demonstrate diatonic and chromatic modulatory methods equally well – not to mention introducing new modulatory norms[2] – I restricted my attention to classical repertoire for two reasons. First, "western" art music, for better or worse, remains dominant in collegiate music programs, and not all teachers are in a position to substantially alter this state of affairs.[3] As such, having easy access to Black classical music is crucial to diversifying the curriculum. Second, while European American classical music is predominantly White (and male), I wish to demonstrate that Black classical music not only exists but is also plentiful and more accessible than ever.

While most textbooks present modulation in a similar order – modulations to closely related keys first, with discussions of chromatic techniques and remote keys interspersed throughout later chapters – there are some terminological disagreements.[4] For example, authors frequently use different terms to describe the same technique, or the same term but with a different definition.[5] As such, I will clarify the following terms:

- *Diatonic pivot chord*: a harmony that is diatonic in both keys. In minor keys, the pivot chord may use notes from either the natural minor or melodic minor scale.[6]
- *Chromatic pivot chord*: a harmony that is chromatic (e.g., mixture, Neapolitan, or applied) in one or both keys but is not enharmonically reinterpreted.
- *Enharmonic pivot chord*: a harmony (usually a dominant seventh, augmented sixth, or diminished seventh chord) with at least one enharmonically reinterpreted chord member.
- *Direct modulation*: a modulation with no pivot chord or emphasized common tone between keys.
- *Phrase modulation*: a direct modulation occurring between phrases.
- *Sequential modulation*: a modulation executed through a diatonic or chromatic sequence. Usually contains at least one plausible pivot chord.
- *Linear modulation*: a modulation executed through parsimonious, nonfunctional voice leading, such as through a passing augmented triad or chromatic wedge progression.[7]

Part 1: Modulating to Closely Related Keys

In Parts 1 and 2, I present and discuss annotated excerpts demonstrating the relevant modulatory techniques. These analytical vignettes may be used to introduce concepts during a lecture or to reinforce them as part of homework or in-class activities. Additional analytical, ear-training, and singing exercises are found on the Supplemental Materials website.

To introduce major-mode modulations to the dominant, Figure 8.1 presents two sentential phrases from Joseph Bologne's (Chevalier de Saint-George, 1745–99) String Quartet op. 1, no. 1, II. The pivot-chord modulation in measure 43 of the first phrase, vi⁶→ii⁶, is clear and convincing for several reasons. First, the pivot chord precedes the following key's new accidental, F♯, as well as its dominant harmony. Second, the pivot chord is a predominant in the new key. Third, vi⁶ chords are somewhat unusual in the classical style, and thus, its presence further destabilizes C major. The second phrase retains F♯, as well as the opening tonic-dominant alternation (now reversed in order), and confirms G major with a predominant–dominant–tonic progression and perfect authentic cadence (PAC).

Figure 8.2a examines the opening sentential antecedent of the fourth movement of Nathaniel Dett's (1882–1943) piano suite, *In the Bottoms*. The excerpt not only begins in the same C major key as the Bologne passage but also uses the same pivot chord, vi⁶. Dett, however, reinterprets the A minor triad as iv⁶ in the mediant key of E minor, launching a two-measure dominant drive to a PAC. Although the modulation is rather swift, it is strengthened by both a cadential six-four and the new key's raised fourth scale degree (A♯) – two elements students can incorporate in their own composed modulations.[8] The

Modulation 83

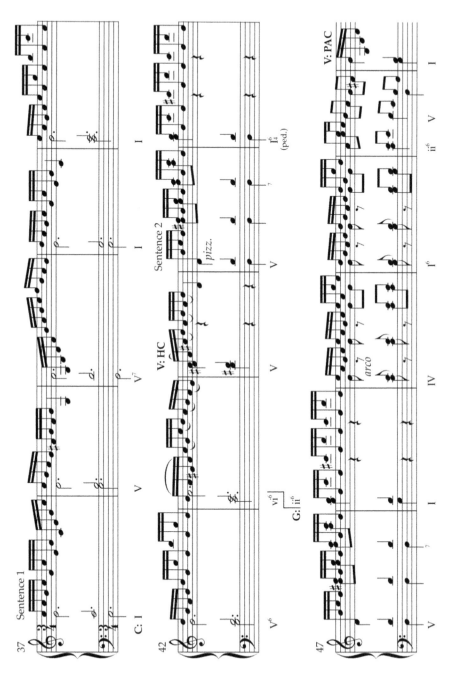

Figure 8.1 Joseph Bologne, String Quartet, op. 1, no. 1, II, mm. 37–52.

Figure 8.2 (a) Nathaniel Dett, *In the Bottoms*, no. 4, "Barcarolle," mm. 5–12; (b) Clarence Cameron White, *Bandanna Sketches* for violin and piano, op. 12, no. 2, "Lament (I'm Troubled in Mind)," mm. 17–25.

passage also features a tonicization of ii through both an applied dominant (V⁶/ii) and the fleeting, decorative E° triad in measure 6. This brief tonicization of D minor, brought to a swift end by the subsequent C major scale and G⁷ in measures 6–7, can be contrasted with the longer and cadentially reinforced modulation to E minor.

Supplemental Figure 8.1, from Coleridge-Taylor's piano setting of the spiritual "Wade in the Water," presents a more chromatically complex pivot-chord modulation from E minor to its relative major. By tonicizing VI and iv within the opening descending-third bass line, Coleridge-Taylor destabilizes the original key – a common tactic when modulating. This is especially true in measures 19–22: A minor alternates with its own dominant above a bass pedal, suggesting a potential modulation to iv. However, at the last moment, the passage swerves to G major, reinterpreting iv as ii and executing not one but *two* cadential confirmations. The mixture harmony after the pivot, marked by an asterisk, will probably be unfamiliar to students just learning diatonic modulation, so I recommend a re-harmonization after playing the original, replacing ii°⁴₃ with V⁴₃/V. This demonstrates how chromatic predominants in the new key strengthen modulations.

Like tonicization, sequences can also destabilize our sense of key, paving the way for a convincing modulation. Figure 8.2b analyzes a transitional passage from Clarence Cameron White's (1880–1960) *Bandanna Sketches*, op. 12, no. 2. The excerpt begins just after a C minor PAC and launches a descending-fifth sequence tonicizing both v – note the enharmonic renotation of F♯ as G♭ – and iv, each through their own vii°⁷ chords.[9] Such a progression suggests multiple potential paths: Do we stay on the C minor highway or, after tonicizing another triad, take the exit for a new key? White chooses the latter, remaining in F minor and setting up the new theme beginning in measure 25. The progression features two additional challenges for the student. First, the syncopated melodic bass line makes determining the "main" bass note for each harmony unclear; Figure 8.2b offers only one plausible interpretation. Second, measure 24's V⁴₂ can generate discussion on its cadential potential: do rhetorical cues – decreased rhythmic activity, the end of an eight-measure unit – outweigh the unusual inversion? Could there be an implied C in the bass, or is B♭ the *true* bass note?

Supplemental Figure 8.2 presents one final modulation to a closely related key. In the sonata-form first movement of his fourth quartet, Bologne concludes the transition section with a C minor half cadence, complete with the requisite triple hammer blows in measure 20. After the quarter-rest medial caesura, the second theme begins immediately in E♭ major; there is no pivot chord. Such phrase modulations to the relative major are common in Bologne's output: as shown in the appendix, he uses the technique in all three of his minor-mode string quartets (nos. 3, 4, and 5).

Additional Activities on the Supplemental Materials Website

- **Analysis:** Analyze three modulating excerpts by Joseph Bologne, Samuel Coleridge-Taylor, and Nathaniel Dett. Students will provide both score annotations and written responses.
- **Singing:** Sing two unaccompanied modulating melodies by Samuel Coleridge-Taylor.
- **Ear Training:**
  - **Identifying Modulations:** Aurally analyze the modulations in four excerpts by Samuel Coleridge-Taylor, Nathaniel Dett, and Joseph Bologne.
  - **Transcription:** Transcribe the bass and melody lines and provide a Roman numeral and cadential analysis of the opening of "The Big Red Shawl" by J. Rosamond Johnson, with lyrics by Bob Cole.

Part 2: Chromatic Techniques and Remote Keys

While harmony textbooks tend to present the preceding modulatory techniques within a single chapter, chromatic modulation receives a more varied treatment: such procedures may be consolidated within a single end-of-the-book chapter or scattered throughout the textbook's second half.[10] In this section, I first present examples of chromatic and enharmonic pivot chords before moving on to common-tone modulation and various linear techniques.

Modal or simple mixture allows for smooth modulations to remote keys: shifting to the parallel mode opens up a new neighborhood of closely related keys. To introduce this technique, Figure 8.3 analyzes the opening of the middle section of Samuel Coleridge-Taylor's final *Fairy Ballad*, "Fairy Roses." After a four-measure piano outro in C major, a sudden shift to C minor, along with an abrupt halt in accompanimental motion, disturbs the preceding lullaby. Fortunately, the singer quickly calms the eponymous flowers – "Fairy Roses, don't be frighten'd" – with a move to E♭ major: Fm^7, borrowed from C minor, functions as ii^7 within the new key. In measures 53–60, a melodic variant of measures 45–52, the flowers' fears return with a predominant-to-dominant motion in G minor mirroring measures 48–50. However, V^7/iii resolves deceptively to V^7 and concludes with another reassuring imperfect authentic cadence in E♭ major.[11]

Supplemental Figure 8.3 analyzes a passage from "A New Hidin'-Place," the finale of Harry Burleigh's *From the Southland*. In the excerpt, only a single mixture harmony initiates the modulation, here from VI (B major) back to I (D major). Burleigh precedes the climactic PAC in measure 36 with a typically romantic ii^{ø7} borrowed from B minor. In measure 37, this same harmony, now in third inversion, returns as a pivot chord (ii$^{ø4}_{2}$→vii$^{ø4}_{2}$) during an energy-gaining post-cadential drive back to the opening tonic key. The triumphant cadential six-four that follows is extended and elaborated, ultimately leading to the return of an earlier theme from measure 15. In addition to chromatic modulation, this except also features tonicization, common-tone chords, added ninths, and pedal point.

Enharmonic reinterpretation, particularly of dominant seventh chords as augmented sixths (and vice versa), is another strategy commonly used to visit remote (or even closely related) keys. Figures 8.4a and b both feature advanced uses of the technique; they are more suitable for reinforcing rather than introducing the concept of enharmonic pivots.[12] Figure 8.4a reduces the transition to and opening of the lyrical central theme from Florence Price's Symphony no. 3 in C minor, second movement. The returning A♭ major theme sets up a potential authentic cadence in measure 60, but E♭^{9} instead resolves to D^7 with a raised fifth (A♯, notated as B♭). Thus, E♭^{9} functions as a German augmented sixth in the new key of G major: the E♭–D♭ minor seventh is reinterpreted, though not explicitly respelled, as E♭–C♯. Moreover, this German sixth has an added ninth, hence the rather-foreboding figured bass in my analysis.

Figure 8.4b examines the opening of the tonally roving transition section from Coleridge-Taylor's sonata-form Ballade in D minor, op. 4. Using the primary theme's principal motive, the excerpt modulates from D minor to B major, with brief detours through F and B♭ major. D minor is established through both plagal motion – the opening i–VI^6–i progression – and a quick suggestion of a vii$^{o4}_{2}$ (C♯^{o7}) in measure 56 during a swift scalar run up an octave. That same C♯^{o7} returns more overtly in measure 57 but resolves to an F major triad, revealing C♯ as D♭ and, thus, C♯^{o7} as E^{o7}. However, F major quickly gives way to B♭ major once A^{o7} sounds in measure 58. B♭ major seemingly has more staying power, as the alternation with its own subdominant-functioned ♭VI recalls the tonal stability of measure 55. And yet when that same G♭ major triad returns in measure 60, now respelled as F♯ major and affixed with an E♮, it resolves not as a German augmented sixth chord but as a dominant

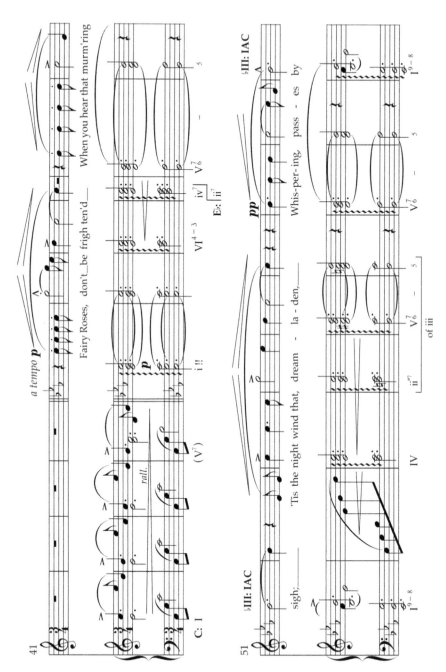

Figure 8.3 Samuel Coleridge-Taylor, *Five Fairy Ballads*, no. 5, "Fairy Roses," mm. 41–59. Words by Kathleen Easmon.

88 Alan Reese

Figure 8.4 (a) Florence Price, Symphony no. 3 in C minor, II, mm. 57–62, reduction; (b) Samuel Coleridge-Taylor, Ballade in D minor for violin and piano, op. 4, mm. 55–64.

seventh within B major. With a new key secured, the violin returns with a scalar ascent. In sum, Coleridge-Taylor uses two enharmonic pivot chords in combination with intermediate keys to move from D minor to the remote key of B major.[13]

Moving away from pivot chords, Supplemental Figure 8.4 looks at the common-tone modulation in the verse of Robert Allen "Bob" Cole's (1868–1911) song "Everybody Wants to See the Baby." After a restated tonicized half cadence, Cole repeats D in both the piano and vocal parts, transforming it from $\hat{5}$ in G major to $\hat{3}$ in the chromatic mediant key of B♭ major. The common-tone connection is accompanied by a stepwise descent in the bass, smoothing out the remote modulation. The reduction in Figure 8.5, taken from the second movement of William L. Dawson's (1899–1990) *Negro Folk Symphony*, combines common-tone modulation with linear techniques. Upon achieving a PAC in B minor, the passage begins a short post-cadential phrase modulating to the relative major. The intervening B♭ augmented triad in measure 40 serves as a voice leading connector between the B minor and D major triads: D and F♯ are held as common tones, while B passes to A through B♭ (this is particularly clear in the string arpeggiations).[14]

Figure 8.6a offers one more chromatic modulation, here from the transition to the C section of Scott Joplin's ragtime waltz "Bethena." In the passage, Joplin uses linear techniques, in particular the chromatic wedge progression known as the "omnibus," to modulate from G major to F major through several short-lived intermediate keys.[15] To clarify the passage, Figure 8.6b derives Joplin's transition from four five-chord omnibus progressions, each of which is framed by a single dominant seventh chord. Two voices move in chromatic contrary motion, while the other two, related to one another by minor third (or major sixth), are sustained throughout. As a result, each harmony, labeled by its position within the progression, is either a major-minor seventh chord (functioning as a dominant seventh or augmented sixth) or a second-inversion minor triad. As shown on the second line of Figure 8.6b, the "Bethena" transition is derived by recontextualizing chord 5 in one omnibus as chord 2 in another; the concluding dominant seventh chord is therefore reinterpreted as an augmented sixth in order to launch the next omnibus. Moreover, this recontextualization creates an uninterrupted chromatic descent in the bass.

The voice leading logic that governs the transition in Figure 8.6a is straightforward – hold two notes, move the other pair in contrary motion – but the result is a highly ambiguous tonal and harmonic-functional environment. That said, fleeting tonicizations emerge in the passage, particularly through the three Ger$^6_5$–i$^6_4$ motions, suggesting three minor-third-related keys: G♯, F, and D minor. Once the transition reaches D minor, it exits the chromatic carousel through circle-of-fifths motion and diatonic pivot chords: i–iv^7 in D minor becomes vi–ii^7 in F major. In sum, Joplin's modulation combines several of the techniques discussed previously: diatonic pivots, enharmonic reinterpretation, and nonfunctional (or semifunctional) linear logic.

Additional Activities on the Supplemental Materials Website

- **Analysis:** Analyze four modulating excerpts by Joseph Bologne, Samuel Coleridge-Taylor, and Scott Joplin. Students will provide both score annotations and written responses.
- **Singing:** Sing two complete songs, accompanied or unaccompanied, by J. Rosamond Johnson, with lyrics by Bob Cole and J. W. Johnson.
- **Ear Training:**
  - **Identifying Modulations:** Aurally analyze the modulations in five excerpts by Samuel Coleridge-Taylor.
  - **Transcription:** Transcribe the bass and melody lines and provide a Roman numeral and formal analysis of an excerpt from Samuel Coleridge-Taylor's *Four Characteristic Waltzes*, op. 22, no. 3, "Valse de la Reine."

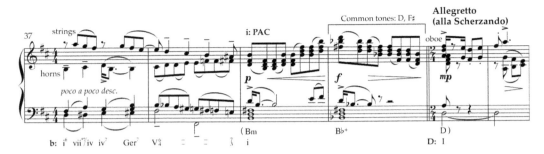

Figure 8.5 William Dawson, Negro Folk Symphony, II, "Hope in the Night," mm. 37–42, reduction.

Figure 8.6 (a) Scott Joplin, "Bethena, a Concert Waltz," mm. 66–77; (b) Four omnibus progressions and their role in Scott Joplin's "Bethena," mm. 68–74.

Part 3: Modulation and Futility in Samuel Coleridge-Taylor's "Tears"

This section examines the modulatory maneuvers in Coleridge-Taylor's "Tears: A Lament," the second of his *Southern Love Songs* (op. 12), and how the resultant key scheme supports the text – in other words, how modulation is used expressively. While teachers may present my analysis in a lecture-like format in class, there is also a sample analytical assignment on the Supplemental Materials website.

Supplemental Figure 8.5 presents an annotated score of "Tears." The text is an English translation of "Ich habe, bevor der Morgen" by Adelbert von Chamisso:

> In tremor, ere the morning
> With Orient light is grey,
> I tarried at the window,
> And look'd for coming day.
>
> Full in the glow of noontide
> I shed a bitter tear
> And to my fond heart whisper'd,
> "My Love will soon be here."
>
> The night, the night is o'er me,
> Whose gleams I shun in dread,
> The day has now departed,
> My dream of joy is fled![16]

In the poem, the narrator awaits the return of their beloved, with each stanza marking the passing of time – waiting anxiously in the morning, searching for hope at noon, and falling into despair at night. These emotional states are reinforced by imagery in the text. A gloomy, hazy dawn suggests uncertainty, while "the glow of noontide" correlates with the narrator's short-lived, somewhat-performative optimism. The poem's tripartite structure is carried into the song: each of its three vocal phrases, labeled A–B–A' on the annotated score, corresponds with the stanzas.

The key scheme is crucial to interpreting "Tears." The song's A and A' sections begin in D♭ major yet conclude in B♭ minor, meaning "Tears" seemingly begins and ends in different keys. The B section, meanwhile, begins in B♭ minor but concludes in a distant, ecstatic F major. Thus, the apparent global tonic of D♭ major, representing an uncertain present, is flanked by two mediants, one chromatic and major (F), the other diatonic and minor (B♭). Within the narrative, far-off F major seeks refuge in fantasy ("my beloved might return!"), while nearby B♭ minor is firmly grounded in reality ("ah, never mind . . .").

The A section (mm. 1–10) is harmonically stagnant. The opening D♭ major triad controls most of the phrase, while scales and arpeggios meander in the right hand, reflecting the anxious thoughts and literal pacing of the narrator. No dominant appears to add a sense of movement; the only tonic interruption is a plagally functioned submediant triad in measures 5–6, adding to the phrase's lack of direction. This B♭ minor triad returns four measures later as a new tonic to close the phrase, eliding with the start of the B section. The modulation is smooth but swift – the G♭ major pivot chord transforms from IV into VI – and the post-cadential music confirms the tonic with additional plagal motion. There's a sense at measure 10 that the opening phrase functions as an *introduction* to the B material – that the song truly starts once B♭ minor arrives. I will return to this idea at the end of my analysis.

Having reached a minor key, the narrator lays bare their emotional state ("I shed a bitter tear") and sings a melody based on the A section's – note the D♭–B♭–A♮–B♭ in measures

9–10 and 12, as well as the general rise to a quarter-note F_5 in measures 3–4 and 13–14. In measure 16, the narrator turns to another character, their heart, setting up a duality, and perhaps a disagreement, between mind and body, or reason and emotion. With a seemingly diatonic pivot (i⁶→iv⁶) and modulation-reinforcing German augmented sixth in measure 17, Coleridge-Taylor sets up a modulation to the closely related and similarly dour key of F minor. As the narrator reassures their heart – "My Love will soon be here" – a less-than-subtle cadential six-four in F major creates a modulation more remote than expected.

A few factors, however, undermine the narrator's asserted optimism. First, the piano and vocal parts create a metrical clash: while the voice maintains a triple meter, the pianist projects a duple meter, particularly in the left hand. Second, harmony and melody are likewise misaligned at the cadence, with tonic resolution occurring in the piano on the second beat of measure 19 (with a short plagal extension afterwards), while the voice concludes on the downbeat of measure 20.[17] As a result, while many surface elements suggest hope – the major-mode surprise, the extended phrase length, and the striking cadential six-four – the metrical and cadential misalignment indicates that the narrator may just be trying to convince their heart of something their mind knows to be untrue. Finally, the remote modulation is short-lived: after some post-cadential noodling based on measures 1–2, the piece is swiftly yanked back into the five-flat world through a common-tone F in the right hand. F major's optimism, sincere or otherwise, quickly dissipates.

The A' section retreads much of the opening, with only a few small rhythmic and melodic changes in the first several measures. The parallel musical setting reflects textual relationships between the first and third stanzas, such as "morning" vs. "night," "Orient light" vs. "gleams," or "in tremor" vs. "in dread." Moreover, as stated earlier, A' concludes in B♭ minor, maintaining the tragic tonal trajectory from before. However, there are several important alterations at the cadence. First, the G♭ major triad of measure 9 is transformed into a major-minor seventh in measure 31, changing its function from a diatonic pivot (IV⁷→VI) into an enharmonic pivot (IV♭⁷→Ger⁶₃), strengthening the modulation to B♭ minor. Although one could read the preceding D♭ major triad as the pivot chord, as indicated in Supplemental Figure 8.5, I argue that while IV♭⁷ is uncommon in late romantic music (though not without precedent),[18] the parallels between measures 9 and 31 create the expectation that the returning G♭ harmony, despite the added E♮, will serve once again as a pivot chord. In addition to the harmonic change, the phrase is extended by one measure, paralleling the extension at the end of the B section. However, *unlike* the end of B, there is no accompanying cadential or metrical misalignment. Heart and mind are now unified; the "dream of joy" expressed at the end of the second stanza "has fled."

The previous analysis emphasizes the expressive role of the modulatory maneuvers and key scheme in "Tears" and specifically tracks the song's moves from the principal tonic key, an uncertain D♭ major, toward two potential futures: an optimistic F major *chromatic* mediant vs. a pessimistic B♭ minor *diatonic* submediant. The song's conclusion in B♭ minor confirms the poem's tragic direction. Figure 8.7a graphically summarizes this tonal narrative; measure numbers indicate where modulations take place. Figure 8.7b, meanwhile, proposes an alternative: What if B♭ minor was the global tonic all along? As shown in the graphic, D♭ major and F major are subsumed into B♭ minor as III and V, respectively – as mere projections of a large-scale B♭ minor triad. Despite D♭ major launching the A sections, its tonal primacy is weakened not only by the B♭ minor ending but also by the lack of both cadential confirmation and its very own dominant. In other words, D♭ major is only asserted and sustained by repetition and plagal motion. B♭ minor, on the other hand, is confirmed by two PACs, and the song's only other cadence is in B♭ minor's dominant key (albeit recast unexpectedly in the major mode). Thus, within this framework, D♭ major is no key at all but simply part of a large-scale III–VI–V⁷–i progression in B♭ minor.[19]

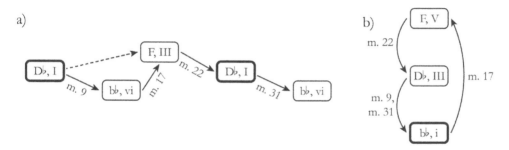

Figure 8.7 (a) D♭ major trajectory in Samuel Coleridge-Taylor's "Tears"; (b) B♭ minor trajectory in Samuel Coleridge-Taylor's "Tears."

Such a monotonal interpretation pays narrative dividends. While the D♭ major reading ends tragically, it initially offers two plausible outcomes, including one where the beloved returns. But if B♭ minor was the tonic all along, there never was any possibility of reunion: D♭ major is just as illusory a key as F major. This sense of hopelessness, of a future already written, is found in the text. As mentioned previously, the narrator's reassuring whisper to their heart, coming on the heels of a "bitter tear," seems forced and insincere – a soothing lie intended to prolong an optimism they know to be delusional. Moreover, the routine presented in the poem – tarry in the morning, cry at noon, lose hope at night – suggests that this is not the first day following such a schedule (and likely won't be the last). The narrator is simply going through the motions; Figure 8.7b's looping design captures this circularity. With all that said, I still see value in both the D♭ major hearing (an off-tonic *ending*) and the B♭ minor hearing (an off-tonic *beginning*): the former is a likely perspective on a first hearing of the song or read-through of the poem (when hope is alive), while listeners can pursue the latter interpretation on subsequent hearings (when hope is dead). Such a multidimensional approach to the song's tonal organization reinforces the notion that theory and analysis, despite their potential to clarify, can also *complicate* our understanding, making the listening and analytical processes more dynamic and personal.

Conclusion

With the aforementioned analytical vignettes, as well as the appendix and additional activities on the Supplemental Materials website, I have demonstrated how modulation can be introduced and reinforced using primarily (or only!) common-practice music by Black composers. Moreover, I hope to have shown not only that there is a significant number of pedagogically appropriate pieces and excerpts to choose from but also that there is a variety of Black composers available to us, something that can prevent potential tokenism in the classroom. While I agree with Ewell and others that substituting in non-White composers is insufficient in the quest for an antiracist music theory pedagogy, it remains a necessary step, and I believe this chapter has made that step easier to take for ideologically inclined but materially burdened instructors.[20]

Notes

1. Ewell, for example, writes that such an approach "actually reinforces our [W]hite frame" (2020, [3.4]).
2. For example, on "expressive modulation," see Doll (2011). On the "pump-up modulation," see Ricci (2017).

3. For instance, the mission of the Cleveland Institute of Music, where I teach, is "to empower the world's most talented classical music students to fulfill their dreams and potential" (Cleveland Institute of Music, n.d.).
4. For this chapter, I consulted five popular textbooks: Burstein and Straus (2020), Clendinning and Marvin (2021), Kostka et al. (2018), Laitz (2016), and Roig-Francolí (2020).
5. For an example of the former, a sudden modulation with no common chord or tone is described as "direct" (Clendinning and Marvin 2021, 484), "abrupt" (Burstein and Straus 2020, 306), and/or "unprepared" (Laitz 2016, 537). For an example of the latter, a "chromatic pivot chord" may be defined as a mixture chord in the original key becoming a diatonic chord in the new key (Laitz 2016, 532) or, more broadly, as any pivot chord that is not diatonic in one or both keys (Roig-Francolí 2020, 599). As Yosef Goldenberg (2018) notes, even the notion of "diatonic modulation" has distinct definitions that often (but not always) overlap: (1) a modulation to a closely related key, and (2) a diatonic pivot-chord modulation. An explicit distinction between these two meanings is "missing from all major harmony textbooks" (37–38).
6. I borrow this liberal definition of "diatonic" from Burstein and Straus (2020, 255). Clendinning and Marvin (2021) restrict pivot chords to the natural and harmonic minor scales (474), while most other authors draw pivot chords only from the natural minor scale. In addition, Laitz (2016) disallows six-four chords (470), while Roig-Francolí (2020) seems to omit VII and v as possibilities (481).
7. "Linear modulation" is my own term. Some textbook authors account for similar techniques: Laitz (2016) references using "semitonal voice-leading" to visit remote keys (667–70), while Clendinning and Marvin (2021) discuss modulation through "chromatic inflection" (610–11). Unfortunately, such modulatory techniques remain under-theorized.
8. The German augmented sixth chord (Ger$^6_5$) marked by the asterisk, often alternatively labeled as Ger^{+6} or Gr^{+6}, is likely to be an unfamiliar chord to students first learning diatonic modulation, so I recommend adding in alternative harmonizations, e.g., replacing Ger$^6_5$ with vii^{o7}/V or V^7/V.
9. I interpret the applied vii^{o7} chords as substitutions for V^7 chords, allowing for the descending-fifth reading.
10. Burstein and Straus (2020), for example, place all chromatic techniques within the final chapter on chromatic harmony (300–09). Laitz (2016), on the other hand, generally pairs a new modulatory technique with the introduction of the relevant harmony or harmonies, e.g., Neapolitan pivots in the Neapolitan chapter and enharmonically reinterpreted augmented sixth chords in the augmented sixth chapter (562–66, 583–87).
11. This deceptive motion works particularly well because a G minor triad, the desired resolution of the preceding D^7, is contained within B♭^{7} as an unstable upper structure, to use jazz parlance.
12. For introducing enharmonically reinterpreted augmented sixths or dominant sevenths, see Coleridge-Taylor's *African Suite*, op. 35, no. 4, mm. 31–41; *Four Characteristic Waltzes*, op. 22, no. 3, mm. 93–128; and/or *Twenty-Four Negro Melodies*, op. 59, no. 20, mm. 28–34. For introducing enharmonically reinterpreted diminished seventh chords, see Coleridge-Taylor's *Three-Fours*, op. 71, no. 6, mm. 127–47.
13. In the previous analysis, I am taking Coleridge-Taylor's notation at face value. However, one could also read the B major notation as an enharmonic respelling, one done for purely visual convenience, of the *true* key of C♭ major (♭♭VII!). In other words, the Ger$^6_5$ in m. 60, G♭–B♭–D♭–E, is not enharmonically reinterpreted as F♯–A♯–C♯–E but as G♭–B♭–D♭–F♭. This makes sense, given that we just heard a G♭ major triad in m. 59 and are unlikely to hear it as F♯ major in m. 60. All that said, I see little pedagogical downside here with assuming B major as the "true" key, as enharmonic reinterpretation is still at work.
14. I omitted a Roman numeral label for the augmented triad so as to emphasize its voice leading function, but one could analyze it as a dominant-functioned III$^6_4$ (D$^+$) in B minor becoming a subdominant-functioned VI (B♭$^+$) in D major. In this interpretation, the augmented triad would be an enharmonic pivot, with A♯ reinterpreted as B♭.
15. For introductions to chromatic wedges and the omnibus progression in textbooks, see Clendinning and Marvin (2021, 613–16), Kostka et al. (2018, 455–57), and Laitz (2016, 708–11). For an in-depth exploration of the omnibus, see Yellin (1998).
16. The author of Coleridge-Taylor's English translation is unknown.
17. This is an example of "grouping dissonance," a type of metrical dissonance. See Krebs (1999, 31–33).
18. For example, see m. 38 of Edvard Grieg's (1843–1907) "Ein Traum" (op. 48, no. 6), where a IV♭^{7}–Ger^7 progression creates a chromatic wedge into a particularly transcendent cadential $^6_4$. In the early twentieth century, Florence Price deploys a blues-like and somewhat half-cadential IV♭^{7} in mm. 84–85 of Symphony no. 3, first movement.

19. In Schenkerian terms, we can understand this off-tonic beginning as an auxiliary cadence; for additional information, see Burstein (2005). For an explanation of off-tonic beginnings in undergraduate textbooks, see Laitz (2016, 670).
20. Such resource-sharing is key, and I am encouraged by recent initiatives, such as the Composers of Color Resource Project (n.d.) and Music Theory Examples by Women (n.d.).

Bibliography

Burstein, L. Poundie. Fall, 2005. "Unraveling Schenker's Concept of the Auxiliary Cadence." *Music Theory Spectrum* 27/2: 159–85.

_____, and Joseph N. Straus. 2020. *Concise Introduction to Tonal Harmony*, 2nd edition. W.W. Norton.

Clendinning, Jane Piper, and Elizabeth West Marvin. 2021. *The Musician's Guide to Theory and Analysis*, 4th edition. W.W. Norton.

Cleveland Institute of Music. "Mission and Vision." Accessed December 27, 2021. www.cim.edu/aboutcim/mission#:~:text=The%20CIM%20mission%20is%20to,fulfill%20their%20dreams%20and%20potential

Composers of Color Resource Project. "Welcome." Accessed June 7, 2021. https://composersofcolor.hcommons.org/

Doll, Christopher. 2011. "Rockin' Out: Expressive Modulation in Verse-Chorus Form." *Music Theory Online* 17.3. https://mtosmt.org/issues/mto.11.17.3/mto.11.17.3.doll.html#FN18

Ewell, Philip. 2020. "Music Theory and the White Racial Frame." *Music Theory Online* 26.2. https://mtosmt.org/issues/mto.20.26.2/mto.20.26.2.ewell.html

Feagin, Joe. 2013. *The White Racial Frame: Centuries of Racial Framing and Counter-Framing*, 2nd edition. Routledge.

Goldenberg, Yosef. 2018. "When and How Are Modulations Diatonic?" *Intégral* 32: 37–58.

Kostka, Stefan, Dorothy Payne, and Byron Almén. 2018. *Tonal Harmony: With an Introduction to Post-Tonal Music*, 8th edition. McGraw-Hill.

Krebs, Harald. 1999. *Fantasy Pieces: Metrical Dissonance in the Music of Robert Schumann*. Oxford University Press.

Laitz, Steven G. 2016. *The Complete Musician: An Integrated Approach to Theory, Analysis, and Listening*, 4th edition. Oxford University Press.

Music Theory Examples by Women. "Home." Accessed June 7, 2021. https://musictheoryexamplesbywomen.com/

Ricci, Adam. 2017. "The Pump-Up in Pop Music of the 1970s and 1980s." *Music Analysis* 36/1: 94–115.

Roig-Francolí, Miguel. 2020. *Harmony in Context*, 3rd edition. McGraw-Hill.

Yellin, Victor Fell. 1998. *The Omnibus Idea*. Harmonie Park Press.

Part Three
Form

9 A Jazz-Specific Lens
Methodological Diversity in the Music Theory Core

Ben Geyer

Introduction

Music programs have increasingly revisited their undergraduate theory curricula according to considerations around diversity, equity, and inclusion. These efforts have largely involved inclusion of diverse classical composers and examples from non-classical styles. Such representation is important: our repertoire choices send implicit (but no less strong) signals to each new generation of music majors about what music theory is and whom it is for (Palfy and Gilson 2018). Repertoire substitutions are ultimately insufficient, however, without also introducing diversity in method. In this chapter, I argue that an infusion of methodological diversity must be a substantive component of any curricular reform that hopes to disrupt the status quo of White-centric music theory instruction. Imani Mosley has noted that "[t]hose [non-canonical] names added to our textbooks and syllabi are always understood through the lens of an established majority" (2021). As music theory adds previously excluded names, we must also undermine that majority lens through a wide range of other lenses, each specifically catered to the styles we incorporate.

Many of the positions I lay out here relate to racial diversity. As a White person, my thinking on these matters can only be philosophized: I cannot draw from the lived experience of racial oppression. Further, this chapter relies on my own understandings of jazz, and there is a certain uncomfortable tension in representing an Afrological art form from my subjective position as a White person (Lewis 2002). Cultural insiders may be better suited to make these arguments, and I may well get things wrong. But music theory has work to do before its spaces can be genuinely welcoming, comfortable, or appealing to Black scholars. No one can expect an influx of Black participants in music theory until music theory widely honors Black music. Until the field reflects a sustained commitment to that work, talented scholars will choose other fields and other career paths. I am therefore submitting this chapter, despite its potential failings, in an effort to highlight systemic issues that remain untouched by reforms that center on substituting repertoire without also broadening methods.

I am not alone in calling for methodological diversity. Philip Ewell notes, "The problem of our [W]hite frame in our music curricula concerns not only the repertoire that we study, but also the music theories behind the repertoire" (2020, [3.4]). And as Robin Attas and Margaret Walker put it, "Music instructors must recognize the value of multiple knowledge systems, beliefs, values, and practices in music – all of which are just as valid as Western ones" (2019, 12). These calls for attention to "the music theories behind the repertoire" and "multiple knowledge systems" come against a backdrop of a field that has treated classical music's assumptions, habitual patterns of thought, and ways of knowing as normative and universal, instantiating what Eduardo Bonilla-Silva has termed "color-blind racism" (2003).

DOI: 10.4324/9781003204053-13

As Kimberlé Crenshaw et al. put it, color-blind racism involves "reproducing the notion of the [W]hite subject as the normative standard or 'reasonable person' in academic ... discourse" (2019, 12). It is color blindness that leads us to imply that theories developed for application to classical music are universally relevant. This supposed universality excuses the study of non-classical traditions using classical theories. It leads to an ongoing emphasis on structural characteristics that are essential to classical music, even when those same characteristics are secondary or superficial in those other traditions. It deems the lessons of classical music satisfactory preparation for the study of any number of other traditions, regardless of those traditions' distinct cultural underpinnings, aesthetic values, and performance practices. On a systemic level, music theory continues to center classical music by pushing all other traditions to the periphery, and it establishes classical music as the norm by defining all other traditions in relation to it.

Color blindness is entrenched in the standard music theory curriculum through textbooks, course objectives, accreditation requirements, and the demands of any number of stakeholders. But perhaps the most daunting challenge is that, even if there were broad support for methodological diversity, graduate training in music theory generally does not prepare future instructors to think about (and within) a broad range of non-classical traditions according to catered methods: courses in jazz, popular music, and musical theater are rarely required, and courses in non-western musical theories are scarcely offered even as electives (VanHandel 2021; Kajikawa 2020, 49). Without methodologically diverse training, the onus falls to individuals and communities to guide each other. To those ends, this chapter pursues two functions: as a commentary on the need for methodological diversity and as a resource to help prepare music theory instructors to teach a catered approach to jazz.

Part I of this chapter discusses essential differences between the structure of "straight-ahead jazz" and "European common-practice" (ECP) music, demonstrating how these differences motivate distinct methods and, in turn, how those methods lead to different modes of listening and analytical conclusions. I go on in Part II to describe how a jazz unit in my textbook, *Music Theory in Mind and Culture* (MTMC) (Geyer 2021), introduces methodological diversity by emphasizing what is unique about jazz rather than teaching it as a tangent in support of methods that are ultimately centered on classical music. Part III extrapolates from the specific case of this jazz unit to explore how curricular design on a broader scale might undermine color-blind racism through methodological diversity.

Part I: Jazz Form Is Not European Common-Practice Form

It is not a coincidence that music theory on jazz is often founded on classically derived methods: structural forces shaping music theory's institutions have ensured it. Graduate programs continue to center classical music, and it is impossible to override such a powerful influence on a person's thinking, myself included. Until recently, even scholars who later specialized in jazz often wrote dissertations on classical topics, and music theory journals generally did not accept research on traditions outside of classical music. The eventual inclusion of jazz was preconditioned on its treatment through classical methods: jazz research did not begin to be accepted until scholars justified its value according to the standards of classical music. Yet I maintain that jazz structure is fundamentally different from classical structure and requires an entirely separate method – from first assumptions to final conclusions. This section describes how a catered approach to jazz theory can circumvent classically based method by emphasizing aspects that are special to jazz performance practice and different from classical music.

Jazz has many stylistic branches from all aesthetic corners, but in this chapter, I focus on "straight-ahead jazz" – a stylistic umbrella including swing, bebop, hard bop, and cool jazz that continues to thrive as a common language for jazz musicians. When jazz topics are included in music theory classes, they tend to draw from straight-ahead jazz because its tertian and metrical organization resembles ECP music. Unfortunately, these commonalities can easily tempt music theory instructors to teach jazz as a tangent within a curriculum otherwise focused on ECP music. Treated with care, however, these apparent structural similarities can make jazz an especially interesting foil to classical music precisely because they seem so alike yet manifest so differently in practice.

Studying form in jazz depends on identifying relationships between two distinct layers of text: a framework for elaboration, called the "scheme," and the performance of that elaboration, called the "realization" (Love 2013, 48; Smither 2019). The scheme exemplifies what Lawrence Zbikowski has described, in music-specific context, as the "conceptual model" (2002). Zbikowski notes that the conceptual model functions as "a set of cognitive resources for performance, as a basis for negotiations on how musical practice should proceed, and as a focus for how musical practice can be regulated" (216). Because the scheme directly regulates realization, realizations should be analyzed in relation to their underlying scheme.

A scheme is a mental representation of a particular tune's mandatory elements (Geyer 2020). A "mandatory" element is one that must be incorporated into each realization as a defining characteristic of the tune being played. Ongoing references to mandatory elements allow experienced listeners to track the scheme as they hear the realization. There are two mandatory elements. First, in the absence of predetermined content, the "time-span structure" measures and regulates the passage of time during a performance. "Time-span" refers to the interval between successive beats at any structural level, drawing its shape from metrical structure; "time-span *structure*" refers to a hierarchy of time-spans at various timescales (Komar 1971, 36; Lerdahl and Jackendoff 1983). In straight-ahead jazz, the eight-bar time-span tends to be a particularly important temporal unit: it allows performers to track the passage of time and remain coordinated, even in the absence of precomposed and recognizable content. Figure 9.1 presents the "container," a diagram that I have developed in previous work to represent the eight-bar time-span, both as a theoretical concept and as a practical framework for analysis (Geyer 2020, 3–4). Each numbered box represents one measure, and time-spans at distinct levels – the one-measure, two-measure, four-measure, and eight-measure levels – are represented through different types of borders: respectively, dotted lines, solid lines, an indentation, and double lines (Love 2012, 7).

A second mandatory element of the scheme is a framework of essential harmonies, positioned at specific localities within the time-span structure. These harmonies form a middle-ground progression that is elaborated in the realization process through flexible, and often improvised, foreground harmonies. Essential harmonies are reliable auditory signposts

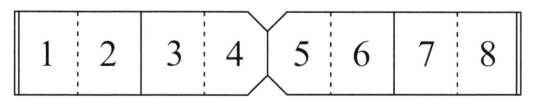

Figure 9.1 The container diagram, representing time-span structure from the one-measure to the eight-measure level.

that occur within an otherwise-flexible harmonic foreground. Foreground harmony is an important (and undertheorized) locus of improvisation, and one emphasis of the method in MTMC is to help students develop a sense of the wide harmonic flexibility built into the realization process. Thus, jazz harmony is shaped around two types of mandatory elements – harmonic objects and the temporal structure that situates them – and both are conceptually prior to any particular pitch details of the realization, including voice leading.

Whereas ECP music is generally theorized according to voice leading structures that manifest in varying rhythms, jazz involves fixed temporal units that are filled with wide-ranging pitch contents. In jazz, surface voice leading is a subtlety of elaboration, not a structural determinant. This jazz-specific conceptual frame is not a recalibration of ECP theory; it is a fundamental opposition to an ECP conception of voice leading as the primary communicator of structure, liable to unfold according to the needs of a given piece, with flexible scale and proportions. Voice leading is a syntactical foundation of formal communication in ECP music, which justifies the dominance of voice leading in the undergraduate theory curriculum; a method founded primarily on voice leading, however, is insufficient for the study of jazz harmony.

These differences between the conceptual structures of jazz and ECP music have ramifications even for seemingly basic tenets of harmony. Jazz musicians use a set of idiomatic foreground harmonic progressions to get from one essential harmony to the next, reserving substantial leeway to personalize local harmonic pathways. Different musicians sometimes choose similar pathways or adjust to each other's choices midstream. However, each musician has the prerogative to improvise foreground harmonies that are different from what might be found in a lead sheet, different from previous performances, different in each successive pass through the scheme, and even different from the foreground harmonic pathways that other musicians are playing simultaneously. The harmonic discrepancies that can result from multiple, incongruous foreground progressions are not only legitimate but also represent an astounding achievement of the jazz tradition: an improvisational system that maximizes each musician's harmonic freedom while maintaining communal coordination and comprehensibility.

Whereas ECP harmony and voice leading are characterized by a general state of agreement among all voices, the various voices in jazz harmony often seem to contradict on the surface. This harmonic incongruence can short-circuit analysis from an ECP perspective, but it is unproblematic from a jazz-specific method: rather than relating the various voices to each other at each given moment, each musician's individual improvisations should be independently compared to a scheme, understood as a flexible conceptual model that each performer can manifest differently. The structures of jazz performance practice assure a realization that is just as organized as ECP music, only that organization follows a different set of parameters, operating at different structural levels, conceived through a different conceptual frame, and deciphered from different kinds of auditory cues.

These allowable incongruities between voices undermine the importance of the consonance–dissonance and stability–instability relationships that are so important to ECP theory. In ECP theory, structure at every level – from moment-to-moment comprehension to large-scale tonal structure – are communicated by dissonances resolving to consonances, and by unstable scale degrees giving way to stable ones. Although jazz includes vestiges of these dissonance–consonance and stability–instability dichotomies, they are simply not primary determinants of structure. Instead, in the absence of literal resolutions on the surface, particular localities within the scheme attain structural weight through a shared understanding that they are essential harmonies or time-span boundaries. The classically based assumption that these kinds of tension and release determine structure can lead to an impression of jazz as disorganized, mysterious, or even ill-formed, based on its lack of regular points of agreement among different voices. However, this is an error of misplaced emphasis: it is the mutual understanding of the mentally constructed scheme, and that scheme's expression through individual choices in content, that communicate structure.

Owing to these differences in the communication of structural organization in classical music and jazz, the traditions demand distinct listening strategies. Listening for structure in classical music requires a focus on voice leading processes, with special attention to processes that might remain open (as in a tonic prolongation) or attain closure (as in a perfect authentic cadence). In contrast, listening for structure in jazz involves maintaining attention to meter and time-span structure – grooves, measures, containers, and larger forms – to create a playing field for contextualizing the specific pitch contents that fill those spaces. In the absence of a precise agreement of predetermined content and voice leading processes, jazz listening prioritizes the unflappable march of the groove and its accumulation into predictable and comprehensible temporal spaces.

Part II: Teaching the Jazz Unit from MTMC

As a tactic toward undermining color-blind racism in music theory, instructors should aim to teach jazz (and any other non-classical tradition) on its own terms – not as an extension of ECP music. Unit 5 in MTMC, "Jazz Theory," attempts to introduce such a catered perspective in a manner accessible to first-year undergraduates. Part II of this chapter can be seen as a teacher's supplement to that instructional unit. The unit's first three lessons extend topics from the standard curriculum into jazz-specific tangents. Lesson 5.1 expands on a previous unit's introduction of triad chord symbols, now adding seventh chords and sixth chords. Lesson 5.2 introduces the jazz-specific voicings "four-way close" and "drop-2," which I categorize as "complete voicings" based on their inclusion of all four chord tones (the root, third, fifth, and either sixth or seventh). Lesson 5.3 introduces the "shell voicing": this is an especially useful component of functional musicianship since it provides the basic aural information of a chord in a configuration that is efficient and relatively accessible at a piano keyboard – namely, with the root in the left hand and the chordal third and seventh (or sixth) in the right hand. Students realize these voicings in one-off problems, but they also realize them in progressions, reinforcing voice leading skills from the standard curriculum and demonstrating how the same processes manifest differently in a non-classical context.

If this jazz unit were to stop at chord symbols and voicings, it would achieve little in the way of methodological diversity. Jazz musicians are certainly concerned with spelling chords, realizing them into voicings, and connecting them through attention to voice leading. However, when a curriculum marked by a preoccupation with classical harmony and voice leading continues to emphasize those same parameters when it turns to jazz, students are merely experiencing tangents to the same prioritized methods. Further, these lessons would lack any jazz-specific musical context without the unit's subsequent lessons. While I support diversity of styles for the sake of representation, a presentation of jazz topics that omits mention of the characteristics that distinguish it from ECP music, as discussed previously, does nothing to destabilize the color-blind notion that the assumptions we have about ECP structure are normative and universal.

This unit's real gambit for methodological diversity, then, comes in Lessons 5.4–5.7. Lesson 5.4 describes some of the basic mechanics of jazz performance practice, addressing what I have described previously as the mandatory elements of a scheme. I center the container (introduced earlier in MTMC) and characterize it according to three functions: as a guide for performance, a context for understanding improvised content, and a background setting to which essential chords are tethered. A discussion of essential chords highlights their capacity to form essential harmonic motions within a container's boundaries and demonstrates the variety with which these harmonic plans can manifest, covering I–I, I–V, IV–V, V–I, I–III, I–ii, and vi–V progressions.

A harmony-first method might not emphasize this variety of middleground harmonic motions. Instead, it would reveal harmonic pathways more akin to the tonic–dominant–tonic norm of ECP music, which do occur at a deeper structural level, cutting across multiple containers. The historic harmonic palette of jazz standards undeniably retains these connections to ECP music, and this lesson subsequently points out how container-level harmonic motions combine into these progressions at the scale of multiple containers. But identifying this variety of middleground departures and arrivals emphasizes an important listening strategy for jazz musicians: a prioritization of containers as temporal frames, and the harmonic motions that fit within them. This exemplifies the methodological diversity I am calling for: even if a non-ECP style *could* be characterized in terms of ECP theory, I am proposing that we focus instead on methods that are catered to the tradition in question and the distinct ways of knowing and hearing that make it unique.

Lesson 5.5 builds on this discussion of jazz-specific conceptual models, presenting an analytical deep dive into a single container from "Just Squeeze Me" by Duke Ellington. This analysis has two objectives: reducing a particular set of foreground harmonies into its essential harmonies and learning more generally about the musical logic of the elaboration–reduction relationships involved. Both objectives resonate with aspects of a tune-learning process important to jazz practice (Berkman 2013, 108–11). The method here is based on a brand of time-span analysis developed by Steven Strunk in his "Layered Approach" (1979). Strunk's method intuitively captures a vital trait of jazz performance practice: that the temporal spaces created by groove, meter, and hypermeter form viscerally experienced boundaries for harmonic elaboration. Thus, this method ensures that harmony will be contextualized within a prior temporal structure, in contrast to a classical conception in which a prior voice leading structure is rhythmicized.

Where Lesson 5.5 offers a general description of the analytical method, Lesson 5.6 supplies more detail by introducing a set of seven harmonic idioms that are common in jazz. Rather than using Roman numerals to name each chord's relative role within the key, as is common in jazz theory, students identify idioms according to novel labels. For example, instead of labeling Em7–A7 as a "ii–V progression," I call it an "m7–dom7 pair" according to its succession of qualities. I represent each idiom according to four characteristics – root motion, chord quality, hierarchy, and meter – and assign each idiom a symbol for the purpose of annotation in analysis. The choice to avoid Roman numerals is a matter of pedagogical pragmatism. The ii–V progression is ubiquitous in jazz but frequently occurs at a pitch level other than its nominal roots of $\hat{2}$ and $\hat{5}$. The Roman numeral assigned to any given chord can therefore include a wide array of relationships to the operative key. Further, harmonies in jazz often have nested meanings, leading to multiple levels of interpretation. For example, in the progression Em7–A7–Dm7–G7–C6, the first two chords might be identified as iii–VI in C major, but they also function as an applied ii–V progression leading to Dm7. In another layer of abstraction, this same chain of m7–dom7 pairs can just as easily lead to an arrival chord other than I: this is what would happen if this same progression occurred in a global key of G major, with the terminal C chord functioning as IV.

By avoiding Roman numerals and emphasizing quality and root motion instead, students maintain focus on the particular cues needed to identify idiomatic harmonic cells without being bogged down with extraneous layers of interpretation. This way, the jazz unit can be placed prior to chromatic classical harmony within the curriculum; this unit actually introduces concepts of chromaticism, including mixture and applied chords, without wrestling with chromatic spelling. The resulting delay in ECP topics helps to undermine the primacy of classical music in the curriculum (discussed next). By avoiding complicated Roman numeral nomenclature, including the tricky orthography of applied chords (e.g., "V of ii"), students can keep their attention on the mechanics of the analytical system. Further, the flexibility granted by this focus on chord quality and root motion lends itself to the analysis of more challenging jazz repertoire with nonfunctional harmonic systems, such as John Coltrane's "Giant Steps" and the subsequent postbop style (Coltrane 1959).

The jazz unit ends with Lesson 5.7, which synthesizes the foregoing lessons and describes the procedures involved in analyzing a jazz tune through this method. In lieu of a single assignment, as is typical for each lesson in MTMC, the corresponding portion of the workbook provides container templates for a collection of jazz standards. These analyses scaffold the skills necessary for lead-sheet analysis, gradually incorporating the idioms presented in this unit in a controlled, cumulative ordering. On one hand, the analytical system is somewhat open-ended and includes a few tasks that may seem tricky for a first-year theory class: students are asked to track structural levels within a time-span hierarchy and to distinguish similar-looking idioms based on fine details. On the other hand, these tasks are no *more* difficult than the intricate part writing and analysis tasks of the standard curriculum. In any case, I have found that sustained attention to the issues I have described here make this unit approachable in Theory 2. More importantly, this instructional unit – catered as it is to jazz performance practice – offers a layer of diversity that transcends style and composer by additionally diversifying method.

Part III: Rethinking "Fundamentals" for a Methodologically Diverse Curriculum

Students will infer an understanding of what music theory is, what it does, and whom it is for, based on their experience with the curriculum as we present it to them. At least within the undergraduate instruction, then, the normativity assumed of classical music can be disrupted by undermining its typical primacy (teaching it first) and proportion (teaching it the most). Instruction through culturally catered methods in as many styles as possible should begin prior to classical instruction and, ideally, with a greater proportion of overall curricular space dedicated to it. In this way, students might come away with a prism of understandings that dismantle the impression of classical music as normative.

As it stands, music theory instruction implicitly prioritizes classical music even in the first days of Theory 1, based on what is included in and excluded from music theory fundamentals. The standard theory curriculum betrays color-blind assumptions according to four distinct connotations embedded in the typical conception of "fundamentals": that they are easy, requisite, essential, and universal. I am suspicious of the notion that fundamentals are *easy*, in the sense of being accessible to novices and appropriate as beginning topics. Success with these topics, as they are typically presented, is correlated with prior access to translatable musical instruction. A second connotation of fundamentals, that these topics are *requisite* to further study, is baked into curricular structure: students who do not rapidly acclimate to these topics are often barred from progression, not only in the theory curriculum, but also sometimes in their music programs as a whole. Third, fundamental knowledge is treated as *essential*, suggesting that if you do not know it, you cannot know music theory. This is only true if music theory is defined narrowly, as a specific analytical tradition for notated classical music. Yet musical knowledge outside of our narrowly conceived fundamentals is dismissed as extraneous, and our judgments of value leave out the skills and experience that so many musicians from non-classical traditions bring to the table (such as audio production) – sometimes skills and experiences that many of us lack. A

106 *Ben Geyer*

fourth connotation of "fundamental" is the implication that the contents of a fundamentals unit are in any way universal – all a person needs to know to study any music.

ECP theory is not fundamental. Even setting aside the losses in translation between ECP music and jazz, as described previously, the problem with assuming the fundamentality of ECP music is evident in our own backyard: by intention, the music of the Second Viennese School, for example, deliberately avoids the structures presented as fundamental in theory instruction. Our classification of certain concepts and procedures as easy, requisite, essential, or universal would be uprooted if we were to suddenly find ourselves teaching hip-hop to the current generation of college-age students, who are often so well versed in that tradition. Suddenly, *we* would be the ones finding the material difficult and idiomatic (that is, non-universal), and ways of knowing that are typically treated as subsidiary and extraneous would suddenly be of the most requisite and essential kind.

A curriculum based on the premise of methodological diversity would involve rethinking what is "fundamental" in two senses, based on a distinction between what I will call "standard fundamentals" and "conceptual fundamentals." To the extent that standard fundamentals units teach a taxonomy of musical structures, a methodologically diverse curriculum would need to incorporate a wide-enough range of structures to accommodate whatever traditions might be included. The major sixth chord, for example, is not a recognized category in ECP theory and is generally excluded from fundamentals units, yet it is essential to jazz. A curriculum that excludes the major sixth chord as a fundamental structure could only ever teach jazz as a tangent to more centralized priorities. A second, equally important set of fundamentals – what I call "conceptual fundamentals" – is a motivating theme of MTMC, with the goal of fostering flexible, critical thinking about theoretical questions. In just the first four units, MTMC foregrounds concepts drawn from acoustics, geometries of music, music psychology, musical metaphor, style theory, schema theory, rhythm and meter, and theories of musical hierarchy – all concepts that are essential to a humanistic approach to music theory and generalizable beyond classical music.

MTMC addresses both of these critiques of fundamentals by spreading out the introduction of standard fundamentals topics – sometimes rather deeply into the curriculum – and using the curricular space this opens to intersperse conceptual fundamentals. This design achieves four goals. First, the conceptual fundamentals align undergraduate instruction with issues and questions that motivate music theory research rather than maintaining focus on the topics of classical music literacy that typically dominate the standard curriculum. Second, these conceptual fundamentals set the stage for an ongoing critical examination of catered theories of music, attending to the distinct clusters of analytical parameters that are most relevant to any given tradition. That means focusing on time-span structure and chord quality in the jazz unit while focusing on voice leading in the classical units. Third, this prolonged treatment of standard fundamentals and inclusion of conceptual fundamentals undercuts classical music's primacy by delaying classical-specific instruction: wherever possible, MTMC trains the typical theory skills through styles with greater relevance and diversity than classical music, delaying classical-specific treatment of those same skills. This makes it possible to teach issues relevant to a wide range of styles before classical music gets specialized treatment. And fourth, by spreading out standard fundamentals, MTMC addresses inequity among students by building in differentiated instruction: students with less prior access have time to digest the peculiar kinds of thinking required for standard fundamentals, and students with the privilege of prior access remain challenged with the ongoing introduction of the new-to-them topics of conceptual fundamentals.

I sense that the pooled resources of music theory – a research field with increasingly pluralistic tendencies – could pave the way for a curriculum that foregrounds critical discussion of theoretical systems and analytical tools in favor of the long-standing norm:

ever-deeper extrapolations of the same classically derived principles of harmony and voice leading. In this way, music theory could be presented as an enterprise capable of morphing into style-specific configurations that emphasize human, cultural, aesthetic, performative, and structural characteristics of widely contrasting traditions and highlighting their differences as mutual lenses onto each other, presented on equal footing.

As music programs continue to work toward diversity in their music theory courses, it is not enough to substitute examples from non-classical styles, or even to add non-classical theory as tangential topics in support of a method otherwise centered on classical music. Instead, to the greatest extent possible, music programs should be seeking ways to teach non-classical traditions from catered, culturally specific methods. When instructors incorporate methodological diversity, each non-classical repertoire should open conceptual frames and patterns of thought that are distinct from those of classical music. I have attempted to demonstrate how a catered approach to jazz, in particular, might open such divergent thinking, but a methodologically diverse curriculum would incorporate similarly catered approaches to the widest possible range of musical traditions. If we want our curricula to nurture musicians who think flexibly, critically, and with an awareness of the many ways that humans experience music, we must begin to optimize the methods we teach to emphasize what makes each tradition unique.

Works Cited

Attas, Robin, and Margaret E. Walker. November, 2019. "Exploring Decolonization, Music, and Pedagogy." *Intersections* 39/1: 3–20.

Berkman, David. 2013. *The Jazz Harmony Book*. Sher Music Co.

Bonilla-Silva, Eduardo. 2003. *Racism Without Racists: Color-Blind Racism and the Persistence of Racial Inequality in the United States*. Rowman & Littlefield Publishers, Inc.

Coltrane, John. "Giant Steps." On *Giant Steps*, Atlantic 1311–2. Recorded 1959. Compact disc.

Crenshaw, Kimberlé Williams, Luke Charles Harris, Daniel Martinez HoSang, and George Lipsitz. 2019. "Introduction." In *Seeing Race Again: Countering Colorblindness Across the Disciplines*, edited by Kimberlé Williams Crenshaw, Luke Charles Harris, Daniel Martinez HoSang, and George Lipsitz, 1–19. University of California Press.

Geyer, Ben. 2020. "A Theory of Jazz Performance Practice." In *A-R Online Music Anthology*. https://www.armusicanthology.com/ViewerPlus.aspx?&music_id=954

———. 2021. *Music Theory in Mind and Culture*. Self-published textbook and workbook. www.bengeyer.com/teacher

Kajikawa, Loren. 2020. "Leaders of the New School? Music Departments, Hip-Hop, and the Challenge of Significant Difference." *Twentieth-Century Music* 18/1: 45–64.

Komar, Arthur. 1971. *Theory of Suspensions: A Study of Metrical and Pitch Relations in Tonal Music*. Princeton University Press.

Lerdahl, Fred, and Ray Jackendoff. 1983. *A Generative Theory of Tonal Music*. MIT Press.

Lewis, George E. 2002. "Improvised Music after 1950: Afrological and Eurological Perspectives." *Black Music Research Journal* 22: 215–46.

Love, Stefan. Spring, 2012. "An Approach to Phrase Rhythm in Jazz." *Journal of Jazz Studies* 8/1: 4–32.

———. Spring, 2013. "Subliminal Dissonance or 'Consonance'? Two Views of Jazz Meter." *Music Theory Spectrum* 35/1: 48–61.

Mosley, Imani. 2021. "Diversity Is a Tool." In *Panel Talk Delivered as Part of Decentering the Canon in the Conservatory*. Oberlin College-Conservatory of Music.

Palfy, Cora, and Eric Gilson. 2018. "The Hidden Curriculum in the Music Theory Classroom." *Journal of Music Theory Pedagogy* 32: 79–110.

Philip A. Ewell. 2020. "Music Theory and the White Racial Frame." *Music Theory Online* 26/2.

Smither, Sean R. 2019. "Flexible Conceptual Maps: A Schema-Based Approach to the Analysis of Jazz Tunes." *Theory & Practice* 44: 83–118.

Strunk, Steven. Fall–Winter, 1979. "The Harmony of Early Bebop: A Layered Approach." *Journal of Jazz Studies* 6/1: 4–53.

VanHandel, Leigh. 2021. "The 21st-Century Theory Graduate Student." Plenary talk delivered at the Society for Music Theory Annual Meeting.

Zbikowski, Lawrence. 2002. *Conceptualizing Music: Cognitive Structure, Theory, and Analysis.* Oxford University Press.

10 Of Simple Forms and Firsts
On Francis Johnson and Harry Burleigh

Horace J. Maxile, Jr.

In an essay on musical form, William Grant Still wrote the following:

> There is a lesson for us all in the simple little ABA form. It was known to peasant musicians long before the classicists analyzed it and put it into the textbooks. The lesson that it brings is that there must be a recurrence of thematic material in any musical composition before any listener, trained or untrained, can detect the form, or plan, that underlies the work. This recurrence of theme brings a well-defined unity – which, however, must not be made monotonous.
>
> (Cited in Spencer 1992, 175)

These views reflect the perspective of a Black composer who, after the successes of historic symphonic works, seemed disinterested in newer currents in contemporary music around the late 1940s. The Black American presence in the composition of concert music dates back to the early decades of the nineteenth century, and many works from that century adhere to the structural principles outlined by Still. It should be noted that Still's views on form are not novel and were likely shared by other neo-romanticists; however, including the perspective of an Black American composer who garnered widespread acclaim during the twentieth century is fitting for an essay on simple forms by Black American composers.

This contribution seeks to offer teaching commentaries on simple forms as realized in selected works by Francis Johnson (1794–1855) and Harry Burleigh (1888–1939). I focus on these particular composers because of the historical "firsts" with which they are associated. Johnson was the first published Black American composer, and Burleigh is credited as being among the first Black American composers to musically espouse Black nationalistic tenets. In the Burleigh pieces, discussions of vernacular *musical emblems* will aid in exploring interpretive stances based on intra- and extra-musical readings. "Musical emblems" are sonic markers that denote vernacular culture or close connections to it. "Emblem," for this author, seeks to acknowledge and esteem the progenitors, plights, processes, and values from which Black musical devices derive; it assumes more substantive context and agency for such signifying markers in analyses and interpretations that engage and/or foreground Black historical, cultural, or social issues.[1] Thus, the "discussion notes" offered after the analytical vignettes sometimes employ considerations of historical and social contexts surrounding the composers, offering intriguing counterpoints to or expansions upon associations often aligned with the nineteenth century. All scores can be found on the Supplemental Materials website.

Bingham's Cotillion (1811?) and *A Collection of New Cotillions*[2] (1818)

Francis Johnson was one of the most celebrated musicians and personalities in Philadelphia during the early nineteenth century. He amassed many historic "firsts" for a Black musician during his career:

> [F]irst to develop a "school" of [B]lack musicians, first to publish sheet music . . . and first to appear in integrated concerts with [W]hite musicians. . . . [H]e was the first to take a musical ensemble abroad to perform in Europe and the first to introduce the promenade concert to the United States.
>
> (Southern 1997, 107)

A highly reputable leader of social and military bands and a prolific composer, he authored over 200 compositions, including patriotic songs, marches, quadrilles, stylized dances, and cotillions. Johnson's cotillions belong to a tradition of nineteenth-century dance music for upper-class Americans, where Black musicians composed and performed much of the music (Floyd and Reisser 1980, 161–62).

Given the function of cotillions, elements of return and symmetrical phrase structure are essential. Without these aspects of return, how would dancers know when to return to the beginning of the "figure" – the set of instructions for the dancers to follow? Each of the 12 cotillions in the *Collection of New Cotillions* and *Bingham's Cotillion* features thematic restatements and/or harmonic frameworks that contribute to primarily ternary structures. The only exception is a rounded binary structure ("Johnson's Jig Cotillion" from the *Collection*), which will be discussed in more detail in the following passages. The predictability in these simple forms does not detract from Johnson's novel tunes and inventive sectional demarcation. He facilitates contrast by one or more of the following: changes in mode or key (most often to the relative minor), shifts in accompaniment texture, and changes in melodic figurations.

The ternary designs encountered in the *Collection* are varied. Some feature A and B sections of relatively equal length, such as #3, "Augustus"; #4, "Caroline"; and #10, "Fort Erie." Other pieces have A sections with embedded rounded or ternary forms. The cotillions that employ extended A sections feature enough melodic deviation in the repeated sections to warrant a separate designation but remain in the tonic key. In others, the B section features a shift to the parallel or relative minor key: #1, "The Cymbals"; #5, "William"; #7, "Ford"; #9, "Francis"; and #11, "The Arrival." Other cotillions in Johnson's output reveal more complex ternary designs, where each section of the global ABA contains its own smaller ABA form, such as *Bingham's Cotillion*.

Bingham's Cotillion (1810?–1819)

One of Johnson's earliest compositions, this work for piano with violin or flute accompaniment features a complex ternary design where each of the larger formal units have smaller ternary forms within them: A (aba) B (cdc) A (aba). Each phrase is four measures in length, and relationships between phrases are mostly parallel. The A section, marked *moderato*, begins in C major, and the contrasting section within the larger A (mm. 6–16) migrates toward a cadence in G major. Grace note gestures characterize the charming, buoyant melody in C major, while scalar sixteenth passages provide rhythmic and harmonic contrast.

The larger B section (mm. 17–40) features harmonic shifts between A minor (c section) and C major (d section), as well as contrasting treatments of melody. A stately eighth-note melody highlights a dramatic tonicization of the dominant in measures 19–20. As the E_6 (in the violin/flute) is the highest note in the piece and appears in various harmonic and melodic contexts, the arrival in measure 20 is heightened by the only chromatic chord in the piece (V^7/V). The move to C major in measure 25 is direct, and running sixteenth notes meander through simple harmonic progressions for the entire section, resting only at the authentic cadence at measure 32. Other than subtle changes in the direction of the bass line in the return of the c section in measure 33, there is virtually no change in the harmonic profile or melodic line.

Discussion Notes and Further Assignments

1. **Modulation to G:** Does it happen? If so, how and when? There is a lot of F♯ after measure 12, and the accompanying C and B in the violin/flute certainly do not sound like *do–ti* at this point.
2. **Implied harmony, even with a missing pitch?:** The cadences in A minor in the larger B section (mm. 23–24 and 39–40) both highlight a cadential $^6_4$–V–i progression. However, neither cadential $^6_4$ in the score contains the pitch A. This presents an opportunity to incorporate listening strategies, as the eye will only see the pitches E and C. Students' ears will hopefully recognize this particularly strong cadential gesture and stave off a strange Roman numeral.

"The Cymbals" (no. 1) and "Johnson's Jig Cotillion" (no. 6) from *A New Collection of Cotillions*

"The Cymbals"

"The Cymbals" features a ternary design, where the larger A section contains a smaller rounded form (a1–a2–a1). Compared to the relatively thin texture of the running sixteenth notes against the simple bass line, the fortissimo chords in measures 1–2 and 5–6 articulate the beginnings of phrases and also offer sonic markers that lend somewhat programmatically to the title. Measures 9–16 are designated as "a2" because of the lack of tonal/harmonic contrast and the florid right hand's more improvisatory character, advancing melodic ideas from the sixteenth-note passages in a1 and continuing in the key of C major. The B section, in C minor, involves contrasting thematic material, although the supporting harmonic progressions are almost exact restatements of the progressions in the opening measures of the piece. Johnson's preference for the melodic form of the minor scale in the B section, employing A♮ exclusively, contributes to this near-duplicate tonal profile; the only harmony altered from the opening A section is the tonic chord (I to i).

Discussion Notes and Further Assignments

1. Why the A♮ in the B section? This question presents the opportunity for students to think critically, not only about the harmonic implications of the F♯ in the bass in measure 19, but also about melodic trajectories. Some pieces in the *Collection* have progressions of block chords that do not adhere to conventional voice leading principles, but in this case, Johnson avoids A♭, perhaps because it would create an augmented second in the melodic line (m. 23). Favoring the melodic form of the minor scale also aids in maintaining the festive essence of the theme.
2. Compare and contrast this movement with #3, "Augustus," and #12, "Castillian."

As there is not much harmonic adventure, asking students to describe or compare offers an opportunity to explain their ideas and practice writing about music. Students can share their ideas/prose about one piece on index cards and give them to the instructor. Ideas shared with the class could serve as catalysts for discussions of other pieces in the collection. These are not long pieces, so the teacher may wish to extend this exercise to even more cotillions in this collection.

"Johnson's Jig Cotillion"

In addition to being the only rounded binary piece in the *Collection*, "Johnson's Jig Cotillion" has other attributes that distinguish it from the others. The persistent dotted syncopations and ornamented melodic figures contribute a rhythmic vivacity that is distinctive within the set. Rhythmically modest bass lines afford ample space for the sprightly theme's perpetual dance. Composed of sixteen measures without da capo return, the piece is markedly shorter than the others in the set. The B section (mm. 13–16) is only four measures in length. We do not move away from C major in the B section, but it is the most harmonically elaborate and decorative moment in the entire *Collection*. Beginning on vi, "Johnson's Jig" cycles through a falling fifths progression that ends on tonic in measure 10 and then, with a dramatic tritone leap in the bass, tonicizes the dominant for a measure and a half before landing on V^7 in measure 16. V is tonicized in the A sections, but the inflated statement in the B section certainly captures the listener's attention, generating an expectation for an arrival on V and ultimately to the rounding out of the playful tune.

Discussion Notes and Further Assignments

1. Why might this be the only rounded binary piece in the *Collection*? This question presents an opportunity for students to consider the musical reasons behind Johnson's choice of formal structure. Perhaps he did not want to belabor the dotted, snapped rhythm any longer than necessary. Or maybe he thought the relatively vibrant colors of the B section would remain so by not extending thematic ideas any longer than necessary. There is also the possibility that he wanted the cotillion that bore his name to stand out, formally, rhythmically, and harmonically, in the set.
2. Recompose the B sections by adding four additional measures. Ensure a contrasting period structure, and make sure it is harmonically closed. (In the interest of contrast, would students venture away from the prevailing snapped syncopations?)

Harry Burleigh, *From the Southland* (1907)

Harry Burleigh is the first among a notable group of Black American composers whose works exhibited the tenets of Black nationalistic compositional thought that burgeoned during the early decades of the twentieth century. In the words of Eileen Southern, composers "consciously turned to the folk music of their people as a source of inspiration for their compositions" (268). Spirituals, folk songs, dance rhythms, and other musical emblems of vernacular culture served as inspiration and source material for vocal and instrumental works.

Whereas Burleigh is celebrated for his vocal works, particularly the art song spirituals that blossomed after "Deep River" (1917), he wrote a few instrumental works that also suggest nationalistic influences. One such work is *From the Southland*, a set of six piano sketches. Each sketch possesses a distinctive character through statements of spiritual tunes, pentatonic collections, offbeat melodic phrasings, and other emblems that signify an African American vernacular presence – sometimes explicitly and, at other times, implicitly. As Burleigh's lone work for solo piano, this piece predates his pivotal "Deep River" and highlights harmonic progressions that show late-romantic influences as well as chordal complexes that presage the modernist leanings of the following school of composers associated with the New Negro Movement (William Grant Still, Florence B. Price, and William Levi Dawson). Each piece in the set features either a ternary design or an extended binary (ABAB) design, and most conclude with a coda. In addition, each piece is prefaced with epigraphs, written in a Black-folk dialect, by Louise Alston Burleigh. It is not known whether the epigraphs were to be spoken/performed before the pieces, but they do provide compelling forage for interpretative stances that actively engage historical and cultural topics. The following will discuss two pieces that exhibit the formal designs mentioned previously and also illustrate potential interpretive pathways that may be incorporated into class discussions.

"On Bended Knees" (no. 5, *From the Southland*)

Oh I look away yonder_what do I see?
A band of angels after me.
Come tote me away from the fiel's all green;
'Cause nobody knows de trouble I've seen!

The themes in this epitaph are suggestive of a poetic subject that is ready to be carried away. The "fiel's all green" are likely fields of plantation and sharecropping servitude, as the subject looks upward or afar toward angelic dwelling places. "Away yonder" insinuates that the angels are at a distance, but that sought-after relief and peace are in sight. The title, therefore, evokes a religious position of prayer and petition and/or a posture of weariness and fatigue on the part of the subject.

A ternary design, "On Bended Knees" features an original melody in the A section (G minor, mm. 1–13) and settings of a pre-existing spiritual tune, "Nobody Knows the Trouble I've Seen," in the B section (G major, mm. 14–38). The final A section (mm. 39–52) features a modified restatement of the primary theme in the tonic, as well as fragmented statements of the B section material, with which Burleigh highlights changes of mode, rhythm, and contour. Burleigh's treatment of texture at the beginning of the piece is suggestive of a tripartite band of angels. The homophonic accompaniment pattern primarily comprises triads above a somber left-hand melody. An ethereal quality is generated by the undulating rhythmic character of close-voiced triads in the piano's upper register. Harmonic activity in the opening A section is modest in comparison to the B section; the only striking sonorities are three passing augmented triads that appear in measures 5, 10, and 12. In each case, the preceding chords are functional and are approached by way of conventional voice leading.

Burleigh's setting of "Nobody Knows the Trouble I've Seen," particularly moments that correspond to the words "trouble I've seen," supports interpretations that coincide with the poetic subject's troubled condition, from which they long to be freed. The Supplemental Materials website provides a copy of "Nobody Knows the Trouble I've Seen," as rendered in an 1874 volume that chronicled the history and the lives of students at Hampton Normal and Agricultural Institute, a historically Black college now known as Hampton University. Following an initial eight-measure statement of "Nobody Knows" in G major, fragments of the tune are developed harmonically and melodically until the recapitulation of the A material (m. 39). Toward an interpretation of ultimate resolve amid the troubles experienced by the poetic subject, I draw attention to the five instances of the "trouble I've seen" figure in the piece.

114 *Horace J. Maxile, Jr.*

The first two statements of the "trouble I've seen" figure appear in the opening eight measures of the B section (mm. 14–21). The first chromatic event occurs on "seen," although the G pedal and meandering inner voices slightly temper this fleeting mode mixture. Each of the inner voices is a half step away from resolving to a member of the tonic triad in the following chord, but the colorful sonority functions similarly to the pedal IV$^6_4$ in the preceding measure. The next setting of "seen" (m. 19, beat 3) prepares a circle of fifths progression toward the cadence in measure 21. Whereas the inverted secondary dominant (V$^4_3$/vi, m. 19, beats 1–2) prepares the E sonority (m. 20), the altered chord on "seen" (m. 19, beats 3–4) serves a similar function, offering an even more strident suggestion of the troubles facing the poetic subject. This chord could be viewed as a Fr^{+6} with a local resolution to a chord based on $\hat{6}$, or as an altered dominant with a lowered fifth. Whereas the upcoming "Glory Hallelujah" offers a moment of relative repose, the F♮ from "seen" is kept as a common tone, becoming a chromatic extension (♭9) in the E^7 chord and somewhat complicating the subject's sentiment of praise.

The next two settings of the "trouble I've seen" figure occur in transitional episodes that visit the mediant (B minor) and expand the dominant (D major). The statement in measure 23 is chromatic in the context of G major, functioning as a dominant harmony in a brief modulatory passage in B minor. Chromatic events and other episodes of harmonic adventure often occur around structural dominants in Burleigh's piano suite, and measure 29 is illustrative of this tendency. After the brief jaunt to B minor, G major is reasserted in measure 28. "Troubling" begins on an inverted G^7 chord (m. 29) and continues through the C♯°sonority on "seen" to a chromatic descent in the bass, until an arrival on the dominant prepares the return to G minor.

The fifth and final statement of "trouble I've seen" occurs in the last measures of the piece (mm. 51–53). Burleigh utilizes a circle of fifths progression to approach the final cadence. The progression is similar to the one that concluded the initial statement of the tune in the B section, but all the chords are major triads with extensions – essentially a sequence of secondary functions ultimately leading to the tonic triad. Whereas "Glory Hallelujah" was the corresponding text for the circle of fifths progression earlier, "trouble I've seen" corresponds to this final cadence.

A series of quarter note attacks in this statement alters the spiritual tune's rhythmic profile, which has been maintained throughout. Burleigh's plodding, steady rhythmic treatment essentially dissolves the contraction "I've," now accentuating both "I" and "have," suggesting a sense of irritation and/or perseverance. The culminating sonority (G major), the expressive charge of chromatic harmonies toward the final cadence, and the evocative blending of major and minor modes with motivic fragments from the spiritual tune before this utterance suggest that the angels are surely in sight and approaching – that there is salvation amid the troubles.

Discussion Notes and Further Assignments

Tracing "Trouble"

1. Tracing the harmonic underpinnings of the "trouble I've seen" figure, from signifying chromatic complexes to a conclusive authentic cadence, sheds interpretive light on the exclamation mark at the end of the poet's epigraph. Whether it is a mark of triumph or emboldened determination, the exuberant cadence and the corresponding text from the epigraph are compelling and invite readings that invoke not only the tune's quotation but also its intra-musical contexts. Burleigh's revision of "Nobody Knows" amplifies the prayerful and/or belabored petition of the poetic subject by way

of associations with the text of the tune, as well as chords that chromatically "trouble" harmonic progressions.

2. Ask students to think about the "troubling" moments in (or aspects of) the piece. Are there troubling aspects of rhythm, harmony, texture, etc.? If so, where do they occur? Do these coincide with the text of the tune? Are they not involved with the text at all?

   The "trouble," for some, may be the augmented triads or some of the harmonies that are encountered in the fully chromatic bass descent in the B section. There are a number of passages that could be attached to trouble or troubling. A discussion of why such passages are troubling might lead to discussions about chromatic harmony and intra-musical contexts, as well as topics that pertain to aesthetics and culture.

3. Ask students to consider their understanding of *repose* and *resolution*. Are they the same? If the instructor chooses to incorporate some of the interpretive stances given in the preceding text, is the resolve based in triumph or frustration? This is a leading question that could delve into considerations of past and contemporary associations attached to "Nobody Knows the Trouble I've Seen." Such a jaunt could be foreshadowed with video clips that place the tune in various contexts. (For example, one might show video clips of Zazu singing it to Scar in *The Lion King*, or Sheldon singing the tune in *The Big Bang Theory*.)

"A New Hidin' Place" (no. 6, *From the Southland*)

In an expanded binary (ABAB) design, Burleigh explores thematic and motivic developmental possibilities of two spiritual melodies: "My Lord, What a Morning" and "The Rocks and Mountains." The epigraph utilizes text from both tunes.

> My Lord, what a mornin' –
>   When de stars begin to fall!
>   * * * * * * * *
>
> De rocks an' de mountains shall all flee away;
>   But you shall have a new hidin'-place dat day.

The piece begins with a somber homophonic treatment of "My Lord, What a Morning" in D major (mm. 1–10). This statement is followed by a brief developmental episode (mm. 11–14) that prepares the introduction of "The Rocks and Mountains" (mm. 15–26). Although "The Rocks and Mountains" ushers in no change in key, thematic and textural changes warrant designation of a B section. Another developmental episode prepares a restatement of the A theme in the chromatic mediant, B major – one of the most adventurous and colorful excursions in the suite (mm. 27–41). Burleigh's restatement also features a return to the opening homophonic texture and tune of "My Lord, What a Morning" in the upper register, with countermelodic fragments from "The Rocks and Mountains" sounding in the lower register. The ending of the second A section features a brief chromatic episode, as the fragments of "Rocks and Mountains" move from the lower register through the middle register, ultimately foreshadowing the return of the tune in the tonic key in a thicker homophonic texture (the final B section, mm. 42–56). As treatments of texture are highlighted as markers of sectional delineation in the overview offered previously, the following offers some historical and cultural context and carries the discussion of texture further, illuminating select harmonic and structural elements as they relate to interpretive stances.

In *Harry T. Burleigh: From Spirituals to the Harlem Renaissance*, Jean Snyder views "A New Hidin' Place" as a portrayal of the Last Judgement (2016, 263). Considering the epitaph, this reading is plausible; the Last Judgement, according to some Christian denominations, is the second coming of Christ and God's final judgment of the world, which results in the joyous receiving of His church and the damnation of others. One might also draw intriguing parallels to the plight of African Americans, both during the time this piece was composed and for the preceding generation of enslaved Africans in the United States.

The work of scholar and activist W. E. B. Du Bois is also relevant here, as it aids in considerations of historical context. Attempting to trace potential personal and political (dis)associations between Du Bois and Burleigh is far beyond this chapter's scope, but there are some points of intersection that warrant brief discussion. Incipits of both tunes, *sans* text, appear as epigraphs in Du Bois's classic tome *The Souls of Black Folks* (1903).[3] Drawing on the work of Eric Sundquist, Richard Rath submits that Du Bois's strategic omissions of the text "evoked certain feelings" and "also invoked the words to those who knew them. . . . The subversive power of the songs thus lay in the African time and melody, whose muteness could be more eloquent than words" (Rath 1997, 493–94).[4] In another analysis of the incipits, Rath suggests that "My Lord, What a Morning" "refers to the morning when the dead will be raised, or the slaves emancipated, but also the false dawn of reconstruction failed. The trumpet sounds will wake the nation of underground Americans both [B]lack and [W]hite to challenge racism and segregation."[5] Regarding "The Rocks and Mountains," Rath states that the tune "echoes" sentiments "of a time when all men, [B]lack and [W]hite, will rise up together and be free. The new hiding place is heaven/the North and it is the place for the risen up slave, the escaped slave." For those who rise above the veil of prejudicial thinking and second-class citizenship, "the rocks and mountains – the place that sufficed in lieu of a home for [B]lacks during slavery – will all flee away."[6]

Returning to the A section, the homophonic and homorhythmic setting of "My Lord, What a Morning" suggests communal singing. The deceptive progression (m. 8), followed by perfect authentic cadence (m. 10), relays an uneasy resolution or cautious optimism on the part of the poetic subject(s), as "the stars begin to fall." In keeping with the themes of liberation evoked in the text of "The Rocks and Mountains," the thinner texture and lighter rhythmic air in Burleigh's jubilant treatment proposes a sense of movement or mobility; this new texture opens registral space for an important musical emblem to signify an announcing of sorts. Notice the horn fifths in the right hand of measure 18. Continuing with the parallel sixths of measures 15 and 16 would have held true to printed versions of the tune that were in circulation at that time, but Burleigh highlights the text "you shall have a new hidin' place that day" with an emblem suggesting a reference to heralding brass instruments – to, perhaps, awaken the masses to a new place and a new day.

An increase in rhythmic density and a progression of harmonies that land on an F♯ major triad in measures 15 and 16 characterize the transitional episode that prepares the arrival of "My Lord." The presence of B minor (mm. 23–25) points to a clever pivot from D major toward the ultimate arrival of the second A section in B major. Marked fortissimo and maestoso, the second statement of "My Lord" features a homophonic texture similar to that encountered in the opening measures, but the doubled melodic line, upward registral shift, and "Rocks and Mountains" counterstatements distinguish this moment as an expressive apex in the piece. The parallel moments of deceptive resolution (m. 8) and PAC (m. 10) return in measures 34 and 36 in the second A section. Here, the slight upward shift in melodic contour – which ironically corresponds to the word "fall" – and the accompanying colorful sonority (D♯ major) continue the climactic charge toward the final, triumphant statement of "Rocks and Mountains" (mm. 42–45). Returning to the community singing suggested by homophonic textures in this piece is compelling, as the number of voices assigned to the melodic line are doubled in comparison to the initial statement, and the chorus of accompaniment voices in the left hand affirms the glorious message of the new hiding place.

Discussion Notes and Further Assignments

Departures And Arrivals: Getting Into And Out Of B Major

Harmonic analyses of the transitions into and out of B major (the second A section) will involve discussions on modulation. Following the motivic fragment from "Rocks and Mountains" on the subdominant (G) in measure 22, the transitional episode highlights three B minor chords in various inversions before arriving on the F♯ major triad. The immediate D♯s give us a clue that we've moved away from D major, but where is B major confirmed? And where is F♯ destabilized as a key center? If so, how? Such questions will hone harmonic analysis and enhance discussions about cadences, arrivals, and departures. The modulation from B major back to D major may be understood as a direct modulation because of the immediate shift to D♮ in measure 38, but the chord on beat 4 in measure 37 could be analyzed as a pivot chord involving modal mixture in B major. Passing chromatic chords meander around the B pedal after the authentic cadence in measure 36. Modal mixture involving the ♭$\hat{6}$ (G♮) occurs on beats 2–3 of measure 37, altering the diatonic ii$^4_2$ chord to a half-diminished sonority. This chord can be reinterpreted as a diatonic vii$^{o4}_2$ in D major.

Coda: "Morning" Or "Mourning"?

There has been some speculation on the actual title of "My Lord, What a Morning," as there are some versions of the title that use "Mourning." Such distinctions could prompt discussions surrounding culture, race, history, and social conditions for all American citizens at the turn of the twentieth century. Possible questions could invoke thoughts about who is actually mourning when the "stars begin to fall," or what morning symbolized for the poetic subject or the succeeding generation of a once-enslaved people – the creators of the body of song we refer to as Negro, Black, or folk spirituals.

To round out the discussion of "A New Hidin' Place" and to explore potential interpretations of the epigraph, the instructor might refer to the final measures. Following the ascending horn fifths at the penultimate cadence, Burleigh offers one final utterance of a "Rocks and Mountains" melodic fragment. The gesture stalls on a vii^{o7} that borrows B♭ from the parallel minor mode and has a dominant function, but the voicing of the chord (with G in the bass) alludes to a quasi-plagal treatment that obscures a punctuating "Amen" upon arrival at the new hidin' place. However, the arrival is further complicated by the augmented triad before the final statement of tonic harmony. Does Burleigh's cadence allude to a cautious optimism and aspiration (morning)? Or does the unconventional final utterance signal rest but ultimately no resolution to the plight of many Black Americans (in the Southern United States – the *Southland*?) at the turn of the twentieth century (mourning)?

* * * * * * * * *

Consideration of these pieces, others within their respective collections, and additional works by Black composers for teaching simple forms will require a little time in preparation – as would any unfamiliar music. As the instructor listens and learns in preparing, students could partner in moving beyond the excerpt to uncovering works and histories of a compositional tradition that dates at least 115 years before William Grant Still's

Afro-American Symphony (1930). Other points of departure could be Johnson's "Victoria Gallop" (1839), Thomas "Blind Tom" (Bethune) Wiggins's "Water in the Moonlight" (1866), or the folksy first movement of Burleigh's *Southland Sketches* for violin and piano (1916). In conjunction with examinations of cadence types, elements of contrast, and structural peculiarities, brief and incisive historical sidebars into the lives of the composers could augment those discussions and point toward a true revisiting and revaluation of the musical imaginations that shape the broader tradition of concert music.

Notes

1. Toward a more literal association with the term, these emblems have been employed for generations, across genre and style, fortifying grounds for studies ranging from performance practice in secular and sacred music to gestures in western classical frameworks that signal Black culture. For more information on emblems in Black American music, see Maxile (2008).
2. The author acknowledges both the work of Dr. Megan Lavengood in preparing the version of *A Collection of New Cotillions* used for this chapter, as well as her gracious permission for its use. It can be found on IMSLP.org.
3. The corresponding chapter in the Du Bois for the "My Lord What a Morning" incipit is "Of the Dawn of Freedom" (Chapter 2), and the corresponding chapter for "The Rocks and Mountains" incipit is "On the Wings of Atlanta" (Chapter 5). "Nobody Knows the Trouble I've Seen" also appears as the epigraph to Chapter 1, "Our Spiritual Strivings."
4. See also Chapters 5 and 6 of Sundquist 1993.
5. Richard Rath, interactive website devoted to Du Bois's *The Souls of Black Folks*: https://way.net/SoulsOfBlackFolk/index.html.
6. Richard Rath, interactive website devoted to Du Bois's *The Souls of Black Folks*: https://way.net/SoulsOfBlackFolk/index.html.

Works Cited

Du Bois, W.E.B. (1903) 1968. *The Souls of Black Folk: Essays and Sketches*. Reprint, Johnson Reprint Corporation.

———. 1903. "W.E.B. Du Bois." In *The Souls of Black Folks*, edited by Richard Rath. Musical Hypertext Edition. Accessed July 31, 2021. http://way.net/SoulsOfBlackFolk/

Floyd, Samuel A., Jr. and Marsha J. Reiser. 1980. "Social Dance Music of Black Composers in the Nineteenth Century and the Emergence of Classic Ragtime." *The Black Perspective in Music* 8/2: 161–93.

Maxile, Horace J. 2008. "Signs, Symphonies, Signifyin(G): African-American Cultural Topics as Analytical Approach to the Music of Black Composers." *Black Music Research Journal* 28/1: 123–38.

Rath, Richard Cullen. 1997. "Echo and Narcissus: The Afrocentric Pragmatism of W.E.B. Du Bois." *The Journal of American History* 84/2: 461–95.

Snyder, Jean E. 2016. *Harry T. Burleigh: From the Spiritual to the Harlem Renaissance*. University of Illinois Press.

Southern, Eileen. 1997. *The Music of Black Americans: A History*, 3rd edition. W.W. Norton & Company.

Spencer, Jon Michael, ed. 1992. *The William Grant Still Reader: Essays on American Music*. A Special Issue of *Black Sacred Music: A Journal of Theomusicology* 6/2. Duke University Press.

Sundquist, Eric J. 1993. *To Wake the Nations: Race in the Making of American Literature*. Belknap Press/Harvard University Press.

11 A Trio of Art Songs on Texts by Langston Hughes

Melissa Hoag

Introduction

At my institution, Form and Analysis is an upper-level elective. Students have had four semesters of music theory and know the basics of phrase structure, as well as binary, ternary, sonata, and rondo forms, and are proficient in labeling Roman numerals. This course is about coalescing what students learned in previous courses and taking those basic concepts to the next level. Art songs present a unique opportunity to study not only form but also poetic meaning and interpretation at a deep level.

Both poems set to music in this chapter are by the well-known African American poet Langston Hughes (1901–67). Born in Joplin, Missouri, Hughes saw his parents separate shortly after he was born, and his father moved to Mexico. He was raised primarily by his maternal grandmother until she passed away when he was 13; at that time, he moved with his mother to several cities, including Lincoln, Illinois, where he began writing poetry, and finally Cleveland, Ohio. He began college at Columbia University but dropped out to travel. He held a wide variety of jobs and continued to write and publish poetry, short stories, and plays. As a writer who was proud to reflect the Black American experience, he became a major figure in the Harlem Renaissance.

"The Negro Speaks of Rivers": Margaret Bonds (1913–72) and Howard Swanson (1907–78)

"The Negro Speaks of Rivers" was Hughes's first published poem, and it was critically acclaimed.[1] He wrote it at the age of 17, while crossing the Mississippi River on his way to visit his father in Mexico (see the following text).

Students should first analyze the text on its own, so that they can consider the poem's form, themes, possible metaphors, and meaning, before encountering any musical setting. In my experience, engaging with the poem alone, before even listening to the musical setting, greatly increases students' appreciation of the decisions composers make when setting a text. I always remind students that it is often possible to interpret a poem on multiple levels and that musical settings of poems are themselves poetic interpretations; thus, a composer might choose to intensify or undermine any of the possible meanings of a poem. Instructors might use the following questions to guide discussion, or students might answer them in small groups or individually, perhaps on the LMS, before a class discussion about the song.

1. Study the poem. Write at least two paragraphs of well-constructed prose in which you discuss the following:
    - Is it possible to interpret the poem literally, or is there something more than meets the eye (metaphor, for example)? Could both be true?

DOI: 10.4324/9781003204053-15

- Does the poem tell a story, or is it mainly focused on imagery or abstract concepts?
- What are the central images of the poem?
- Choose several adjectives that you think describe the mood of the poem, and with as much specificity as possible, explain why you think they describe the poem.

2. Describe how you might set the poem as a composer. Write at least two paragraphs of well-constructed prose in which you discuss the following:

   - What form might you use to set the poem, and how would you divide up the text among the musical sections? Why would you do this?
   - What sort of accompaniment would you use? You can also consider instrumentation beyond the piano if you wish.
   - Would the accompaniment change for each section or stay the same throughout?
   - What other musical devices (e.g., imitation, canon, ostinato, ground bass) would you use?
   - What mood or atmosphere would be appropriate, and how would you accomplish this?
   - What words seem to invite special musical attention, and how would you set these words?

3. Read about Margaret Bonds's life.[2] In your own words, craft a one- to two-paragraph biography summarizing her life and achievements, similar to what you might read in a recital program.

I've known rivers:
I've known rivers ancient as the world and older than the
flow of human blood in human veins.

My soul has grown deep like the rivers.

I bathed in the Euphrates when dawns were young.
I built my hut near the Congo and it lulled me to sleep.
I looked upon the Nile and raised the pyramids above it.
I heard the singing of the Mississippi when Abe Lincoln
went down to New Orleans, and I've seen its muddy
bosom turn all golden in the sunset.

I've known rivers:
Ancient, dusky rivers.

My soul has grown deep like the rivers.

– Langston Hughes, "The Negro Speaks of Rivers"

The poem features the central image of a river that flows ceaselessly through time, symbolized by the repeated text "I've known rivers." The text references rivers around the world and throughout history: the Euphrates, along whose banks civilization dawned; the Congo, the second-longest river in Africa, along which the poem's narrator builds a hut and is lulled to sleep; the Nile, near which the majestic pyramids were built; and finally, the Mississippi, a river of central significance to the history of the United States and slavery. Hughes directly references Lincoln's trip down the Mississippi to New Orleans, where

A Trio of Art Songs on Texts by Langston Hughes

Lincoln saw enslaved people being bought and sold to the highest bidder. In a recording of his reading of this poem, Hughes describes hearing his grandmother, daughter of a former enslaved person, explain that being "sold down the Mississippi" was the worst thing that could happen to an enslaved person.[3]

The river is also used as a metaphor for the protagonist's soul – a soul that, like a riverbed, has persisted through the ages and accrued much wisdom. The mood of the poem is one of pride and perseverance, an ode to the many ways in which people of the African diaspora have shaped, and in many cases literally built, the world's civilization and culture.

Twentieth-century composers Margaret Bonds and Howard Swanson were friends with Hughes and set many of his poems to music. Bonds was a student of Florence Price and studied at Northwestern University but had a difficult time at the school due to racism and segregation (Toppin 2021, 1). She never held a university position but composed and published music throughout her life. While a student at Northwestern, Bonds won a prestigious composition award for her art song "Sea Ghost" (now lost) and became the first African American pianist to perform with the Chicago Symphony Orchestra. It was also at Northwestern University that Bonds discovered Hughes's poem:

> I was in this prejudiced university, this terribly prejudiced place. . . . I was looking in the basement of the Evanston Public Library where they had the poetry. I came in contact with this wonderful poem, "The Negro Speaks of Rivers," and I'm sure it helped my feelings of security. Because in that poem he [Langston Hughes] tells how great the [B]lack man is. And if I had any misgivings, which I would have to have – here you are in a setup where the restaurants won't serve you and you're going to college, you're sacrificing, trying to get through school – and I know that poem helped save me.[4]

Students could either prepare for an in-class discussion of Bonds's 1942 setting by answering the following questions in advance, or the instructor could use these questions to guide discussion.

1. Listen to the song. Consider how Bonds's compositional vision compares to your own. What surprises you about her setting?
2. There is an ostinato in the piano part. Identify it, and write several paragraphs describing the ostinato and its relationship to the text, as well as the ways in which it changes throughout the song.
3. Where does the ostinato break? Why do you think this happens?
4. What is the form of the song? What musical elements create these divisions? Why do you think the composer chose this form for this text?
5. Is this song tonal or pitch-centric? Argue for your choice using musical evidence from specific score locations.
6. What musical techniques appear in this song that haven't been covered by the previous questions? Describe at least three, being sure to reference precise measure numbers.
7. Describe at least four ways in which text painting is used in this song. Consider not only literal text painting (like a trill for a poem's reference to a lark) but also the overall tone that the music sets for the poetry. Consider also what the overall musical ambience adds to the meaning of the poetry.

Bonds's setting is in D minor and uses an ABACA form (see Table 11.1). It features an ostinato throughout most of the piece that represents the river. In the piano, the indication "muddy bass" not only directs the pianist to embrace the murky turbidity of the bass line's repetitive low pitches (D_1–A_0) but also references the "muddy" Mississippi River, as

Table 11.1 Bonds, "The Negro Speaks of Rivers," Form Diagram

Section	Text	MMs	Key	Accompaniment	Melody
A	I've known rivers: I've known rivers ancient as the world and older than the flow of human blood in human veins. My soul has grown deep like the rivers.	1–21	D minor	Ostinato, with added-note chords and parallel triads (planing) in the right hand	Mostly pentatonic
B	I bathed in the Euphrates when dawns were young. I built my hut near the Congo and it lulled me to sleep.	21–30	D major	Reharmonized ostinato with shades of whole tone, mode mixture, and jazz harmonies (example: IV has whole-tone extensions, mm. 22, 24, 26; AMm♭13 in m. 29; ♭6 in m. 30)	D major, with chromatic pitches and mode mixture
A'	I looked upon the Nile and raised the pyramids above it.	31–50	D minor	Ostinato reharmonized, now with open 5ths and 4ths	Large leaps outlining Dm, depicting strength
C	I heard the singing of the Mississippi when Abe Lincoln went down to New Orleans, and I've seen its muddy bosom turn all golden in the sunset.	51–62	F major	Ostinato absent for the first time, although neighbor motion present (m. 51, F–G–F); score states "picked bass," a reference to the use of banjo in early ragtime music	Syncopated, ragtime style
A"	I've known rivers: Ancient, dusky rivers. My soul has grown deep like the rivers.	66–77	D minor	Similar to A section	Similar to A section

it has long been known to locals. The sections divide up the text according to geographic location. The A section (mm. 1–21) comprises the ostinato refrain that accompanies the text "I've known rivers." The melody is almost entirely pentatonic, a pitch collection often associated with African American musical idioms. The B section references the Euphrates and Congo Rivers and ushers in a lush D major version of the ostinato that evokes not only the fertility and growth created by the Euphrates's annual flooding, which enabled the establishment of early cities, but also the gentle lull of the Congo, by which the narrator chooses to build their hut (mm. 21–30).

The A' section reintroduces the D minor version of the ostinato, along with the description of the Nile and the pyramids (mm. 31–50), with an emphasis on open fourths and fifths in both the melody and the ostinato that embody the sense of strength and accomplishment in Hughes's poem. Large leaps and long notes in both the left hand of the piano and in the voice act as massive blocks of sound that call to mind the massive blocks of stone used in building the pyramids, as well as the incredible feats of strength required to heave them. In fact, the voice part in this section uses only the pitches of an ascending tonic triad in long notes, culminating in a downward leap of a minor tenth accompanying the text "raised the pyramids above it" – a very effective musical analog to slowly and laboriously hauling a huge stone up the side of a pyramid, then finally heaving it into place. The C section (mm. 51–62) introduces the key of F major and references the simplified bass line and syncopated rhythms associated with ragtime music to depict Lincoln's trip down the Mississippi; on the word "sunset," the music turns reflective, as a rolled B♭^{7} chord accompanies a recall of the original ostinato, and shortly thereafter, the final return of the opening material (A" section, mm. 66–77).

Students can then compare Bonds's 1942 setting with Howard Swanson's 1949 setting.[5] Like Bonds, Swanson never held a university position. Swanson worked for the US Postal Service after high school to support his family after his father passed away when Swanson was 17. He then earned degrees in composition and music theory from the Cleveland Institute of Music and received a fellowship to support composition study in Paris with distinguished composition teacher Nadia Boulanger, an enterprise that was cut short due to the German invasion of France in World War II. Swanson returned to the United States and began to work for the Internal Revenue Service, until he won a Guggenheim Fellowship in 1952 that allowed him to return to Paris, where he lived until 1966. His setting of "The Negro Speaks of Rivers" was performed by contralto Marian Anderson at Carnegie Hall in 1950, which launched his composition career. His *Short Symphony* was premiered by the New York Philharmonic later that year, to much acclaim (Southern 1995, 543–44).[6]

Swanson's ternary setting is in G minor; although the first simultaneity in the piano introduction is a DM^7 chord that sounds like a tonic, it gradually morphs into a dominant seventh chord over the course of the piano introduction's five measures. The A section, which sets the text "I've known rivers . . . Ancient as the world and older than the flow of human blood in human veins . . . My soul has grown deep like the rivers," features a persistent eighth-dotted quarter motive, which almost always sets the interval of a minor second. Repetitions of this motive combine to create an ostinato that repeats throughout the A section. (This ostinato is most clearly heard in the piano's melodic line; it almost functions like a lament bass, as it travels from F♯$_4$–G$_4$ down to $\hat{5}$ [D$_4$], then briefly down to $\hat{4}$ before repeating.) Like the ostinato in Bonds's setting, Swanson's ostinato serves as a musical analogue to the image of a deeply gorged riverbed, worn down through years of relentless repetition.

References to the blues abound in the A section, with melodic emphasis on most of the pitches in the G blues collection, in particular C–C♯–D, as well as vocal cadences that toggle between $\hat{1}$ and $\hat{3}$. Instructors should certainly grasp this opportunity to review the blues collection by singing and spelling it in the key of G. (The setting is not entirely blues-focused, however; the major caveat involves the raised leading tone, which is consistent throughout both A sections.) In addition, the harmonies of the A sections are almost all based on G, C, or D – the i, iv, and V in G minor, thus aligning the song with the blues from a harmonic standpoint as well. In terms of chord qualities, there are not only seventh, extended tertian, and added-note chords but also augmented triads and other whole tone-derived sonorities, all of which retain a measure of harmonic function that boils down to i, iv, or V. Students should be reminded that they should trust their ears and not their eyes when determining the chord roots of these complex, intense harmonies. Due to the pervasive half-step motive in the ostinato (and plenty of occurrences of the ostinato's main motive in the bass as well), some simultaneities are extremely dissonant.

The two-part B section, which sets all the text describing specific rivers, presents a stark contrast to the relentless rhythmic grind of the outer sections. The vocal part of B$_1$ (mm. 34–43) rises consistently throughout and is bounded by the pitches E♭$_4$ and E♭$_5$. Likewise, the piano part rises consistently, featuring ascending leaping gestures that connect blocked triads (most of which are major or minor, though there are a couple of augmented triads) and a quarter–eighth–eighth motive. While the harmonic succession might at first appear random (partially due to the constant register shifts), there are many instances of common tones between these harmonies. With its muscular rhythms and relentless ascending contours, this music evokes exertion, strength, and a sense of perseverance and achievement.

The B$_2$ section (mm. 44–55) sets the portion of the text that describes Lincoln's trip to New Orleans. It is improvisatory and clearly references jazz. For example, measure 52 emulates an improvised clarinet solo, while the piano's left hand plays parallel half-diminished seventh chords. The B section ends on a nostalgic G^{ø7}, setting the text's image of a golden setting sun.

The A section returns on a iv chord in G minor, as though the blues from the A section have been playing in the background throughout the B section, only to re-emerge in the middle of a chorus. This return on the subdominant certainly invites one to reflect on a narrative to support the feeling that the blues have been ongoing, and instructors should ask students why the blues resume on a iv chord, as if in the middle of a chorus. I will try to propose one possible narrative. In the A section, one might imagine the song's protagonist in the present tense, ruminating upon the rivers they have known in a general sense, while perhaps listening to the blues or even singing the blues themselves. While the blues continue to play, the protagonist is swept away by the collective memory of the various rivers in the B section, only to be nudged back to the present on the half-diminished seventh chord that sets "sunset." One imagines the protagonist becoming aware of their actual surroundings and rejoining the present tense and, mid-chorus, the blues. Once the blues have resumed, the music quickly crescendos, culminating in a dissonant fortissimo crash on the word "soul."[7]

Florence Price: "Songs to the Dark Virgin"

For the final exam, I distributed two compositions by Florence Price for students to study in advance. They were allowed to bring analyzed scores and as many notes as they wanted to the exam. This song, "Songs to a Dark Virgin," sets a poem by Hughes of the same name.

The poem was originally published in Hughes's collection *The Weary Blues* (1926):

I.

Would
That I were a jewel,
A shattered jewel,
That all my shining brilliants
Might fall at thy feet,
Thou dark one.

II.

Would
That I were a garment,
A shimmering, silken garment,
That all my folds
Might wrap about thy body,
Absorb thy body,
Hold and hide thy body,
Thou dark one.

III.

Would
That I were a flame,
But one sharp, leaping flame
To annihilate thy body,
Thou dark one.
      – Langston Hughes,
  "Songs to a Dark Virgin"

Because this analysis was for a final exam, I instructed students to read a brief analysis of the poem first, so that the focus of the exam could be on music analysis and song interpretation rather than poetic interpretation, but an instructor might use the same questions about "The Negro Speaks of Rivers" for this poem. The plural "songs" in the title "Songs to a Dark Virgin" refers to the three short poems that make up the larger poem, as delineated by the Roman numerals preceding each stanza. Aside from the adoration and sensuality that is obvious if one takes the poem at face value, it can also be read as a metaphor for the difficulty and alienation facing Black Americans in the early to mid-twentieth century.[8] Additionally, the fact that there are three "songs" could be read as three possible ways for a Black individual to make their way through, or position themselves in, White society. The fact that there are three songs in a single poem (instead of just three separate poems) could reflect the inner turmoil resulting from constantly having to work so hard to navigate the world as a Black individual.

I also provide the following excerpt from a letter Price wrote to Boston Symphony conductor Serge Koussevitzky in November 1943, just two years after composing "Songs to the Dark Virgin," in which she tried to convince him to look at one of her scores. This excerpt demonstrates her frustration with being both Black and a woman in American society in the mid-twentieth century, especially when one realizes that this was the fourth such letter she had written to Koussevitzky (the first was in 1935):

> Unfortunately the work of a woman composer is preconceived by many to be light, frothy, lacking in depth, logic and virility. Add to that the incident of race – I have Colored blood in my veins – and you will understand some of the difficulties that confront one in such a position. . . .
>
> I ask no concessions because of my race or sex, and am willing to abide by a decision based solely on [the] worth of my work.[9]

Price's setting, also titled "Songs to the Dark Virgin," is the second of four songs in Price's 1941 song cycle *Four Songs from the Weary Blues*, named for Hughes's 1926 poetry collection *The Weary Blues*.[10] "Songs to the Dark Virgin" is dedicated to her daughter, Florence. In contrast with the poem by itself, Price's interpretation takes on a protective tone, befitting a mother's concern for a daughter who will inherit the same racist and sexist world that Price referenced in her letter to Koussevitzky. In my reading of Price's setting, the narrator is a mother figure who occupies the various physical objects in the poem (a jewel who worships her; a garment that wraps, absorbs, holds, and hides her; and finally, a flame that annihilates her). Each stanza of this modified strophic form begins similarly but develops in a unique fashion based on its text.[11] The modified strophic form highlights, rather than conceals, the asymmetry in length, tone, and meaning among the poem's three stanzas.

Stunning examples of text painting abound, as do more generalized musical reflections of Price's interpretation of the poem's dramatic situation. The song begins with a tender, almost-nurturing A♭ harmony with added sixth that students could mistakenly analyze as an Fm$^4_2$ chord, especially if they do not realize that the second measure introduces an A♭$_1$ below it that clarifies measure 1's ambiguous harmony.[12] (There are several opportunities for such misreadings, which are wonderful fodder for reminding students of the difference between chord spelling and function – measures 11 and 15–17, for example, each contain a dominant chord with a sixth substituted for the fifth, which thus might be erroneously analyzed as iii^6 instead of V.) The song is characterized throughout by descending sixteenth-note arpeggios that evoke warm embraces. In the first strophe, this pattern pauses only in measure 5, with the words "Might fall at thy feet," in preparation for the cadence and transition to strophe 2.

In the second strophe, the reference to a garment whose folds wrap around the poetic object's body is accompanied by a "draping" motive in the vocal part. In measure 11, the vocal line drops down a fourth and resolves up by step on the text "wrap around thy body"; this motive is then sequenced in measure 12 on the text "Absorb thy body," as though the melody itself is shrouding the body. These motives culminate with a larger leap down a perfect fifth, followed by a step *downward* on the word "hide" in measures 13–14. In all these measures, the words "thy body" are metrically and durationally de-emphasized, appearing in the last three eighth notes of each measure, as though the music is literally trying to hide, and protect, the poetic object's body. Additionally, the descending arpeggio pattern that has been nearly consistent since the song's opening disappears beginning in measure 12, thus further setting these measures apart. The harmony as well points toward the climactic nature of these measures; in contrast with the wholly diatonic landscape of the first strophe, the middle of the second strophe emphasizes several chromatic harmonies. In measure 13, the word "hold" is accompanied by an arpeggiated fortissimo B♭^{9} harmony. This B♭^{9} harmony is followed not by a dominant in the key of A♭, as one might expect, but instead by a harmonically distant G♭^{9} sonority on the word "hide," as though the music itself were seeking a remote refuge in which to conceal itself. The words "Thou dark one" at the end of the second stanza both rhythmically augment and reverse the order of the draping motive from measures 11 and 12, and the stanza ends harmonically open on a lingering four-measure dominant.

Strophe 3 returns to the diatonic framework of strophe 1. None of the desperate chromaticism or texture changes from strophe 2 appear here, despite the powerful word "annihilate." There is much that can be read into this; I hear a sense of resignation in the third strophe, a recognition that all the attempts to protect and hide the poetic object in strophe 2 are really powerless against the world. Strophe 3 seems to realize that there is no choice but to allow the world to do what it will, and hope and pray for the best.

From a pedagogical perspective, the important thing is that students engage deeply with both the poem and the song and try to come up with meaningful insights. The song is quite brief – only 30 measures – and while there are a few challenging harmonies, most are relatively straightforward, and the form is not difficult.

Conclusion

Teaching the music of these and other Black composers has not only expanded the diversity of the music I teach but has also greatly enriched my experience as instructor, and I know, from their comments in class, that it has certainly enriched my students' experiences.

That said, curricular change takes time, and I am not, and hopefully will never be, finished evolving. I will continue to work toward a broader vision of what a class with the title "Form and Analysis" should include. Just reading the title of the course makes me ask, "Form and analysis of which music? Form and analysis of whose music?" And so, in the future, I hope to broach other genres like popular music and jazz in Form and Analysis, if it is possible to do so in a way that does not tokenize these other genres. I want to go beyond what Robin Attas has called the "plug and play" approach (Attas 2019) – taking a broader view of what musical form is, and can be, both within and outside of the western tonal canon. A future version of this course might include more categories of formal types: a unit on improvised genres, for example, would allow for inclusion of jazz, gospel, and possibly non-western music, and the unit on song could be expanded to include jazz standards and popular songs.

As a scholar and teacher who was fully trained in the White western art music tradition, I feel it is incumbent upon me to fill in the gaps in my training instead of allowing my training to limit what I teach, to push myself to learn new music and new approaches that will benefit my students, who are themselves diverse and who live in a diverse world, instead of taking the easier path of teaching what I was taught, and, therefore, to do my best to ensure that the same tacit messages of White supremacy are not passed along to my own students.

Notes

1. "The Negro Speaks of Rivers" was originally published in 1921, in the magazine *The Crisis*.
2. The assignment (available on the Supplemental Materials website) includes a hyperlink to a website with information about Bonds's life.
3. A link to this recording of Hughes is available on the Supplementary Materials website. For more on the meaning of "sold down the river," see Gandhi (2014).
4. Margaret Bonds, from a 1971 interview with James V. Hatch. Cited in Kilgore 2013.
5. Questions for this song have been posted to the Supplemental Materials website to save space and, like the questions about Bonds's settings, could be adapted for an assignment or used by the instructor to guide class discussion.
6. *Short Symphony*, premiered by conductor Dmitri Mitropoulos and the New York Philharmonic on November 23, 1950, won the Music Critics Award for best new orchestral work of the previous season. Competitors for the award included Arthur Honegger's Fifth Symphony and William Schuman's Sixth Symphony, among others (Reisser 1989, 10).
7. With all its parallel voice leading, ostinati, extended harmonies, and the references to the blues, combined with the leading tones and major dominants associated with tonal function, Swanson's "The Negro Speaks of Rivers" would make an excellent pairing with music by Debussy and/or Bartók in a post-1900 unit or course.
8. Penelope Peters (1995, 80–81) provides two relatively succinct readings of the poem, which I will not reproduce here due to length but which I encourage readers to look up for themselves before teaching this song. A link is provided on the Supplemental Materials website.
9. See Brown (2020, 187). Price did receive a note from his office telling her that if she sent in a score, he would consider her work (never mind the fact that she had already sent some copies of her work, which were very expensive to make at that time, back in 1935, when she first wrote to him!). However, she never received any other correspondence, and he never performed any of her works, although he did perform works of many other American composers and even commissioned new American pieces (Brown 2020, 188).
10. Leigh VanHandel discusses the first song of this cycle, "My Dream," in Chapter 19 of this volume.
11. Peters draws parallels between the melodic style of "Songs to the Dark Virgin" and the melodic style of plantation songs, the characteristics of which she defines earlier in her essay using "Sometimes I Feel Like a Motherless Chile" as an example. "Each vocal phrase ends with a sustained pitch, the altered and sustained pitches within the phrases accompany expressive words in the text ('hold,' 'hide,' 'flame,' 'annihilate,' etc.), the text-setting is syllabic, and there are three short varied strophes" (1995, 81).
12. Peters reads the voicing of the initially harmonically ambiguous A♭add6 sonority as a musical analog to the dual interpretations she cites in the poem (1995, 81).

Works Cited

Attas, Robin. 2019. "Music Theory as Social Justice: Pedagogical Applications of Kendrick Lamar's *To Pimp A Butterfly*." *Music Theory Online* 25/1.

Bonds, Margaret. 2021. "The Negro Speaks of Rivers." In *Rediscovering Margaret Bonds: Art Songs, Spirituals, Musical Theatre and Popular Songs*, edited by Louise Toppin, 100–07. Classical Vocal Reprints.

Brown, Rae Linda. 2020. *The Heart of a Woman: The Life and Music of Florence B. Price*. University of Illinois Press.

Gandhi, Lakshmi. 2014. "What Does 'Sold Down The River' Really Mean? The Answer Isn't Pretty." NPR Code Switch. www.npr.org/sections/codeswitch/2014/01/27/265421504/what-does-sold-down-the-river-really-mean-the-answer-isnt-pretty. Last accessed February 5, 2021.

Hughes, Langston. 1994. *The Collected Poems of Langston Hughes*. Edited by A. Rampersad and D. Roessel. Vintage Press.

Kilgore, Alethea N. 2013. "The Life and Solo Vocal Works of Margaret Allison Bonds (1913–1972)." Ph.D. diss., Florida State University.

Peters, Penelope. 1995. "Deep Rivers: Selected Songs of Florence Price and Margaret Bonds." *Canadian University Music Review* 16/1: 74–95.

Price, Florence. 1984. "Songs to the Dark Virgin." In *Anthology of Art Songs by Black American Composers*, compiled by Willis C. Patterson, 98–101. Edward & Marks Music Company.

Reisser, Marsha J. 1989. "Howard Swanson: Distinguished Composer." *The Black Perspective in Music* 17: 5–26.

Southern, Eileein. 1997. *The Music of Black Americans: A History*, 3rd edition. W.W. Norton.

Swanson, Howard. 1984. "The Negro Speaks of Rivers." In *Anthology of Art Songs by Black American Composers*, compiled by Willis C. Patterson, 77–81. Edward & Marks Music Company.

Toppin, Louise. 2021. "Editor's Note." In *Rediscovering Margaret Bonds: Art Songs, Spirituals, Musical Theatre and Popular Songs*, 2–5. Classical Vocal Reprints.

12 Teaching Sonatas Beyond "Mostly Mozart"

Aaron Grant and Catrina Kim

Two decades ago, William Caplin's *Classical Form* (1998) and James Hepokoski and Warren Darcy's *Elements of Sonata Theory* (2006) sparked a renaissance of theories of musical form. The last decade, in particular, has seen this "new *Formenlehre*" movement reach a new maturity. Recent research has expanded the purview of sonata form research to include non-canonic composers, both within the Viennese classical style and outside it, and new time periods and geographical regions[1] – in other words, beyond *Formenlehre*'s "Mostly Mozart" repertoire.[2] Moreover, nearly all major textbooks teach concepts from these theories, such as the medial caesura, pre-core, and core.[3] Beyond textbooks, pedagogical scholarship routinely incorporates current *Formenlehre* research (Monahan 2011a; Richards 2012; Alegant 2008).

Despite these changes, the repertoire of sonata form pedagogy remains impoverished: Wolfgang Amadeus Mozart, Joseph Haydn, and Ludwig van Beethoven wrote an astonishing 84% (27 out of 32) of sonata form examples in three current leading textbooks, suggesting that student learning centers only on the sonata form practices of three White male composers from Germany and Austria, all writing music around the same time (ca. 1780–1810).[4] The motivations for this homogeneity seem clear from both theoretical and pedagogical perspectives. Theoretically limiting the corpus to three geographically, stylistically, and chronologically linked composers produces a more consistent set of norms, which in turn enables clear learning outcomes within the typical sonata form unit.

Yet this consistency comes at a cost. Poundie Burstein (2020), for one, notes that focusing on too few composers distorts one's understanding of history and style.[5] In other words, teaching sonata forms by only three composers gives our students a skewed view of what a "normal" sonata is and the impression that the music of all non-canonical composers is somehow "odd." Furthermore, only studying the works of cisgender White men continues to reify what Philip Ewell (2020) calls music theory's "White racial frame." Students' perception of this value system can marginalize students, the majority of whom are not White *and* male. To tie both points together, whose norms are we teaching and why?

This question also raises a final critique of current approaches to teaching sonata forms. One of the principal learning outcomes of most sonata form units is to ask students to internalize the sonata form norms of the "high-classical style."[6] Given that most sonata form units last only two weeks, can any student truly be expected to gain mastery of these norms? Indeed, Seth Monahan specifically notes that acquiring such norms requires significant time, suggesting four to six weeks minimum (2011a, 80–81). As *scholars* of form ourselves, we sympathize with this goal. Internalizing norms allows thought-provoking hermeneutic enterprises to emerge that help move the classroom beyond mere labeling. Yet as both *students* and *teachers* of form, we have found it next

DOI: 10.4324/9781003204053-16

to impossible to implement in a typical three- or four-semester curriculum. Two weeks is simply not enough time to develop a sophisticated understanding of the sonata form norms of three distinct composers, even with their stylistic similarities.

Our chapter responds to these problems by offering a two-week unit on sonata form suitable for an undergraduate core theory course or graduate review that focuses on works by a more diverse set of composers: Guadeloupe-born French composer Joseph Bologne (1745–1799), Afro-British composer Samuel Coleridge-Taylor (1875–1912), and African American composer Florence Price (1887–1953). In contrast to other approaches, we focus specifically on four pieces and take what Kris Shaffer (2013) calls an inquiry-based learning approach.[7] Our unit has the following learning outcomes:

1. Recognize how the distinct logics of small-scale and large-scale forms interact.
2. Gain a preliminary understanding of dialogic form and how sonata form norms are created and interact with each other.
3. Understand how large-scale formal deviations can link to hermeneutic interpretations.
4. Apply modern approaches to analyzing sonata forms.
5. Acquire the foundational analytical framework, tools, and questions for future study of sonata and other large-scale forms.
6. Optional: obtain tools to begin a lifelong journey of internalizing sonata form norms.

We offer four lesson plans that can be implemented directly as a sonata form unit. Each lesson plan takes roughly 80 minutes to implement, allowing for coverage of up to two movements per week. Instructors should do each lesson plan in order, but our approach is flexible. If the instructor can only spend three 80-minute lessons on sonata form, we recommend skipping either the second Bologne example or the Coleridge-Taylor movement. Similarly, if an instructor has three weeks to devote to sonata forms, these lesson plans can be expanded so that students gain an even more detailed understanding of these rich works and their contexts.

Lesson 1: Joseph Bologne's String Quartet op. 1, no. 1/i (1773)

Overview

We feel strongly that a student's first classroom experience with sonata forms should focus on diving headfirst into the music. However, such situations require pieces that balance pedagogical clarity with captivating music. The first movement of Bologne's first string quartet is fairly straightforward. The exposition (mm. 1–42) has a periodic primary theme (P); energetic, modulatory transition (TR); lyrical secondary theme (S); and clear EEC. Similarly, the development (mm. 43–67) and recapitulation (mm. 68–72) are clearly delineated.[8]

However, some parts may still be difficult for students. In particular, the many cadential evasions within S make for a doable challenge in terms of understanding both the phrase structure and boundaries of the action space. As shown in the annotated score, one may interpret the S-space's phrase structure in multiple ways: (1) as an unusual large-scale sentence with multiple sentential continuations;[9] (2) as a period-like structure (mm. 18–25) followed by two continuations, creating a hybrid-like S-theme;[10] or (3) as not following typical classical norms.[11] The ambiguity surrounding S-space can engender profitable discussions about not only how to parse a movement but also the drama that can occur within a sonata form.

Pre-Class Preparation

- Read either a textbook overview or handout that introduces different parts of a sonata form. We use formative testing to allow students to reinforce their understanding as well;[12] while this is encouraged, it is not strictly necessary.
- Students should listen to the entire movement several times, marking any cadences.
- We encourage students to try applying the labels they just learned to this piece. This is optional, but some will try.

Lesson Plan

A Brief Overview of Sonata Form Terminology (15 Min.)

Given the prep work, the class can use Bologne's op. 1, no. 1/i to reinforce the readings. We find it helpful to move from broad to specific. As such, focus the first half of class on the three main portions of the sonata (exposition, development, and recapitulation) and their formal functions. The initial discussion should move quickly, given the preparatory readings. We begin by reviewing the definitions in the abstract but move to encouraging students to apply these definitions to op. 1, no. 1/i together through class discussion as early as possible. This initial foray into analysis tends to focus on how to look for formal markers, like repeat signs and repetition of initial thematic material, that can help students scan a movement and parse it quickly. However, we like to reinforce the textbook definitions with real-life music. This approach allows us to explore questions such as why the development sounds like a development, what makes a recapitulation distinct from an exposition, and how each area expresses a particular temporal function.

An Exposition Deep Dive (35 Min.)

The remaining class time should focus on the exposition. Like the previous section, we begin by reviewing characteristics of each section, but such discussions should only last five to ten minutes. Most of class time should be spent with students in groups applying labels to the exposition. In our experience, this goes quickly. Once complete, students post their analyses to the class discussion board so that we can compare interpretations, debate the merits of each, and come to a consensus about where and why we should apply each label.

Students tend to be confused about where S-space begins. For example, our students were split about whether the MC was at measure 17 or measure 25, given the clear caesura that occurs following both cadences. This particular mix-up, though, allows for a discussion about how we should rely on more than one parameter when analyzing form.

Cadence Games (30 Min.)

We often conclude class by focusing on S-space, because this provides us with the opportunity to devote a large portion of class to the important question of *why* labels matter. One way to do that is to discuss the types of cadence games that composers can play within expositions to play on expectations.

Begin by re-emphasizing how the entire exposition can lead toward an eventual PAC within S-space. It can be helpful to use an analogy to current popular music. Most students intuitively understand how prechoruses lead to choruses. Play a song with a prechorus, stop before the chorus begins, and ask what they expect to come next, prior experiences lead them to expect a chorus, even if they don't know the song. This demonstration illustrates how one can build innate expectations through listening and how, once we listen to enough sonatas, we expect S-space to accomplish a PAC in the dominant or mediant after an MC occurs. Composers can play on those expectations in a multitude of ways.

Many cadential evasions throughout Bologne's S-space shape the drama of the piece. Yet it is not always obvious where cadences – particularly EECs – *could* have happened. As such, students try to find every evasion they can in small groups. We then discuss as a class to summarize our findings. Finally, we listen again to bring that drama to life.

Lesson 2: Bologne's String Quartet op. 1, no. 5/i (1773)

Overview

This movement's large-scale rotational structure is fairly clear, with a two-part exposition and a corresponding recapitulation, but it also poses some new and engaging challenges. In particular, there are several features requiring more sustained attention and interpretation than op. 1, no. 1/i. These features include several EEC deferrals, recapitulatory cuts, and a reference to the composer's own op. 1, no. 4/i in the development.[13]

Students will be familiar with EEC deferral, given the first lesson's focus on S-space in Bologne's op. 1, no. 1/i. As shown in the annotated score, S (mm. 19–33) exhibits an internal sentential structure. A potential III: IAC (m. 27) elides with a second continuation.[14] This second continuation itself leads to a "one-more time" technique (mm. 30–33), leading, finally, to a III: PAC EEC (m. 33). A light codetta-like C-theme follows (mm. 33–37).

Discussion of the recapitulatory cuts in TR and S offers the chance to discuss common sonata form issues at stake at the level of the movement, in addition to phrase- or exposition-level formal considerations. For example, the post-MC recapitulatory cuts should also be discussed in tandem with the expositional EEC deferrals. Comparison of the expositional and recapitulatory S-themes may stimulate discussion about retrospective reinterpretation of the expositional S's formal structure, compositional processes, and hermeneutic interpretations of the entire movement.

The development begins with P-based material in the relative major, features a dramatic cadential evasion with modal mixture (m. 45), and drives toward an MC-like gesture (mm. 52–54). After the caesura, a statement of P from Bologne's op. 1, no. 4 begins a modulatory section that gives way to the retransitional V and caesura at measure 73. The developmental drama is marked by cadential punctuation, modal mixture, and the intertextual reference to the fourth string quartet.

Pre-Class Preparation

- Listen to the movement several times and mark all cadences.
- Apply theme labels to the exposition. The instructor might offer extra guidance, depending on the textbook or handouts used, student ability, and time constraints. In op. 1, no. 5/i, the exposition's TR immediately begins in the relative major in measure 9; this TR's lack of modulation differs from many textbook examples and definitions. As such, it may be helpful to prepare students for this possibility.
- Track correspondences between the exposition and recapitulation by writing in correspondence measures.[15] Apply theme labels to the recapitulation, and note divergences from the exposition. We suggest asking students to have two copies of the score available: one for taking notes, and one for reference.
- Mark expositional themes or entirely new themes in the development.

Lesson Plan

Having parsed op. 1, no. 5/i on their own, students will be equipped to discuss the movement in depth. In our first lesson, students mainly focus on the exposition. This second lesson reinforces the first by reviewing expositional norms using op. 1, no. 5/i, followed by a discussion of the development. It concludes by analyzing the recapitulation. This class, therefore, suggests several ways of thinking about sonata narratives on the level of the movement.

The follow-up assignment builds on in-class work by revisiting op. 1, no. 1/i and applying their skills to its development and recapitulation. Our goals are for students to gain fluency with the nuances of expositional analysis, to practice analysis of a development and recapitulation in a somewhat-familiar work, and to recognize the hermeneutic potential of sonata form analysis.

Reviewing the Exposition (30 Min.)

In small groups, students discuss the themes and cadences of the exposition and put their agreed-upon answers on the board. While P is straightforward, TR requires more discussion. First, students may need guidance on how to group "caesura-fill" material (see previous discussion of MC placement in op. 1, no. 1/i). For example, a downbeat i: PAC (m. 8) is followed by three beats of parallel thirds, which bridge the gap to the onset of TR (m. 9). It is worth discussing how this bridging function might allow the material to be grouped either with P or with TR.[16] Second, the nested sentential 1 + 1 + 2 phrases within TR are both indicative of Bologne's style and a method for TR's characteristic "energy gain." And third, the modal mixture (mm. 15–18) is a common characteristic in dominant pedals.

S also merits separate discussion. Students have identified cadential evasions in op. 1, no. 1/i, so this activity will build on the first lesson. We ask students to analyze S and diagram the small-scale formal structure. Review as a class and discuss.

Development (20 Min.)

We begin the next section by listening to the development once together. Then, we ask students to take five minutes to compare notes – based on their preparation – with their groups: What expositional themes did you identify? Were there any new melodies? What are the main developmental sections? Many students will have noticed that the development begins with P in the relative major (a highly normative choice), and they will likely identify boundaries at measure 45, measure 54, measure 73, possibly measure 64, and the dominant arrival at measure 69. In addition to these points, large-group discussion of the previous might include:

- Measure 45 marks a boundary where a cadence is evaded. Note the mixture in measure 46, which prepares the modulation to F minor. This inaugurates a section that contrasts melodically and rhythmically with the development's opening.
- The caesura in measure 54 paves the way for A♭ major! This section starts with the primary theme from op. 1, no. 4 – what is called an "intertextual" reference. Note that mixture again occurs for dramatic effect at measure 57. It also initiates more harmonic adventuring (like the mixture at m. 46!) toward C minor.

Overall, this discussion can reinforce an understanding of the development in three main sections, following Burstein and Straus (2020): (1) a harmonically and thematically stable section, which leads into (2) a less stable section featuring modulation, sequences, and mixture, before the (3) retransition, which typically concludes with the dominant to prepare the recapitulation. We encourage a final hearing of the development, with some minimal commentary to make these points audible.

Recapitulation (30 Min.)

We begin the final section of class by surveying student observations regarding the recapitulation. They have likely noticed that the transition and secondary theme have been rewritten. As a group, review the correspondence measures. Then, have students discuss the following questions in small groups: What are the effects of these cuts to TR and S? How do you experience these sections differently in the recapitulation, compared to the exposition? What might motivate these changes?

It may be worth relistening to the exposition and recapitulation before discussion. It may also be helpful to use a Padlet for groups to post answers, or ask groups to report at least two answers to each question.

Once most groups have generated enough answers, reconvene for discussion. Answers will vary, but responses may include:

- S in the exposition had many delays, and the recapitulation's S gives the sense of bringing us more swiftly to a conclusion.
- Bologne might have changed the recapitulation to create variety in such a short piece.
- Bologne may have made the recapitulation as concise as possible to add more propulsion toward the ESC, hence the shortened TR and eliminated delays in S.
- The recapitulation provides a retrospective clarifying effect; there is now no question about where ESC should be placed – unlike the EEC.

This last point is particularly important. We encourage the instructor to emphasize that compositional changes in the recapitulation always beg comparison with the exposition and a consideration of the movement's trajectory as a whole. In this case, the relative brevity of the recapitulation evokes the possibility of form-functional clarification or transformation.

Homework – *Due Week 2, Class 1*

Due to its length, this assignment works best as a weekend assignment posted on an LMS discussion thread. We recommend adjusting settings so that students cannot view classmates' responses until they have posted first. It should take about two hours for most students to complete. This assignment synthesizes their learning from week 1 and also serves as a springboard for class 3.

1. (Target: 2–3 paragraphs.) What compositional strategies are shared between the expositions of op. 1, no. 5/i and op. 1, no. 1/i? What is different? For example: cadences as formal markers; modulation and modal mixture; and contrasts in texture, melody, rhythm, articulation, and dynamics.
2. (Target: 2–3 paragraphs.) Revisit op. 1, no. 1/i, the movement discussed in our first lesson on sonatas. Write correspondence measures in the recapitulation, add in theme labels, and parse the development. Then answer the following questions:

    a. What expositional themes occur in the development?
    b. How does the recapitulation diverge from the plan laid out by the exposition? What narratives or motivations might there be for these changes? Don't hesitate to reference the development if it presents evidence for a large-scale narrative.

Lesson 3: Florence Price's Symphony no. 1, mvt. 1 (1932)

Overview

The previous lessons focused on relatively straightforward movements. Yet few sonata forms are so clear-cut. While this may seem like a problem, we embrace the situation, because deviations from conventional norms offer excellent opportunities to expose undergraduate students to hermeneutic analysis. The first movement of Florence Price's Symphony no. 1 offers a perfect example. As shown in the form chart (Figure 12.1), the exposition, though expansive, is relatively uncomplicated, with a few tricky moments. Following a six-measure introduction, the small-ternary primary theme stretches through measure 41, where it melts into the transition with no cadence but a clear textural shift. The modulating TR continues for 39 measures, concluding with a III: PAC MC (m. 70). Of interest here is the seeming de-energization of TR following a blocked MC (m. 60) – a clear departure from the classical style seen in Bologne, but part of a nineteenth-century tradition of de-energizing transitions (Hepokoski and Darcy 2006, 116).

S-space includes three other tricky moments. For one, while it begins in the expected key of G major, the entire action space counter-generically waffles between G major and E minor (the original tonic).[17] The exposition's conclusion complicates matters further. Measure 105 offers a clear sense of departure from the profoundly lyrical S-space. However, two things make this moment challenging: (1) measure 105 ends in the original tonic, and (2) S-space concludes on a second-inversion I chord – not much of an EEC. Finally, the post-"EEC" music can be considered closing but also has a somewhat-retransitional feel, offering up the possibility of an exposition with no C. These moments are made more approachable given the texturally and thematically clear action-space boundaries. As such, they are worthy of discussion and a challenging but approachable step-up in difficulty from sonatas. Moreover, it provides an opportunity to address interesting questions of narrative and convention.

These questions only intensify as the movement progresses. The massive development (mm. 117–230) ends with a dominant lock (m. 223). This section, roughly the same size as the exposition, suggests an equally long recapitulation. However, the 114-measure-long development is answered by a 53-measure-long recapitulation: less than half the length of the exposition. Adding to the confusion is the thematic material that comprises the recapitulation. Varied P motives saturate the recapitulation, making no attempt at S and leading directly into a P-based coda (m. 284). The recapitulation is a clear departure from anything seen in the previous lessons. But like the exposition, these moments offer opportunities for students to tackle meaningful questions. Rather than trying to pinpoint the exact moment of EEC, they can ask *why* a composer might choose to drastically break from conventional norms and thus experience the power of formal analysis in shaping their hearing.

Pre-Class Preparation

Because students will be completing a lengthy homework assignment prior to this class, prep work for this third lesson will be rather minimal. As such, we recommend that students:

- Come to class having listened several times to the movement.
- Mark where the exposition, development, and recapitulation begin.

136 *Aaron Grant and Catrina Kim*

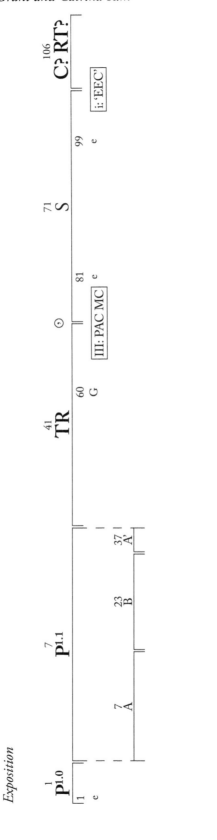

Figure 12.1 Price, Symphony no. 1 in E minor (exposition and recapitulation).

Lesson Plan

The lack of preparation necessitates a more instructor-led class than previous lessons. That, however, can be a benefit to students. We suggest structuring the class as a masterclass in top-down analysis. Students will have begun this process by listening and marking large-scale sections; the rest of class can clarify the rest of the movement. Given the confines of an 80-minute class, this lesson will focus on the exposition and recapitulation, as they present some of the most intriguing formal questions.

Context *(10 Min.)*

We first historically contextualize this work. Many students will not have looked up the date or location of this composition, and those who have may not understand the significance of looking at a sonata form written over a hundred years after the Bologne works from the previous week. As such, a brief summary of the symphony's context is in order, as is a brief discussion of dialogic form. In particular, we focus on the following questions: What is dialogic form, and how are forms disseminated? How should questions about form change for post-classical sonata forms? What other factors impact the norms against which we measure this form?[18]

Exposition *(40 Min.)*

With that context in mind, we analyze the exposition together from the top down, starting with the exposition boundaries. Then, we listen twice to the exposition to find the first cadential goal: the MC.[19] We ask them to mark, while listening, large cadences, textural shifts, new themes, and especially key changes. The ensuing back-and-forth demonstrates that what makes the MC so special is the confluence of factors that tend to occur at that moment.

We then analyze P/TR and S, focusing on parsing the tricky spots previously mentioned. P/TR may not pose too much of a struggle. Rather, students may need to listen on a larger scale than previously encountered. Worth pointing out is the way in which the B section of the small ternary can feel almost like TR in the moment, allowing you to discuss the distinction between diachronic (processual) and synchronic (bird's-eye view) modes of listening.

By contrast, students probably need guidance through the S-space, both in terms of parsing its structure and the ensuing narratives. We first foreground the uniqueness of this action zone and ask students how it diverges from both Bologne's S-spaces and the textbook definition. Among other things, they should notice the move toward other keys within S and the lack of a clear EEC. Discussion should, therefore, focus on the ways in which this piece does and does not follow the norms we set up last week and norms for the time. Some guidance will be necessary for the latter. For instance, instructors might point out that moving to tonic within S-space does occur in music of romantic composers like Franz Schubert (Grant 2018, 54 and 2022, 13), and that Gustav Mahler often leaves symphonic expositions formally open (Monahan 2011b). Yet these precedents do not stop these moments from conveying profoundly expressive narrative implications of tragedy and failure in light of classical norms.[20] For instance, the move back to the original tonic within S is so counter-generic that it at least invokes a sense of trying to turn back the clock – the piece is so tonic- and P-centric that it fights against the typical journey from tonic to dominant or mediant – and at most suggests a narrative in which the piece is trying to break down the entire premise of a sonata and its norms altogether. Both narratives are strengthened by the other two oddities of post-MC material. The lackluster tonic "EEC" certainly bolsters both views, and the retransition-like C-material implies a rushing to get back to P-material with the repeat sign or development.

The instructor may fruitfully link this narrative to Price's pursuit of a compositional career in a world that was generally uninviting to both Black and female artists. To this end, we suggest having students read a letter Price wrote to the conductor of the Boston Symphony, Serge Koussevitzky, accompanied by Rae Linda Brown's analysis of the same:

Letter from Price to Koussevitzky, and analysis by Rae Linda Brown[21]

My dear Dr. Koussevitzky,

To begin with I have two handicaps – those of sex and race. I am a woman; and I have some Negro blood in my veins.

Knowing the worst, then, would you be good enough to hold in check the possible inclination to regard a woman's composition as long on emotionalism but short on virility and thought content; – until you shall have examined some of my work?

As to the handicap of race, may I relieve you by saying that I neither expect nor ask any concession on that score. I should like to be judged on merit alone – the great trouble having been to get conductors, who know nothing of my work (I am practically unknown in the East, except perhaps as the composer of two songs, one or the other of which Marian Anderson includes on most of her programs) to even consent to examine a score.

I confess that I am woefully lacking in the hardihood of aggression; that writing this letter to you is the result of having successfully done battle with a hounding timidity. Having been born in the South and having spent most of my childhood there I believe I can truthfully say that I understand the real Negro music. In some of my work I make use of the idiom undiluted. Again, at other times it merely flavors my themes. And at still other times thoughts come in the garb of the other side of my mixed racial background. I have tried for practical purposes to cultivate and preserve a facility of expression in both idioms, altho I have an unwavering and compelling faith that a national music very beautiful and very American can come from the melting pot just as the nation itself has done.

Will you examine one of my scores?

Yours very sincerely,

[signed] (Mrs.) Florence B. Price

The letter is a masterpiece of economy, decorum, and, in its way, authority. Price tackles the issues of gender and race up-front by mentioning, then dismissing, them. She invites Koussevitzky to set aside prejudice and judge her work on its merits. In this approach, she reveals her understanding of what she is up against. And she ends her letter with a deeply personal statement, touching on her own character and personal history, the place of "Negro music" in her work, and her firm belief ("unwavering and compelling faith") that she has been a participant in Koussevitzky's own quest to support American composers in their search for a national identity in music. Price's letters to Koussevitzky spanned nine years (1935–44). In October 1944 Koussevitzky did look at one of her scores, but no performances resulted from Price's efforts.

This letter provides a valuable snapshot of how the composer advocated for her work to be performed, against the currents of sexism and racism. Brown draws out Price's strategic acknowledgment of both, which evocatively displays the type of fighting and maneuvering Price had to do to get her music performed or even looked at during her time, due to issues of sex and race. How might our narrative, that this sonata is intent on destroying previously held sonata norms, be impacted by this letter?

Recapitulation *(25 Min.)*

Such narratives make perfect starting points for discussion of the recapitulation. We ask students where they placed the recapitulation and why, and then listen to it twice. While listening, we ask them to track how the recapitulation does or does not correspond with the exposition. What themes do they hear? Anything newly composed? Discussion will reveal that only the primary theme is heard, and just as problematically, the entire recapitulation is significantly shorter than expected.

Yet noticing this unique feature of the exposition is only half the story. We divide the class into groups and ask them to consider either how the recapitulation furthers the narratives discussed in the exposition or to propose another explanation as to why Price decided to make such a stunning formal decision in her recapitulation.

Lesson 4: Samuel Coleridge-Taylor's Violin Sonata, Finale (1898)

Overview

Coleridge-Taylor's violin sonata finale presents an ideal mixture of challenge and familiarity for the student at the end of a sonata form unit, featuring multiple blurred boundaries, attenuated cadences, EEC deferral, and sonata failure. After the Bologne and Price movements, students are sufficiently prepared to discuss these issues and to construct compelling, evidence-based narratives about this movement.

Within the exposition and recapitulation, the boundaries of P, TR, and S are clear (Figure 12.2).[22] However, the "winding-up" opening deserves comment: an open-fifth violin vamp is joined by a short ascending piano motive. It repeats twice, and the second repetition becomes the basis of the primary theme.[23] P is sentential, with an attenuated cadence in measure 8, and after a fragmentary codetta, it almost exactly repeats with differing orchestration.[24] TR begins like a repeat of P before dissolving via modulating repetitions of the presentation phrase: to C major, E major, and finally, the target key of A minor.

S-space is in three parts, all based upon the first sentential theme (mm. 31–38) (Figure 12.3). The continuation (mm. 33–38) initially articulates a potential v: HC (m. 34) but only truly achieves closure with a v: PAC (m. 37). While this is a clear EEC candidate, students should recognize that the dissolving repetition of the theme at measure 39 reopens and defers structural closure. The more literal repeat at measure 48 brings about the EEC at measure 54.

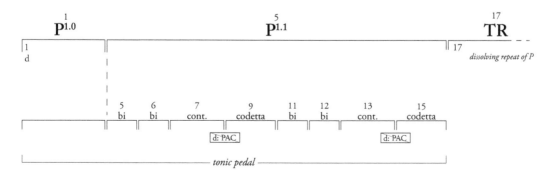

Figure 12.2 Samuel Coleridge-Taylor, Violin Sonata, op. 28, iii. *Poco meno mosso*, expositional P.

140 *Aaron Grant and Catrina Kim*

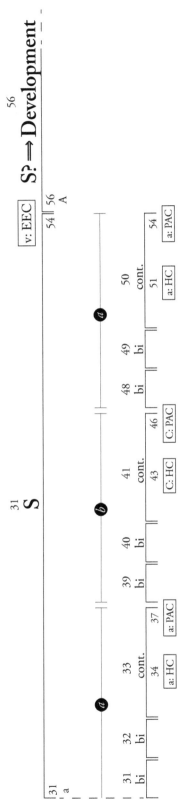

Figure 12.3 Samuel Coleridge-Taylor, Violin Sonata, op. 28, iii. *Poco meno mosso*, expositional S.

There is no real closing material, as the development begins at measure 56 with a repeated passage extending to measure 79. This may be the most puzzling passage for students, given that (1) it begins in A major, (2) the opening melody is clearly based on S, and (3) it repeats. On the basis of the key and thematic content, we hear this as a continuation of S-space, with a modal twist to major. Moreover, students may mistakenly interpret the repeat signs at measure 79 as the end of the exposition, given their prior experience with Bologne. However, as the passage modulates to C major (m. 60), it *becomes* the first section of the development. This passage's status as development is confirmed by more modulations, a prominent dominant arrival in D minor – confirmed by a lengthy wedge progression – at measure 70, and the arrival of P/TR material (m. 74). The second portion of the development (mm. 80–96) is relatively straightforward. It begins with the opening of P in A minor, followed by fragments of S and P in alternation. S-material embellishes the dominant arrival at measure 87, trailing off into the recapitulation at measure 97.

Most of the recapitulation corresponds to the exposition. TR is slightly recomposed, but it begins and concludes with corresponding thematic and harmonic material. The most significant change occurs at the end of the recapitulation (mm. 150–52). The EEC occurred in the corresponding expositional measures (mm. 54–56), with the violin performing a melodic cadential gesture twice, each time supported by the piano. Here, the piano undercuts the ESC twice. First, the violin performs an obvious cadential gesture, but the piano fails to resolve *sol* to *do* in the bass (m. 150). Following this, the piano takes over the melodic gesture – as though attempting to fix its earlier error – but the cadential dominant collapses into an A^{ø7} as the coda begins, marked *più lento*. The melodic *ti* is pulled down to C♮ – *te* in D minor, but *fa* in the coda's starting key of G minor.

The movement's failure to attain closure is heightened by its status as the conclusion of a three-movement sonata, and the coda does not offer a solution, as no satisfying PAC emerges. Instead, we find reminiscences of the earlier two movements: the opening theme of the second movement forms the basis of the coda's start (m. 156), and the sonata concludes with an extended diminuendo over P from the first movement (m. 185). When related to the finale's failure to produce an ESC, this powerful conclusion can spark thought-provoking conversations and narratives.

Pre-Class Preparation

- Listen with the score several times. Mark large-scale sections, themes, and cadences.[25]
- Post answers to the following questions on the LMS the evening before class:
  - There is a PAC in A minor at measure 37. Why can't this PAC be the EEC?
  - Where does the development begin, in measure 56 or measure 80? Be prepared to discuss your choice.
  - In the coda, mark the main melodies. Then, listen to the openings of the first and second movements. Can you locate the origins of the melodies in the finale's coda in these earlier movements?

Lesson Plan

The trickiest passages are the first section of the development (mm. 56–79) and the end of the recapitulation to the end of the movement (mm. 150–200); our lesson highlights these passages, in addition to reviewing the movement's overall structure. Students should have no trouble identifying the beginnings of the recapitulation and coda, but they will need guidance on the start of the development. We spend most of class on this passage, as it invokes questions about romantic boundaries and liminal spaces, practically demanding formal narratives.

Exposition: P and TR (15 Min.)

We begin by reviewing the structure of P. We ask students to notice the opening vamp, parse the theme's sentential structure, identify its one internal repeat, and recognize the dissolving repetition that initiates TR. Students may notice a kind of additive layering effect. The piano introduces the new melodic material (mm. 3–5), while the violin retains the vamp; then, in the internal repetition (m. 11), the violin repeats the piano's theme, while the piano takes up a new, descending chromatic line.

P contains no clear cadences. At the end of measure 8, for example, a proposed cadence is undercut by the piano's repetition of *sol* in the bass. At the end of the P-zone, persistent tonic pedals undercut possible cadential motion. We prompt students to bookmark these moments, as they may portend the recapitulation's ESC failure.

TR is clearly P-based; ask students to identify *how* P is transformed. An obvious standing on the dominant begins at measure 26, and students should hear how this dominant leads into the MC effect. In order to aurally reinforce these points, we have students listen to P and TR at least once more.

Expositional S and the Development (30 Min.)

We discuss the status of measure 37's PAC as a class and review how thematic repetition can reopen a proposed EEC. Then we consider the end of measure 54. Help students discover how the later cadence – the actual EEC – is weaker than the earlier one, due to the bass's delayed resolution to *do*.

Following this review, we form small groups to discuss the question: Where does the development begin? Allot about ten minutes for this activity. If students agree that measure 56 is correct, ask them to consider the possibility of measure 80, and vice versa. From our experience, students will gravitate toward measure 80 as the beginning of the development.

Either way, however, it is worth problematizing measures 56–79. As a class, review the thematic material, modulations, and repetition. Students might also note that this section concludes much like the expositional MC. Discuss the pros and cons of classifying this section as expositional versus developmental. We argue that it is crucial to emphasize the formal ambiguities of this section.

If time allows, discuss the second section of the development (80–96). Identify thematic material, key areas, and the retransition's move to the recapitulation.

Sonata Failure: Recapitulation and Coda (35 Min.)

The last portion of class can be devoted to the concept of sonata failure and narrative motivations and interpretations. After briefly reviewing the recapitulation's mostly straightforward course, focus on the moment of the proposed ESC and discuss how the syntax of a PAC is undercut at the end of the recapitulation as it leads into the coda.

Students will have identified the coda's thematic references back to the first and second movements in their pre-class preparation. In small groups, have students discuss the question: How does the coda reinforce the recapitulation's failure to produce an ESC? During the large-group debrief, note the harmonic course from G minor back to D minor, corresponding with the thematic references. It may also be helpful to discuss the concept of cyclicism as it pertains to the coda's thematic material. Taking this discussion a step further, you may wish to extend the discussion to the finale as a whole and how its form may be understood in light of the ESC failure *and* the coda.

Prompt small-group discussion by referencing several earlier moments: the lack of cadences in P-space, EEC deferral, and the ambiguous zone in measures 56–79. We encourage students to connect narratives to other models they have seen and tried during the previous lessons. One example is the concept of retrospective clarification or transformation – discussed earlier with respect to Bologne's op. 1, no. 5/i – where the coda's arrival might clarify the status of measures 56–79 as development rather than exposition. Another possible narrative thematizes the idea of failure on three levels. The attenuated cadences found in P and S are at the smallest scale, and the lack of ESC is at the level of the movement. The coda might be interpreted as a last-ditch attempt to attain cadential closure via themes external to the finale's sonata form, but even this tragically and quietly fails.

Conclusion

These lessons ask students to think about the ways sonatas are situated in particular contexts. While we think that no student can internalize sonata form norms in two weeks, we firmly believe that thinking critically about such norms is a worthwhile endeavor beyond the study of sonata form per se. In shifting the focus from internalizing norms to thinking about the contexts of a small number of sonatas, we free ourselves to reflect on higher-level questions. We want students to understand that norms change, most music is dialogic, and norms are bound to the repertoire by which they are defined. Moreover, any analysis must engage with that dialogic context. As such, we feel that a rewarding way to conclude this unit is to intentionally guide students to think about these issues through in-class discussions and LMS discussion boards.

First, we suggest asking students to think about the juxtaposition between the works in week 1 and week 2 and to relate that to their own consumption of music. For example, much of the discussion in week 2 focused on how both sonatas broke the norms we teased out of week 1 in highly evocative ways. How might that relate to pop form's evolution from the verse-chorus forms that have dominated the genre since the 1960s to today? We have students read Nate Sloan and Charlie Harding's essay in the *New York Times* about these changing norms and relate that to what they just learned.[26]

In addition, we ask students to reflect more on the juxtaposition among all works in this unit and the music that defined the "textbook norms" we teach. In particular, it is valuable to reveal that textbook norms are almost entirely derived from White male composers, and to have students reflect on the suitability of applying these norms uncritically to distinct, though related, repertoires. As such, we either ask students to read their textbook or provide them with an example textbook chapter on sonata forms if handouts were used for this unit. Students should answer the following questions:

1. Record the (1) gender, (2) race, (3) time period, (4) location, and (5) class of the composers represented in your textbook. This will require some research.
2. Choose one piece from the last two weeks and write a few sentences summarizing the context of the composer's life using – at minimum – the parameters in the previous item. Feel free to explore other avenues, though. Who were they? What music did they admire?
3. In a couple of sentences, compare your composer's context to the tally that you generated for question 1.
4. Review the norms that your textbook suggests are typical for sonata forms and compare those norms to the piece you chose. Write a few sentences describing your findings.
5. How do your answers to Parts 3 and 4 relate? Cite specific examples.

In asking these questions, these two weeks become so much more than a sonata unit. Indeed, in explicitly foregrounding race, gender, and class as part of a composer's "context," we ask students to engage with aspects of music that have been historically overlooked. In other words, this unit culminates not just in students learning to apply labels to sonatas; rather, this final assignment asks them to consider how form is disseminated and developed over time, how norms are established, and what formal labels actually mean. Moreover, it lays foundations for students to investigate how race, gender, and class contribute to the development of formal norms. Finally, it invites students to think about their role in the changing of those norms and the proliferation of labels.

Notes

1. See, for instance, Vande Moortele (2013), Pedneault-Deslauriers (2016), Burstein (2020), and Brody (2020).
2. The phrase comes from the title of William Drabkin's (2007) review and refers to Sonata Theory's overreliance on Mozart at the expense of other sonata form composers, despite the supposed breadth of their claims about classical norms. This critique was reiterated in Wingfield (2008). The same is true of Caplin (1998), who focuses on the music of Haydn, Mozart, and Beethoven.
3. Clendinning and Marvin (2016), Burstein and Straus (2020), and Laitz (2015) employ the term "medial caesura." While no textbooks use the terms "core" and "pre-core," Burstein and Straus (2016, 348), for instance, clearly describe the events of a development using these concepts.
4. This number comes from a survey of musical examples, both in-text and otherwise, from three leading textbooks as well as their accompanying workbooks and anthologies: Clendinning and Marvin (2016), Burstein and Straus (2020), and Laitz (2015). Of the five remaining examples, all are composed by White men. Note that this fact remains true in spite of Burstein and Straus's conscious push for a more inclusive repertoire in their section edition of *Concise Introduction to Tonal Harmony*.
5. Burstein writes, "[C]oncentrating too much on just two composers would create a distorted view of the style. Too often, owing to a lack of familiarity with the broader style, a standard Galant layout in a Haydn or Mozart piece is described by musicians today as radical or inventive" (2020, 13).
6. See, for instance, Richards (2012), which focuses on students learning cadential norms.
7. In doing so, we align with Brian Alegant's (2014) call for "scuba diving" rather than "snorkeling" and contrast with Monahan's (2011a) approach to "expose students to as many pieces as possible in the time we have" (81).
8. For a clear overview of these terms, see Burstein and Straus (2020, Ch. 39).
9. Hearing mm. 18–25 as a presentation requires hearing the cadences in mm. 21 and 25 as of limited scope. While such phrase structures are possible in the romantic style (see Grant 2022; Vande Moortele 2013; Martinkus 2021), they would be much more unusual in the classical style. However, one may certainly argue that the classical style is the wrong norm to judge Bologne against, given that he was writing at the end of the Galant period. See Burstein (2020) for a discussion of these issues.
10. Mm. 18–25 cannot technically be a period, given that the first phrase ends with a stronger cadence than the second. Both phrases are clearly linked, however, by their motivic content. As such, we can hear mm. 18–25 perhaps functioning as a large-scale antecedent, followed by a continuation phrase, creating one of Caplin's (1998) hybrid phrases.
11. This last may be the most historically accurate, given that Bologne was writing at the tail end of the Galant period. See Burstein (2020) for a discussion of phrase structure in this period.
12. For details on formative vs. summative assessments, see Elise Trumbull and Andrea Lash (2013), Michael Theall and Jennifer Franklin (2010), and David J. Nicol and Debra Macfarlane-Dick (2006).
13. Depending upon time, the instructor might choose to prioritize these features in the order listed.
14. Mm. 27–29 feature an audible example of a parallel-tenth tonic expansion (I–V$^4_3$–I^6), which may be useful as a harmonic dictation example in aural skills.
15. The supplementary materials include a mostly clean score for students, which includes several correspondence measures intended to model the task for the student to complete. See mm. 76–77, which correspond to mm. 1–2, and m. 85, which corresponds fairly closely to m. 16. The annotated instructor score includes all correspondence measures.

16. We have also found that some students find it challenging to locate phrase-formal boundaries without a literal gap or a very obvious change in texture. This pertains to the beginning of TR, as well as to the location of the MC; this latter example will be discussed shortly.
17. This use of the original tonic is common in Schubert's expositions (Grant 2018, 54 and 2022, 13).
18. Answering these questions goes beyond the scope of this chapter. However, for a concise primer on the unique issues in analyzing romantic form, see Vande Moortele (2017, 1–14).
19. The students should have the music in their ears, but given that the exposition is only roughly 4 minutes and 30 seconds long, we play it a couple of times to continuously link listening and analysis.
20. See Monahan (2011b) for an example of how to make narrative claims with late-romantic symphonies in light of conflicting norms.
21. See Brown's commentary in Price (2008, xxxv–xxxvi). See also Brown's more recent, posthumously published discussion – including another letter Price sent to Koussevitzky – in Chapter 15 of her biography of Florence Price, edited by Guthrie Ramsey (2020).
22. Coleridge-Taylor's Violin Sonata, op. 28 may be accessed via IMSLP.
23. Comparison might be made with the opening Allegro measures in Beethoven's Fourth Symphony or Felix Mendelssohn's op. 13 String Quartet; this kind of "wind-up" beginning is but one of many novel introductory strategies that emerged in the nineteenth century. See Hepokoski and Darcy (2006, 298), Vande Moortele (2017, ch. 4), and Kim (2020).
24. Note that the measure numbers reflect the solid bar lines and 3/2 meter. If the instructor prefers to work with the 2/4 meter, they may change the written-in measure numbers using the formula $m = 3n - 2$, where n is the written-in measure number and m is the new measure number assuming 2/4 meter.
25. You may include the following note: The bar lines are unusual in this movement. There are solid and dotted bar lines. We will treat the solid bar lines as the boundaries between measures, and the dotted bar lines like they are subdividing each measure into three parts. Near the end of the movement, the meter changes and there are no more dotted bar lines.
26. Nate Sloan and Charlie Harding, "The Culture Warped Pop, For Good," *New York Times*, March 14, 2021, www.nytimes.com/interactive/2021/03/14/opinion/pop-music-songwriting.html. Most students should have enough familiarity with pop forms to understand Sloan and Harding's article. However, it would be helpful to have a pop form unit planned prior to sonatas.

Bibliography

Alegant, Brian. 2008. "Listen Up!: Thoughts on iPods, Sonata Form, and Analysis without Score." *Journal of Music Theory Pedagogy* 22: 149–76. https://jmtp.appstate.edu/listen-thoughts-ipods-sonata-form-and-analysis-without-score

———. 2014. "On "Scuba Diving," or the Advantages of a Less-Is-More Approach." *Engaging Students: Essays in Music Pedagogy* 2. http://flipcamp.org/engagingstudents2/essays/alegant.html

Bologne, Joseph. 1988. *String Quartet, op. 1, no. 1*. Edited by Neal Richardson and William Bauer. Africanus Editions.

———. 1988. *String Quartet, op. 1, no. 5*. Edited by Neal Richardson and William Bauer. Africanus Editions.

Brody, Christopher. 2020. "Two Langerian Sonata-Form Problems, with Solutions by Beach and Medtner." Paper delivered at the 43rd Annual Meeting of the Society for Music Theory (Virtual Conference).

Brown, Rae Linda. 2020. *The Heart of a Woman: The Life and Music of Florence B. Price*. Edited by Guthrie P. Ramsey. University of Illinois Press.

Burstein, L. Poundie. 2020. *Journeys Through Galant Expositions*. Oxford University Press.

———, and Joseph Straus. 2020. *Concise Introduction to Tonal Harmony*, 2nd edition. W.W. Norton & Company.

Caplin, William. 1998. *Classical Form: A Theory of Formal Functions for the Instrumental Music of Haydn, Mozart, and Beethoven*. Oxford University Press.

Clendinning, Jane, and Elizabeth Marvin. 2016. *The Musician's Guide to Theory and Analysis*, 3rd edition. W.W. Norton & Company.

Coleridge-Taylor, Samuel. 1917. *Sonata in D Minor for Violin and Piano*. Edited by Albert Sammons. Hawkes & Son.

Drabkin, William. 2007. "Mostly Mozart." Review of *Elements of Sonata Theory: Norms, Types, and Deformations in the Late-Eighteenth-Century Sonata*, by James Hepokoski and Warren Darcy. *The Musical Times* 148/1901: 89–100.

Ewell, Philip. 2020. "Music Theory and the White Racial Frame." *Music Theory Online* 26/2. https://doi.org/10.30535/mto.26.2.4

Grant, Aaron. 2018. "Schubert's Three-Key Expositions." Ph.D. Dissertation, University of Rochester.

———. 2022. "Structure and Variable Formal Function in Schubert's Three-Key Expositions." *Music Theory Spectrum* 44/1.

Hepokoski, James, and Warren Darcy. 2006. *Elements of Sonata Theory: Norms, Types, and Deformations in the Late-Eighteenth-Century Sonata*. Oxford University Press.

Kim, Catrina. 2020. *The Romantic Introduction*. Ph.D. Dissertation, University of Rochester.

———. 2021. "Issues in Teaching Music Theory Ethically: Under the University's Directives of Antiracist and Decolonized Curricula." *Theory and Practice* 46: 23–45.

Laitz, Steven. 2015. *The Complete Musician: An Integrated Approach to Theory, Analysis, and Listening*, 4th edition. Oxford University Press.

Martinkus, Caitlin. 2021. "Schubert's Large-Scale Sentences: Exploring the Function of Repetition in Schubert's First-Movement Sonata Forms." *Music Theory Online* 27/3. https://doi.org/10.30535/mto.27.3.2

Monahan, Seth. 2011a. "Sonata Theory in the Undergraduate Classroom." *Journal of Music Theory Pedagogy* 25: 63–128. https://jmtp.appstate.edu/sonata-theory-undergraduate-classroom

———. 2011b. "Success and Failure in Mahler's Sonata Recapitulations." *Music Theory Spectrum* 33/1: 37–58.

Nicol, David J., and Debra Macfarlane-Dick. 2006. "Formative Assessment and Self-Regulated Learning: A Model and Seven Principles of Good Feedback Practice." *Studies in Higher Education* 31/2: 2–19.

Pedneault-Deslauriers, Julie. 2016. "Bass-Line Melodies and Form in Four Piano and Chamber Works by Clara Wieck-Schumann." *Music Theory Spectrum* 38/2: 133–54.

Price, Florence. 2008. *Symphonies No. 1 and 3*. Edited by Rae Linda Brown and Wayne Shirley. *Recent Researches in American Music* 66 & *Music of the United States of America* 19. A-R Editions.

Richards, Mark. 2012. "Teaching Sonata Expositions Through Their Order of Cadences." *Journal of Music Theory Pedagogy* 26: 215–54. https://jmtp.appstate.edu/teaching-sonata-expositions-through-their-order-cadences

Shaffer, Kris. 2013. "Flipping the Classroom: Three Methods." *Engaging Students: Essays in Music Pedagogy*. http://flipcamp.org/engagingstudents/shafferintro.html

Sloan, Nate, and Charlie Harding. 2021. "The Culture Warped Pop, For Good." *New York Times*. www.nytimes.com/interactive/2021/03/14/opinion/pop-music-songwriting.html

Theall, Michael, and Jennifer L. Franklin. 2010. "Assessing Teaching Practices and Effectiveness for Formative Purposes." In *A Guide to Faculty Development*, edited by K.J. Gillespie and D.L. Robertson. Jossey-Bass.

Trumbull, Elise, and Andrea Lash. 2013. "Understanding Formative Assessment: Insights from Learning Theory and Measurement Theory." WestEd.

Vande Moortele, Steven. 2013. "In Search of Romantic Form." *Music Analysis* 32/3: 1–28. https://doi.org/10.1111/musa.12015

———. 2017. *The Romantic Overture and Musical Form from Rossini to Wagner*. Cambridge University Press.

Wingfield, Paul. 2008. "Beyond 'Norms and Deformations': Towards a Theory of Sonata Form as Reception History." Review of *Elements of Sonata Theory: Norms, Types, and Deformations in the Late-Eighteenth-Century Sonata*, by James Hepokoski and Warren Darcy. *Music Analysis* 27/1: 137–77.

Part Four
Popular Music

13 Expanding the Scope of Analysis in the Popular Music Classroom

Zachary Zinser

Introduction

Instructors should continuously reassess curricula with a critical eye. As music educators in the twenty-first century, experiencing music with the technologies and access of our time, we should extend our re-evaluation to the inclusion of popular music in our teaching. The extent to which we can access and experience music is significantly different in the present with extensive implications. These changes in experience necessitate changes to our pedagogy. Beyond the notion of *how* we experience music, there is an equally important question of *whose* music we are engaging. Addressing the lack of music by underrepresented composers and artists in the classroom has been long overdue. Such change, however, does not happen overnight. It occurs through individual teachers, one class at a time. This chapter provides an overview of my experience leading what I hoped would be one of those classes and considers how we can learn from our students in rewarding ways if we create the appropriate pedagogical space.

After a broad description of the course and its goals (Section 1), this chapter provides a sample analysis and the course's core content (Sections 2–3), procedures and assessment (Sections 4–7), and course evaluation responses from students (Section 8). While these materials could be adapted for use as a module in other classes, their design as presented here demonstrates the benefits of realizing them as an entire course.

Course Philosophy

In fall 2020, I led an upper-level undergraduate music theory elective course titled "Sound, Syntax, and Space in Popular Music," where I introduced 13 students to a variety of topics relevant to how we listen to studio-produced popular music. Our objectives were twofold: first, to build a foundation of concepts and vocabulary to enhance how we listen to, experience, and think about this music on our own, and also to hone our ability to describe and communicate the nature of those experiences to others. In addition to fostering the exploration of new ideas, I maintained and encouraged a dialogue on what we might call more "traditional" music theory concepts along the way. By entertaining a mixture of familiar and unfamiliar analytical tools, students grew receptive to recalibrating their notion of what "music theory" is and can be. The tremendous variety among popular music repertoire demands additional and alternative methods to address topics essential to our listening experiences, topics that are likely unfamiliar to students whose *analytical* exposure is rooted in structural aspects of western European tonal music. Without dismissing the effectiveness and importance of that knowledge, students could engage with familiar, current pieces of popular music and creative analytical methodologies in ways that inspired their curiosity in all styles of music. Many concepts of this course – virtual

DOI: 10.4324/9781003204053-18

spaces, spatial impressions, agency, and musical texture, to name a few – are not limited by genre or style, as they are universal to the act of listening to recorded musical sound in general.

While most discussions of underrepresentation and repertoire choices in music classrooms have centered on composers as traditionally defined, popular music pedagogy is not necessarily any less susceptible to the same pitfalls. We must be wary of establishing a tradition, Juliet Hess urges, that is similarly "colonial" or "a new hegemony" following centuries-long convention in teaching western European art music. She observes that such perspectives may lead to pedagogy that "replicate[s] bands from the 1960s or 1970s, and center[s] the music of predominantly [W]hite men and utilize[s] guitar-based styles featuring guitar, bass, and drum kits" (Hess 2019, 33–36). This is, of course, advice for teachers, given under the assumption that teachers will determine all classroom content. While educators can (and should) make more significant strides to incorporate the music of different cultures and demographics in their classrooms, the effort will inescapably remain the perspective of one individual. I chose to relinquish control over this aspect of the course to let my students generate their own musical examples. Every class's student body represents a unique collection of wonderfully diverse musical backgrounds and experiences. Why not grant agency to this potential collaborative network? By giving students the power to choose repertoire, we ensure that the music being discussed in the classroom resonates with them. They know it. They like it. They *care* about it. When students are genuinely invested – socially, culturally, emotionally, academically – in the content, they become far more likely to continue engaging with it beyond the classroom in meaningful ways.

Sample Analysis

Popular music education does not share the luxury of notated scores and score analysis that traditional music theory courses typically rely on, because the compositions under scrutiny are intangible (i.e., audio recordings). Both instructors and students must develop effective verbal communication (and perhaps their own visual representations) as a way of producing analyses that attempt to convey their experience to others. These skills are essential to this course. Together we worked through a variety of topics that demand close, guided listening as a means of developing a vocabulary to describe our experiences in different ways.

A sample analysis on agency and embodied cognition from week 7 of the semester is provided next. The analysis incorporates concepts from previous weeks on virtual spaces, musical texture and recording techniques, and demonstrates the music-theoretical framework of the class as a whole. As one of my own analyses, it gives students an idea of the type of analysis they are invited to replicate or build on in their own analyses throughout the semester. This and other sample analyses are designed to empower students to craft creative and new analytical techniques that differ from more familiar music theory tools geared toward classical music.

* * *

Vocal parts, like instrumental parts, have long been altered and enhanced through studio technology. With so many standard tools designed to modify the sound of a vocalist, the sonic possibilities are vast even with a solo voice, let alone when multiple voices are combined. Imagine listening to a song with both solo and harmony vocals. It feels intuitive that those moments of harmony vocals would cause a perceived spatial expansion to some degree, an impression likely informed by our natural tendency to attribute human agency to human voices. The more voices we hear, the more our metaphorical performance space enlarges to accommodate those active (virtual) bodies (see Figure 13.1). Even so, I'm sure we've all had listening experiences that are not so straightforward. Features like the degree of effects applied to the vocals, who we perceive as singing the additional voices, and the pace at which additional voices are introduced can have a significant impact on how we ultimately interpret their placement and function in the metaphorical performance environment.

The chorus of Michael Jackson's "Rock with You" (1979) provides an example of how syntactically equivalent material can be sonically reshaped in significant ways that go beyond the traditional perspectives of music analysis and music theory. Jackson's chorus vocals reuse all melodic and harmonic gestures heard in the song's introduction, then produced instrumentally (see Figure 13.2a). Formally, they are both parallel periodic phrase structures lasting eight bars. Their harmonic structures are identical, and their melodic designs are nearly so, save for a slight variation in Jackson's lead vocal at the conclusion of the chorus phrase (replacing the string gesture from the introduction). But while these observations elucidate details of formal design, they are not able to address some vital experiential aspects of the passages. While many of the traditional analytical tools of music theory would represent these passages as essentially the same, aural experience is quite different. The *sensation* created by the chorus vocals eclipses syntactic familiarity, as the chord progression is given a powerful, new sonic context.

For me, one of the most powerful features of this record is Jackson's harmony vocals. There is no process or buildup that prepares them; instead, they function as a call-and-response juxtaposition to the solo vocal. All voices being Jackson's own, the harmony vocals create an aural sensation that is almost entrancing. Their dynamic power and wider stereo placement in the mix makes them feel significantly closer, facilitating an impression that the overall textural space has momentarily been contracted. I feel enveloped by these vocals, something I don't feel with any other aspect of the record. Jackson's mixing engineer, Bruce Swedien, sheds light on this sensation when he explains his process for recording these vocals using "early reflections to create both presence and depth of field" by having Jackson perform multiple takes, each one a bit further away from the mic, and then raising the gain on those tracks to match the level of previous ones. This technique "raises the ratio of early reflections to direct sound" (Swedien 2009, 19). Swedien's sonic result is impossible in natural acoustic environments, an aural paradox of proximity and presence with concurrent impressions of depth and fullness.

Swedien's harmony vocals recording technique contributes to their incredibly vivid sonic character. One important factor that makes these moments feel more intense is perceived movement in space (toward greater proximity relative to the solo vocal). Following studies of interpersonal distance in virtual contexts, Nicola Dibben points to the "intensification of emotional reactions to spaces where affective scenes are imagined to approach," suggesting an analogous effect in virtual musical spaces specifically (Dibben 2012, 116). If a sensation of greater proximity, or even envelopment, is felt with these harmony gestures, each return to the solo vocal texture would then feel like an *expansion* back to a larger space (and a potential lessening of emotional intensity) (see Figure 13.2b). This sensation challenges the hypothetical proposed at the beginning of this analysis that adding harmony vocals to a texture will likely result in an expansion of perceived space. In this case, the ways that multiple voices are contextualized have the opposite effect, demonstrating that more parts do not necessarily create more space.

152 *Zachary Zinser*

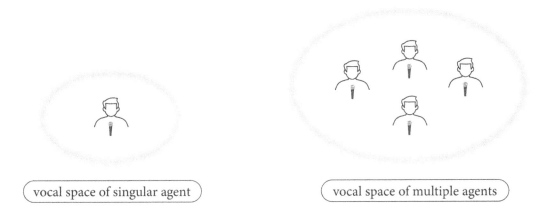

Figure 13.1 Hypothetical spatial effect of agential population.

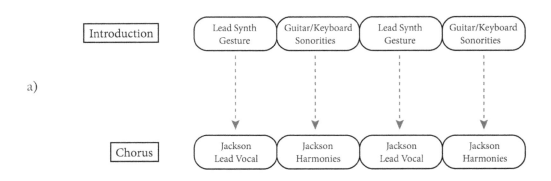

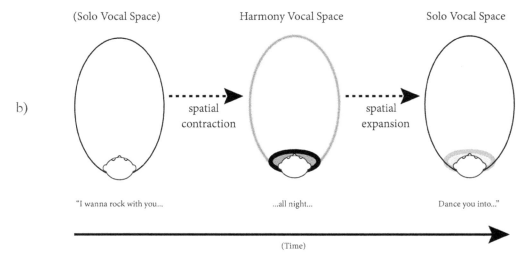

Figure 13.2 Michael Jackson, "Rock with You" (1979), (a) syntactic equivalence of introduction and chorus, (b) spatial cues of chorus vocals.

Expanding the Scope of Analysis in the Popular Music Classroom 153

The striking harmony vocals also impact my experience of metric emphasis. My anticipation for the next moment they enter shifts the relative strength I perceive on certain bars relative to what I felt throughout the introduction (see Figure 13.3a). While I have no doubt that this phrase maintains the same periodic structure as the introduction, I nevertheless feel my attention shift toward the metrically "weak" bars of each four-bar unit – a kind of hypermetric backbeat.

Another element in the chorus further reinforces this backbeat emphasis: handclaps on the fourth beat of every bar (an addition to the typical snare hits on beats 2 and 4 already present). Considering its consistent metric placement, this gesture immediately precedes and rounds out every gesture of harmony vocals in the chorus by framing them on either side. This new component is significant in two ways: from a purely sonic perspective, the handclaps engage the upper frequency range of our hearing (16 kHz and above) for the first time on the record, and the temporal location of that addition serves to highlight the already powerfully presented harmony vocals. Furthermore, the descending contour of Jackson's lead melodic gestures result in a natural decay in volume as they descend, making the (initially) unexpected and aurally contrasting handclaps that follow all the more salient.

The handclaps emphasize a metric backbeat by drawing attention to an additional metric level. While the harmony vocals occupy (and sonically highlight) the traditionally "weak" *bars* of a four-bar unit (i.e., bars 2 and 4), the handclaps occupy a traditionally "weak" *beat* of each bar (in traditional models of accentual hierarchy within a bar, the weakest) (see Figure 13.3b). As a result, there is an interesting negotiation between syntactically

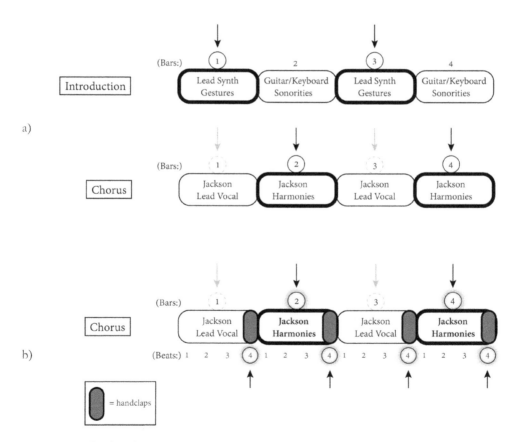

Figure 13.3 Michael Jackson, "Rock with You" (1979), (a) comparison of hypermetric emphasis, (b) layers of backbeat emphasis in the chorus.

oriented knowledge and expectations a competent listener brings to this style; while the expected metrical accent pattern in a four-bar unit remains clearly intact (i.e., strong-weak-strong-weak), how the material is sonically contextualized has the potential to subvert that normative hearing.

From shifting metric emphasis to spatial transformations, this analysis demonstrates a synthetic approach that incorporates different aspects of stylistically informed musical knowledge and auditory perception. Together, these considerations shape how we interpret and represent listening experiences in ways directly related to musical texture in virtual spaces. The analytical statements presented here are by no means prescriptive; they represent one potential hearing among many. Music that presents dynamic, multidimensional virtual spaces invites us as listeners to hear them in different ways.

***

Course Content

Weeks 1–11

While presenting a comprehensive account of every detail discussed throughout the entire semester is beyond the scope of a single chapter, I will provide what became the core concepts of the class (organized by week):

Week 1

- "New"-ness in popular music
- Ontology of the record, of music
- Acousmatic experience and its implications

Week 2

- "Primary" vs. "secondary" materials of composition; sound and syntax
- Analytical techniques for music recordings

Week 3

- Repetition (e.g., within a song, between songs, listening habits)

Week 4

- Musical texture as experienced

Week 5

- The metaphorical performance environment
- Virtual space (aural spatial cues); cross-modal nature of spatial perception
- The listener's position in relation to "the music"/virtual space

Week 6

- Expansion of the idea of a "part" in virtual spaces
- Specific mixing techniques (e.g., the "monocentric" mix), celebrity culture in pop

Week 7

- Agency and embodied cognition

Week 8

- Ecological perspectives on how we hear/interpret foreign sounds
- Electronic music and its implications for analysis

Week 9

- Modes of listening: mono/stereo, headphones/loudspeakers
- Spector's Wall of Sound, Swedien's Acusonic recording process; comparing sonic textures

Week 10

- Sonic functions, "genre modulation"

Week 11

- Covers, remix culture, intertextuality

These topics were generated primarily through the assigned reading for each week, although some arose spontaneously through student interest in later parts of the semester. For greater details on specific reading sources and writing prompts that accompanied these topics, I invite readers to visit this book's website to access my supplemental materials. Articles or chapters were seldom assigned in their entirety. Instead, I curated excerpts to help students maintain focus and allow them time to process and apply these new ideas to their own musical examples. The enthusiasm students consistently showed for this content reflects its applicability to twenty-first-century musicians, despite being rarely found in undergraduate music theory training. These subjects are essential aspects of the popular music idiom and, by extension, music theory pedagogy that seeks to incorporate popular music. Many are also modes of inquiry that are readily applicable more generally to other repertoires.

Weeks 12–16

Week 12 class sessions were reserved for each student to present a five- to ten-minute "lightning talk" to describe the nature of their final project (see Sections 6–7 for more details). Week 13 served a culminating role. Instead of assigning new material, I asked students to reflect on the course topics as a whole and apply some of these new ideas to musical examples. Students were encouraged to demonstrate new analytical insight while synthesizing the many different topics covered throughout the semester. Weeks 14–16 were dedicated to one-on-one consultations and final presentations.

Repertoire

As with any music analysis course, the topics of study are only part of the equation. Application of newly learned theoretical concepts to repertoire is a critical next step in the learning process. In the popular music domain, current repertoire and the context that shapes its consumption are likely more intimately known and experienced by the students themselves.

> The musical practices of the twenty-first century are changing rapidly and in many instances students may be better apprised of new developments than faculty members. A learning partnership thus requires the lecturer to use their experience to guide the student toward critical reflection on new developments rather than always insisting on control of the content and context.
>
> (Henson and Zagorski-Thomas 2019, 22)

As David Henson and Simon Zagorski-Thomas suggest, we should consider the potential benefits of approaching popular music education as a partnership rather than a dictatorship. I believe the confidence and strength students exuded were a direct result of the agency they enjoyed in directing musical content, as well as the conversational manner of live sessions. The repertoire was entirely student generated, save for only a few contributions from me. A complete list of the repertoire that comprised the entirety of this course can be accessed through this book's website. I found that my students' collection of musical artists turned out to be more interesting and diverse than anything I might have devised on my own. I suggest viewing this specific collection of music as one manifestation of a unique time and place, displaying what *can* be rather than what *should* be. In other words, the repertoire for this type of course will change every time it is taught, because the students will be different every time. I think that is wonderful. Since this is music they consume frequently, I also believe they will be far more likely to retain the information explored throughout the course and continue to explore and apply it.

The student-led aspect of the course also benefited the instructor–student dynamic. Classes felt much more *collaborative* than prescriptive, and much more collective than asymmetrical. We had conversations instead of lectures. Moreover, giving students the freedom to bring in any repertoire they wanted resulted in, as one might expect, a *wide* variety of styles and artists. From 2pac to 2cellos, Aretha Franklin to Ariana Grande, Beyonce to Bob Marley, Frank Ocean to Fiona Apple, Lana Del Rey to Lil Nas X, it was exciting to watch our eclectic repertoire grow week after week. Were there some very common rock and pop contributions? Of course. But at the same time, there was plenty of music I had never heard before – music that *they* were the experts on. By the end of the semester, I felt like I had learned as much from my students as they had learned from me.

While a course that allows students to generate the repertoire provides an opportunity to explore a more diverse collection of musical artists, it also leaves open the possibility that will not be the case. The backgrounds and experiences of one's students and different institutional contexts are all variables that will undoubtedly inform student choices. If it seems as though the repertoire being chosen is predominantly by White artists, instructors should be prepared to encourage students to discover more non-White and Black artists as musical examples for their assignments. Challenging students to seek out unfamiliar music and apply new analytical concepts to it might at first feel like a daunting task for some, but with proper guidance I am confident the benefits of doing so would be great both during and beyond this specific course.

Course Procedures

The exploratory spirit of this course lends itself well to a seminar format. Live class sessions were carried out over Zoom (due to the global pandemic), and all other course business occurred through the Canvas platform. As a hybrid of synchronous class discussions and asynchronous written discussions (posted on the discussion board of our Canvas site), the course created an environment that encouraged ongoing discussions both within and outside of live meetings. Additionally, the Zoom platform for live sessions had an unexpected benefit in students' ability to screen-share musical examples quickly (via YouTube or their preferred streaming service) during a conversation – something that, while possible in a traditional, in-person classroom context, would be far less efficient. The simple act of allowing students to do this spontaneously contributed to an empowering learning environment. The basic structure of course operations during a given week is shown in Figure 13.4.

Expanding the Scope of Analysis in the Popular Music Classroom 157

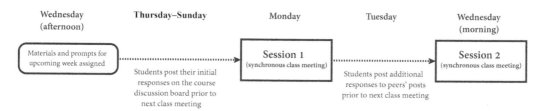

Figure 13.4 Weekly course activity.

A typical week consisted of two 75-minute class sessions (held via Zoom). In the time between the end of a week and the start of the next (i.e., the end of session 2 and the next session 1), students read assigned material, listened to musical examples (from the reading and their own), and composed written responses to prompts I provided. These initial posts to our Canvas discussion boards were expected to be at least two substantial paragraphs in length, though in most cases students far exceeded this minimum. Then, in the much shorter time between sessions 1 and 2 during the week, students would respond to at least two peers' responses in a constructive, thoughtful way. These follow-up posts were allowed to be shorter, because the expectation was for students to comment and build upon the ideas and musical examples of others. These asynchronous discussions fueled our live meetings with a wealth of material to address and work through together. It was, of course, up to me to determine what responses and topics to raise, and in what order, as I planned our live sessions. I viewed my role as a mediator to guide and bolster student conversations in ways that allowed them to explore and try out new ideas through sharing among themselves.

Both the synchronous and asynchronous aspects of this course were incredibly important in their own ways. Allowing students ample time – about 4.5 days – to become acquainted with foreign concepts on their own in preparation for each session 1 class made for engaging live discussions, which served to refine their understanding as well as gain further insight from others. Their online responses to peers between sessions 1 and 2 consistently benefited from the first live session of each week. The synchronous class meetings provided spontaneity and freedom for students to explore the application of new concepts while the asynchronous discussion board became an outlet for progress and growth through ongoing conversations.

Assignment Prompts for Asynchronous Discussions

Knowing that many of the writing styles and concepts presented to students through the readings are likely quite challenging, I assigned only what I believed to be absolutely necessary to prevent overwhelming them (i.e., many components of the assigned reading are excerpts rather than complete chapters or articles). The questions in my prompts served to focus their reading, thinking, and listening toward core concepts and ideas that accumulated week by week. Additionally, sometimes incorporating more open-ended questions or instructions gave students the opportunity to interrogate concepts that inspired their curiosity most. The assignment prompts for this course are available in the supplemental materials for this chapter online.

If the prompts seem in danger of presenting *too much* material, that is by design. I have found that providing students with many potential avenues for discovery often results in a more multifaceted discussion informed by their own unique subject positions. While they were expected to, at the very least, address all questions in a given prompt, different students will be drawn to explore different questions in greater depth than others. The live meetings (particularly session 1 of a given week) then functioned to both expand on the content generated by students on the discussion board and fill in any conceptual gaps I felt necessitated deeper scrutiny.

Assessment

Assessment of student work in this course poses certain challenges if approached with the mindset of a more conventional class involving questions with absolute answers. The nature of the subject matter requires us to grapple with the fact that, in many cases, there is no "right" or "wrong" answer – only a thoughtful, informed, inevitably subjective, experiential account. This exploratory approach was new and unusual for most of my students, given their prior experiences in traditional theory classrooms (e.g., chord spelling, voice leading, dictation, etc.). I worked to mitigate any sense of anxiety from the students regarding how they were being graded in an experimental context without definitive answers. I wanted them to feel comfortable to try out new concepts and discover new ideas without fear of judgment or quantifiable ramifications. I found it effective in this seminar-style class to assess holistically with a focus on process and progress. It was in this spirit that I weighted various aspects of this course, as shown in the following.

Grading

Canvas Discussions	50%
Final Paper	30%
Final Presentation	10%
Attendance/Participation	10%

The final project components – presentation and paper – represented a culminating demonstration of each student's most well-formed and developed ideas. With significantly different topics to evaluate, I assessed based on effectiveness of communication and depth of ideas about each topic. As the only consistent "assignment" work throughout the semester, the Canvas discussions (both initial post and responses to peers) represented the clearest evidence of engagement, comprehension, and genuine effort every week. My approach to assessing these exploratory, albeit guided, responses was holistic. Students earned full credit if they addressed (on time) all questions posed by the prompt and demonstrated a genuine effort to engage with the concepts and ideas at hand. In conjunction with participation in live class sessions, these asynchronous discussion posts gave me a way to plan each live session effectively and review a given student's progress over the entire semester. My expectations were not that my students "master" this material by the end of the course, because these are challenging concepts that take time to digest well beyond a matter of weeks. I did my best to inspire this perspective of beyond-the-classroom application and extend this enjoyment to my students.

In short, assessment for this type of course necessitates ongoing communication between instructors and students. Consistent transparency about expectations and timely feedback are absolutely critical. The pedagogical benefits of maintaining this transparency cannot be overstated. I felt like I got to know my students in a meaningful and lasting way, and as some of their course evaluation responses will suggest (see Section 8), I think they appreciated steady interaction and encouragement from me as they navigated challenging new concepts.

Final Project

There were no traditional exams for this course. Students instead developed a final project consisting of two components: (1) a 20-minute formal presentation to the class on their topic, with an extra 5 minutes for Q&A, and (2) a 10- to 15-page analytical paper. The paper, due after all presentations, was expected to represent the most developed and polished form of their presentation ideas. I established several benchmarks for students to guide their approach as their ideas developed over a number of weeks. First, I encouraged them to start thinking about potential topics early and reminded them at the end of each week that I was available to discuss final project ideas. I had them prepare for a brief discussion with me about their ideas during week 9, outside of class sessions, if I had yet to hear from them before then. Week 12 was reserved for "lightning talk" presentations during our synchronous class sessions. Students were expected to informally share their preliminary ideas with the class. The question-and-answer time was invaluable for many at this stage of the process, as each student was able to receive helpful feedback from both me and their peers with several weeks left to continue developing their work toward its final form. The last opportunity for students to workshop their project came in week 14, which I reserved for one-on-one consultations with me. By then, students were expected to arrive at our meeting with substantive work to demonstrate.

The only content requirement for the final project was to include some analysis of musical examples through incorporating any concepts explored throughout the semester relevant to their specific topics. Allowing students the freedom to choose and develop their own topics for this project using music they are passionate about yielded incredibly rewarding results. The 13 final topics were:

- EDM production techniques
- "Breakdowns" in heavy metal
- Perception of electronically altered and computer-generated voices
- Layering and multidimensionality in aural experience
- Modes of listening and the effects of repetition
- Intersections of extramusical information and production techniques
- Music as context in video games
- Experiential ramifications of automatic double tracking
- Potential impact of semantic content on spatial perception
- Genre-specific types of repetition
- Musical qualities of various K-pop genres
- Engagement and accessibility through the riot grrrl genre
- Space as a disorienting device

The breadth and variety of final project topics is a testament to these students' abilities to use the content of the class and apply it creatively and effectively in new directions. I believe the fact that these fascinating topics are rarely found in traditional music theory classes provided additional motivation and inspiration to interrogate their experiences in fresh and rewarding ways.

Instructor Reflection and Comments from Students

For the educator considering incorporating popular music in their classroom, choices regarding pedagogical approach, assessment, and repertoire have the potential to encumber and deter rather than inspire confidence. There is, however, a growing collection of resources available with helpful discourse on these very topics, such as the annual conference for the Association for Popular Music Education, the *Journal of Popular Music Education* and *Journal of Popular Music Pedagogy*, as well as *The Routledge Research Companion to Popular Music Education* and *The Bloomsbury Handbook of Popular Music Education*. At the same time, many educators who do not have extensive familiarity with popular music in their own educational background and experiences might feel apprehensive leading a classroom of students likely more immersed in and knowledgeable about this repertoire than we often assume. As John Kratus puts it:

> [T]he music teacher with little understanding of hip-hop music needs to be humble enough and willing to accept student expertise in sharing knowledge to teach the class. This is not an admission of weakness on the teacher's part; it is a sign of strength.
> (Kratus 2019, 462)

While a teacher's role in relation to their students is arguably defined by expertise, Kratus invites us to entertain the idea that a lack of expertise in certain contexts can be an asset rather than a liability. "Taking popular music seriously will change the role of the music educator, who can hardly presume any longer to be an authoritative purveyor of factual insights in a field notable for its effervescence, fluidity, polysemy, hybridity, and mutation," states Wayne D. Bowman. "What students bring to the educational experience will of necessity become much more central, a fact that will arguably alter in positive ways what they take away as well" (Bowman 2004, 43). It is on that note that I now turn to sharing comments from the students themselves.

The following questions were posed to students as part of their course evaluations at the conclusion of the semester. Responses were not mandatory, so the response rates were not consistent across all questions. Since evaluations are done anonymously, it is impossible for me to definitively link responses of the same individual across multiple questions. Nonetheless, I have labeled each response numerically for ease of reading and reference.

Question 1: What did you like most about the course?

Student 1: "The various articles we read introduced ideas, but our discussion-based format and getting to hear musical examples from classmates."
Student 2: "Getting introduced to new music and gaining new ideas to reflect on when I listen to music."
Student 3: "The open-ended discussions were great. I also loved that we all got to share our own musical examples to cultivate different ideas."
Student 4: "Class discussions and the flexibility they had to get into topics that interested us as a class."
Student 5: "I really liked how different this course was, compared to everything else in the music school. The thing that attracted me more to this course was how different and out of my comfort zone, knowledge-wise, it was. I wish we'd have more courses like this, because music is constantly changing and I would love to see more variety of genres and artists besides the ones constantly talked about in theory or music history. It was a nice break from the repetitive teachings we got from previous courses, and it really challenged me as a student to think in a different perspective that I was not used to."

Question 2: How did you feel this class compared with other music theory classes you have taken in the past?

Student 1: "I loved this class so much more because of how different it was. I also feel like this class will be more applicable when looking at how we, as performers, must adapt to how music is changing in our culture."

Student 2: "Completely different and absolutely fascinating . . . practical intersections between what we've learned in the past and applying it in a different medium."

Question 3: To what extent did you feel your prior theory knowledge was applicable to the eclectic collection of musical styles and analytical perspectives we explored?

Student 1: "I don't think this class would have been nearly as interesting or beneficial to someone who didn't have that sort of background knowledge. Knowing the conventions of form and compositional construction gave me more appreciation for the nuanced elements of the music. That being said, I think most of the concepts could be learned from someone without a background in music theory, but what made the course so interesting was how we could compare our previous ideas about music and how sometimes theoretical analysis can be short-sighted when only looking at eighteenth- to nineteenth-century tonal music."

Question 4: Do you think a class like this should be required for music majors? Music minors? Both? Neither?

Student 1: "YES TO BOTH – if it was required for minors, I think there should be a separate section with more time spent on explaining basic concepts of form and analysis before diving into the material. I definitely think music majors should be able to talk about this kind of stuff, though!"

Student 2: "Yes for both! Pop music is an inevitable part of the future of music as a whole."

Student 3: "I do not think it should be required, but definitely offered more."

Student 4: "I think everyone should take it. I guess I don't like the word 'required,' but I think more people should know about this class and take it if they are interested (both music majors/minors)."

Student 5: "I think it should be required for music majors to take at least one course dealing with contemporary or non-classical topics in an analytical or overview format. The reality is that we live in a world where lines are blurred between genres and disciplines, and the more aware we are of developments and technologies out there, the better equipped we'll be to contribute in a meaningful way with our career."

Question 5: Please feel free to share any other thoughts you have about your experience with this course.

Student 1: "Wonderful experience. Would highly recommend to any of my colleagues."

Student 2: "I loved this class. Definitely among my favorite courses I've taken. Super interesting ideas were presented each week, and the open-discussion format of class made it easy to ask questions/discuss ideas with other students (apt for learning)."

Student 3: "I love the course. It's the first time I felt like I had a lot to offer."

Student 4: "Absolutely loved this course. Was by far one of my favorite classes to take in my degree."

* * *

Conclusion

These students' impressions of this course appear overwhelmingly positive, as the evaluation responses suggest. Their learning and creativity flourished under an exploratory, student-led approach to musical repertoire, rather than a more prescriptive approach. A delightful variety of students with different backgrounds and experiences resulted in a similarly eclectic repertoire. With this freedom, students demonstrated their interest in the diversification of "music theory" repertoire.

The students also viewed the general format of the course – a seminar with both synchronous and asynchronous discussions – as beneficial to their learning process. Thinking more globally about this type of course in the context of music degrees, I found student 5's response to question 4 particularly insightful. It is evident that, yet again, the students themselves are well aware of the ongoing, significant changes to the twenty-first century musician's professional landscape. I believe my students enjoyed this course because it felt deeply relevant to what they do every day as musicians who compose, perform, and most importantly, *listen.*

Popular music is an omnipresent, continually evolving, and influential facet of our culture. As such, it is as interesting as it is valuable to study both its production and our listening experiences from a growing variety of perspectives. Introducing new topics to popular music analysis, particularly those that engage aspects of our listening experiences in fundamental ways, can be an effective way to inspire an exploratory spirit in students that lasts well beyond the classroom.

Works Cited

Bowman, Wayne D. 2004. "'Pop' Goes . . .? Taking Popular Music Seriously." In *Bridging the Gap: Popular Music and Music Education*, edited by Carlos Xavier Rodriguez, 29–49. MENC.

Henson, David, and Simon Zagorski-Thomas. 2019. "Setting the Agenda: Theorizing Popular Music Education Practice." In *The Bloomsbury Handbook of Popular Music Education*, edited by Zack Moir, Bryan Powell, Gareth Dylan Smith, 11–28. Bloomsbury Academic.

Hess, Juliet. 2019. "Popular Music Education: A Way Forward or a New Hegemony?" In *The Bloomsbury Handbook of Popular Music Education*, edited by Zack Moir, Bryan Powell, Gareth Dylan Smith, 29–44. Bloomsbury Academic.

Kratus, John. 2019. "On the Road to Popular Music Education: The Road Goes on Forever." In *The Bloomsbury Handbook of Popular Music Education*, edited by Zack Moir, Bryan Powell, and Gareth Dylan Smith, 455–64. Bloomsbury Academic.

Sample Analysis Bibliography

Dibben, Nicola. 2012. "The Intimate Singing Voice: Auditory Spatial Perception and Emotion in Pop Recordings." In *Electrified Voices: Medial, Socio-Historical and Cultural Aspects of Voice Transfer*, edited by Dmitri Zakharine and Nils Meise, 107–22. Vandenhoeck and Ruprecht.

Swedien, Bruce. 2009. *In the Studio with Michael Jackson*. Hal Leonard.

Sample Analysis Discography

Michael Jackson. 1979. "Rock with You." In *Epic*.

14 Formal Structures and Narrative Design in Janelle Monáe's *The ArchAndroid*

Cora S. Palfy

Introduction

When teaching phrase forms and formal functions, it can be useful to connect topics like phrase forms and formal functions to contemporary popular music. Genres within this category create familiar connections for students, increasing retention (Ausubel 2012; Rovee-Collier et al. 2001) and motivation (Wentzel 2020, Driscoll 1994). Crucially, popular music genres often afford examples where samples and ostinati shape a piece's entire formal structure. Songs with such straightforward formal designs can prompt discussion of formal structures dependent on a well-designed phrase, easing the transition between formal structural levels for students. These types of pieces can, more importantly, foster dialogue about the way in which storytelling, the audience's attentional focus, and empathy with a narrator-artist contribute to the effectiveness of a musical work.

Work on narrative, attentional direction, and artist–audience engagement has previously been done,[1] but the methodology has not yet been discussed in the context of the classroom. Janelle Monáe's concept album *The ArchAndroid* (2010) is rife with examples of such musical storytelling. In this chapter, I will examine the album's use of narrative in conjunction with the structural simplicity of its songs. I provide structural analysis of two pieces, "Cold War" and "Come Alive (War of the Roses)," and provide dialogue prompts that highlight the interactive storytelling facilitated by the phrase-form bound music.

Janelle Monáe, *The ArchAndroid*

Since she entered the popular music scene around 2005, Janelle Monáe has quickly become the standard for musical innovation. Monáe is multiply awarded[2] for her Afrofuturist[3] multimedia albums, and she has become a Black and queer American icon. Her style, which is not easily defined, is characterized by adventurous genre-mixing; clever intertextuality among music, literature, art, and film; and high-profile collaborations with artists such as Big Boi, Sean "Puffy" Combs, George Clinton, and Esperanza Spalding. Her top tracks include "Tightrope" (feat. Deep Cotton), "Q.U.E.E.N." (feat. Erykah Badu), and the queer anthem "Pynk."

The ArchAndroid (2010) is the second and third suite in a seven-part concept album series which follows the story of Monáe's alter ego, android Cindi Mayweather. The story line follows Cindi's journey to become a savior figure within the Star Core Metropolis, a city in which society is divided into oppressed, disenfranchised androids and human beings. Inspired by science fiction and Fritz Lang's *Metropolis* (1927), the narrative serves as an allegory for and commentary on the systematic oppression of BIPOC and LGBTQ+ people in American society.[4]

> Monáe borrows from [Octavia] Butler a focus on reclamation and restoration of the past as a path to both claiming individual identity and living with and within an oppressive society. In Monáe's work, finding a connection to a history that's been taken from you is a crucial part of resistance and self-empowerment. Monáe uses her access to black culture and history to unite herself out of diaspora, drawing strength from her alter ego, Cindi (Romano 2018).

Purposeful Curricular Transitioning: From Phrase to Formal Structure

It is crucial to consider moments of transition and opportunities to integrate new information with ideas reinforcing previous concepts in curricular design. By melding old and new information, which curriculum researchers call "bridging" (Richland 2005; Sawyer et al. 2014), "interleaving" (Fleming and Grant 2020; Wiggins et al. 2005; Rohrer et al. 2015), or "spiral curriculum" (Ambrose et al. 2007; Gosper and Ifenthaler 2014), instructors can encourage organically occurring, logical responses to new material. For example, the transition from smaller phrase forms to large-scale formal structure can be confusing: many students need to be guided through listening for markers of larger sections and their formal functions. Students can become mired in small-scale processes (like hearing cadential closure or expectations for 8- or 16-bar structures) and can miss features that distinguish longer-span sections.

In my classroom, I bridge between these two conceptual areas (phrase form and large-scale formal structure) by inserting larger formal structures heavily reliant on phrase structure, such as simple verse form, simple verse-chorus form, sampling practices from hip-hop, rap, and EDM, or the 12-bar blues. By drawing attention to larger formal structures reliant on regular, overt repetition of phrases, I am able to reinforce phrase structures while drawing attention to larger structures. Research in educational psychology demonstrates that such scaffolded knowledge transfer leads to deeper intellectual engagement with concepts.

> [Students] need opportunities to connect their prior knowledge and experiences with new information through their own thought processes and through interactions with others and the environment. Such opportunities allow students to use their schema as a basis on which to build a framework for understanding new ideas and information. Through this gradual building or *scaffolding* of knowledge and skills, students can be supported to move beyond rote knowledge and develop depth of understanding (Childre et al. 2009, 6).

Using popular music and media to achieve such curricular transfer has added benefits that can make a curricular transition more intellectually invigorating. Students familiar with songs, albums, or artists are likely to feel more motivated and engaged. Students may feel a sense of intrinsic motivation because of affinity for or identification with Monáe and her background, the album's complex narrative, or the ease of the formal structures – this motivation is crucial for deep learning. Wentzel and Brophy note:

> When we are intrinsically motivated, we do something not for *its* sake but for *our* sake – because doing so provides us with enjoyable stimulation or satisfaction. Interest in particular content implies the arousal of a desire to explore or to know more about the content, while *interesting activities provide learners with forms of input or opportunities for response that they find rewarding and want to pursue* (Wentzel and Brophy 2014, 99 [emphasis original]).

Stimulating students with familiar content creates opportunities for a deeper critical engagement alongside learning to listen at a larger formal level; students may feel empowered to draw connections to similar structures in other songs, engage in more complex interpretation, or think about cultural topics and events that parallel the narrative events.

A final crucial consideration is the way in which familiar popular music can increase feelings of inclusion and belonging in the classroom. Studies investigating "culturally responsive" or "culturally relevant teaching" within higher education suggest that inclusions of diverse activities, faculty, students, and curriculum contribute positively to campus climate (Milem 2001, 247) and contribute positively to life skills beyond the classroom.[5] Further, benefits abound within the classroom; collaborations and dialogue with students from wide-ranging backgrounds importantly improve classroom performance (from engagement, to motivation, feelings of empowerment and ownership of material, to overall curricular success) in a number of different subjects, from math, science, writing, and pertinently, music (Steele 2011, Peters 2016; Huang 2009; Adams 1992). Educational researchers Margery B. Ginsberg and Raymond J. Wlodkowski note, "Just as cultural wealth in everyday life generates the opportunity to leverage personal interests, in the classroom, it enhances the opportunity for academic success" (2011, 23–24).

Narrative, Empathy, and Attentional Focal Points

Working with structurally simple musical works provides an opportunity to engage with topics that are less frequently discussed, such as timbre, narrative, and empathy. In the case of Monáe's *The ArchAndroid*, the structural simplicity of selected pieces encourages listeners to focus on the complexity of the words and poignant narrative. Further, the loops and layers are minimal, thereby directing listener attention to changing, unexpected, or challenging elements within the piece.[6] This compositional design raises questions about where the artist is expecting an audience's attention to focus and how an artist might direct focus strategically with music. Design simplicity can further encourage deeper thought about the way in which an artist and listener have an empathetic, communicative bond despite the mediated distance of a recording. Finally, it can encourage listeners to think carefully about the ways in which the artist, in this case Monáe, is creating moments within the work to create empathy with an artistic persona or character spotlighted in the narrative.[7]

I now spotlight two examples within *The ArchAndroid*, "Cold War" and "Come Alive (War of the Roses)," that use a layered texture built of repetitive phrase loops. In both examples, musical elements like narrative, timbre, and empathy leap to the fore against these repetitive structures. For each, I have provided a formal structural design of the overall piece, a breakdown of the melodic loops, and a concise analysis of the lyrical narrative. I follow these analyses with guiding discussion questions.

"Cold War"

Formal Structure

The basic shape of "Cold War" is (arguably) simple verse-chorus form (Figure 14.1). There are six prominent loops layered and reused throughout "Cold War." The loops are recombinant, as they show up in different iterations and combinations throughout the piece. Because of the recombinatorial nature of the loops throughout the song, the form may be interpreted as simple verse-chorus; however, this may be an interesting point of discussion with students.

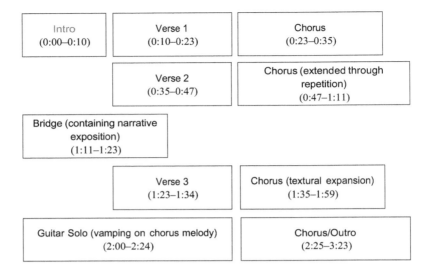

Figure 14.1 Janelle Monáe, "Cold War," from *The ArchAndroid*, formal structure.

The energy of the piece takes on a *crescendo-decrescendo* shape. As the form progresses, the texture thickens, the timbres distort, and the pitch level of Monáe's voice rises. Two sections in the piece, the bridge and the final chorus/outro, abruptly bring the energy down and are not reliant on looping structures. They deserve their own examination.

The bridge (1:11–1:23), which serves as a moment of peace and prayer, introduces a simplified contrapuntal texture (Figure 14.2).

The final outro (2:50–3:23) also introduces a chorus of singers reassuring Mayweather's listening audience (Figure 14.3). After the explosive guitar solo and escalating energy of the chorus, this outro again calms the texture and slows the rhythmic intensity.

Loop Design

The first loop centers on F minor but consistently sustains B♭ (Figure 14.4a). This ever-present tension between F and B♭ as tonal center holds narrative potential: it could represent literal separation between humans and androids, the war inside Cindi Mayweather as both android and savior, or perhaps a rift between Mayweather and her ignorant audience, who she encourages to educate themselves throughout the song.[8] This loop appears prominently within the introduction (0:00–0:10) and verse 2 (0:35–0:47).

These simultaneous loops do not close with a clear, shared cadence, especially in the introduction. The electric organ appears to stop on a plagal half cadence or authentic cadence in B♭ minor. The bass guitar loop is more obviously an authentic cadence, ending with a scalar descent in F minor. When the loop returns in verse 2 (0:35–0:47), Monáe's voice has established itself more firmly in B♭ minor (adding a consistent G♭), creating even more ambiguity. The tension between these two tonics is never resolved, which can be prominently seen in the use of both G♮ and G♭ in the outro (seen in Figure 14.2).

The second loop (Figure 14.4b), which consists of held organ notes (with harmonics), enters at verse 1 (0:10–0:23). It is later reused in the chorus sections. It, too, emphasizes B♭ minor through the addition of G♭.

The third loop adds in a choral component and occurs at the choruses (Figure 14.5a). The second chorus, which is formally expanded through the addition of loops (Figure 14.5b and c), gives Mayweather an opportunity to improvise and spurs the subsequent guitar solo.

Formal Structures and Narrative Design in The ArchAndroid 167

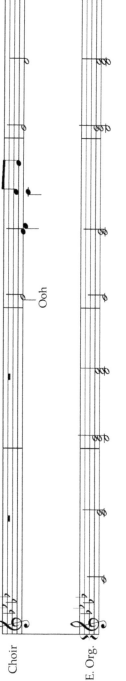

Figure 14.2 Monáe, "Cold War," bridge texture, which thins and slows.

168   Cora S. Palfy

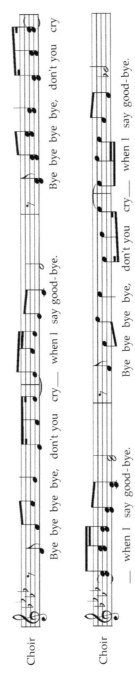

Figure 14.3 Monáe, "Cold War," outro vocals, reassuring and calming the audience/Mayweather.

Formal Structures and Narrative Design in The ArchAndroid   169

Figure 14.4 Monáe, "Cold War": (a) organ and electric bass loop from introduction and verse 2; (b) organ harmonics loop introduced in 0:10–0:23.

170 Cora S. Palfy

Figure 14.5 Monáe, "Cold War": (a) choir, organ, and bass loop from chorus 1; (b) augmentation of chorus loop with organ harmonics loop; (c) final repetition of chorus loop (1:00–1:11), which adds introductory organ melody.

Narrative and Lyrics

In this piece, Cindi Mayweather grapples with the reality of being an android in Star Core Metropolis. Androids are objectified and forced into servitude, are routinely hunted and killed for relationships with humans, and can only know freedom by escaping underground. "Cold War" is the first on the album to expose that Mayweather is fated to be a messiah figure who restructures the social hierarchy and norms of Star Core Metropolis. Throughout, Mayweather implores her fellow android and human rebels to educate themselves about the rebellion and join the fight – she invites them to join her "underground," in a not-so-subtle reference to the American Underground Railroad (Romano 2018; Sterritt 2013). Themes of escape, freedom, and rebellion are foregrounded throughout the album but are especially prominent in this piece; "Cold War," therefore, provides an excellent opportunity to connect culturally responsive dialogue about American social justice movements (such as the civil rights movement, Black Lives Matter, or the #MeToo movement).

The lyrics reflect Mayweather's inner turmoil as she reflects on the abusive nature of her culture: in Star Core Metropolis, "you spend life fighting for your sanity"; she was "taught to believe there's something wrong with [her]"; and she foreshadows the underground rebellion she instigates later in the album and series ("If you want to be free, the underground's the only place to be"). The repetitive loop structures could be narratively interpreted as the habitual and interchangeable nature of androids, or their repetitive tasks.

Perhaps the most important narrative section is the bridge (1:11–1:23), in which the texture slows, allowing focus on Mayweather's prayer to the higher power, "The Maker" (revealed in track 9, "Oh Maker," on *The ArchAndroid*). Invoking strength and wisdom, Mayweather asks that her efforts find success and her enemies be foiled. The thinner texture and simpler rhythms in this section encourage focus on the lyrics and can lead to a constructive discussion about empathy: in this passage, despite the swirling frenzy of formal sections that have come before and which follow, Mayweather finds a moment of quiet to pray and hope.

In the final chorus, it becomes clear that the "Cold War" in the title is not a simple metaphor for discontent. Mayweather's voice escalates with the pitch and timbre of the electric guitar solo, with the repeated titular lyrics reflecting the fervor of beginning a movement to restructure Star Core Metropolis. Mayweather's intensity contrasts with the outro (2:50–3:23). As the texture calms in the outro, singers repeat the words "Bye bye bye bye, don't you cry when I say goodbye." This implies that, despite Mayweather's later capture, she will eventually return to continue fighting for the freedom of her fellow androids. These lyrics also draw attention to the song's position within the album (track 6) – a larger point of discussion, highlighted in the questions provided at the end of the chapter, is what role this song plays in the plot and advancement of the narrative.

"Come Alive (War of the Roses)"

Formal Structure

"Come Alive" is a simple verse-chorus form in C minor (Figure 14.6). One prominent loop is used throughout, introduced by the electric bass in the introduction to the piece. This loop is frequently doubled at the octave by the electric guitar and is also used as a point of improvisation in the solo section.

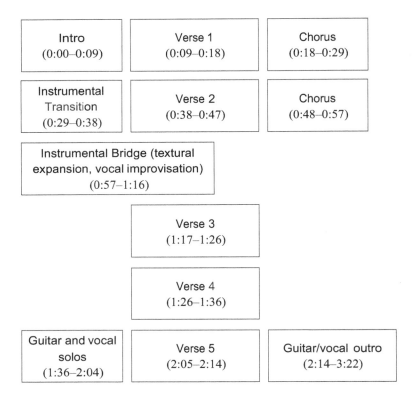

Figure 14.6 Monáe, "Come Alive," from *The ArchAndroid*, formal structure.

A lesson on this song might focus on the escalation of vocal timbre and electric guitar distortion between verses 3 and 4 (1:17–1:36). In these sections, Mayweather moves from whispered, agitated declamation to outright screaming. This escalation mirrors the terror and aggression displayed in the lyrics as Mayweather's mood shifts from that of a subdued patient to that of an enraged rebel across the course of the song.

As in "Cold War," moments of calm and contrast within the intensifying formal structure are crucial for analysis. The instrumental bridge provides just such a moment, introducing an organ playing in a bell timbre, mixed choir, and vocal improvisation (Figure 14.7). The section provides an excellent point of conversation about timbre and spatiality; the mixing choices for this section make the bells and voices sound ethereal, as if Mayweather was far away and in a large, echoing space. This contrasts sharply with the following verse 3, in which Mayweather's whisper is close and centered in the quiet mix, as if she is restrained and in a smaller room.

Loop Design

The primary loop in "Come Alive" is the electric bass melody featured in the introduction (Figure 14.8).

Narrative and Lyrics

In this punk- and blues-inspired piece, Mayweather is restrained in an institution after being captured by bounty hunters. The lyrics reflect her experience of being medicated

Formal Structures and Narrative Design in The ArchAndroid 173

Figure 14.7 Monáe, "Come Alive," instrumental bridge (0:57–1:16).

Figure 14.8 Monáe, "Come Alive," loop featured in the introduction.

as she is detained ("Tommy thinks the crazies are back in my mind"; "You want to see me crazy, takin' my meds"). In true punk spirit, Mayweather reacts to her inhumane treatment by threatening her doctors and caregivers ("And if you come and find me, I'll color you red"; "You better leave town because I'm coming for you"). The repetitive loop, which ends prominently on a phrygian half cadence, could reflect Mayweather's repetitive daily routine within the institution, recurrent thoughts of escape and anger, or her deep and recurrent distress through the repeating *pianto* gesture.

Like "Cold War," "Come Alive" contains references to themes of rebellion, escapism through mental dissociation, and imagined freedom. In this song, however, her restraint and medication are immediately occurring. This could provide an interesting point of discussion about the difference in and intensity of Mayweather's reaction in "Come Alive"; she is vocal, aggressive, and actively furious. While Mayweather is passionate in "Cold War," the vocal timbre is markedly different during her struggle in the institution.

The immediacy of Mayweather's restraint relates to the song's escalating formal structure. While the opening verses are pitched low and with clear timbre, the solo sections rapidly escalate as Mayweather literally screams over the repeating bass loop (2:23–end). The guitar, which increases reliance on the distortion pedal through the end of the song, is either reflective of Mayweather's fraying mental state or an extension of her frantic vocalizations. The pairing of guitar and vocals within the solo sections reflects the intense physical exertion Mayweather uses to fight her restraints. This provides an excellent opportunity to discuss the correlation of force and physical exertion on timbre – indeed, it is difficult not to empathize with the escalating pitch, harsh vocal timbre, and distorted guitar. Students may find that, as they empathize with the character, they feel aggressive, angry, and overwhelmed; the instructor can encourage students to use physical discomfort as a listener or player to inform arguments about musical meaning. This is an opportunity to discuss how empathy and embodied topics, such as timbre, can connect a listener to the artist and characters in a musical narrative; the artist has designed it that way.

The ethereal section introduced at the instrumental bridge is rife with narrative possibilities because of its repetition in the form as well as its contrasting energy level. It prompts analysis of timbre, spatiality, and empathy with Mayweather and can encourage discussion about the dehumanizing treatment Mayweather is receiving. The ethereal instrumental section returns following the guitar solo at 1:55, after Mayweather's outbursts and aggressive threats. Prior to the bridge, Mayweather declares, "Now let's go wild!" Similarly, at the close of verse 4, the lyrics state, "I'm getting wild on you, you better go and call the law." This raises the question of whether the sections at the bridge and 1:55 are related to dissociative escape within Mayweather's mind ("When everything is wrong, I dance inside my mind."). The section could also be interpreted as a medicated stupor because of the spatial distortion, new and calming instrumental timbres, and the mention of medication in verse 3 following the bridge. Encourage students to embrace ambiguity in this section; it is not clear what has occurred, and there is no clarification in the remainder of the album.

Guiding Discussion Questions

The following questions are meant to be a starting point for a broader discussion and may be augmented based on the information previously presented.

1. Monáe uses **textural thickening** in piece X – this means that, throughout the piece, Monáe adds or subtracts loops and sample layers. Describe how piece X is shaped based on changes in **texture**. (Hint: it may be helpful to look up "orchestration" and "texture." Feel free to **paraphrase** any definitions you find useful.)

2. What is the phrase structure of the _____ in piece X? Would you characterize it as a simple or complex formal structure? Explain your choice.
3. How does the repetitive nature of the loops in piece X manipulate your attentional focus? Reflect on your engagement with the different pieces of the texture that we've studied, highlighting any that you thought were either memorable (caught your attention) or unmemorable (faded from your attention).
4. How might the structural simplicity of piece X's compositional design force your attention to the words and narrative?
5. Where does piece X fall within the larger concept album's structure? Reflect on why this piece falls where it does in the album, taking into account the previous two questions.
6. The voice of Cindi Mayweather (sung by Monáe) becomes increasingly strained throughout both songs. By the end of "Cold War," Mayweather is screaming her improvisation. Listen closely to the electric guitar's timbre; defend or reject the interpretive position that **the guitar is acting as an extension of Mayweather's voice in these pieces.** (Note: there is no "correct" answer to this question, just a well-defended and evidenced answer!)
7. Piece X's narrative explores issues of identity as they intersect with systematic oppression through the lens of android Cindi Mayweather (you can read a summary of the storyline in Wanak 2019 or Félix 2018). Draw at least one connection to a current event of your choice and explain how Monáe's narrative helped you think about that event. Please provide a link to a news article from an approved source.

Conclusion

This chapter has examined how structural simplicity can foster rich dialogue and interpretive thought in the classroom. By incorporating transitional materials that allow simultaneous reinforcement of old material alongside newer concepts, students can be encouraged both to continue engaging prior material and to create moments in which students practice professional music theoretical interpretation.

Notes

1. Palfy (2020) describes how ostinati can become memory devices for narrative, increasing empathy with an artist by engaging reminiscence.
2. Monáe has earned eight Grammy Award nominations alongside 48 other awards, including an ASCAP Vanguard Award in 2010, two Soul Train Music Awards in 2010 and 2013, two Billboard Women in Music Awards in 2013 and 2018, the NAACP Image Award in 2014, and the GLAAD Media Award for Outstanding Artist in 2019.
3. "Both an artistic aesthetic and a framework for critical theory, Afrofuturism combines elements of science fiction, historical fiction, speculative fiction, fantasy, Afrocentricity, and magic realism with non-Western beliefs. In some cases, it's a total re-envisioning of the past and speculation about the future rife with cultural critiques" (Womack 2013, 9).
4. "From her first reference to Metropolis, the cold, dystopian, slave droid-powered city that looms over each of her albums, Monáe has built her discography through sci-fi tropes codified by 20th-century white male writers. In the process, as great women of sci-fi have done before her, she's mapped those narratives onto her own identity, claiming them for 'androids' like herself. 'I speak about androids because I think the android represents the new 'other',' she told the *Evening Standard* in 2013. 'You can compare it to being a lesbian or being a gay man or being a black woman'" (Romano 2018).
5. "All told, the student-reported outcomes strongly suggest that interacting with diverse peers, faculty, and curricula as an undergraduate has a substantial positive effect on the development of skills needed to function in an increasingly diverse society as well as other academic skills important to the learning process" (Hurtado 2001, 199).

6. This is similar to the way the simplicity of a recitative texture forces attention on the singer's declamation of plot context.
7. Palfy (2016) explores the idea of "artistic agency" in more depth.
8. See also Spicer (2017).

Bibliography

Adams, Maurianne. 1992. "Cultural Inclusion in the American College Classroom." *New Directions for Teaching and Learning* 49: 5–15.
Ambrose, Susan A., Michael W. Bridges, Michele DiPietro, Marsha C. Lovett, and Marie K. Norman. 2010. *How Learning Works: Seven Research-Based Principles for Smart Teaching*. John Wiley & Sons.
Anderson, Reynaldo, and Charles E. Jones. 2015. *Afrofuturism 2.0: The Rise of Astro-Blackness*. Lexington Books.
Ausubel, David Paul. 2012. *The Acquisition and Retention of Knowledge: A Cognitive View*. Springer Science & Business Media.
Benassi, Victor, Catherine E. Overson, Chris Hakala, John Hattie, Slava Kalyuga, Chee Ha Lee, Jennifer J. Stiegler-Balfour, et al. 2014. *Applying Science of Learning in Education: Infusing Psychological Science into the Curriculum*. Society for the Teaching of Psychology.
Childre, Amy, Jennifer R. Sands, and Sandra Tanner Pope. 2009. "Backward Design: Targeting Depth of Understanding for All Learners." *Teaching Exceptional Children* 41/5: 6–14.
Cox, Arnie. 2016. *Music and Embodied Cognition: Listening, Moving, Feeling, and Thinking*. Indiana University Press.
Driscoll, Marcy Perkins. 1994. *Psychology of learning for instruction*. Allyn & Bacon.
Félix, Doreen St. 2018. "The Otherworldly Concept Albums of Janelle Monáe." The New Yorker. Accessed June 14, 2021. www.newyorker.com/culture/culture-desk/the-otherworldly-concept-albums-of-janelle-monae
Fleming, Amy, and Aaron Grant. December 2020. "The Rest Is Noise : A Historically Integrated Approach to Post-Tonal Pedagogy." *Journal of Music Theory Pedagogy* 34. https://jmtp.appstate.edu/rest-noise-historically-integrated-approach-post-tonal-pedagogy
Gilroy, Paul. 1991. "Sounds Authentic: Black Music, Ethnicity, and the Challenge of a 'Changing' Same." *Black Music Research Journal* 11/2: 111–36.
Ginsberg, Margery B., and Raymond J. Wlodkowski. 2015. *Diversity and Motivation: Culturally Responsive Teaching in College*. John Wiley & Sons.
Gosper, Maree, and Dirk Ifenthaler. 2014. "Curriculum Design for the Twenty-First Century." In *Curriculum Models for the 21st Century: Using Learning Technologies in Higher Education*, edited by Maree Gosper and Dirk Ifenthaler, 1–14. Springer.
Hoard, Christian. 2010. "Artist of the Week: Janelle Monae." *Rolling Stone*. www.rollingstone.com/music/music-news/artist-of-the-week-janelle-monae-186564/
Huang, Min-Hsiung. 2009. "Classroom Homogeneity and the Distribution of Student Math Performance: A Country-Level Fixed-Effects Analysis." *Social Science Research* 38/4: 781–91.
Hurtado, Sylvia. 2001. "Linking Diversity and Educational Purpose: How Diversity Affects the Classroom Environment and Student Development." In *Diversity Challenged: Evidence on the Impact of Affirmative Action*, 187–203. Harvard Education Publishing Group.
Lyden, Jackie. 2013. "'Electric Lady' Janelle Monae On Creating The Unheard." *NPR.Org*. www.npr.org/2013/09/07/218617976/electric-lady-janelle-monae-on-creating-the-unheard
Milem, Jeffrey F. 2001. "Increasing Diversity Benefits: How Campus Climate and Teaching Methods Affect Student Outcomes." In *Diversity Challenged: Evidence on the Impact of Affirmative Action*, 233–49. Cambridge: Harvard Education Publishing Group.
Monáe, Janelle. 2010. *The ArchAndroid*. Bad Boy Records.
Palfy, Cora S. 2016. "Human After All: Understanding Negotiations of Artistic Identity through the Music of Daft Punk." In *The Oxford Handbook of Music and Virtuality*, edited by Sheila Whiteley and Shara Rambarran, 282–305. Oxford University Press.
———. 2020. "Formal Reminiscence Space and Memory in Sufjan Stevens's Storytelling." *Music Theory Online* 26/1.

Peters, Gretchen. 2016. "Do Students See Themselves in the Music Curriculum?: A Project to Encourage Inclusion." *Music Educators Journal* 102/4: 22–29.

Pitchfork. 2013. "Take Cover: Janelle Monáe's The Electric Lady." *Pitchfork*. https://pitchfork.com/thepitch/62-take-cover-janelle-monae/

Pulliam-Moore, Charles. 2018. "From Metropolis to Dirty Computer: A Guide to Janelle Monáe's Time-Traveling Musical Odyssey." *Gizmodo*. Accessed June 14, 2021. https://gizmodo.com/from-metropolis-to-dirty-computer-a-guide-to-janelle-m-1825580195

Rohrer, Doug, Robert F. Dedrick, and Sandra Stershic. 2015. "Interleaved Practice Improves Mathematics Learning." *Journal of Educational Psychology* 107/3: 900–08.

Romano, Aja. May 16, 2018. "Janelle Monáe's Body of Work Is a Masterpiece of Modern Science Fiction." *Vox*. www.vox.com/2018/5/16/17318242/janelle-monae-science-fiction-influences-afrofuturism

Rovee-Collier, Carolyn K., Harlene Hayne, and Michael Colombo. 2001. *The Development of Implicit and Explicit Memory*, vol. 24. John Benjamins Publishing.

Sawyer, R. Keith. 2014. *The Cambridge Handbook of the Learning Sciences*. Cambridge University Press.

Singer, Tania. 2006. "The Neuronal Basis and Ontogeny of Empathy and Mind Reading: Review of Literature and Implications for Future Research." *Neuroscience & Biobehavioral Reviews* 30/6: 855–63.

Singer, Tania, and Claus Lamb. 2009. "The Social Neuroscience of Empathy." *Annals of the New York Academy of Sciences* 1156/1: 81–96.

Spicer, Mark. 2017. "Fragile, Emergent, and Absent Tonics in Pop and Rock Songs." *Music Theory Online* 23/2. https://mtosmt.org/issues/mto.17.23.2/mto.17.23.2.spicer.html

Stainback, Susan Bray, and William C. Stainback. 1996. *Inclusion: A Guide for Educators*. P.H. Brookes Publishing Company.

Steele, Claude M. 2011. *Whistling Vivaldi: And Other Clues to How Stereotypes Affect Us (Issues of Our Time)*. W.W. Norton & Company.

Sterritt, Laura. 2013. "Metropolis: Janelle Monáe's Hidden Sci-Fi Epic." *TransChordian* (blog). www.transchordian.com/2013/10/metropolis-janelle-monaes-hidden-sci-fi-epic/

Wanak, LaShawn M. October 18, 2019. "Metropolis Meets Afrofuturism: The Genius of Janelle Monáe." *Tor.Com*. www.tor.com/2019/10/18/metropolis-meets-afrofuturism-the-genius-of-janelle-monae/

Wentzel, Kathryn, and Jere E. Brophy. 2014. *Motivating Students to Learn*. Routledge.

Wiggins, Grant P., Grant Wiggins, and Jay McTighe. 2005. *Understanding by Design*. ASCD.

Womack, Ytasha L. 2013. *Afrofuturism: The World of Black Sci-Fi and Fantasy Culture*. Chicago Review Press.

Yaszek, Lisa. 2006. "Afrofuturism, Science Fiction, and the History of the Future." *Socialism and Democracy* 20/3: 41–60.

15 Diving Deeper into Rhythm and Meter Through Drum Parts in Twenty-First-Century Pop

David Geary

Popular music is becoming increasingly prevalent in today's music theory classrooms in response to the artistic goals and interests of current students. A pedagogical implication of this repertoire diversification is that we, as teachers, should be providing our students conceptual models, musical skills, and analytical and creative opportunities focused on popular music's defining characteristics. Rhythm and meter are considered the cornerstone of many popular styles – particularly those pioneered and performed by Black musicians, such as funk, rap, and, more recently, pop. The drums are commonly cited as the rhythmic and metric foundation of popular music, and this chapter provides a pedagogical overview of drum parts in twenty-first-century pop songs by Black artists. In short, the drums are often mischaracterized as just a timekeeper, establishing a song's metric grid while other parts fluctuate more regularly. In reality, the instrument is also a primary driver of one of the genre's hallmark attributes: textural variety within individual tracks. Today's pop hits typically include multiple drum patterns and other sounding components that create different expressions of meter, articulate musical form, and fulfill other syntactical and affective functions.

In two lessons, this chapter provides students an overview of the norms and artistic potential of drum parts with analysis and composition as the primary musical skills. The first day starts with an introductory activity before focusing on individual drum patterns, their sounding characteristics, and their functions within individual formal areas. The second day surveys how drum parts operate across larger spans of music. These lessons are designed for an undergraduate music theory elective on American popular music, though I have taught an abbreviated version during a popular music module in Music Theory II. The activities described hereafter are moderately flexible in terms of both depth and placement, and instructors are encouraged to shrink, expand, reorder, or otherwise amend them to fit their specific educational environments. Students will need a computer or laptop with internet access and headphones for some activities. Instructors will need to be able to operate BandLab, an online digital audio workstation; distribute audio files to students through a learning management system, email, or other method; and possibly perform basic audio editing.

I begin the first lesson by summarizing many of the introductory points previously mentioned for students. Studying rhythm and meter involves much more than meter classifications and time signature designations. In fact, in many repertoires, a song's rhythmic and metric attributes can be equally or more expressive, variable, and syntactical than pitch characteristics such as melody and harmony. Popular music is a great example, and we will study how a single instrument, the drums, can fulfill temporal, affective, and rhetorical functions through its sounding components and their variation across a song.

Pivoting to the opening activity, I inform students that this and our next class will focus specifically on drum parts in twenty-first-century mainstream pop. American popular music drumming has evolved over the past century, and today's top pop hits are based upon the two drum patterns in Figure 15.1a. The standard rock drum pattern alternates bass drum and snare drum attacks with steady eighth notes in the hi-hat, which can be heard in Michael Jackson's "Billie Jean" (1982). Alternatively, the four-on-the-floor pattern has a steady, repeating bass drum rhythm. An example is Technotronix's "Pump Up the Jam" (1989) that has the bass drum ostinato and, not an uncommon addition, various cymbals and other drums interspersed throughout the track.

These two drum patterns can be heard in today's mainstream pop hits, but rarely as identical and fixed realizations. This first activity asks students to listen to the introduction and first verse-chorus unit (VCU) of Lizzo's "Good as Hell" (2016) and describe how the drum part varies throughout the excerpt. This task is likely an unfamiliar mode of listening for students, so I encourage them to respond informally with whatever ideas come to mind as we begin developing new musical skills. We listen to the excerpt once, and students exchange initial ideas in pairs. After a second hearing, we discuss "Good as Hell" together, and I strive to facilitate and foster dialogue before, if necessary, sharing my own observations. I also project Figure 15.1b at some point to serve as a visual aid and motivate more conversation. The main takeaway is that the drum part has multiple drum patterns that sound different combinations of instruments and rhythms, influencing each section's temporal, rhetorical, and expressive effect. A few drum fills, and an instance of text painting through the drums, also contribute to the song's impact. The introduction and postchorus have no drums, which creates a sparsity that parallels the typical functions of these formal areas. The verse has a variation of the standard rock drum pattern: omitting the hi-hat, substituting snaps for snare drum, and embellishing the bass drum's standard rock rhythm. Verse 1 is also preceded by a brief drum fill, a suspended cymbal roll, and eighth-note sandpaper blocks depict the phrase "dust your shoulder off." The prechorus's drum pattern is snaps alone, thinner and quieter than what precedes and follows. The chorus, also prepared with a drum fill, includes the excerpt's fullest drum pattern. It introduces the hi-hat for the first time and performs more syncopated snare drum and bass drum rhythms compared to the verse. Despite being difficult to aurally identify, the bongos also help instrumentally and rhythmically densify the focal formal area's drum pattern.

The primary purpose of Lizzo's excerpt, and the module as a whole, is not to be able to identify every detail of every drum part. It is to show how the drums' rhythmic and metric characteristics are significant and communicative facets of today's pop hits and to demonstrate that studying these attributes provides new ways to hear, create, and appreciate popular music. I conclude the introductory activity by providing students with the big-picture plan for our two-day module. Today's goals are to learn more about individual drum patterns, their variable characteristics, and their functions and affordances within individual formal areas; and the second class shifts to analyzing and creating drum parts across verse-chorus units in order to see more patterns and possibilities for how drums vary across excerpts like Lizzo's "Good as Hell."

The first lesson's remaining activities include an overview of the four primary characteristics of drum patterns, analysis with two new methods of annotation, and composition of a drum pattern with BandLab. Before jumping in, however, I quickly define a few terms. The "drum set," or "the drums," is the instrument used to perform or create drum parts, which includes acoustic kits, electronic drums, and digital audio workstations. A "drum part" is the totality of what the drums perform throughout a song. "Drum patterns" are repetitive ostinatos, and they are the main component of drum parts in twenty-first-century mainstream pop. "Drum fills" are decorative connectors at phrase and formal boundaries which are used intermittently in this genre. Finally, though a rarity in pop, "drum solos" spotlight the instrument's melodic potential.

180 David Geary

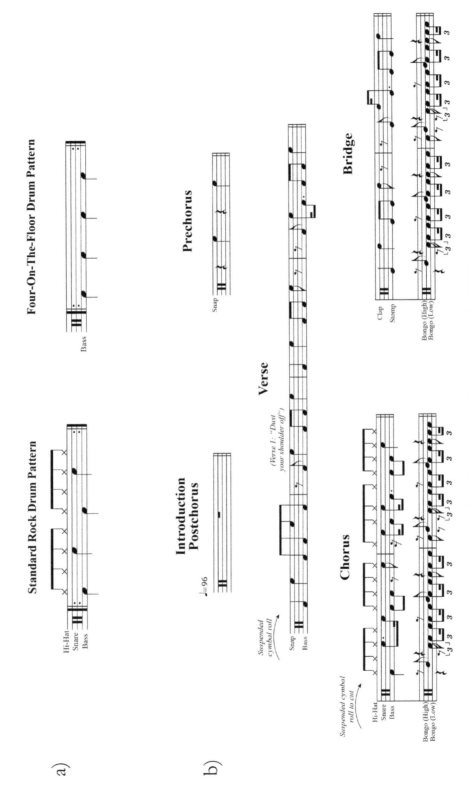

Figure 15.1 (a) The standard rock and four-on-the-floor drum patterns; (b) Lizzo's "Good as Hell."

The introductory activity typically takes about 10 to 15 minutes. The next ten-minute activity is an overview of a drum pattern's four primary characteristics, followed by two informal analytical examples. Projecting Table 15.1, I begin by telling students that these attributes are not meant to be a comprehensive account of every detail for every drum pattern; rather, they provide an effective foundation for both analysis and composition. First, drum patterns can perform different combinations of high, middle, and low drum layers. Common options include zero layers (a tacit "pattern"), a one-layer snare drum backbeat, a two-layer bass drum and snare drum combo, and a three-layer standard rock realization. Multiple instruments occasionally work interdependently to fulfill a single layer, such as doubling a backbeat rhythm with snare drum and claps. The second characteristic is instrumentation, and Table 15.1 lists the prevalent options for each drum layer. Third, each drum layer also has a set of common rhythms, all of which can be varied by adding, subtracting, or shifting certain attacks: eighth notes or sixteenth notes in the high layer; backbeat (most common), straight four, or tresillo in the middle layer; and standard rock (most common), four-on-the-floor, or tresillo in the low layer. Also, it is not unusual for there to be a change in drum feel among a song's multiple drum patterns, such as shifting from a common-time feel to a half-time feel for contrast in a bridge section. Finally, drum patterns vary in duration.[1] For example, the four-on-the-floor pattern in Figure 15.1a is one quarter note long, and the standard rock ostinato is two quarter notes in duration. Lengthier options are also possible based upon instrumental and rhythmic variation.

Next, students listen to two excerpts and practice describing drum patterns according to the four characteristics. The first is the chorus of Beyoncé's "Halo" (2009). As students respond, I notate their answers on the board according to the format in Figure 15.2. Shown on the left, "Halo" has a two-layer pattern composed of claps and stomps. The claps

Table 15.1 Four Primary Characteristics of Drum Patterns in Twenty-First Century Mainstream Pop

Number of Layers	• Different combinations of high, middle, and low drum layers. • Multiple instruments can fulfill a single layer (i.e., snare drum + claps). • Tacit "patterns" (zero layers) are possible.

Instrumentation	• Different instruments are common for each drum layer:
	  • High: hi-hat and other cymbals
	  • Middle: snare drum, claps, and snaps
	  • Low: bass drum and stomps

Rhythm	• Different rhythms are common for each drum layer:
	  • High: eighths and sixteenths
	  • Middle: backbeat (most common), straight four, and tresillo
	  • Low: standard rock (most common), four-on-the-floor, and tresillo
	• Rhythms can vary by adding, subtracting, or shifting attacks.
	• Half-time feel (more common) and double-time feel patterns are possible.

Length	• ½ measure, 1 measure, 2 measures, and 4 measures are common.

Beyoncé's "Halo"
Drum Pattern (four measures)
Claps: backbeat rhythm
Stomps: embellished standard rock rhythm

Rihanna's "Umbrella" featuring Jay-Z
Drum Pattern (two measures)
Hi-hat (open and closed): embellished sixteenth-note rhythm
Snare drum: embellished backbeat rhythm
Bass drum: embellished standard rock rhythm

Figure 15.2 Beyoncé's "Halo" and Rihanna's "Umbrella" featuring Jay-Z.

182 David Geary

perform a backbeat rhythm, while stomps embellish the standard rock rhythm. Difficult to quickly identify, the drum pattern is four measures long. As a final analytical point, I draw students' attention to the rhythmic parallel between the voice and drums during the song's title text ("I can feel your halo, halo, halo/I can see your halo, halo, halo") to show how a drum pattern's rhythm is often motivated by its relationship to other parts of the track.

The second example is the chorus and postchorus of Rihanna's "Umbrella" featuring Jay-Z (2008). In a few hearings, students notate the drum pattern's characteristics on their own, using the same format as "Halo." Shown on the right of Figure 15.2, the two-measure drum pattern has open and closed hi-hat attacks performing an embellished sixteenth-note rhythm, snare drum embellishing the backbeat rhythm, and bass drum embellishing the standard rock rhythm. I also highlight this song's rhythmic parallel during Rihanna's postchorus statement of "eh, eh, eh."

The Beyoncé and Rihanna excerpts help students practice what is likely a new type of aural analysis, and the previous annotative method succinctly depicts a drum pattern's four characteristics in general terms. The next activity continues developing the same skills, but through a second and more detailed transcriptive system. I begin by telling students that dictating music is a valuable skill and that different types of visual representation can be better suited, easier to create, and more stylistically relevant than others for certain repertoires and musical tasks. For instance, we use staff notation to depict melodies and Roman numerals to communicate harmonies because they effectively and efficiently illustrate what they aim to represent. For drum patterns, staff notation can be cumbersome to create, and our informal method previously shown may not always provide sufficient detail. At this point, I introduce students to table notation by projecting Figure 15.3a and Figure 15.3b and describing their representations of the Beyoncé and Rihanna drum patterns.[2] In short, each row depicts an instrument, every column represents a sixteenth note, and an "X" designates an attack within the metric grid. Addendums and modifications can be used as needed, but this basic design can depict most drum patterns with great accuracy. As a pedagogical aside, this setup is also similar to BandLab's drum machine and other DAWs, allowing for a smooth transition to composition later in the lesson. The summary of table notation is followed by a dictation of verse 1 from Flo Rida's "My House" (2015). Figure 15.3c provides the answer. Though teachers may choose to provide the instrumentation, meter, and drum pattern length upfront for class time efficiency, I prefer to have students determine these features through a few initial hearings. Next, we isolate each instrumental layer and dictate its rhythm. As a fairly straightforward example, the activity should move quickly.

The first lesson's last activity moves from analysis to composition, where students create their own drum patterns with BandLab. BandLab is a free online digital audio workstation that allows students to learn many popular music essentials, such as recording vocal melodies, creating instrumental parts with MIDI input, and editing tracks. For this module, students compose drum parts with the platform's drum machine as a way to deepen their command of the instrument's norms and artistic potential through creation. Before class, students are given a homework assignment to make a BandLab account and watch a short YouTube tutorial about the program's drum machine. In class, I begin this activity by recreating Flo Rida's drum pattern on BandLab for students to review the process and ask questions. Figure 15.4 provides a snapshot of my project. The top of the interface has the playback, tempo, time signature, and metronome features. The bottom of the screen defaults to opening the instrument window, which looks similar to table notation. Different drum kits can be selected on the far left, specific instrumentation can be changed in the left column, and the grid's 16 steps represent sixteenth notes in a $\frac{4}{4}$ measure.[3] The instrument window also shows that BandLab can store up to eight one-measure patterns, allowing

Rhythm and Meter Through Drum Parts in Twenty-First-Century Pop 183

Figure 15.3 (a) Beyoncé's "Halo" with table notation; (b) Rihanna's "Umbrella" featuring Jay-Z with table notation; (c) Flo Rida's "My House" with table notation.

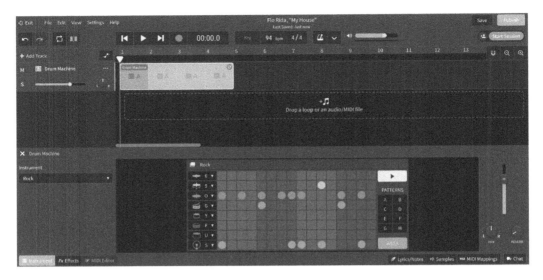

Figure 15.4 Snapshot of BandLab.

users to create a handful of one-measure and multi-measure drum patterns as well as drum fills. Once created, a drum pattern can be added to the drum machine track in the middle of the screen, where it can be looped, moved, and edited in other ways.

The prompt for the composition activity is to create a drum pattern for an excerpt of The Weeknd's "Blinding Lights" (2020) that has the drum part removed.[4] The goal is for students to demonstrate a command of the four drum pattern characteristics and to have their drum pattern creatively work interdependently with the other parts of the track. Half the class is assigned the first verse, and the other half is assigned the first chorus. Students begin by creating a new project on BandLab, setting the tempo to 171 beats per minute (BPM), and importing an mp3 file of their excerpt from our learning management system.[5] Next, I tell students that this activity also foreshadows aspects of our next lesson, which focuses on how drum parts vary across longer passages of music. For this composition, they should select characteristics from Table 15.1 based upon how they think drum patterns may differ between verses and choruses. Finally, we listen to the first verse-chorus unit together before students begin working independently. It typically does not take them long to create their drum pattern and add it to their drum track alongside the provided audio, resulting in a rewarding collaboration between them and The Weeknd.[6] The activity concludes with listening to and discussing each other's creations – first in pairs, and then as a class, where I ask for volunteers to share their work. Students typically create wonderful and widely varying drum patterns, which ignites lively discussion about their artistic decisions and preferences. If instructors run out of class time, they may choose to have students complete the activity as homework or at the beginning of the next class.

Again, the first lesson introduces students to the rewards of studying the rhythmic and metric features of music through a survey of drum parts in twenty-first-century pop hits. It also teaches skills for analyzing and composing individual drum patterns. I start the next class by quickly summarizing these points and by framing the remaining goals and activities. In the second lesson, students analyze and create drum parts across verse-chorus units as a way to better understand how drums can vary within and across sections. A deeper dive into fewer activities, it begins with an overview of pop's typical formal structure and the drum part's paralleling characteristics. Then, we analyze one song that exemplifies these norms and another song that demonstrates some extensions commonly at play in the genre. Finally, the lesson concludes with students composing a complete drum part for a verse-chorus unit in groups, crafting a series of drum patterns and drum fills that they decide effectively fulfills the instrument's temporal, syntactical, and expressive functions.

Analyzing and creating drum parts across multiple sections of a song requires a general knowledge of form. The challenge, however, is that no structure perfectly encapsulates the many layouts of individual hits. The result, as I tell students, is that formal analysis often requires flexible and interpretive application of a genre's general consistencies. Figure 15.5's diagram and table outline the layout, section labels, and rhetorical functions of a typical song. Tunes often begin with a brief, prefatory, and texturally thin introduction that presents some of a song's main temporal, melodic, and harmonic features. Songs then progress through two verse-chorus unit rotations, the latter possibly presenting subtle changes. VCUs are commonly characterized as growing from expository verses to climactic choruses, which can be linked by an intensifying prechorus. In twenty-first-century pop hits, it is also possible to have a section after the chorus. A postchorus continues some chorus material while removing other parts in order to connect smoothly to the next rotation. Alternatively, a dance chorus continues a VCU's build by sustaining or growing texturally from the preceding chorus while replacing most or all of the vocal text with a song's melodic hook. A pop song's third rotation begins with a contrasting bridge that introduces original material before returning to a final chorus iteration, which almost always functions as a track's high point. If present, the outro provides a section of repose.

My description of musical form is succinct in order to move quickly to a group discussion about how drum parts can work alongside a track's vocal and other instrumental parts to create a cohesive and expressive whole. In twenty-first-century mainstream pop, this most regularly entails having multiple drum patterns throughout a track. With the goal of generating ideas rather than prescribing definitive answers, I ask students to hypothesize how varying each drum pattern characteristic in Table 15.1 can match the rhetorical function of different sections and how drum fills can contribute to a sense of flow between formal areas. Adding or subtracting the number of drum layers can quite directly project growth or decay between successive drum patterns. Similarly, increasing rhythmic density,

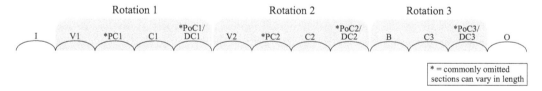

Figure 15.5 An analytical guide for twenty-first-century mainstream pop.

embellishments, and syncopation can create a sense of accumulation. Shifting from a common-time feel to a half-time or double-time feel drum pattern can create contrast. Some changes in instrumentation may be more straightforward than others in terms of their effect, such as using snaps in verses and snare drum in choruses. Some students intuit that longer drum patterns can parallel more focal sections, yet there is typically more consensus that it can be difficult to aurally identify a drum pattern's length, making its rhetorical impact less clear. Finally, drum fills in pop hits have diverse characteristics, placements, and effects. Again, the goal of this discussion is to provide students with a framework and an invitation for analysis and creation rather than a rigid depictive or prescriptive formula.

The conversation flows into an analytical example that follows Figure 15.5's layout and supports ideas from our discussion. Together, our goal is to identify the form, drum patterns, and drum fills for the first verse-chorus unit of Nelly's "Just a Dream" (2010) and to describe how the drum part, through its variability, functions throughout the excerpt. After a first hearing, students identify the passage's layout of verse, prechorus, and chorus. Next, I ask students to try identifying the number of drum patterns on the second hearing. Is there one throughout the VCU, one for each section, or something else? Though usually unable to pinpoint all the sounding components immediately, students can often hear that there are three drum patterns, one for each section. We next isolate each drum pattern and depict its characteristics with our informal method of annotation from Figure 15.2. We also discuss the impact of the drum patterns' varying characteristics as we progress through the excerpt. Shown in Figure 15.6, verse 1 begins with a clap backbeat rhythm and an embellished standard rock bass drum rhythm. Prechorus 1 maintains these layers while adding sixteenth notes in the hi-hat, creating both continuity and accumulation across the drum pattern change. Finally, moving from the prechorus to the chorus also has continuity and growth. Drum pattern 3 preserves the same composite rhythm as drum pattern 2 while substituting snare drum for claps. Once we have analyzed and discussed the drum patterns, we listen to the excerpt again to identify any drum fills. The verse and prechorus end by briefly removing the drums, providing a sonic gap that invites the instrument's return at the beginning of the next section.

"Just a Dream" gives students the opportunity to hone their analytical skills through an archetypal example with a relatively straightforward drum part. It is paired with a second analytical example, Nicki Minaj's "Right by My Side," featuring Chris Brown (2012), that illustrates some of the idiosyncrasies that permeate twenty-first-century mainstream pop.[7] Additionally, students complete the second analysis in small groups of two to four, in order to give them more independence and ownership over the analytical process.[8] We start the activity together by identifying the form of the opening 1' 26" through an initial listening. "Right by My Side" begins with an introduction, verse, prechorus, and chorus. I then describe two analytical goals for students to complete in their groups. The first goal is to identify and depict, with our informal method of annotation, the excerpt's drum patterns, drum fills, their sounding characteristics, and their formal locations. The second

Verse 1 (eight measures)
Drum Pattern 1 (two measures)
Claps: backbeat rhythm
Bass drum: embellished standard rock
   Drum fill (fourth measure): drums cut
   out for third and fourth quarter notes

Prechorus 1 (four measures)
Drum Pattern 2 (two measures)
Closed hi-hat: sixteenth notes
Claps: backbeat rhythm
Bass drum: embellished standard rock
   Drum fill (last measure): drums cut out

Chorus 1 (eight measures):
Drum Pattern 3 (two measures)
Closed hi-hat: sixteenth notes
Snare drum: backbeat rhythm
Bass drum: embellished standard rock

Figure 15.6 Nelly's "Just a Dream."

goal is for students to take these musical observations and create an informal descriptive interpretation. How does each drum pattern function temporally, rhetorically, and expressively within its section? Does the drum part accumulate steadily throughout the VCU, or is there another design? Do you find any drum patterns or drum fills particularly interesting or effective? What other similarities and differences are there between the drum parts in "Right by My Side" and "Just a Dream"? Though unlikely, if any group completes these tasks quickly, they can transcribe the drum patterns with table notation.

I typically let students work in their groups for 15 minutes while I circulate around the room to answer questions, guide listening, and foster dialogue. We reconvene once groups have made sufficient progress, even if everything is not fully completed. Before launching into our discussion, I remind students again that a comprehensive and precise depiction of every aspect of the drum part is exceptionally difficult and not our main goal. Our goal is more process-oriented, learning new ways to study and appreciate rhythm and meter through drum parts in today's top pop hits. We next proceed through the excerpt chronologically and create Figure 15.7, listening again to passages as needed. This depiction

Introduction 1.1 (five measures)
Drum Pattern 1
No layers

Introduction 1.2 (four measures)
Drum Pattern 2 (two measures)
Snare drum: embellished backbeat rhythm
Claps: backbeat rhythm
Bass drum: embellished standard rock rhythm

> Drum fill (last quarter note before Verse 1): clap on fourth quarter note followed by snare drum thirty-second notes

Verse 1.1 (four measures)
Drum Pattern 3 (four measures)
Closed hi-hat: embellished sixteenth notes rhythm
Snare drum: embellished backbeat rhythm
Claps: backbeat rhythm

Verse 1.2 (four measures)
Drum Pattern 4 (four measures)
Closed hi-hat: thirty-second notes rhythm
Snare drum: embellished backbeat rhythm
Claps: backbeat rhythm
Bass drum: embellished standard rock rhythm

> Drum fill (last quarter note before Prechorus 1): same as before Verse 1

Prechorus 1 (four measures)
Drum Pattern 5 (two measures)
Claps: backbeat rhythm
Bass drum: embellished standard rock rhythm

> Drum fill (last measure): drums cut for first two quarter notes; suspended cymbal for third and fourth quarter notes

Chorus 1.1 (four measures)
Drum Pattern 2 (two measures)
Snare drum: embellished backbeat rhythm
Claps: backbeat rhythm
Bass drum: embellished standard rock rhythm

> Drum fill (last two quarter notes before Chorus 1.2): suspended cymbal

Chorus 1.2 (four measures):
Drum Pattern 6 (two measures)
Tambourine: eighth notes rhythm
Closed hi-hat: thirty-second notes rhythm
Snare drum: embellished backbeat rhythm
Claps: backbeat rhythm
Bass drum: embellished standard rock rhythm

> Drum fill (last quarter note before Verse 2): same as before Verse 1

Figure 15.7 Nicki Minaj's "Right by My Side," featuring Chris Brown.

portion of the activity then transitions to discussing students' analytical interpretations. There is more to talk about than class time allots, so I let students respond freely while highlighting the following four broad points. First, there are notably more drum patterns in "Right by My Side" than "Just a Dream." Regularly having multiple patterns within sections creates a faster rate of change that impacts the VCUs sense of timing. This fastness relates to the second analytical point, which is that the hi-hat's thirty-second notes activate a rapid pulse layer not seen in many pop songs. Third, Figure 15.7 shows that this song occasionally has two instruments for its high and middle drum layers: tambourine and closed hi-hat, and snare drum and claps. This creates dense drum patterns, where the paired instruments work interdependently by performing related, but not identical, rhythms and sounds. Finally, I like to have students discuss ways that the drum part in "Right by My Side" differs from pop's typical rhetorical design in Figure 15.5. One difference is that changing drum patterns more frequently creates variety within rather than just across sections. Another dissimilarity is that the prechorus's drum pattern 5, rather than serving as an intensifier between the verse and chorus, serves more as an intervening moment of repose by removing two drum layers from drum pattern 4 before returning to a three-layer realization in chorus 1.

Like the first lesson, our final activity switches to composition, in which students demonstrate their command of and creativity with the day's learning objectives. In small groups with a collaborative BandLab project, students create a drum part for the first verse-chorus unit of Taio Cruz's "Break Your Heart" (2009). The goal is for groups to decide how they want their excerpt to flow – rhetorically, rhythmically, and expressively – and to create drum patterns and drum fills that fulfill their artistic vision. Depending on how much time remains, instructors may decide to complete the activity in class, begin the activity and assign its completion as homework, begin the activity and complete it during the next class session, or complete the activity entirely as an assignment.

After groups are formed, the first step is for one student to create a new BandLab project, set the tempo to 122 BPM, and download and import the mp3 file.[9] The student also needs to invite their other group members with the "Collaborators" button shown toward the top right of Figure 15.4. Next, we listen to the verse-chorus unit together to determine the form. The track has an introduction (m. 2), verse (m. 10), prechorus (m. 18), chorus (m. 26), and postchorus (m. 34). I then provide students more concrete directives and suggestions before they begin working. I recommend that groups start by forming a plan for their composition. Do they want steady growth throughout or a different design? Do they envision one drum pattern per section, more, or fewer? And do they think drum fills would be effective at any formal junctures? The second directive is for students to divide the creative labor by having group members compose different drum patterns and drum fills and insert them onto their collaborative track. As groups work, I again circulate around the room to answer questions and provide feedback. If we are able to complete the activity during class, we conclude by hearing and discussing each other's projects. If we are unable to fit everything into our remaining time, I have students finish their compositions as homework, and we conclude the activity at the beginning of the next class.

Studying drum parts in twenty-first-century mainstream pop is one way to show students the depths and possibilities of music's rhythmic and metric attributes. It also introduces a new and specific lens for analyzing, creating, and otherwise appreciating the norms and nuances of a particular style of music. At the same time, these lessons also teach concepts that stretch across the undergraduate curriculum, for example, that theories of music are foundational and guiding rather than dogmatic and rigid, and that analysis is a performative blend of observation and interpretation. They also develop generalizable musical skills, such as aurally isolating and notating individual instruments, coordinating parts of an ensemble, and arranging through music technology. Finally, this module is also an explicit step toward incorporating more repertoire by more peoples, and thus to better equip students as musicians and citizens of the twenty-first century.

Notes

1. A drum pattern's length is technically not an independent characteristic but rather an outworking of its number of layers, instrumentation, and rhythm. It is treated as a fourth primary characteristic in Table 15.1 and throughout this chapter because I have found it to be more pedagogically efficient and effective.
2. If preferred, teachers can have students notate open and closed hi-hat attacks on a single "Hi-Hat" row with "O" and "X" symbols.
3. Other time signatures can be created in BandLab by changing the $\frac{4}{4}$ designation at the top of the screen and using the appropriate number of sixteenth notes for a measure. For example, a $\frac{3}{4}$ measure uses the first 12 sixteenth-note steps.
4. Several popular songs have drumless versions available on YouTube to view and download. There are also free and paid apps and websites that can isolate and remove various parts of a track, including the drums. As another option, many karaoke websites have covers of popular songs with the drums extracted available for purchase. Finally, instructors with the technical capacity can remove the drum part from songs themselves using programs such as Adobe Audition.
5. The BPM of "Blinding Lights" is slightly faster than 171 BPM but slower than 172 BPM. The tempo discrepancy does not dramatically offset within the sixteen-measure sections, but it becomes more noticeable after about twenty measures.
6. Sample creations for this and the second lesson's composition activities are provided on the Supplementary Materials website.
7. Table notation transcriptions for the drum patterns in "Just a Dream" and "Right by My Side" are provided on the Supplemental Materials website. There is also a brief list of additional songs for analysis.
8. Students, therefore, will need an electronic device and headphones to listen to "Right by My Side" individually.
9. I created a drumless version of "Break Your Heart" with an app called Moises.

16 Developing Contemporary Rhythm Skills Through Contemporary R&B

Trevor de Clercq

Introduction

If the contents of current music theory textbooks reflect the structure of the modern-day music theory classroom, then an outsized majority of teaching is currently devoted to topics related to pitch as compared to rhythm. This emphasis on pitch is especially pronounced in textbooks that focus on European art music of the extended common-practice period (i.e., classical music).[1] Yet it persists in textbooks that include a good, if not great, deal of popular music as well.[2] One factor may be that rhythm is normally considered more of a skill than a concept, and so its teaching is relegated to dedicated skills-based courses. This distinction between skill-based and conceptual topics may represent tradition more than anything else, however.[3] And even in textbooks devoted specifically to aural skills, the imbalance between pitch and rhythm remains.[4]

As a counterbalance, I offer in this chapter some classroom activities that shift students' attention away from pitch and toward aspects of rhythm. Specifically, I suggest ways to help students develop contemporary rhythm skills in the context of contemporary R&B music. Although conventional approaches to teaching rhythm may be adequate for developing the skills needed for understanding classical music, these approaches do not adequately address the skills needed for popular music. In other words, understanding rhythm in popular music requires an expanded skill set and, as I detail next, a corresponding expanded set of pedagogical approaches. Contemporary R&B seems like a logical style in which to develop these skills, given that R&B – which stands for "rhythm and blues" – is the only major style of popular music to include the word "rhythm" in its name.

What exactly do I mean by "contemporary R&B"? Like the term "rock," contemporary R&B can be construed in various ways. In this chapter, I adopt a fairly broad definition of contemporary R&B, using it as a catchall term for music that grew out of the early R&B styles of the 1950s and '60s, such as doo-wop, Motown, and funk.[5] Contemporary R&B traces its roots to the progressive soul movement of the 1970s, championed by singer-songwriters such as Marvin Gaye and Stevie Wonder; in the '80s, technological advancements helped R&B blossom in the music of artists like New Edition, Janet Jackson, and Whitney Houston; the style reached maturity in the '90s, as heard in the music of Boyz II Men, Babyface, and Mariah Carey; and contemporary R&B artists such as Beyoncé, Justin Timberlake, D'Angelo, and Rihanna continue to dominate popular music of the twenty-first century. Generally speaking, contemporary R&B is notable for its blend of hip-hop production styles, melismatic and soulful vocal melodies, jazz-influenced harmonies, and funk-derived rhythms – all combined with a polished, pop sensibility.

In what follows, I discuss how contemporary R&B can help develop rhythm skills in three areas. The first is the ability to map the form of a song in real time, focusing on hypermeter and phrase rhythm rather than harmonic function. The second is a more modern approach to meter identification, using a method that goes beyond normal categorization schemes by having students listen for different drum feels and levels of swing. The third is dedicated transcription assignments to engage with the high levels of syncopation often found in vocal melodies of the style.

Given a conventional curriculum, most of these activities are perhaps best suited for an aural skills class. In my current department, however, there is no separate written theory and aural skills tracks; each course in our theory sequence includes both conceptual topics and skill-based exercises, and no particular days are set aside for one versus another. Each of the activities described in the following text, therefore, requires some explanation of concepts prior to asking the student to perform the task. In a curriculum with separate written theory and aural skills classes, some cross-pollination may thus be necessary, whether through coordinated schedules or more blended teaching.

Contemporary Form Charts

In traditional textbooks, the teaching of large-scale form is normally reserved until later chapters, coinciding with a student's final semesters in a theory sequence.[6] This delay occurs because form has historically been taught through the lens of harmonic areas and cadences, which thus need to be understood first. This order of topics is not necessary for popular music, however. While harmony sometimes participates in delineating the form of a song, it often does not. Instead, other factors – such as lyrics, texture, and timbre – will offer sufficiently strong markers of section boundaries. As a result, the study of form can begin early in a student's studies. In my first-semester theory course (which has no pre-requisites), song form is introduced in the third class meeting.

When teaching song form, I do not assign the students any reference text to read, since form labels can be difficult, if not impossible, to define. (That said, for those who would like an overview of form in popular music, see Chapter 8 in Temperley 2018). Instead, I present students with relatively straightforward examples – primarily through listening and discussion activities – and I then ask the students to make their own form charts by ear for homework (typically one song assigned a week). On the day their form chart is due, we talk about the song in class, weighing the pros and cons of one analysis versus another; usually, multiple readings of the song are reasonable. As the students' musical vocabulary increases, their arguments (and my explanations) become more nuanced.

For beginner students, the critical skill to develop is an intuition for the hypermetric structure of the song. Much like four beats group into a bar of $\frac{4}{4}$, four bars commonly group into a hypermeasure in popular music. This four-bar hypermeter is so pervasive that students need to feel the regularity of it in a similar way as they feel the regularity of four beats in a bar of $\frac{4}{4}$. The form charts I ask them to create thus track not only the section names but also the hypermetric structure, which mostly (but not always) operates in four-bar units.

For instance, after about a week of introductory exercises devoted to identifying the beat and the bar by ear, the students and I will work together in class to create something like Figure 16.1a, which shows a drummer's chart for the album version of "Nothin' on You" by B.o.B., featuring Bruno Mars (2009). A drummer's chart is simply a list of song sections spanning two columns, each section separated by a horizontal line, with an underscore for each bar and the bars organized into hypermeasures. The opening chorus (abbreviated "Ch"), for example, includes four four-bar hypermeasures, for a total of 16 bars. In creating this chart, the students and I will first discuss how we might divide the song into sections, what names for these sections might be appropriate, and what musical factors might influence our decisions. We then work to determine the length of each section in

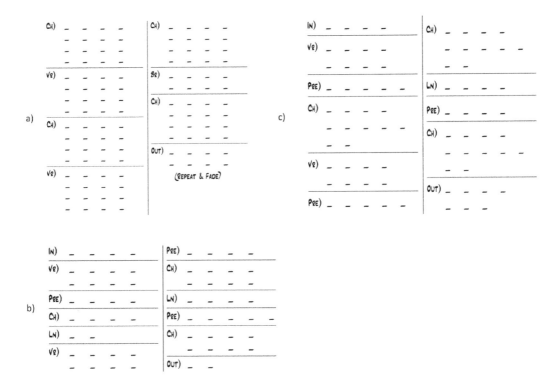

Figure 16.1 (a) Drummer's chart for "Nothin' on You" by B.o.B. ft. Bruno Mars (2009); (b) drummer's chart for "Good as Hell" by Lizzo (2016); (c) drummer's chart for "When Can I See You" by Babyface (1993).

bars, thinking about whether we hear these bars grouping together in any consistent way. This discussion then leads to an introduction of the concept of hypermeter.

From the perspective of form, "Nothin' on You" is a good starting example because of its relative simplicity. The bars organize into repeating four-bar hypermeasures, and the song uses only a handful of section types. But even in a song this simple, there is room for discussion about issues of form. Is the opening chorus, for example, also an intro? Are the last eight bars in the verse (Vr) something leading into the chorus, like a prechorus? Should we have called the bridge (Br) just another verse?[7] Harmony would not provide much help in answering any of these questions, since the song consists entirely of a repeated eight-bar, four-chord loop. So although we could add chord symbols to the drummer's chart (thus creating a Nashville number chart), having a map of the hypermetric structure is sufficient to guide the discussion.[8]

Creating a drummer's chart may seem like a fairly easy task, but the goal is to have students be able to create these charts (using pencil and paper) *in a single hearing*. To do this, the student must develop a solid internal feel for both the regularity of the meter as well as the hypermeter, such that hearing the succession of beats, bars, and hypermeasures can essentially be on "autopilot" while the student considers what section labels might be most appropriate. A student also needs to develop good intuitions about the typical forms found in popular music, such as the large-scale AABA pattern seen in "Nothin' on You" (where each verse-chorus unit stands as a single A group). All these skills, of course, develop through regular listening practice.

Drummer's charts also provide an opportunity to distinguish between hypermeter and phrase rhythm. Contemporary R&B, like much popular music, does not consistently delineate phrase boundaries through traditional cadential formulas, so students must think about how melodic and harmonic events interact with the hypermetric structure. Figure 16.1b, for instance, shows a drummer's chart for "Good as Hell" by Lizzo (2016), which employs the additional section types of prechorus (Pch) and link (Ln). Prior to the first full bar of each chorus (including the intro chorus), Lizzo sings a brief pickup – either "I do my/hair toss" or "and do your/hair toss" – with the word "hair" landing on the downbeat. Where, then, does the chorus officially begin? Other questions can lead into teasing out the difference between hypermeter and phrase, for example: How many bars are in each phrase? What makes the phrase structure clear here? Does the phrase structure in the song change? If so, where and why? In whatever way one chooses to define "phrase," it is worth noting how the music in this song generally organizes into two-bar units, as determined by the pacing of the lyrics and the piano loop. These shorter phrases (or subphrases) can be contrasted with the longer eight-bar phrases heard in "Nothin' on You," even though both songs display (for the most part) a regular pattern of four-bar hypermeasures.

Harmony, of course, is an important factor in thinking about phrase structure. As students begin to learn about chord progressions, drummer's charts can also help direct attention to harmonic rhythm. In this regard, consider the chart for "When Can I See You" by Babyface (1993), shown in Figure 16.1c. Notice that the hypermeter here is not simply a regular succession of four-bar units. Nonetheless, a beginner student might posit that the chorus has a 4 + 4 + 3 structure, automatically creating a new hypermeasure every four bars within the section. What are the factors, then, that lead to the more musically appropriate 4 + 5 + 2 structure shown on the chart? One central aspect is the harmonic rhythm, with a sustained chord that extends the second hypermeasure of the chorus to five bars. This realization can lead to a larger discussion of *where* the chords are changing in the song, even if the students cannot yet identify *what* those chords are.

The examples of drummer's charts shown here have all been in $\frac{4}{4}$, which is by far the most common meter found in contemporary R&B (and popular music more broadly).[9] That said, it is worthwhile for students to do at least a few charts in different meters, particularly a compound meter like $\frac{6}{8}$. The duple nature of $\frac{6}{8}$ requires a different internal expectation for the succession of beats and bars as compared to a quadruple meter like $\frac{4}{4}$, so it can take some practice for a student to get sufficiently comfortable to make a drummer's chart in a single hearing. Examples of contemporary R&B songs that can be considered in $\frac{6}{8}$ include "Kiss from a Rose" by Seal (1994), "Red Light Special" by TLC (1994), "Fallin'" by Alicia Keys (2001), and "Right Thru Me" by Nicki Minaj (2010). Note that some of these examples could alternatively be considered in a different time signature, such as $\frac{12}{8}$, so let's turn now to a discussion of meter.

Contemporary Meter Identification

Not much time, if any, is typically devoted to meter identification by ear in modern aural skills or fundamentals textbooks.[10] Perhaps the task seems fairly trivial given the limited number of options. After all, the categorization of regular meter (i.e., not complex, mixed, additive, fractional, or irrational) involves determining only the number of beats – which are limited to duple, triple, or quadruple – and how those beats are divided – either simple or compound. That gives only six possible combinations, some of which are not very well differentiated in any obvious way. It's not always clear just by listening, for example, whether a passage might be a bar of slow $\frac{2}{4}$ versus a bar of $\frac{4}{4}$ at a faster tempo, or two bars of $\frac{2}{4}$ versus one bar of $\frac{4}{4}$ at the same tempo. Teaching meter identification by ear also may

194 *Trevor de Clercq*

not seem worth the effort, since performers are traditionally provided with a notated score that explicitly states the time signature at the outset.

In popular music, however, there is rarely any official score, although even that is not the main issue. The bigger problem is that conventional time signatures alone cannot comprehensively describe the metric organization of many songs, especially those in the R&B genre. Two other factors are critical – drum feel and swing – and it is important that students are attuned to these factors if they hope to understand the various ways that rhythm and meter are organized in this style.

To introduce drum feels to students, it is easiest to use a song that shifts between different patterns. One good example in this regard is the song "Closer" by Ne-Yo (2008). Around 0:46, a full version of the main drumbeat appears, making it clear that the song is in 4/4 at a tempo of about 126 BPM. In particular, the handclaps on beats 2 and 4 follow a normal backbeat pattern, as shown in Figure 16.2a, which in other songs might be played by the snare drum.

Notice in "Closer" that around 3:33 (the final chorus), the electronic drum pattern changes dramatically, such that the handclap rate is cut in half. The customary way to understand this change is as a different drum feel.[11] The backbeat – which was previously occurring on beats 2 and 4 – shifts up a metric level to beat 3, thus creating a half-time feel. An idealized version of a half-time drum feel is shown in Figure 16.2b. The students should notice that nothing aside from the drum pattern has changed; the pacing of the harmony, melody, and instrumental lines remains the same in the final chorus as it was in the rest of the song. The best approach is thus to retain the same tempo and bar lengths, despite the slower "feel" conveyed by the drum pattern.

Once a student is introduced to the idea that drum patterns do not always have the snare (or backbeat) on beats 2 and 4, they are primed to consider that an entire song may use a half-time feel. The song "Human Nature" by Michael Jackson (1982) is a good example of this situation. The song's tempo is clearly 93 BPM, and the meter is clearly 4/4, so the snare is clearly hitting on beat 3 of each bar. But how do we know this? What aspects make the 93 BPM tempo so clear? Ideal beat rates are one factor, and this can start a conversation about what tempos are easier to dance to than others. Harmonic rhythm is also an important factor, and this can lead to a discussion about what rates of chord changes are typical in popular music. It is extremely rare, for example, for chords in popular music to regularly change on every beat in 4/4 (unlike, say, in a Bach chorale).

Figure 16.2 Different prototypical drum patterns in 4/4: (a) a normal drum feel, (b) a half-time feel, and (c) a half-time shuffle.

A follow-up activity would be to play songs and decide as a class whether each song is best thought of as a half-time feel – such as "My All" by Mariah Carey (1997), "Bills, Bills, Bills" by Destiny's Child (1999), "Fly" by Nicki Minaj (2010), and "The Hills" by The Weeknd (2015) – or as a normal drum feel. This task helps develop a student's sense for how bar lengths are determined in the absence of a score, encouraging them to think about harmonic and melodic pacing. Students should also begin to develop a rough sense for "absolute tempo," such that they can estimate the tempo of a song by ear to within about 10–20 BPM of the correct answer (without recourse to a metronome).

The other important aspect of meter that usually does not receive much attention in a traditional curriculum is swing, especially the difference between swing and compound meter. A good introductory example in this regard is the song "Higher Ground" by Stevie Wonder (1973). If students are asked to choose the best time signature for the song, some will probably say $\frac{12}{8}$ based on how the synthesizer lines seem to divide each beat into three equal parts. But what about the drums? More rhythmically savvy students will hopefully notice that the drum part – particularly noticeable in the long-short shuffle rhythm of the tambourine – is playing a rhythm that is *not* congruent with a beat evenly divided into three parts. Specifically, the long note is longer and the short note is shorter than a standard quarter-eighth long-short rhythm in a true $\frac{12}{8}$. As a result, the best way to categorize the meter of "Higher Ground" is as $\frac{4}{4}$ with eighth-note swing. In essence, swing offers a more flexible timing framework than compound meter. For students having trouble hearing the non-congruence of the drum part in "Higher Ground" with $\frac{12}{8}$, the song "Girl They Won't Believe It" by the blue-eyed soul artist Joss Stone (2007) offers an example of a shuffle rhythm with particularly hard swing, despite the clear triplet fills throughout.

As with different drum feels, a worthwhile follow-up activity is having students distinguish between songs with straight (non-swung) rhythms and those with eighth-note swing. Students are also then prepared to learn about the half-time shuffle, as idealized in Figure 16.2c, which combines a half-time drum feel with swung eighth notes. (Note that the triplets in Figure 16.2c are to be taken as an approximation of the real rhythm.) Particularly good R&B examples of a half-time shuffle include the songs "The Thing About Love" by Alicia Keys (2007) and "Pretty Wings" by Maxwell (2009).

Although some musicians may think of swing as limited to the eighth-note level, it's important for students to realize that swing in popular music, especially in contemporary R&B, is very common on the sixteenth-note level as well. Good examples abound from the new jack swing era, including "Every Little Step" by Bobby Brown (1988), "Alright" by Janet Jackson (1989), "Someday" by Mariah Carey (1990), "Poison" by Bell Biv DeVoe (1990), "Queen of the Night" by Whitney Houston (1992), and "The Halls of Desire" by Tevin Campbell (1993). Detecting sixteenth-note swing can be difficult for many students, since sixteenth-note swing is mutually exclusive of eighth-note swing. So if a student is listening only to the eighth-note level, they may incorrectly assume that songs such as these are entirely straight. To hear the sixteenth-note swing, it's helpful to have the student focus on the hi-hat part, which usually reveals the uneven sixteenth notes, or the student can test straight versus swung sixteenths while listening to other instrumental parts of the song.

Swung sixteenths are not limited to time signatures of $\frac{4}{4}$. Many, if not most, contemporary R&B songs in a compound meter (like $\frac{6}{8}$) include swing on the sixteenth notes. Clear examples by Mariah Carey alone include "Vision of Love" (1990), "So Blessed" (1991), "And Don't You Remember" (1991), and "Never Forget You" (1993). Although $\frac{6}{8}$ meters are traditionally considered to have two beats per bar, it can help students feel the sixteenth-note swing if they switch to feeling the eighth note as the primary pulse. This is especially useful in slower $\frac{6}{8}$ songs, such as "End of the Road" by Boyz II Men (1991) or

"If I Ain't Got You" by Alicia Keys (2004), where the eighth-note pulse is slow enough to allow the sixteenth notes to be felt as the "ands" of six eighth-note beats.

Ultimately, students should learn that conventional time signatures address only a limited aspect of common metrical organizations in popular music. Meter categorization thus becomes more nuanced, including not just what time signature might be most appropriate but also whether the drum pattern aligns or departs for the norms of that time signature as well as whether the eighth-note and sixteenth-note levels are straight or swung. Aural identification exercises help with internalizing these various meters, but other activities – such as transcription and performance – are also useful, as addressed in the next and last section.

Contemporary Syncopation

From my own apprenticeship teaching at various institutions, activities focused on rhythm in the aural skills classroom normally consist of two tasks: rhythmic dictation exercises and one- or two-part rhythm reading exercises. These are very fruitful activities, and it does not take much effort to adapt them for teaching more contemporary rhythm skills. In addition, it can also be useful to include longer transcription exercises to help students internalize contemporary rhythms.

Rhythm reading exercises, for example, are traditionally performed without swing in the aural skills classroom. There is, however, no reason an instructor cannot ask students to perform these exercises with swing on the eighth notes or swing on the sixteenth notes. Some students, such as jazz majors, can presumably shift to this performance practice without much effort. For those students who need additional support, using a pre-existing groove as a metric backdrop can facilitate them getting the right feel. Suitable metric backdrops can often be found at the beginning of R&B songs, prior to the entrance of the vocal part.

The song "Isn't She Lovely" by Stevie Wonder (1976), for instance, provides a good example of eighth-note swing in $\frac{4}{4}$, and especially convenient, there are 12 bars of instrumental vamp at the beginning of the song (from about 0:14 to 0:36) that can serve as a background groove for a student performance.[12] Creating four or five minutes of instrumental vamp by looping eight bars from this passage is not too difficult using digital editing software (such as Audacity or Pro Tools). In essence, the looped passage becomes a contemporary metronome, giving the student not just the beat but the complete feel of the meter. For a good background groove involving sixteenth-note swing, the song "That's the Way Love Goes" by Janet Jackson (1993) has an introductory section (from about 0:14 to 0:34) that can be looped to create a longer groove. Without too much additional effort, these loops can be pitched-shifted up or down to create grooves at different tempos.

Performing rhythms from a sight-singing manual or rhythm reader – even when done with a contemporary groove in the background – is, of course, still limited to the types of rhythmic patterns found in these books. And while syncopation is a topic covered in every aural skills text, the depth to which it is explored usually does not reflect the extent and difficulty of syncopation in contemporary R&B songs. For this reason, it is helpful for students to transcribe the rhythms of R&B melodies, so as to internalize and realize the prevalence of syncopation in this style. (Be aware that transcribing the rhythms of a real vocal melody can be difficult, due in part to variations and subtleties in timing, so exercises like this are probably best for more advanced undergraduate students.)

A good starting place for developing syncopation skills is in a song with a half-time feel, since half-time songs typically involve syncopation on the eighth-note level only. Figure 16.3a, for instance, shows the rhythms for the first line of the first verse in "Soon as I

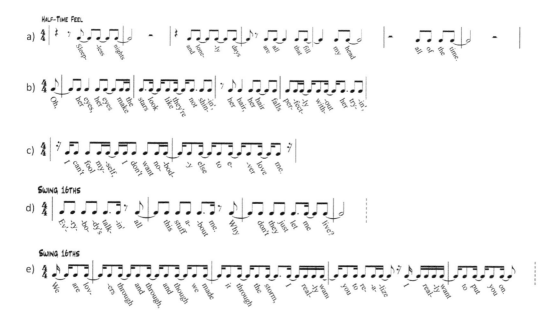

Figure 16.3 (a) Rhythm and lyrics for opening vocal melody (starting at 1:04) in "Soon as I Get Home" by Faith Evans (1995); (b) rhythm and lyrics for opening vocal melody (starting at 0:17) in "Just the Way You Are" by Bruno Mars (2010); (c) rhythm and lyrics for opening vocal melody (starting at 0:38) in "Never Too Much" by Luther Vandross (1981); (d) rhythm and lyrics for opening vocal melody (starting at 0:21) in "My Prerogative" by Bobby Brown (1988); (e) rhythm and lyrics for opening vocal melody (starting at 0:22) in "Real Love" by Mary J. Blige (1992).

Get Home" by Faith Evans (1995). To be clear, this is my own transcription of the vocal rhythms, and I can imagine a variety of similar but different interpretations due to the melismatic nature of the melody. (Note that the task here is to identify only when words *begin*; transcribing the full melismas of the lead vocal would be particularly challenging.) That said, it should be apparent that very few words begin on the beat, especially a strong beat, with long chains of words occurring off the beat.

Figure 16.3a transcribes only a short passage, but a normal assignment would involve transcribing the rhythms of a longer excerpt, either the full verse or the verse and chorus together. In terms of assessment, students can be asked to just turn in their transcriptions. But a better method might be to ask students to perform their transcription with the original recording. Rather than simply singing along, though, I would suggest asking students to perform on rhythm syllables while conducting. This ensures they are thinking about rhythmic locations with respect to the beat. These performances can be spot-checked in class or submitted as recorded skills proficiency assignments, graded on a pass/fail system.

Syncopation becomes trickier, of course, when it involves sixteenth notes. The opening line to "Just the Way You Are" by Bruno Mars (2010), as shown in Figure 16.3b, involves a moderate level of sixteenth-note syncopation. Although this example may not appear difficult given a slower tempo, it is not trivial at the tempo of the song (around 109 BPM) to perform even just these two bars on rhythm syllables while conducting. The speed of these examples is thus part of the challenge, not only for the performance, but also the transcription task itself. My advice to students is to try to memorize the melody, slow it

198 *Trevor de Clercq*

down, and then work carefully lyric by lyric. I also suggest that they can tap their fingers, index through pinky, for each sixteenth-note pulse, so as to identify the exact rhythmic location of each syllable.

Sixteenth-note syncopation can get especially heavy in contemporary R&B songs. Consider, for example, the opening line to "Never Too Much" by Luther Vandross (1981), as shown in Figure 16.3c. On one hand, the syncopation is fairly straightforward, in that most notes are shifted offbeat. On the other hand, the regularity of the syncopation may trick students into assuming that many of these notes are occurring on (rather than off) the beat. It requires a very solid internal metronome to not get fooled here. Once students are exposed to these chains of sixteenth-note syncopation, they will hopefully be primed to better identify and reproduce them when they are encountered again.

To raise the stakes, sixteenth-note syncopation can be studied in the context of sixteenth-note swing. A relatively simple starting example is in the opening chorus line of "My Prerogative" by Bobby Brown (1988), as transcribed in Figure 16.3d. Most of this melody involves eighth notes, which are not affected by the swing (since, as has just been noted, eighth notes are straight when sixteenth notes are swung). But the end of each measure includes what is essentially a tresillo rhythm (3+3+2), here within a metric framework of swung sixteenths. As a result, the timing of the note right before the fourth beat in each bar is slightly later than it would be in a straight context.

For a more complex example of sixteenth-note syncopation with sixteenth-note swing, consider the song "Real Love" by Mary J. Blige (1992). My best attempt at transcribing the rhythms of the opening line of the verse is shown in Figure 16.3e. As in Figure 16.3c, the basic rhythmic organization here is fairly simple; essentially, it involves a chain of eighth notes displaced by a sixteenth note. But there is enough variation by the end of the second bar and into the third bar to challenge even the stronger students.

The transcriptions presented here were all in $\frac{4}{4}$, so as to model the progression of increasingly difficult syncopated rhythms that can be found in contemporary R&B songs. A similar progression of exercises could be modeled for songs in $\frac{6}{8}$ as well. The previous transcriptions also focused solely on vocal melodies, but the task could be extended to bass lines, synthesizer parts, or drumbeats. What exactly, for example, is the rhythm of the kick and snare in "Real Love" or the rhythm of the synth bass? Moreover, notated transcriptions and performances are not the only modes by which a student could show an understanding of the rhythms in these songs. For a student population that is savvier with music sequencing and audio production, one could ask students instead to recreate the drumbeat in "Real Love" from scratch using computer software. Unfortunately, strong music technology skills are not always developed in undergraduate programs, nor are those skills usually coordinated with music theory coursework beyond the use of notation software.

Conclusion

As a final reminder, the focus on rhythm here has been meant to remedy (in an admittedly small way) what has historically been an overemphasis on pitch in the music theory and aural skills curriculum. This is not to say that rhythm is inherently more interesting than pitch in contemporary R&B, or that there are not extremely interesting and challenging materials to be found in the pitch domain of this style. Indeed, the pitch organization of R&B music is (perhaps not surprisingly) much different than in classical music. Harmony in contemporary R&B, for example, is heavily influenced by jazz, although it would be overly reductive to say that jazz and R&B share the same patterns of harmonic vocabulary, syntax, grammar. Ultimately, more work needs to be done to understand both rhythm and pitch in a variety of modern popular music styles.

I expect that some readers will wonder exactly how and where to incorporate the skills and associated activities described previously into their own teaching. In my own teaching, students are asked to create drummer's charts, identify drum feels, and perform with swing in their first semester. This first semester also includes simple rhythmic transcription exercises, which prepare students for more heavily syncopated rhythmic transcriptions (such as those described above) in their second semester. Admittedly, activities such as these may not currently exist in an established music theory curriculum, so incorporating them may be more complicated than simply swapping in new examples. Instead, I am advocating for a rebalancing of topics in a music theory curriculum. Given the finite amount of time in any curriculum, this rebalancing effort will require adjustment on a larger scale than merely a single lesson plan. But that is the kind of adjustment needed when we start by thinking about the musical styles we want to teach, asking what sort of skills and concepts need to be taught to understand those styles, rather than assuming that the topics we currently teach are appropriate and adequate for all musical styles.[13]

Notes

1. See, for example, Laitz (2015) and Kostka et al. (2018).
2. See, for example, Holm-Hudson (2016) and Snodgrass (2020).
3. For a compelling counterfactual argument along these lines, see Cohn (2015).
4. See, for example, Karpinski (2017) and Jones et al. (2014).
5. The closest overview to my understanding of contemporary R&B can be found on the web page "Contemporary R&B," Wikipedia, accessed July 5, 2021; for a narrower definition of contemporary R&B, see Bogdanov et al. (2003).
6. Binary and ternary forms, for example, are not taught until Chapter 20 of 27 in Kostka et al. (2018); in Laitz (2015), ternary, rondo, and sonata form are not covered until Part 7 of 9.
7. For more on the multivalent and ambiguous nature of section labels, see de Clercq (2017a).
8. For more on Nashville number charts, see de Clercq (2019).
9. For a statistical analysis of different meters in three different corpora of popular music, see de Clercq (2016).
10. See, for example, Clendinning et al. (2017) and Phillips et al. (2021).
11. For more on different drum feels in different meters, see de Clercq (2017b).
12. For more on using background music for aural skills activities, see de Clercq (2014).
13. For an exceptional discussion of the way the topics we teach influence the styles we teach, see Palfy and Gilson (2018).

Works Cited

Bogdanov, Vladimir, John Bush, Chris Woodstra, and Stephen Erlewine, eds. 2003. *AllMusic Guide to Soul: The Definitive Guide to R&B and Soul*. Backbeat Books.

Clendinning, Jane, Elizabeth Marvin, and Joel Phillips. 2017. *The Musician's Guide to Fundamentals*, 3rd edition. W.W. Norton.

Cohn, Richard. 2015. "Why We Don't Teach Meter, and Why We Should." *Journal of Music Theory Pedagogy* 29: 5–22.

de Clercq, Trevor. 2014. "Grooves, Drones, and Loops: Enhancing Aural Skills Exercises with Rock Music Contexts." *Engaging Students: Essays in Music Pedagogy* 2.

———. 2016. "Measuring a Measure: Absolute Time as a Factor for Determining Bar Lengths and Meter in Pop/Rock Music." *Music Theory Online* 22/3.

———. 2017a. "Embracing Ambiguity in the Analysis of Form in Pop/Rock Music, 1982–1991." *Music Theory Online* 23/3.

———. 2017b. "Swing, Shuffle, Half Time, Double: Beyond Traditional Time Signatures in the Classification of Meter in Pop/Rock Music." In *Coming of Age: Teaching and Learning Popular Music in Academia*, edited by Carlos Rodriguez, 139–67. Maize Books.

———. 2019. "The Nashville Number System: A Framework for Teaching Harmony in Popular Music." *Journal of Music Theory Pedagogy* 33: 3–28.

Holm-Hudson, Kevin. 2016. *Music Theory Remixed: A Blended Approach for the Practicing Musician*. Oxford University Press.

Jones, Evan, Matthew Shaftel, and Juan Chattah. 2014. *Aural Skills in Context: A Comprehensive Approach to Sight Singing, Ear Training, Harmony, and Improvisation*. Oxford University Press.

Karpinski, Gary. 2017. *Manual for Ear Training and Sight Singing*, 2nd edition. W.W. Norton.

Kostka, Stefan, Dorothy Payne, and Byron Almén. 2018. *Tonal Harmony with an Introduction to Twentieth-Century Music*, 8th edition. McGraw Hill.

Laitz, Steve. 2015. *The Complete Musician: An Integrated Approach to Theory, Analysis, and Listening*, 4th edition. Oxford University Press.

Palfy, Cora, and Eric Gilson. 2018. "The Hidden Curriculum in the Music Theory Classroom." *Journal of Music Theory Pedagogy* 32: 79–110.

Phillips, Joel, Paul Murphy, Jane Clendinning, and Elizabeth Marvin. 2021. *The Musician's Guide to Aural Skills*, 4th edition. W.W. Norton.

Snodgrass, Jennifer. 2020. *Contemporary Musicianship: Analysis and the Artist*, 2nd edition. Oxford University Press.

Temperley, David. 2018. *The Musical Language of Rock*. Oxford University Press.

Wikipedia. "Contemporary R&B." Accessed July 5, 2021. https://en.wikipedia.org/wiki/Contemporary_R%26B

17 Structural Shifts and Identity in Music by Ester Rada

Rosa Abrahams

Introduction

In a first-year undergraduate theory core curriculum, students are often encouraged to practice moving between local and global analysis. Music by Ethiopian Israeli jazz and soul artist Ester Rada provides an excellent opportunity for students to both build analytical skill sets through recorded music and think about structural shifts as aspects of musical narrative. While generally following conventional pop forms, Rada often structures her music through stylistic shifts that include distinct modal, metrical, timbral, and textural changes between sections, in addition to lyrical variation. In this way, her music not only invites students to focus their analysis on a single section but also offers avenues for thinking about how the combination of sections complicates, reinscribes, or deepens findings from local analysis.

In this chapter, I provide a variety of approaches to teaching first-year theory topics through two of Ester Rada's recordings: a Nina Simone cover, "Four Women" (2015), and Rada's original composition "Life Happens" (2014). In addition to analytical discussion of these two pieces, lesson plan outlines are provided for each piece on the Supplemental Materials website. These assignments offer a variety of types of engagement with Rada's work, from short in-class activities to a full-topic unit to a longer project or paper. They can be tailored to both music major and nonmajor courses and encourage socially responsive and self-reflexive teaching in the music theory classroom.

Further, these lessons, and my suggestions around teaching Rada's music more generally, demonstrate the fruitfulness of these pieces as components of a spiral curriculum, wherein they might be brought back at multiple points in the first-year undergraduate core for continued engagement.[1] Since Rada's music is popular music created without a foundational score, I also encourage instructors to use these pieces as an opportunity for transcription and the development of close listening skills. Because these songs are highly structured and segmented in nature, they work well for repeated listening and study. Further, they provide an opportunity to model ways to work with non-notated music, which helps to de-center score notation as the only way of engaging analytically with music in a theory classroom. For the music theory professor, Rada's music offers engaging, complex soundscapes for analysis and skill-based instruction examples, as well as intricate, nuanced musical narratives that open classroom discussion toward the extra-musical, political, and affective power of music.

Historical Background

It is common for Ethiopian Israeli musicians like Ester Rada to use the medium of popular music as a space to address political, religious, and identity issues. Rada has gained renown as an Ethio-jazz and soul artist, both internationally and in Israel. Understanding

DOI: 10.4324/9781003204053-22

some of the historical, social, and political background of Ethiopian Israelis can help students better understand the significance of Rada's music, whether presented prior to or following engagement with her music in the classroom. In this and the following section, I offer a brief background that may be helpful for instructors wanting to teach Rada's music in the theory classroom. In the accompanying lesson plans, I offer suggestions for how to engage students with this background, depending on your classroom and learning goals.

Ethiopian Jews, like other Jews throughout the African continent, trace their ancestry to the Ten Lost Tribes of Israel. These peoples migrated via ancient trade routes to the African continent after being expelled from Samaria, now known as northern Israel. While this foundational narrative situates African Jews as members of the global Jewish diaspora, the mythical aspect of the story has historically provoked skepticism from Jews in other, majority-White parts of the world. This tension is foregrounded in Israel, where it was not until 1975 that Ethiopian Jews – sometimes known as Beta Israel – were recognized as Jews by the State of Israel. This was the case even though, since the founding of the Jewish State in 1948, Jews throughout the African continent had attempted to make *aliyah* (gain Israeli citizenship) based on the Law of Return: an Israeli statute declaring that all Jews living in the diaspora have equal access to Israeli citizenship. Sadly, in the case of the Ethiopian Jews, due to international relations and identity politics, it wasn't until Ethiopian civil war and famine created crisis for the Beta Israel that their right-of-return was granted.

Between the 1980s and 1990s, thousands of Ethiopian Jews immigrated to Israel through Law of Return. The majority arrived in Israel through two major rescue operations conducted by the Israeli government, intended to free the Beta Israel from persecution and political instability in Ethiopia during the regime of revolutionary Marxist leader Mengistu Haile Mariam (Weil 2012, 207). By moving secretly from Ethiopia into refugee camps in Sudan, several missions between 1984 and 1985, termed "Operation Moses," brought 7,700 Ethiopian Jews from Sudan into the land of Israel. Then, in a 36-hour period in 1991, a single mission, "Operation Solomon," airlifted 14,310 Beta Israel directly out of Ethiopia, bringing them to safety in the State of Israel (Weil 2012, 211). In the time between these operations, and since 1991, Ethiopian Jews have made their way in smaller numbers into Israel. But what they have found is, as Shalva Weil highlights, distinctly different from their idealized homeland.

While the Ethiopian Jews have diasporic yearning for Israel built into their liturgy and festivals, the Israel they have encountered in their immigration marginalizes Ethiopian Israelis as racially distinct others, despite their status as Israeli citizens. As part of the agreement between Chief Rabbis, each Ethiopian Jew that made *aliyah* had to go through a ritual conversion to Judaism, a highly offensive devaluing of their Jewishness. As Israeli citizens, Ethiopian Israelis have faced sociocultural and economic marginalization, thus continually negotiating what it means to be members of the Jewish people living in their Jewish homeland while they are also part of the African diaspora by living in Israel.

Ester Rada

Ester Rada was born in 1985 in Kiryat Arba, a controversial settlement in the West Bank, and raised in Netanya, a city roughly halfway between Tel Aviv and Haifa on the Mediterranean. Her religious upbringing is often brought up in interviews, as is her musical training through her compulsory military service in the Israeli Defense Force (IDF) (Webster-Kogen 2018, 30). Rada's rise from playing her music in the club scene in Tel Aviv to international recognition at the Glastonbury Festival in the United Kingdom in 2013 happened quickly, as did her first EP release, *Life Happens* (2013), and her album *Ester Rada* (2014). Since, she has toured around the world as well as Israel, has released two more albums (*Different*

Eyes in 2017, and חסד in 2020), and has made eight singles and EPs between 2015 and 2021. She is the first Ethiopian Israeli solo star, and notably, writes and performs Afrodiasporic music rather than Israeli pop, which in itself indicates an acknowledgment of the failures of the Israeli state to incorporate Ethiopian Israelis into the mainstream (Webster-Kogen 2018, 24). Rada is thus an example of how many Ethiopian Israelis have reframed their understanding of exile and diaspora, moving from a Jewish exile and diaspora outside of the state of Israel to an African exile and diaspora as Israeli citizens (Webster-Kogen 2018, 24–25). Rada's musical framing and influences are reflected in her original compositions and her choices of songs to cover in her performances and recordings: African American jazz, soul, funk, and blues, reggae, and Ethiopian jazz and pop.

Ethnomusicologist Ilana Webster-Kogen's 2018 monograph offers an in-depth portrait of several modern Ethiopian Israeli musicians and the ways in which they navigate identity politics in the Israeli and global music scenes. Her work undergirds much of this chapter and would be a great companion to these materials were one looking for more in-depth analysis of Ethiopian Israeli music in the twenty-first century. Further, for instructors interested in integrating aspects of ethnomusicology with music theory, Webster-Kogen's text can be a meaningful counterpart and extension to the lessons and discussion offered in this chapter. For instance, she employs the concept of *sem-enna-werq* (wax and gold) when discussing Ethiopian Israeli music and political commentary. This concept relates to the lost-wax casting process wherein wax is poured over gold and the gold is then revealed after the dried wax is sculpted away. As a metaphor, this acts as a vital principle of Ethiopian musical aesthetics, where musicians, particularly the Azmariwoch, use dual meanings to both praise and ridicule the subjects of their songs, concealing various meanings within their musical settings (Webster-Kogen 2018, 30).[2] Rada's avoidance of political statements during her concerts, the fact that she does not often sing in Hebrew, but rather in English and Amharic, and the fact that her lyrical content deals only with relationships and personal experience all allow her to employ this wax-and-gold technique as subtle political critique based only in the subtextual references of music and music videos (Webster-Kogen 2018, 30).

This proves to a be particularly fruitful approach for Rada, given the complex political climate in Israel, the identity politics, racism, and scrutiny Ethiopian Israelis have experienced since their arrival in Israel, and Israel's controversial standing in the world, including difficulties Israeli artists face surrounding the Boycott, Divest, and Sanctions (BDS) movement. Rada's compositions are broadly Afrodiasporic, drawing heavily on African American, Afro-Caribbean, and Ethiopian musical styles and avoiding what might be seen as distinctly Israeli musical markers. However, given her status as one of the most famous international musicians from Israel, this sonic connection to global Afrodiasporic experience, rather than a personal narrative of a Jew returned from the Jewish diaspora to the Jewish homeland, is one that underscores her personal and cultural experiences as an Ethiopian Israeli without overtly discussing specifics. Webster-Kogen notes that "through her musical critique . . . Rada offers an alternative narrative for Ethiopian Israelis that transforms that attribute of [B]lackness into a source of cultural capital" (2018, 27).

Overall, Rada's style of music is often referred to as Ethio-jazz – a combination of Ethiopian music and American jazz – but Webster-Kogen perhaps more accurately describes her soundscapes as Ethio-soul, given Rada's audible influences and singing style from soul and jazz musicians, most notably Nina Simone, as well as Aretha Franklin and even Lauryn Hill (2018, 27). Soul's more religious, less politically overt style lends a retro flair to Rada's music, even while her instrumentation grounds her in Ethiopian pop, global pop, and jazz trends. Beyond soul, Rada includes reggae, funk, gospel, and both American and Ethiopian jazz and pop sonic markers in her compositions, making her music sound more like North American or global pop, due to these various Afrodiasporic elements, rather than Israeli pop or "world music" (Webster-Kogen 2018, 31–32). This not only allows her music to be familiar and accessible to North American music theory students but also opens the door for them to explore the complexities of Rada's Afrodiasporic style.

In addition, Rada sings mostly in English, a choice that connects her to the African diaspora in America, and specifically American popular music, and one that allows her to speak to an audience outside of Israelis and Ethiopians (or, rather, outside of the Hebrew- and Amharic-speaking communities of the world). According to her official website and an interview with BBC News (April 2014), while Rada grew up speaking Amharic and Hebrew, she began singing in Amharic as a way of connecting to her Ethiopian roots and the language of her parents.[3] In doing so, Rada casts herself as globally Black, "othering" herself in Israel and connecting instead to a larger African diasporic community. In fact, not until 2019 did she begin releasing EPs, followed by a 2020 album, wherein she sings in Hebrew, rather than solely in English and Amharic.

With this background in mind, I will offer teaching suggestions for two songs: Rada's cover of Nina Simone's "Four Women" from her 2015 EP *I Wish*, and "Life Happens" from Rada's 2014 self-titled album.[4]

"Four Women"

Rada's cover of this powerful Nina Simone song offers several avenues for exploring meter, formal structure, narrative, and aspects of cover songs, in addition to considering the extra-musical aspects of Simone's text. I have taught this pair of songs (Simone's original and Rada's cover) in a fundamentals class with students of varied racial, ethnic, and gender identities and have found it to be a useful, thoughtful, and memorable teaching tool. While this song is excellent for a first-year theory classroom, I recommend that it be accompanied by a content warning for sexual violence and descriptions of racial oppression. It is particularly important to consider the positionalities and identities of students in the classroom – visible and invisible – to discern whether this example will help students learn, or provide a difficult or triggering experience that could hinder learning.

The song is written in first person, each woman describing herself and her experiences in powerful, often painful imagery. The beginning of each verse begins with a declaration of "my skin is ___" and concludes with "my name is ___." Simone moves through the four perspectives, beginning with Aunt Sarah, an enslaved woman who is "strong enough to take the pain/inflicted again and again," followed by Saffronia, whose "yellow skin" marks her as a living legacy of the rape of her mother by her father, who is "rich and White" (1966, track 2). Then comes Sweet Thing in the third verse, whose text explores the "reminder that [B]lack women migrants to the urban North often had limited economic options or resources beyond their own bodies" (Feldstein 2013, 108).[5] Ruth Feldstein cites a 1969 essay by Phyl Garland, a Black female music critic, discussing the final verse:

> [T]he "loud-talking, no-shit-taking 'Peaches' of the final verse," came "closest to where so many [B]lack women of today stand, regardless of age." By bringing all four women together, Simone rejected the historical degradation of [B]lack women's bodies by [W]hites, and the disparagement of dark skin and hierarchies of color that many women continued to experience in their own families and communities.
>
> (2013, 108)

In Simone's original, she performs the four-stanza song with a similar texture throughout, providing a slow build to the final verse, which ends in an angry yell: "My name is

Peaches!" This outburst is accompanied by minimal instrumentals on the studio recording, though live recordings have varied instrumentation. (My discussion focuses on the studio recordings for the original and Rada's cover.) Simone's performance is grounded by a piano ostinato, which can be perceived in $\frac{4}{4}$, with a 3 + 3 + 2 syncopation in each measure. Aside from a piano solo in the bridge and some changes in the final verse as the climactic moment of the song – its ending on "my name is Peaches" – approaches, this ostinato grounds the song throughout. Other instruments, including percussion, electric guitar, and flute, add texture and variety, but the song has a meditative soundscape that allows the listener to focus on the text and emotion in Simone's measured but fierce vocal performance.

Ester Rada's version, however, plays with meter through extension and explores instrumentation and style to emphasize structural shifts. Rada uses a full band and includes a jazz-and-funk style opening and verses, highlighting these styles with a bass riff and brass chordal harmonies. In the final verse, a guitar solo emphasizes the building climax and hearkens to late-1960s guitar performance style. While still in simple meter in the verses, the line "my name is ___" occurs in a moment of musical stasis that ultimately launches the band into a compound meter instrumental chorus. This could also be described as an interlude, since there are no lyrics other than Rada's repetition of the woman's name freely restated throughout. The reimagining of the breaks between stanzas, demarcating them with a shift from simple to compound meter wherein the addition of the triplet subdivision creates a sense of frenetic energy, allows Rada and her listeners to embody the pain, fear, and anger underlying each woman's narrative, taking the 3 + 3 + 2 syncopation from Simone's original and extending and amplifying it for narrative effect. The extended interludes also allow Rada to include elements of Ethio-jazz, moving sonically from African American to Ethiopian soundscapes (Webster-Kogen 2018, 373–78). To underscore these stylistic shifts, Rada moves from the minor mode of the original in the verses to a hemitonic pentatonic mode in the interludes. As Webster-Kogen observes:

> [T]he [B]lack otherness that Rada expressed through musical vernaculars of soul and Ethio-jazz is represented in the song's lyrics about the abuse of [B]lack women, but she also plays it out in the juxtaposition of African American musical vernaculars (jazz, funk) in the verses and Ethio-jazz in the bridge. The shift from minor scales or hemitonic modes, and the syncopation to triple meter are small but significant adjustments to the instrumental accompaniment, forming the basis of Rada's reimagining, in which Ethiopian-Israelis share the experience of [B]lackness with African Americans.
> (2018, 37)

Again, Rada's own experience links to a broader Afrodiasporic experience that is expressed on the level of the musical texture, structure, and style rather than through text.

Table 17.1 Form Diagram, "Four Women," by Nina Simone, *Wild Is the Wind* (1966, Track 2)

Instrumental Introduction	Verse 1 Aunt Sarah	Verse 2 Saffronia	Verse 3 Sweet Thing	Instrumental Interlude	Verse 4 Peaches
0:00–0:10	0:11–1:10	1:11–2:13 (short instrumental from 2:06–2:13)	2:14–3:07	3:08–3:28	3:29–4:24

$\frac{4}{4}$ with a 3 + 3 + 2 internal syncopation – -- – rit. at close

Table 17.2 Form Diagram, "Four Women," Cover by Ester Rada, *I Wish* (2015, Track 2)

Intro	Verse 1 Aunt Sarah	Interlude	Verse 2 Saffronia	Interlude	Verse 3 Sweet Thing	Interlude	Verse 4 Peaches	Interlude and Outro
0:00–0:27	0:27–0:59	1:00–1:16	1:17–1:48	1:49–2:06	2:06–2:38	2:38–2:55	2:55–3:27	3:27–4:16
$\frac{4}{4}$	$\frac{4}{4}$	$\frac{12}{8}$	$\frac{4}{4}$	$\frac{12}{8}$	$\frac{4}{4}$	$\frac{12}{8}$	$\frac{4}{4}$	$\frac{12}{8}$

Assignments and activities around metrical shifts and the relationship of meter to narrative are possible with this example. I suggest using the metrical shifts from simple to compound to explore how the feel of these different meters changes embodied experience (which can also be seen in Rada's accompanying video performance). The instructor can also include other examples that shift between simple and compound meters, allowing exploration around what metrical shifts can offer to narrative readings of such music.[6] However, metrical and narrative effects can be understood just through a comparison of Simone's syncopation within simple meter and Rada's shifting between simple and compound. Notation is not necessary; students will likely understand the distinctions more effectively through conducting, tapping the 3 + 3 + 2 syncopation, and swaying or otherwise embodying the differences between meters while listening.

Further, this song provides excellent opportunities for core theory, fundamentals, or nonmajor classes to explore cover songs and to discuss Black female experience through Simone's text and Rada's interpretation. Asking students to compare the settings in light of the lyrical content can spark a discussion around how musical setting of text changes the meaning of text – an especially good way into a composition project that includes text setting. Exploring Rada's cover, we can see how her singing style is freer than Simone's, and how her insertion of the extended instrumental sections alludes to internal experience that does not align with the factual, externally focused descriptions that the lyrics in the verses provide. In this way, Rada's recomposition, her cover, is a wonderful way to get students talking about how different aspects of the musical setting can express the unexpressed and can connect to internal experiences, where words sometimes fail. Looking at Rada as connecting her own experience to those of the African American women she is singing about (and also singing *as*) is another avenue to the linkages this song reveals between musical and extra-musical signifiers.

"Life Happens"

Teaching this song, and its accompanying video, in the undergraduate music theory classroom can be approached in several ways. Since the song is also accompanied by a sleek, engaging, and highly produced music video, I encourage instructors to consider including both audio only and audio with visuals so students can understand a range of approaches to the analysis throughout the song.

Billed on her website as "gracefully combining Ethio-Jazz, funk, soul and R&B, with mixed undertones of [B]lack grooves," Rada does indeed integrate several overt musical references in this EP.[7] Webster-Kogen identifies Rada's composition style in this track as cut'n'mix, drawing from Dick Hebdige's 1987 description of music created with a mixture of Afrodiasporic roots, in this case African American and Caribbean musical cultures (2018, 39). She describes "Life Happens" as combining both Ethiopian and African American markers through sound worlds of Ethio-jazz, traditional Ethiopian massenqo, and a gospel-style ending, wrapped together in a generic pop verse-chorus structure (Webster-Kogen 2018, 41). These multidirectional instrumental and sonic markers are further emphasized through Rada's music video, where her costume choices, alongside the instruments she is shown playing, move geographically and chronologically from 1970s Ethiopia to American disco to traditional West African prints and headdress to 1980s United States. This variety of eras, instruments, costumes, and sonic markers allows Rada to present herself as a global Black musician, particularly drawing from Ethiopia and the United States (Webster-Kogen 2018, 41).

I first use this song in an early scales-and-keys unit. As popular, un-notated music, it provides transcription practice by way of the opening melody. This melody, played on the saxophone, outlines an A minor scale but omits $\hat{7}$, repeating often throughout the song. Asking students to sing the motive, identify interval types, and then transcribe the motive offers an excellent, bottom-up processing exercise. Further, it opens discussion about the variations of the minor scale they may have already learned (harmonic, melodic, and natural) and how this melody differs: Is it truly a minor scale without a seventh scale degree? Could it be modal instead? Having students grapple with this ambiguity early on will reinforce minor scale skills while also providing a sense of the utility of transcription and analytical discussion.

The next step could be exploring differences between the verses (minor) and the chorus (major). Since Rada uses relative key areas (A minor and C major), asking students to do some brief transcription of the chorus melody – finding "do" and tracking solfège throughout, perhaps – allows them to discover the relative key relationship through active analysis and close listening. From there, students can track the song's formal structure using key areas, noting alternating minor and major. This requires some knowledge of popular verse-chorus structure, but Rada's song can be a great way to introduce this form if students are not familiar with it, given that it includes prechoruses and postchoruses (the postchoruses can also be considered instrumental interludes and a bridge – another point for analytical discussion!). Table 17.3 outlines how the key areas align with the formal structure and instrumentation or stylistic musical markers.

This song is a good example of a "breakout chorus" as described by Christopher Doll (2011). The chorus continually moves up, includes a change of texture and often instrumentation, and contains lyrics that discuss breaking out and away in various ways. Doll's 2011 article contains many excellent examples of breakout choruses and is so clearly written that it is possible to invite students to engage with ideas from the article, if not with the article directly. Either way, having students explore the diagrams in the article and then try to identify or create their own diagram for Rada's song provides an opportunity to apply Doll's concept to music they are already familiar with. Depending on the curriculum, this module could be easily placed in the key areas unit, or even used as part of a spiral curriculum, to be used again in a future modulation unit.

In exploring modal shifts and key areas in "Life Happens," it becomes imperative to explore timbral shifts as well. Timbre is a key element of popular music identity, and this song uses timbre, in part, to exhibit Rada's Afrodiasporic, Ethio-jazz identity. In this instance, listening before watching is important for student discovery and close listening. Asking students to make a list of the timbres they hear in the song, and then comparing and discussing their lists, will allow them to practice general timbre identification. The next step is exploring which timbres were easy to identify and why: Did they hear the saxophone right away? How did they understand the massenqo? Depending on the students in your classroom, you might find this discussion challenging, so another way to approach it might be for students to list timbres they know within a provided form diagram, then add "unknown 1," "unknown 2," etc., for those timbres with which they are not familiar. At this point, students

208 Rosa Abrahams

Table 17.3 Form Diagram, "Life Happens," by Ester Rada, *Ester Rada* (2014, Track 4)

Section	Time Stamp	Text	Key	Foregrounded Timbre(s)
Intro	0:00–0:22	(no text)	A minor	theme A melody played on sax, chorus echo
Verse 1	0:22–0:43	"sometimes it seems like . . ."	A minor	vocals, bass ostinato on keyboard
Prechorus	0:43–0:52	(no text)	A minor	theme A melody played on sax, chorus echo
Chorus	0:53–1:13	"while you're looking astray . . ."	C major	vocals, flute
Postchorus	1:13–1:23	(no text)	A minor/modal	theme B played on massenqo
Verse 2	1:23–1:43	"you prefer a long walk . . ."	A minor	vocals, bass ostinato on keyboard
Prechorus	1:44–1:53	(no text)	A minor	theme A melody played on sax, chorus echo
Chorus	1:54–2:34	"while you're looking astray . . ."	C major	vocals, flute
Postchorus	2:34–2:44	(no text)	A minor/modal	theme C played on massenqo, flute
Verse 3	2:44–3:03	"no matter how hard . . ."	A minor	vocals, bass ostinato on keyboard
Chorus* note: no prechorus!	3:04–3:44	"while you're looking astray . . ."	C major	vocals, flute, chorus
Tag	3:45–3:55	"while you're looking astray . . ."	C major	a cappella vocals (solo and chorus)

can watch the video and compare how the instruments they see in the video align with the timbral identification they were able to complete aurally. Due to the cut'n'mix style Rada uses in this track, it can be useful for students, especially those familiar with popular music, to tie instrumentation and costumes to specific musical styles that she evokes.

Finally, I offer longer prompts that deal with the music video as a whole, thinking about not only the sonic but also the visual narrative. Several important themes arise in the video, which can augment and extend discussion of Afrodiasporic identity, as the visual effects of the music video narrative reinforce the sonic multiplicity Rada composes into the song. In the video, Rada continually multiplies herself throughout scenes, allowing her clones to take on their own personhood: singing and dancing individually while retaining the coherence of scene and costume, and of course, harmonizing with each other. Where the camera shows her playing instruments, her arms and hands are suddenly doubled or tripled, increasing a sense of futuristic virtuosity. The second chorus finds Rada throwing an acoustic guitar, a cymbal, a speaker, and finally, a vinyl record, which freeze in copies as they fall around her. These symbols of popular music reference analog technology, aligning her with the soul style and embedding her in the Ethio-soul genre that she is most known for when combined with the instrumental sections featuring massenqo. At the same time, by tossing these mediating technologies aside and continuing to sing, Rada "frees" herself from interfaces that might prevent authenticity of sound and self.

Perhaps most obviously, in one shot Rada literally frames herself, leaving trace copies as she moves away from the camera, and leaving the viewer unsure as to her "true" self.

In doing so, Rada foregrounds the process of transmedia (understanding that incorporates multiple forms of media) and the multimedia technology as implicated therein. This technique aligns with the Ethiopian wax-and-gold aesthetic concept discussed previously. As scholar of music and technology Jody Berland suggests:

> The history of communication technology is the history of the increasing separation of singer, sound, and image . . . and the simultaneous history of their reconstructed unity. This technical reconstruction is instrumental in the changing topography of social, cultural and political space.
>
> (1993, 28)

In the "Life Happens" video, acknowledging the deconstruction of sound from source is completed by a reconstruction of Rada's voice and body as diverse identities. Thus, it is only in the world of transmedia that Rada can exist at the levels of multiplicity she embodies: a place where music, video storytelling, and musical historicization all expand Rada's world beyond the music video and into the musical, racial, and religious complexities of her subjective position as an Ethiopian Israeli. The song's cut'n'mix, collage style of composition allows Rada to identify herself sonically and visually as Afrodiasporic, aligning herself with the global African diaspora. While Rada seems to navigate her own identity as multiplicity, any reference to Israel or Jewishness is conspicuously absent from the video. As Webster-Kogen observes, this strategic musical effort allows Rada to demonstrate an implicit critique of Israeli treatment of Ethiopian Israelis, by "othering" herself in Israel and connecting the larger African diasporic community through both spatial and temporal signifiers (2018, 49).

The setting is also indicative of expansion and freedom of identity. Slowly the video moves from inside a stark concrete warehouse to the same building broken down and partially destroyed, to a field, with only the ruins of the warehouse in the background. The video closes with Rada alone in the field, singing and riffing on a gospel-style version of the chorus to a thick backing track of a cappella voices. While the lyrics of the song are non-political (they are about personal overcoming and experience), the sonic and visual aspects of the composition allow for nuanced layers of interpretation.

Incorporating the video into a music theory classroom can be done in a variety of ways. One could provide historical background, ask students to read or listen to an English-language interview with Rada, explore the lyrics and story therein as it works with the video and music, or simply start with students' own, likely varied, readings of the video. Key elements for such lessons would be identifying overt and covert messages that Rada is sending, where these messages stem from (video, music, text, or some combination), and what signifiers point to an Afrodiasporic reading of the video. Instructors might include a discussion of Hebdige's concept of the cut'n'mix style (as illuminated by Webster-Kogen) or of how Rada's video employs a sense of multiplicity of self, both visually and musically. Discussions around chronological as well as geographical space and reference are also possible, particularly in thinking about Rada's costumes and her mixing of analog visual references with digital effects (her clones). I have found this video to be highly engaging and entertaining for students to watch, and as they embark on analyzing it, they can connect the music analysis skills they have learned to visual and narrative analysis, allowing for practice in this multimedia genre.

Conclusion

In this chapter, I have offered suggestions for teaching two songs by Ester Rada in the undergraduate music theory core classroom. Each piece allows for varied levels of engagement, from simply being another nice example of relative keys or metric shifts, to an opportunity to think about Afrodiasporic sound and identity as portrayed through the music of this Ethiopian Israeli musician. In teaching Rada's music, I emphasize the importance of close listening, embodied experience (particularly in thinking about meter), and transcription as ways to help students learn to interact with un-notated, popular music texts. By de-emphasizing notation as the main way to understand musical meaning, not only will students build invaluable critical listening and transcription skills, but they will also broaden their understanding of how timbre, texture, and other musical style markers go a long way into creating meaning and narrative in Rada's music, as in other popular musics. Moreover, by using music video, a medium already deeply familiar to twenty-first-century students, one can help students think more generally about analysis: how visuals and sounds cocreate meaning, express ideas, and engage with the listener in multimedia.

Finally, I find Rada's music particularly exciting to work with because she is a living artist in the prime of her career. She is still touring and releasing albums and EPs regularly. This means that you may have students in your classroom who have heard her live, and that there are numerous, ongoing opportunities to continue to develop and extend discussions of her music by taking into account her newer work. For example, when I first started analyzing Rada's work in 2013, she had only her first EP out, which was then quickly followed by her album. Now, in 2022, she has several albums, and her work produced since 2019 includes music where she sings in Hebrew, complicating her previous downplaying of her Israeli-ness through avoidance of Hebrew in her music. Similarly, the Ethiopian Israeli experience and the politics around race in Israel more generally are also continually growing and changing. This provides rich ground for classes or individual students that truly want to think about music analysis in relation to broader sociocultural contexts. Given how varied, engaging, and complex Ester Rada's musics are, the lessons and teaching suggestions I provide here are only the beginning of what could be a deep and ongoing engagement with her work.

Notes

1. When slotting in these examples throughout a curriculum, I encourage instructors to allow Rada's music to replace music by White male composers, rather than music by composers of other marginalized identities. This will allow for greater equity and balance around diverse examples in the music theory classroom.
2. Azmariwoch (singular: Azmari) are Ethiopian folk-poets and traveling minstrels who are self-accompanied, often on the massenqo, a single-stringed fiddle.
3. https://ester-rada.bandcamp.com/ (accessed July 2021) and www.bbc.com/news/magazine-27071775 (accessed July 2021).
4. The "Life Happens" track was previously released as an EP in 2013.
5. Webster-Kogen (2018, 34–39) also has a thoughtful discussion of Simone's original and Rada's cover.
6. While there are many such examples, two that might be easy to include alongside Rada's are Leonard Bernstein's "America" from his musical *West Side Story* (1961) and the Fleet Foxes's "Mykonos" from their EP *Sun Giant* (2008, track 4).
7. http://esterrada.bandcamp.com/ (accessed July 2021). The song was released first as an EP in 2013 and then on the *Ester Rada* album in 2014. The accompanying music video has over 1.3 million views on YouTube as of July 2021.

Works Cited

Berland, Jody. 1993. "Sound, Image and Social Space: Music Video and Media Reconstruction." In *Sound and Vision: The Music Video Reader*, edited by Simon Frith, Andrew Goodwin, and Lawrence Grossberg, 25–44. Routledge.

Doll, Christopher. 2011. "Rockin' Out: Expressive Modulation in Verse-Chorus Form." *Music Theory Online* 17/3.

Feldstein, Ruth. 2013. *How It Feels to Be Free: Black Women Entertainers and the Civil Rights Movement*. Oxford University Press.

Rada, Ester. 2014. "Life Happens." Track 4, *Ester Rada*. FitFit Records.

———. 2015. "Four Women." Track 2, *I Wish*. FitFit Records.

Simone, Nina. 1966. "Four Women." Track 2, *Wild Is the Wind*. Philips Records, vinyl.

Webster-Kogen, Ilana. 2018. *Citizen Azmari: Making Ethiopian Music in Tel Aviv*. Wesleyan University Press.

Weil, Shalva. 2012. "Longing for Jerusalem Among the Beta Israel of Ethiopia." In *African Zion: Studies in Black Judaism*, edited by Edith Bruder and Tudor Parfitt, 204–17. Cambridge Scholars Publishing.

Part Five
Twentieth-Century Music

18 Inclusivity and the "Perfect Teaching Piece" in the Undergraduate Post-Tonal Classroom

Cara Stroud

Many compositions that music theorists traditionally use to teach post-tonal techniques are structured so that all the analytical data falls into a neat pattern. These tidy explanations are often helpful for convincing students of the value of learning the analytical techniques in question. It can be both engaging and comforting for students when nearly every pitch can be explained as a member of a certain collection, or when it's clear how the composer was using a consistent canonic procedure that neatly works itself out over the course of an entire piece. While there is value in helping students foster their own curiosity and seek understanding of music that they might initially perceive as random or discordant, many of us may find ourselves stuck using the same set of "perfect teaching pieces" over and over in our post-tonal classes. I know I do this: my course syllabus is filled with pieces by Claude Debussy, Béla Bartók, Arnold Schoenberg, and Igor Stravinsky because those pieces are known to work so reliably well to introduce students to basic post-tonal concepts. Let's face it – sticking to the same set of perfect teaching pieces year after year furthers the supremacy of White male composers.

In this chapter, I will briefly explore how the ideal of the "perfect teaching piece" can unnecessarily limit classroom teaching and further narratives of White supremacy, and I include sample lessons with works such as Julius Eastman's *Piano 2* (1986), Dorothy Rudd Moore's song cycle *From the Dark Tower* (1972), Zenobia Powell Perry's Sonatine for Clarinet (1963), and Tania Léon's "Oh Yemanja" from *Scourge of Hyacinths* (1994). Finally, I will discuss strategies for addressing students' (and instructors'!) discomfort with music beyond the "perfect teaching piece."[1]

The Impossible Ideal of the Perfect Teaching Piece

All sorts of pedagogical priorities might influence our choices of course repertoire, and whether we like it or not, those priorities reflect our stated values as well as values that we may not be intending to communicate. Cora S. Palfy and Eric Gilson, building on work by educator Philip Jackson, describe this as the "hidden curriculum in music theory" (2018).[2] Just as there may be unintended values communicated by a curriculum, such as "only music by White composers is worthy of study" if a curriculum only includes work by White composers, our own intended pedagogical values and outcomes can be unnecessarily obstructed when we choose pieces exclusively from the canon of "perfect teaching pieces." Through the lens of the hidden curriculum, limiting post-tonal course repertoire to the standards from Debussy, Bartók, and Schoenberg reinforces the supremacy of White European composers. It also trains students to expect that post-tonal music will always have an underlying organizing principle that can only be revealed through in-depth analysis. Michael Buchler has described ways that including analysis using pitch-class set theory (hereafter "set theory") in the undergraduate post-tonal curriculum unnecessarily

DOI: 10.4324/9781003204053-24

limits and biases our repertoire choices: instead of choosing repertoire because it is interesting and engaging for students, we can end up choosing exclusively pieces that "work" to teach the topic (2017). I suggest that this is also true for many topics in addition to set theory in the standard undergraduate post-tonal curriculum: modes, rhythm and meter, and serialism, to name a few.

While there is value in carefully deploying works from the standard repertoire of "perfect teaching pieces," instructors should be aware of the potential for mistaken conclusions and value judgments that we (or anyone in the classroom) might make. Many of us know well the thrill that comes with finding the perfect teaching piece for a topic: "All the pitches can be interpreted using an (014) prime form, and students can find transpositions and inversions in one piece!" or similarly, "The composer uses both of the all-interval tetrachords in a variety of spacings so students can see their full range of possibilities!" *et cetera*. I don't mean to unnecessarily pick on set theory here: pedagogically sound strategies such as spiral learning, where the "perfect teaching pieces" are the ones that provide easily accessible payoffs from multiple analytical perspectives, can also easily influence our repertoire choices for the classroom in unintended ways.

Thus, curricular preferences can be interpreted as a smaller-scale version of the systemic structures of oppression described by racial inequity scholar Daria Roithmayr in *Reproducing Racism: How Everyday Choices Lock in White Advantages* (2014). Roithmayr describes the "self-reinforcing monopoly" of wealthy White neighborhoods and wealthy White public schools, and I would argue that the same could be said of our existing textbooks and pedagogical research. Current textbooks and pedagogy articles – honestly, including my own work[3] – mostly focus on work by White European men, so that becomes what we teach and what students learn.[4] This perpetuates a system that furthers White narratives.

Indeed, the idea of what constitutes a "perfect teaching piece" for each of us is laden with our own pedagogical values, as well as unintended baggage inherited from our discipline's history and our own educations, of course – a huge part of the problem! Is a teaching piece perfect when the students enjoy it because it reminds them of music they already like? When it is short enough that students can listen to it in 60 seconds or less but also complex enough that it demonstrates multiple uses of a certain technique? When the notation is simple enough that we know that students with visual disabilities will be able to access it through their assistive technology? When it exposes students to the compositional language of an important and influential composer? All these are considerations in choosing repertoire for my own classes, and they all come with hidden assumptions. While we cannot eliminate the values and compromises that accompany our teaching choices, we can be transparent about these choices, our priorities, and the consequences of our choices with our students.

I'll include an example from my own teaching to illustrate this phenomenon. My current post-tonal curriculum includes four model composition projects, and the first one is a composition modeled after a group of Béla Bartók's *Mikrokosmos*. I choose this collection as a source of models because it is so carefully designed from a pedagogical perspective: Bartók's compositional materials are transparent for students, form and phrase structures are familiar to them, they are easy for beginners to play on the piano, and most importantly for me, Bartók emphasizes compositional techniques that are also emphasized in my post-tonal curriculum. The *Mikrokosmos*'s modal scales, symmetrical collections, additive and asymmetrical meters, and use of small motivic cells that are easily analyzable using set theory illustrate these topics in a really vivid way for students, and they can easily digest Bartók's compositional language to create something that sounds more or less like it also belongs in the *Mikrokosmos* collection. But what is the cost of this? I spend about four to six weeks of the semester really living with the *Mikrokosmos*, and there is so much more that I could include in my curriculum without focusing so much on the work of one composer. At the end of the day, this is a project that foregrounds the work of *one European male composer*, above all others, as work that deserves to be emulated. That said, Bartók's culturally sensitive approach to documenting and responsibly taking in inspiration from the musical culture around him in Hungary is something I admire. I hope to share this admiration with my students, so I don't want to entirely take this unit of study out of my class. I counteract the emphasis on Bartók at the beginning of the semester by adding additional model composition projects with a wider range of stylistic models later in the semester, but it is still a curricular investment worth considering and discussing openly with students, without judgment. As Philip Ewell's 2020 blog post "New Music Theory" suggests, we can continue to be aware of the structures of oppression that are present behind our choices as we add compositions and analytical techniques to our curriculum and take away others; this does not mean doing away with any work from White men. Simply, Ewell encourages us to be strategic about what we are teaching. His blog post also contains excellent resources for instructors looking for methodologies developed by Black scholars, and I recommend going there for curricular resources for post-tonal topics theorized by Black scholars (2020).

Instructors may or may not choose to overtly discuss this with their students, but I believe there is a significant pedagogical advantage to openly discussing curricular choices: foregrounding the work of one European male composer above the work of others may be very helpful for learning about post-tonal compositional techniques, but it does so at the cost of furthering narratives of White supremacy. Jay-Z's and Julius Eastman's works are certainly stylistically replicable by undergraduates, if model compositions are as central to your teaching decisions as they are to mine. Why don't they get foregrounded in the same way as Bartók? Without reflecting on this directly, the post-tonal pedagogical canon becomes self-serving, self-replicating, and furthers only music and ideas written by White men. This is how choosing "perfect teaching pieces," semester after semester, crowds out the voices of Black composers.

Sample Lessons

In the following section of this chapter, I'll provide an overview of four pieces by Black composers that are long overdue for inclusion in post-tonal music theory courses. Sample assignments featuring these pieces are available in this book's Supplemental Materials website. Please note that these lessons are designed for inclusion within the traditional post-tonal curriculum that I have historically taught in my own post-tonal classes, accompanied by *The Musician's Guide to Theory and Analysis* by Jane Piper Clendinning and Elizabeth West Marvin. While I strive to address important features of music such as timbre and rhythm in my post-tonal classes, I still primarily focus on pitch-centric topics, such as modes, set theory, and serialism. As the music theory community continues to address long-standing imbalances, I anticipate that many of us will take the opportunity to shift our curricular priorities and take our topics of study in a new direction, but that shift is happening slowly for many of us, including myself. For those of us who are currently constrained to a traditional, pitch-centric curriculum, I will discuss four pieces that are an easy fit for an existing post-tonal curriculum. Even if complete curricular redesign is undesirable or far away, we can still make space to include works by Black composers. For this reason, I include curricular suggestions for similar pieces of repertoire from the standard canon that share common compositional priorities with the compositions in this chapter. Instructors may wish to focus exclusively on music from underrepresented composers, in

218 Cara Stroud

Table 18.1 Common Post-Tonal Topics in Four Select Compositions

Composer	Title (Year)	Teaching Topics
Zenobia Powell Perry	Sonatine for Clarinet and Piano (1963)	Neoclassicism (relating to form, phrase structure, and use of motive), twentieth-century tonality, ostinato, extended tertian harmonies
Dorothy Rudd Moore	*From the Dark Tower* (1972)	Quintal/quartal harmony, quotation and intertextuality, twentieth-century contrapuntal techniques, cluster chords, ostinato, centricity, twentieth-century tonality, bitonality, asymmetrical and changing meters, pentatonic collection, text–music relationships
Julius Eastman	*Piano 2* (1986)	Set theory, innovations in notation, ametrical, perceived vs. notated meter, chorale texture, extended tertian harmonies, quotation and intertextuality
Tania León	"Oh Yemanja," from *Scourge of Hyacinths* (1994)	Quintal/quartal harmony, pentatonic collection and subsets, text–music relationships, extended tertian harmonies, motivic use of intervals, twentieth-century rhythmic techniques

which case these curricular suggestions can be disregarded. In Table 18.1, I summarize the teaching topics that connect with each of the four pieces I discuss in this chapter.

Assignments and annotated scores featuring these four pieces can be found in the ancillary materials for this chapter. Here, I will discuss where to locate some interesting musical features so that instructors can easily include them in class discussion and analysis.

Powell Perry: Sonatine for Clarinet and Piano *(1963)*

This piece by Zenobia Powell Perry is a great one to include in a discussion about neoclassicism. The forms, phrase structure, and use of motives in all the movements strongly relate to classical formal techniques. This piece could easily be a part of a discussion of how neoclassical works are in dialogue with classical forms. Instructors could brainstorm characteristics of a typical classical sonata and discover with students which of those characteristics relate to a selection of neoclassical sonatas, perhaps with Powell Perry's clarinet Sonatine replacing or appearing alongside a piano sonata by Sergei Prokofiev or one of the many solo sonatas by Paul Hindemith. Powell Perry's work includes a lovely cyclic return of material from the first and third movements in the final movement – a fun discovery for students. Instructors could also ask students to highlight material from the first and third movements using two different colors in the finale, for example, and then discuss in class the musical effect and formal implications of recalling the earlier musical material at the end in this piece and in other pieces, tonal and post-tonal. Figure 18.1 shows one example of this. In measure 109 of the fourth movement, material from the retransition of the first movement reappears.

Julius Eastman: Piano 2 *(1986)*

Julius Eastman's compositions, including *Piano 2*, can be found written in his own handwriting and thus constitute an excellent introduction to sketch studies for students.[5] It's

Figure 18.1 Zenobia Powell Perry, Sonatine, iv (mm. 104–18), return of material from mvt. i (mm. 95–100).

easy to get a sense of Eastman's exuberant, wise, iconoclastic personality from the creative notation in his manuscripts, and the way that he intentionally flouts notational conventions in this work and others speaks to his compositional priorities. *Piano 2* can foster a discussion on innovations in rhythm, meter, and musical notation in the twentieth century, since this work is set without a meter and bar lines that do not appear to mark measures. Thomas Feng edited the published version of *Piano 2*, and he maintains some (but not all) of the creative notation from Eastman's manuscripts.[6] *Piano 2* also works well in a discussion with advanced students about the utility of analysis with sets, since Eastman uses symmetrical collections and repeated intervallic patterns that are amenable to set analysis alongside chords that students may prefer to describe as extended tertian harmonies rather than with sets. Eastman's consistent use of the (014) prime form in formally important areas – the beginnings of the second and third movements – make this a good choice for an introduction to set theory, perhaps replacing or appearing alongside Schoenberg's "Nacht" from *Pierrot Lunaire*. These (014) prime forms are shown in Figures 18.2a and b. For students who want to delve into intertextuality, I have included an assignment that guides students through exploring the role the (014) prime form might play in supporting an intertextual connection between "Nacht" and *Piano 2*.[7]

Dorothy Rudd Moore: From the Dark Tower (1972)

Rudd Moore's song cycle *From the Dark Tower* includes many techniques that are commonly discussed in an undergraduate post-tonal course. The exquisite texts of the cycle are assembled by the composer entirely from work by Black poets. Extended study of multiple movements of this song cycle would be rewarding, especially if students have not yet had a chance to study a full song cycle. One efficient but meaningful way to do this would be to devote one class day to analysis and a second class day to student presentations. On day 1, divide the class into eight groups, assign one of the eight movements to each of the groups, and ask them to have "something to say" about their movement in order to present it during the next class. Day 2 would be filled with student presentations and discussion – an especially rewarding opportunity, given the breadth and depth of this song cycle. *From the Dark Tower* could also be part of a summative project at the end of a

Figure 18.2 Julius Eastman, Piano 2: (a) normal order {458}, a member of set class with prime form (014), first system, second movement; (b) normal order {890}, a member of set class with prime form (014), first system, third movement. *Source*: Copyright © 2018 by Music Sales Corporation and Eastman Music Publishing Co. All rights administered by Music Sales Corporation. International Copyright Secured. All Rights Reserved. Used by Permission.

unit on art song if you devote more course time to this topic. Rudd Moore's song cycle easily fits into a discussion of modes, collections, tonality, and centricity in twentieth-century music, making it ideal for replacing or teaching alongside work by Claude Debussy and Maurice Ravel.[8] If your course includes a discussion of twentieth-century contrapuntal techniques, *From the Dark Tower* offers many examples from which to choose. Figure 18.3 illustrates a fugue-like subject (cello) and answer (piano left hand) in the seventh movement of the song cycle, "For a Poet."

Tania León: "Oh Yemanja," from Scourge of Hyacinths *(1994)*

"Oh Yemanja" is a stunning aria that rewards study at all levels. In a fundamentals course, students will be able to find returning intervallic patterns such as the melodic sevenths and ninths shown in Figure 18.4. After discovering the prevalence of these particular intervals in both the interlude and vocal part, students might speculate on the musical effect created by repeatedly hearing or singing so many intervals of a ninth and seventh – to me, they depict the mother Tiatin's yearning supplications to the goddess Yemanja.

"Oh Yemanja" can also serve as a touchstone for a discussion about text and music relationships, since students will notice the "Oh Yemanja" refrain and the changes in the vocal line and accompaniment over the course of the aria that connect with the mother's heart-wrenching pleas to protect her son. The Supplemental Materials website contains assignments in which students can explore the use of the pentatonic collection and ametrical features in this aria.

Strategies for Addressing Discomfort in the Classroom

In the final section of this chapter, I discuss some strategies for addressing student and instructor discomfort that may arise when working with pieces outside of post-tonal pedagogy's typical canon. Many of us rely on the comfort of "perfect teaching pieces" for a reason,

Inclusivity and the "Perfect Teaching Piece" 221

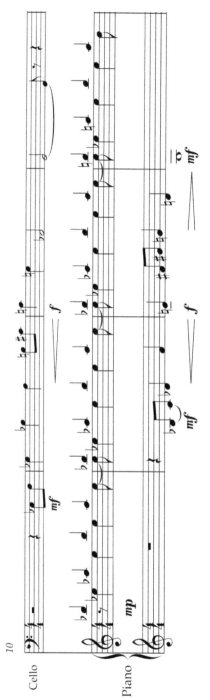

Figure 18.3 Dorothy Rudd Moore, "For a Poet," From the Dark Tower (mm. 10–13), subject and answer. Excerpts, From the Dark Tower by Dorothy Rudd Moore. Reprinted by permission of American Composers Alliance (BMI).

222 Cara Stroud

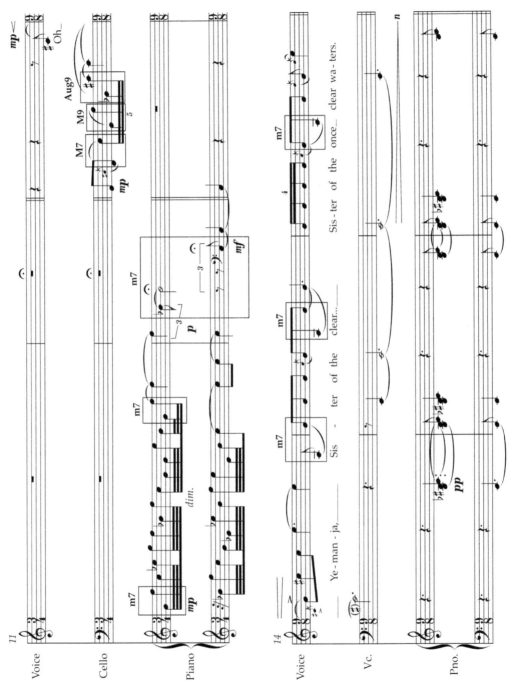

Figure 18.4 Tania León, "Oh Yemanjá" (mm. 11–16), melodic sevenths and ninths in the voice and piano.

and the creative discomfort of exploration can stretch students and instructors in unfamiliar ways. First, I explore contributing factors and solutions relating to student discomfort with unfamiliar repertoire, and then I close with a brief discussion of instructor discomfort.

What contributes to student discomfort in this situation? There are probably many pedagogical, psychological, and developmental reasons for college undergraduates to feel uncomfortable when faced with an unfamiliar post-tonal work. Understanding where students are coming from helps address the discomfort. Are they used to focusing on tests and correct answers in courses earlier in the undergraduate sequence or in high school? If so, it helps to recognize that the earlier scaffolding was beneficial for learning key signatures and ternary forms, but that students are now advanced enough to move past that way of thinking. Are they struggling with anxiety or fear of uncertainty? If so, I find it helpful to ask students to imagine advocating for this piece of music for an audience of non-musicians, such as their future elementary music students or a broad audience. This task works well at many points in the semester, since it prepares them with an advocacy mindset for later works they will encounter, and at the end of the semester, it allows for them to reflect on how far they have come. Advocating for a previously unfamiliar piece of music draws students toward features of the music that they personally find compelling and engaging, which helps them stay focused and motivated. Are students in your post-tonal class feeling overwhelmed with the responsibilities of a junior/senior-level undergraduate, such as student teaching or high-stakes juries? If so, I suggest guiding students toward finding ways to efficiently manage their time and assignments. I recognize that many of us are already doing this for our students and are still seeing signs of stress and overwhelm; however, it bears repeating, since it is so easy to get caught up in the rush of work and life. Are there ways to incorporate their jury repertoire in a listening response assignment or to incorporate their high school's wind band repertoire into their final project for the course? Going the extra mile to help an overwhelmed student or group of students always seems to be worth it. An extra benefit of this blending is that it helps students engage more with the course material when the repertoire they're working on in private lessons, for example, is also included in their theory class.

Above all, fostering a positive classroom culture with open communication goes a long way. Openly discussing students' struggles and discomfort can disarm the power of that discomfort to have an impact on their learning. Simply recognizing the universality of their struggle and brainstorming strategies for overcoming it can help students become more comfortable with ambiguity and the initially overwhelming task of analyzing a piece of music that doesn't easily fit with their current models for thinking about music. Potential topics for a beginning of class icebreaker discussion could be: Why do you think we feel discomfort about studying these pieces where we can't explain or label every note with a function or hierarchical position? I've found that the open discussion on struggle must be followed by work that feels meaningful to the students so that the struggle was worth it.

Remember that you, the instructor, control the narrative. While it is your job to invite students to contribute their own stories to the classroom, you can also carefully curate the discussion. Even when many students are feeling uncomfortable about a challenge or the lack of a single clear answer, some of them will undoubtedly have some creative, insightful ideas that spark further conversation with the class. I suggest choosing to focus our class time productively on these ideas when the opportunity arises. One way to solicit creative insights from students is to ask them each to write a few sentences about the assignment before class: What did they find confusing, surprising, or interesting? This low-stakes preparatory assignment can then be emailed to the instructor or posted to an online discussion board with some lead time for the instructor to read the responses, and then you will know whom to call on to share their juicy insights in class.

Discomfort also often comes up for instructors working with unfamiliar works. Feeling like we must always be the expert is yet another example of perfectionism that defeats the larger goal of inclusivity, since there is no possible way each of us could be experts on pieces about which there is little published work. Working against the idea that teachers must always be experts about everything we teach, and instead promoting the belief that the instructor's role is to guide the students in their own learning, can free up many possibilities for being comfortable with the unfamiliar and for being comfortable when not everything in a piece of music in the classroom lines up perfectly.

For example, Julius Eastman's *Piano 2* prominently features (014) prime forms at the beginning of the second and third movements, while the first movement features a (013) prime form at the opening. A question such as this one might be easy to ask: "Why didn't he use (014) for all three beginnings?" On closer consideration, this question implicitly suggests that post-tonal works *should* aim for a certain level of intervallic consistency – another question that gets at the actual musical effect of this particular work can get the students thinking about their own aesthetic values in relation to that of the music in front of them. A question such as this one can approach the musical effect from a more neutral perspective while still engaging with set theory, for example: "What musical effect is created for you by choosing these two sets, (013) and (014), for the beginnings of the three movements?" The second question gets at something interesting that may be different for different students, generating a helpful discussion about our own differing musical values. In this way, choosing perfectly consistent, limited musical choices only prepares students for repertoire that is limited and consistent in that way. By opening up the repertoire in our post-tonal classrooms to what students will actually encounter in their musical careers, or to the music we hope they will become advocates for, we are preparing them for a full and rewarding musical life.

Notes

1. Many thanks to Alyssa Barna, Esther Cavett, Sam Estenson, and Juliet Hess, who provided valuable insight and editorial comments on this chapter.
2. Palfy and Gilson cite Philip Wesley Jackson's influential work on the hidden curriculum (1990 [1968]).
3. For the sake of accountability, I'll describe here how I wish I had taken a more intersectional approach to my 2018 essay in *Engaging Students*, "Transcending the Pedagogical Patriarchy." The stance in this article excludes Black composers and scholars, and I apologize for this.
4. At the time of writing, there were many exciting changes beginning to happen in the field of music theory, including this volume and planned changes to upcoming textbook editions. I'm looking forward to seeing these changes bear out in what we teach and what students learn.
5. As of this writing, the Music Library at the University of Buffalo is hosting an online summary of an exhibit featuring photographs of Eastman and his compositions, which can be found at this URL: https://library.buffalo.edu/music/collections/detail.html?ID=16.
6. Julius Eastman, *Piano 2*, ed. Thomas Feng (NY: Music Sales Corporation, 2017). This is the version that is used for the assignments in the Supplemental Materials website for this chapter.
7. The intertextuality and quotation assignment including *Piano 2* can be found in the Supplemental Materials website for this chapter.
8. The sample assignments featuring *From the Dark Tower* can be found on the Supplemental Materials website.

Works Cited

Buchler, Michael. 2017. "A Case Against Teaching Set Classes to Undergraduates." *Engaging Students* 5. http://flipcamp.org/engagingstudents5/essays/buchler.html

Eastman, Julius. 2017. *Piano 2*. Edited by Thomas Feng. Music Sales Corporation.

Ewell, Philip. May 1, 2020. "New Music Theory." *Music Theory's White Racial Frame.* https://musictheoryswhiteracialframe.wordpress.com/2020/05/01/new-music-theory/

Jackson, Philip Wesley. 1990 [1968]. *Life in Classrooms.* Teachers College Press.

Palfy, Cora S., and Eric Gilson. 2018. "The Hidden Curriculum in the Music Theory Classroom." *Journal of Music Theory Pedagogy* 32: 79–110.

Roithmayr, Daria. 2014. *Reproducing Racism: How Everyday Choices Lock In White Advantage.* NYU Press.

Stroud, Cara. 2018. "Transcending the Pedagogical Patriarchy: Practical Suggestions for Including Examples from Women Composers in the Music Theory Curriculum." *Engaging Students* 6. http://flipcamp.org/engagingstudents6/essays/stroud1.html

19 Dream Variations

An Analytical Exploration of Florence Price's "My Dream"

Leigh VanHandel

Introduction

Florence Price's 1935 song "My Dream," from *Four Songs from the Weary Blues*, is a sophisticated blend of tonal harmony, chromatic sequences, whole tone, pentatonic and octatonic pitch collections, and characteristics of African American music and popular music.

This lesson focuses on four sequences in the piece, how those sequences relate to one another, and how the sequences express the form of the piece and Price's interpretation of Langston Hughes's poem. Neo-Riemannian analysis techniques are presented in this chapter, but the piece can also be studied by focusing on mediant relationships and common tones.

Florence Price (1887–1953)

Florence Price was one of the first African American composers to achieve critical success in the United States. Born in Little Rock, Arkansas, she received early musical training from her music teacher mother and graduated from the New England Conservatory in 1906 with a degree in piano and organ, while also studying composition and counterpoint. Price taught at several Southern Black colleges until 1912, when she returned to Little Rock to marry and start a family.

Price and her family moved to Chicago in 1927. After her 1931 divorce, she worked as a composer and organist in Chicago and was friends with many prominent African American performers, composers, and other artists. Her *Symphony in E Minor* won the Rodman Wanamaker Prize in 1932, making her the first African American woman to have a symphonic work performed by a major orchestra.

Stylistically, her compositions were informed by her education in the western classical tradition, as well as by characteristic African American stylistic idioms and rhythms. In a letter to Serge Koussevitzky, then-conductor of the Boston Symphony, Price wrote:

> Having been born in the South and having spent most of my childhood there I believe I can truthfully say that I understand the real Negro music. In some of my work I make use of the idiom undiluted. Again, at other times it merely flavors my themes. And at still other times thoughts come in the garb of the other side of my mixed racial background. I have tried to for practical purposes to cultivate and preserve a facility of expression in both idioms, altho [sic] I have an unwavering and compelling faith that a national music very beautiful and very American can come from the melting pot just as the nation itself has done.[1]

DOI: 10.4324/9781003204053-25

Sadly, interest in her music waned after her death in 1953, and much of her compositional output was thought lost. However, a large collection of her work was discovered in 2009 in her long-abandoned former summer home in St. Anne, Illinois, and was gifted to the University of Arkansas library (Steward 2018).

Langston Hughes (1901–1967)

Langston Hughes was an active figure in the Harlem and Chicago Renaissance; his prolific writings often focused on African American identity and racial consciousness. *Dream Variations* was first published in 1926 in *The Weary Blues*, a collection of poetry inspired by the music and language of Black Americans.[2] Price most likely came into contact with Hughes in Chicago in the 1930s–40s, and she set nine of Hughes's poems between 1935 and 1945 (Brown 2020, 205).

> *Dream Variations*
>
> To fling my arms wide
> In some place of the sun,
> To whirl and to dance
> Till the white day is done.
> Then rest at cool evening
> Beneath a tall tree
> While night comes on gently,
> Dark like me –
> That is my dream!
>
> To fling my arms wide
> In the face of the sun,
> Dance! Whirl! Whirl!
> Till the quick day is done.
> Rest at pale evening . . .
> A tall, slim tree . . .
> Night coming tenderly
> Black like me.

Students should be provided with the poem and asked to discuss their interpretation.[3] Among many possible responses, students might recognize several aspects of the poem:

> *Contrasts.* The poem invokes multiple contrasts. Within each stanza there is a contrast between *day* and *night*; the "white" day and "dark" or "black" night intensify that contrast and can be interpreted as a reference to racial identity. The language associated with *day* is more active, whereas *night* brings rest and gentle peace. The "white day" may reference Hughes's reaction to existing in a racist society, and the "dark" night providing coolness and rest may indicate finding a sense of home or peace in the Black community.
>
> *Form.* The second stanza of the poem is a "variation" of the dream presented in the first stanza, with more active and fragmented imagery. Where the first stanza uses the infinitive forms of "to fling," "to whirl," and "to dance," the second stanza uses the imperatives – "Dance!" and "Whirl!" The onset of evening under a tree is present in both stanzas, but the imagery becomes more fragmented and disjointed in the second, where thoughts are introduced but not concluded.

Structure. The rhyme scheme implies pairings of every two lines; in both stanzas, the rhymes occur between *sun/done* and *tree/me*. The lines "Dark like me" and "Black like me" are indented in each stanza for emphasis. The line "That is my dream!" is typeset with the first stanza but is outside of the rhyme scheme for both stanzas.

Before hearing the song, students could discuss how they would reflect the poem's characteristics if they were to compose a setting of this text. How would they represent the contrasts? How might they reflect the variation idea? What lines stand out that they might want to emphasize? For example, they may highlight "That is my dream!" at the end of the first stanza as a potentially important moment and discuss how they might incorporate that in their setting. Students could also compose and perform rhythmic settings of portions of the text to see how they interpret the poetic meter.

Stanza 1, Section 1: Opening, mm. 1–7

To fling my arms wide[4]
In some place in the sun,[5]
To whirl and to dance
Till the white day is done.[6]

Measures 1–7 establish the key and introduce a duality that pervades the piece. Price immediately incorporates the language of early twentieth-century jazz, popular music, and traditional African American song into this art song, even while establishing tonic by traditional harmonic means.

As shown in Figure 19.1a, the first half of each $^6_8$ measure contains an ascending D major arpeggiation but includes a B as part of a descending melodic gesture that crosses from the right hand to the left. Chords with an added sixth appear throughout the song and are common in popular music and jazz in the early twentieth century.[7]

The opening measures provide an opportunity to talk about tonality, context, interpretation, and style with students, whether they are just learning harmonic analysis or have more advanced analysis skills. Students who see a key signature with two sharps and stack the notes in the first half of the measure may assume the key is B minor and analyze the opening arpeggiation as a chord spelled B–D–F♯–A, or i$^6_5$. Even students who identify the key as D major may still stack the notes in thirds and analyze the chord with B as the root, resulting in a vi$^6_5$ chord.

The important question to discuss is: While it may *look* like a B minor chord, do they *hear* B minor as tonic? If they're interpreting it in D major, does the quick appearance of the B really make the piece sound like it's beginning with a vi$^6_5$? The instructor can play the opening arpeggiation with and without the B and have students provide arguments for their tonal interpretation. When combined with the A[7] chord in the second half of each measure, students should understand how D major is established as tonic; through this, students can be introduced to chords with an added sixth, a harmonic language characteristic of early twentieth-century popular styles.

The D major chord with an added sixth introduces four of the five pitches used in the D–E–F♯–A–B pentatonic collection in the opening vocal melody in measures 2–5, set to the poem's first two lines (Figure 19.1b); this pentatonic melody is set over the D major–A[7] progression in the piano. The pentatonic scale is frequently used in African American folk traditions (as well as elsewhere throughout the world), and Price often uses it in combination with and as a contrast to the language of western tonality.

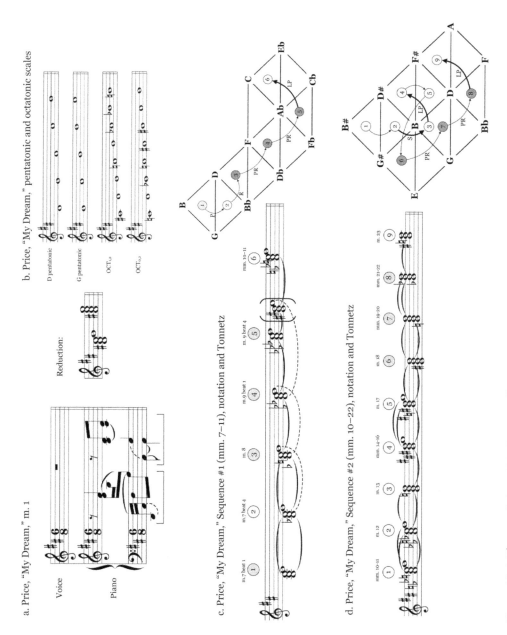

Figure 19.1 Florence Price's "My Dream," first stanza.

In the second half of measure 5, Price transposes the piano and vocal line to G major and G pentatonic respectively (Figure 19.1b) on the lines "To whirl and to dance/Till the white day is done." These two lines complete the initial rhyme of *sun/done* and are compressed into two measures, with an unexpected G minor chord at the end of measure 7 indicating the end of the transposed material.

Stanza 1, Section 2: Sequence #1

Then rest, then rest at evening[8]

The shift away from G major in measure 7 sets up the first chromatic sequence of the piece in measures 7–10. The piano's arpeggiated figuration stays the same, including the now-familiar added sixth in each chord. The harmonic sequence is initiated with the modal shift from G major to G minor in measure 7, then in rapid succession the harmony moves through arpeggiations of B♭ major, D♭ major, E major, and A♭ major (see Figure 19.1c). Students should be asked to attempt a Roman numeral analysis, leading to a discussion of function and whether the Roman numerals reflect how we hear these chords functioning in this piece – for example, do we really hear the D♭ major chord in measure 9 functioning as a lowered tonic, or the E major chord as a major predominant built on the supertonic, or as a V/V that doesn't resolve to V? (Hopefully, the answer to both questions is "no.")

Analysis via Neo-Riemannian Transformations

If students are familiar with neo-Riemannian transformational analysis, they will be able to analyze this harmonic progression as a PR cycle, with the first PR motion between G major and B♭ major made one transformation at a time, and the remainder being made directly (highlighted in gray in Figure 19.1c). The analytic challenges for students will be remembering to account for the added sixths present in each chord and recognizing that the E major chord in the second half of measure 9 can be enharmonically reinterpreted as F♭ major, thus preserving the PR cycle.[9]

The next step after E/F♭ major in the PR cycle would be a return to G major (or its enharmonic equivalent). Instead, Price moves from E/F♭ major to A♭ major, a striking LP transformation, and alters the piano figuration for the first time to highlight the word "evening" on the downbeat of measure 10.

Analysis via Mediant Relationships and Common Tones

Even if students are not familiar with neo-Riemannian analysis, this chromatic sequence can still be meaningfully analyzed by discussing mediant relationships and common tones. Students can be prompted to examine how chords in the chromatic sequence relate to one another, and to examine how common tones help the harmonic progression to sound smooth even as the chords become increasingly distant from the established D major tonic. Students should discover that the overall motion from G major–B♭ major–D♭ major–E/F♭ major outlines a harmonic sequence by ascending minor thirds, and each pair of chords contains one or two common tones (Figure 19.1c).[10] As before, the added sixths and the enharmonic reinterpretation of E/F♭ are likely to cause the most confusion.

Pitch Collections

In this sequence, Price highlights the octatonic scale formed by the aggregate of the chords of the minor third/PR cycle (Figure 19.1b, $OCT_{1,2}$). The chord roots of the sequence make up one of the fully diminished sevenths in the octatonic scale (G–B♭–D♭–F♭/E), and with each chord change the vocal melody emphasizes the other fully diminished seventh (D–F–A♭–B), resulting in a P5 between the bass and the melody at each chord change. The three notes missing from the voice's overall ascending octatonic scale, G, B♭, and C♯, are present in the chord roots, as well as in the right hand of the piano figuration as the added sixths for the D♭ major and E major chords, respectively (mm. 8–9). The C♮ at the melodic climax on "evening" in measure 10, instead of the C♯ expected as part of $OCT_{1,2}$, disrupts the octatonic aggregate as the major third/LP transformation breaks the minor third/PR cycle, marking the end of the sequence. The texture change in the piano and the comparatively long length of the A♭ major harmony also serve to signal the sequence's end.

Interpretation

The opening four lines combine the language of western tonality with that of popular and vernacular music to accompany the imagery of the sun and of the "white day"; the tonal areas are static and last as long as a workday may seem. As the poem shifts to evening, the harmonic language unmoors itself from the tonal harmonies that represented the day and accelerates through a colorful chromatic progression representing the ever-changing evening.

Stanza 1, Section 3: Sequence #2

> *Beneath a tall tree*
> *While night comes on gently,*
> *Dark like me –*
> *That is my dream!*

A modal shift from A♭ major to A♭ minor in measure 12 initiates the second chromatic sequence, which lasts for the rest of the first stanza, including the added line "That is my dream!" This sequence explores a harmonic and melodic landscape largely centered on the pitch B until the end of the sequence. Figure 19.1d shows the second sequence's harmonic path in reduction, with common tones indicated, and on the Tonnetz.

Analysis via Neo-Riemannian Transformations

The first part of the sequence takes place from measures 11–13, on the line, "Beneath a tall tree." On the Tonnetz (Figure 19.1d), the A♭ major and minor chords in measures 10–12 have been respelled enharmonically to illustrate the SLIDE transformation from A♭ minor/G♯ minor to G major. The SLIDE transformation preserves the third of each chord, here C♭/B♮, while shifting the perfect fifth by a semitone. Price places the semitone change from C to C♭/B♮ in the vocal melody from measures 11–12 (spelled as B♮ over the A♭ minor chord) and then holds that B♮ as the common tone between A♭ minor and the G^7 chord (mm. 12–13).

Price again uses an LP transformation, or motion up a major third from G to B, in combination with other cues to signal a change or end to a harmonic passage. With the addition of the dominant seventh to the G major chord in measure 13, the chord could also be interpreted as an augmented sixth chord (G–B–D–E♯) with a nonstandard resolution to a B major chord in second inversion that is functioning as tonic rather than as a cadential $^6_4$ chord.[11] The B major harmony is arpeggiated in the piano's left hand through the line "While night comes on gently," while a pentatonic collection (B–C♯–D♯–F♯–G♯) oscillates in the upper voices of the piano figuration. The tonic function of B major is emphasized by the vocal line's $\hat{3}$–$\hat{2}$–$\hat{1}$ motion and the arpeggiation in the left hand.

232 *Leigh VanHandel*

At the beginning of the dramatic line "Dark like me," a P transformation shifts the mode from B major to B minor, similar to the earlier modal shift from A♭ major to A♭ minor. If Price repeated the previous P + SLIDE transformation from measures 10–13 here, the progression would lead from B major to B minor directly to B♭ major, which is the eventual harmonic goal of this passage. However, Price instead introduces an E⁷ chord, which has three common tones with the B minor chord with added sixth – G♯, B, and D♮.[12]

The E⁷ chord initiates another PR cycle that concludes this chromatic sequence. This time, the cycle uses dominant seventh chords built on E, G, and B♭ (shown highlighted in gray in Figure 19.1d as steps 6, 7, and 8), with the B♭⁷ setting the climactic text, "That is my dream!" in measures 21–22. This arrival is emphasized by the sustained harmony and the stepwise diatonic vocal melody leading to an F₅, the highest note so far in the piece. Thus, instead of moving directly from B minor to B♭ major using a SLIDE transformation, Price extends the sequential passage to include the "extra" line at the end of the first stanza by recalling the PR cycle from the first sequence to delay the arrival to B♭ major. And as in sequence #1, the end of the cycle and start of the next sequence is signaled with an LP transformation, this time from B♭ major to D major (m. 23), providing a return to the opening tonic at the beginning of the second stanza.[13]

Pitch Collections

Since the PR cycle used at the end of sequence #2 is the same as that used in sequence #1, the aggregate of the cycle once again creates an $OCT_{1,2}$ collection. However, in this sequence Price's melody outlines most of the $OCT_{0,2}$ scale (mm. 18–22, shown in Figure 19.1b); the missing notes of F♯ and A are present in the piano part in measures 18–20. The pitches in common between the $OCT_{1,2}$ and $OCT_{0,2}$ scales are D, F, G♯, and B, all of which are present and three of which are prominent in the vocal melody from measures 18–22.

Interpretation

The SLIDE transformation has its origins in romantic harmony and was frequently used throughout the nineteenth and twentieth centuries. Price no doubt encountered this harmonic progression in her conservatory studies, and as it was often present in film scores, she may have also encountered it as she accompanied films on organ in theaters in Chicago and Boston (Lehman 2013, 2; Brown, 99). Frank Lehman describes the progression as being frequently associated "with liminal spaces such as dream and (un)death" and "readily mapped onto oppositions" (2014, 68). Lehman also describes the SLIDE progression as having the "unique ability to connote extreme tonal distance while maintaining extreme pitch proximity[,] render[ing] it especially apt for conveying ambivalence and otherworldliness" (2013, 6).

Students can be prompted to discuss what this striking harmonic progression might indicate to them. Among other responses, the nineteenth- and twentieth-century associations of SLIDE transformations with dreams, opposition, and otherworldliness may reflect the contrasts in the text; that transformation takes place on the line "Beneath a tall tree," highlighting the different worlds of the day and evening and indicating dreams of a world where the narrator is able to rest as evening comes.

This sequence contains the second and third appearance of an LP transformation, or motion up a major third, marking the end of one harmonic sequence (or section) and beginning another. The addition of the dominant seventh to the harmonies initiating the transformation also allows for a potential interpretation as an enharmonic augmented sixth chord that is resolving to a triad in second inversion, which helps emphasize the chords of resolution as important moments of arrival. Each LP transformation is also marked by the new harmony being sustained, as well as by a change in piano figuration and pitch collection.

Stanza 2, Section 4: Sequence #3

To fling my arms wide
In the face of the sun,

The second stanza of the poem opens with a variation on the first two lines (*some place/ the face*), recalling the beginning of the narrator's dream. Price incorporates variation in the second stanza by returning to the opening tonal area of D major via the LP transformation at the end of sequence #2 into measure 23, and by using melodic and harmonic material that can be interpreted as a variation of the processes present in the first stanza.

In the first stanza, the introduction and first two lines established D major and then sequenced to G major on the second pair of lines. In the second stanza, the first two lines themselves contain sequence #3, which is a comparatively tonal sequence of diatonic triads in a descending thirds sequence of D major–B minor–G major, with the B minor and G major chord approached by a tonicizing chord (Figure 19.2a).[14] Thus, where the tonal sequence in the first stanza moved directly from D major to G major, this time Price uses a descending thirds sequence to achieve the overall move from D major to G major. Both the D major and G major chords contain hints of the added sixth that was present in the first stanza; the D major chord in measure 23 has a quick A–B–A neighbor tone motion in the piano's left hand, and the G major chord also contains the added sixth of E on the downbeat of measure 25.

The vocal melody consists of a descending fourth in each measure over the descending thirds sequence; the clear melodic sequence helps make the harmonic sequence audible, since each measure in the piano differs in rhythm and texture (Figure 19.2a).

The sequence is broken in measure 27, as the B major triad at the end of measure 26 does not fulfill its expected function as the dominant of E minor. Instead, an emphatic A♭ major triad on the word "sun" signals the end of the sequence.

Interpretation

The return to an essentially diatonic sequence (with chromatic embellishments) at the beginning of the second stanza mirrors the use of an essentially tonal harmonic and melodic sequence with G major as its goal at the beginning of the first stanza. The motion from G major in measure 25 to A♭ major in measure 26 signals the end of the diatonic harmonic progression and is notable for several reasons. First, an unexpected progression to A♭ major was used in measure 10 to mark the word "evening" at the end of chromatic sequence #1; here, it's marking the word "sun." Second, the motion from G major to A♭ major is the reverse of the P + SLIDE transformation in sequence #2 (mm. 10–13), which transformed A♭ major to G major; here, the reverse is being accomplished in one step. Third, this is the first harmonic sequence ending with something other than an LP transformation; the RP transformation (enharmonic minor third) from B major to A♭ major is the mirror image of the E major to A♭ major LP transformation in sequence #1. The variations in the second stanza have begun.

a. Price, "My Dream," Sequence #3 (mm. 23–26), notation

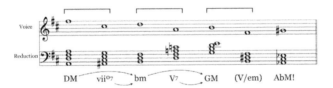

b. Price, "My Dream," Sequence #4 (mm. 27–32), notation and Tonnetz

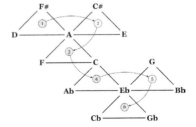

c. Price, "My Dream," octatonic collection connections

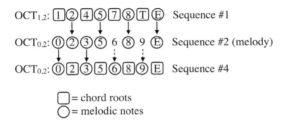

d. Price, "My Dream," diminished seventh sonorities and augmented triads derived from the two octatonic sets

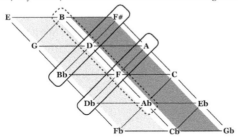

Figure 19.2 Florence Price's "My Dream," second stanza.

Stanza 2, Section 5: Sequence #4

Dance! Whirl! Whirl!
Till the quick day is done.

Immediately following the A♭ major chord that breaks sequence #3, the original tonic of D major returns in measure 27 to initiate sequence #4 on the text, "Dance! Whirl! Whirl! Till the quick day is done." This sequence is another ascending minor thirds, or PR cycle (highlighted in gray in Figure 19.2b), though it features different chords than the previous PR cycles. The D major and A♭ major chords (mm. 27 and 30, respectively) are embellished by their dominant seventh chords; in each case, the melody holds onto the common tone between the chords for the two measures of the implied (but unfulfilled) diatonic motion. The piano figuration distinguishes between the chords of the PR cycle, which have similar piano figurations, and the two embellishing dominant chords in measures 28 and 31, whose figurations are contrasting.

The analytical challenge in this sequence will be separating the embellishing dominant seventh chords from the PR cycle. Neither dominant seventh should be considered part of the cycle, though the implications of using them to emphasize D major and A♭ major (a tritone from tonic, and a structurally important chord at the end of sequence #1 and sequence #3) are worth discussion.

Pitch Collections

While this is the third sequence using a PR cycle in the song, the pitch collection created by this sequence is different than that used in sequences #1 and #2. This PR cycle contains D major, F major, A♭ major, and B/C♭ major (shown in Figure 19.2b), resulting in an $OCT_{0,2}$ collection. This collection was first introduced in the melody only of sequence #2 and is now present as the harmonic and melodic structure of this sequence (Figure 19.2c). Where sequence #1 was constructed with perfect fifths between the bass and vocal line marking each chord change, this sequence has octaves marking the arrival of the first three chords of the cycle.

The vocal melody from measures 27–31 outlines the diminished seventh chord of A–C–E♭/D♯–G♭/F♯, highlighting the other members of the $OCT_{0,2}$ scale.[15] Thus, Price connects these three chromatic sequences together by first using the $OCT_{1,2}$ scale for both the harmonic and melodic content of sequence #1, then using $OCT_{1,2}$ for the harmonic and $OCT_{0,2}$ for the melodic content of sequence #2, then using $OCT_{0,2}$ for both the harmonic and melodic content of sequence #4.

The harmonic and melodic motion to G minor in measure 33 indicates the end of the chromatic sequence. The piano prolongs G minor (with an added sixth of E♮) for five measures, discharging the energy from sequence #4 and providing an extended transition to the second half of the second stanza.

Interpretation

As implied by the imperative verbs of "Dance! Whirl! Whirl!" and the change of text to "Till the quick day," Price's time signature change in measure 27 from $\frac{6}{8}$ to $\frac{2}{4}$, and a notated tempo increase from dotted quarter = 63 to quarter = 108 both results in an acceleration of time through this section. The use of a PR cycle recalls sequences #1 and #2, but Price varies it with a different pitch collection and dominant seventh chord embellishments.

Stanza 2, Section 6: Conclusion

> *Rest at pale evening . . .*[16]
> *A tall, slim tree . . .*
> *Night coming tenderly*
> *Black like me.*

The second half of the stanza uses harmonic language and piano figurations reminiscent of the calm and still evening depicted at the end of the first stanza. While there are no harmonic sequences, this section will likely be more challenging; however, pitch collections and patterns of transformations recall and vary notable melodic and harmonic events from earlier, drawing together the various compositional elements seen throughout the piece. A lesson focusing only on sequences could omit this section, whereas an advanced class could discuss how this section uses material from the first stanza to create variation in the second stanza.

At the *tempo primo* in measure 38, the piano figuration alternates between two pentatonic collections (D–E–F♯–A–B and A♭–B♭–C♮–D–F♮), recalling the structural importance collections and chords built on D and A♭ have had throughout the song. In measure 41, just after the word "evening," the A♭ pentatonic collection changes to a collection (E–F♯–G♯–B–D) that can be interpreted as an E^7 chord.[17] This motion from an A♭ collection to E is the reverse of the LP transformation from E/F♭ to A♭ on the word "evening" at the end of sequence #1 in measures 9–10.

Setting the line "A tall, slim tree," the E^7 collection changes in measure 43 to a D minor chord with added sixth, holding the B♮ in common in the vocal line. The B♮ common tone recalls the pitch's central role in sequence #2, where a common tone in the vocal line (mm. 12–3) bridged the SLIDE transformation from A♭ minor to the G dominant seventh on the analogous text "Beneath a tall tree."

A short piano interlude extends the B♮ common tone, first in an inner voice through a fully diminished seventh chord (E♯–G♯–B–D, mm. 44–45), and then as the melodic arrival point of a chromatic line in the piano's left hand in measures 45–46 as the harmony shifts to a C♯^{7} chord decorated with an inner voice 9–8 motion that echoes the bass voice's motion from D to C♯. The overall harmonic motion from D minor to the C♯^{7} (mm. 43–46) can be interpreted as a SLIDE transformation, recalling the setting of this portion of the text in the first stanza.

Additional melodic and harmonic links to the first stanza include the fully diminished seventh chord in measures 44–45 (E♯/F–G♯/A♭–B–D), which is the same collection of pitches emphasized in the melody in sequence #1 (mm. 7–9) and sequence #2 (mm. 17–21) and which also appeared in the bass in sequence #4 (mm. 27–32). As shown in Figure 19.2c, it consists of the common tones between the OCT$_{1,2}$ and OCT$_{0,2}$ collections used throughout the piece. Figure 19.2d illustrates the two octatonic sets shaded in light and dark gray, and the dotted rectangle indicates the shared pitches between the two collections.

Price also ties these octatonic collections together by using two augmented triads connecting the collections; the B♭–D–F♯ augmented triad is outlined in the melody and bass voice from measures 38–42, and the A–C♯–E♯ and B♭–D–F♯ triads in the piano set the beginning of the rising vocal line. These triads are indicated in Figure 19.2d by the solid rectangles.

The piece culminates with a predominant[18]–V^7–I cadential motion to D major with the added sixth still present, returning to the opening tonality. However, the imperfect authentic cadential progression maintains the influences of the vernacular harmonic languages sharing space in this piece by including the added sixth and the pentatonic figure in the piano's right hand.

Interpretation

Students will likely find this the most challenging section to analyze. The material recontextualizes and fragments melodic and harmonic elements from the first stanza, just as the text of the poem recontextualizes and fragments the evening imagery.

Conclusion

Florence Price's "My Dream" is a powerful song that rewards close study. It illustrates a synthesis of western tonal harmony with the vernacular of jazz, popular song, and African

American traditions. The song contains chromatic sequences that will challenge advanced undergraduate and graduate students and that allow for discussion of how these sequences relate to the text. The dualities of the poem (white/black, day/evening) are represented in the music, in part through the juxtaposition of the tonal and non-tonal elements present in the piece. The concept of "variation" is manifested in the overall harmonic design, with the second stanza providing a reinterpretation of the harmonic collections from the first stanza.

Suggestions for Assignments

Students could complete a compare-and-contrast assignment with Margaret Bonds's setting of Hughes's "Dream Variation." Bonds's setting is included in the collection published by Hildegard and features repeated melodic motives, quartal harmonies, and a setting of the two stanzas that is close to strophic.

Notes

1. Florence Price, letter to S. Koussevitsky, July 5, 1943, cited in Brown 2020, 187.
2. See Hughes (1994, 4). The poem had been published in several periodicals as early as 1924 prior to being published in *The Weary Blues* and was called "Dream Variation" until *The Selected Poems of Langston Hughes* was published in 1959. (*Collected Poems*, p. 624 n. 40.)
3. Students may make a connection to Abel Meeropol's 1937 poem "Strange Fruit," popularized by Billie Holiday's 1939 recording. That poem and song were composed after Hughes's poem and Price's setting, but both "Strange Fruit" and "Dream Variations" use a tree as an evocative symbol – a symbol of rest and peace in Hughes's poem, and a symbol of the horrors of lynching in Meeropol's.
4. The Hildegard edition's opening line is "To fling wide my arms," while the Schirmer edition uses "To fling my arms wide," as it is in Hughes's poem. The Hildegard edition also credits the poem as being from Hughes's collection *The Dream Keeper*, but it had been published six years earlier in *The Weary Blues*, which the Schirmer edition credits.
5. Price changes "of the sun" to "*in* the sun," perhaps to call attention to the contrast between day imagery and night imagery; "some place of the sun" evokes a generic, typically sunny location, whereas "some place *in* the sun" indicates that the location is sunny at the moment the described action is taking place. This change is present in both the Hildegard and the Schirmer edition.
6. The Schirmer edition has a comma at the end of this line.
7. Because of the pervasive nature of the added sixth, and because it does not change the interpretation of the chord root or function, I will refer to chords with added sixths by their triad root and quality, and the added sixth can be assumed. The exception to this is if the chord has the quality of a dominant seventh chord, as in the A^7 chord in Figure 19.1a; even though this could conceivably be considered a C♯–E–G–A chord and still serve a dominant function in D major, its function as a V^7 is clear.
8. Price alters this text from "Then rest at cool evening" to "Then rest, then rest, at evening."
9. Again, this analysis focuses on triad root and quality of chords with added sixths to allow for a neo-Riemannian analysis.
10. In chords 2, 3 and 4, the root of the chord becomes the added sixth of the following chord; this is indicated in Figure 19.1c with a dotted line.
11. As shown in Harrison (1995) and elsewhere, nonstandard resolutions such as this were common in the late nineteenth- and early twentieth-century repertoire.
12. This motion can of course be described as an LRP or PRL transformation, but the important thing to highlight here is that in addition to the common tone of B, the added sixth in the B minor chord (G♯) and the seventh in the E^7 chord (D) are also common between the two chords, making the harmonic distance between these two chords far less substantial than it appears on the Tonnetz!
13. Similar to the motion from G^7 to B in mm. 13–14, the $B♭^7$ chord here could also be enharmonically reinterpreted as an augmented sixth chord (B♭–D–F–G♯), with a nonstandard resolution to a triad in second inversion functioning as tonic rather than a cadential $^6_4$ chord.

14. The sequence also includes the dominant of the expected, but unfulfilled, next step to E minor (m. 25).
15. That diminished seventh collection is also shared between $OCT_{0,2}$ and $OCT_{0,1}$, which is the third possible octatonic scale. $OCT_{0,1}$ is not used in the sequences.
16. The punctuation provided in the Hildegard edition after *evening* and *tree* matches that in Hughes's poem, while the Schirmer provides periods after the first two lines, and a comma after *tenderly*.
17. This interpretation is strengthened by the leap of a fourth from B♮ to E and back in the vocal line, and the voicing of the sustained chord in the left hand of the piano, implying a E^7 chord in third inversion.
18. The chord on the downbeat of m. 48 could be interpreted as an E–G–B–D chord, a ii^4_3 in D major, or as a G major triad (IV^6) with an added sixth. Either way, the chord serves a predominant function.

Works Cited

Brown, Rae Linda. 2020. *The Heart of a Woman: The Life and Music of Florence B. Price.* University of Illinois Press.

Harrison, Daniel. 1995. "Supplement to the Theory of Augmented-Sixth Chords." *Music Theory Spectrum* 17/2: 170–95.

Hughes, Langston. 1994. *The Collected Poems of Langston Hughes.* Edited by A. Rampersad and D. Roessel. Vintage Press.

Lehman, Frank. 2013. "Transformational Analysis and the Representation of Genius in Film Music." *Music Theory Spectrum* 35/1: 1–22.

———. 2014. "Schubert's SLIDEs: Tonal (Non-)Integration of a Paradoxical Transformation." *Music Theory and Analysis (MTA)* 1/1–2: 61–100.

Price, Florence B. 1995. "My Dream." In *Art Songs and Spirituals by African-American Women Composers*, edited by Vivian Taylor. Hildegard Publishing Company.

———. 2021. "My Dream." In *Four Songs from the Weary Blues*, edited by J.M. Cooper. G. Schirmer, Inc.

Steward, Karen Tricot. 2018. "After Lost Scores are Found in Abandoned House, Musicians Give Life to Florence Price's Music." *UALR Public Radio.* www.ualrpublicradio.org/post/after-lost-scores-are-found-abandoned-house-musicians-give-life-florence-prices-music

20 Teaching Twentieth-Century Stylistic Pluralism Through the Music of George Walker

Owen Belcher

In an interview, American composer, pianist, and teacher George Walker (1922–2018) was asked to discuss his compositional approach to melody and harmony. He responded that his pieces are "melodic . . . without being conventional in either a diatonic or chromatic sense," and that, harmonically, he does not compose with "any preconceived ideas" or through a strict pre-compositional system (Baker et al. 1978, 368). Walker's remarks avoid explicit association with any one school of twentieth-century composition. Indeed, his polystylistic *oeuvre* necessitates a variety of analytical lenses: some of his works can be approached from a tonal perspective, while others demonstrate a substantial break with common-practice tonal and formal procedures. The latter works may exhibit pitch centricity but not diatonic tonality, privilege motivic transformation over traditional harmonic relationships, or reimagine traditional classical forms. Walker's stylistic pluralism is representative of numerous twentieth-century composers, and while post-tonal textbooks and pedagogical research are beginning to take into account a broader spectrum of twentieth-century compositional approaches, many post-tonal textbooks, for reasons of space or curriculum, still concentrate primarily on only a small segment of theoretical techniques, with a heavy emphasis on pitch-class sets and twelve-tone techniques as derived from composers of the Second Viennese School.[1]

My chapter extends recent efforts to diversify the repertoire and techniques in courses devoted to twentieth-century music by offering one to three weeks' worth of material that allows students to explore tonal music in the twentieth-century classroom, as well as music that does not fit neatly into tonal and atonal categories.[2] Given the range of institutions and pedagogical contexts in which students might study twentieth-century music and analysis, I attempt to provide theory instructors with maximum flexibility so that they can tailor the material to their own curricula, whether that be an upper-level undergraduate elective course or an introductory graduate survey. I organize the chapter as a series of analytical vignettes which focus on three main areas: tonality and modality, large-scale musical form, and motivic and pitch-class set theory (hereafter set theory). The analytical overviews are modeled after the "Guided Analyses" in Joseph Straus's *Introduction to Post-Tonal Theory* (2016) and can serve as the basis of a class lecture or homework assignment. Additional homework assignments, suggested readings, essay response questions, and musicianship/skills exercises are posted on the Supplemental Materials website. Before each vignette, I list the key topics covered, along with the relevant chapters of several popular textbooks.[3] I have attempted to balance consideration of technical concepts with broader, open-ended questions for either class discussion or in-class writing.

DOI: 10.4324/9781003204053-26

Methodology and Accessibility

The central methodological goal of the chapter is to reinforce to students the benefits of exploring twentieth-century repertoire (and all repertoire for that matter) through multiple analytical lenses, with the understanding that their own analytical adventures will rarely result in the "clean and tidy" analytical examples necessarily promulgated by textbooks.

My approach yields several benefits. I expand existing discussions of twentieth-century compositional practices and create a conceptual bridge between students' knowledge of common-practice procedures and the freely atonal and 12-tone pieces that comprise the majority of many courses devoted to post-1900 music and music theory. Furthermore, I familiarize students and instructors with a major American composer – the first Black composer to win the Pulitzer Prize for music – whose New Grove entry contains only five bibliographic sources.[4] Thus, I engage music that is often cast aside in the curricular rush from the French Symbolists to the Second Viennese School, offering students a fuller picture of twentieth-century American music.

Before moving on, I raise two logistical issues related to accessibility. First, due to Walker's birth in 1922, all his music will remain under US Copyright restriction for some time. Thus, unlike most of the music of Debussy, Bartók, Schoenberg, Webern, and Berg, it is not available on any public domain archive. For this reason, I am unable to reproduce complete movements in either the text of the chapter or the Supplemental Materials website, nor will students be able to download scores in order to complete assignments at their leisure. On the other hand, the pieces examined in this chapter are not particularly expensive to purchase, and therefore it is possible for even smaller libraries to acquire a representative selection of Walker's catalog.

Second, some – but certainly not all – of Walker's works are un- or under-recorded. The instructor may have to dig a little deeper before finding polished recordings to use in class. I can attest to the fact that YouTube contains several excellent options for the works discussed here, often performed by Walker himself or, in the case of the Trombone Concerto, by major orchestras and ensembles. Other pieces, however, including some of the choral music, have few or no professional-quality recordings freely available.

"Prelude," from *Prelude and Caprice* (Published 1975)

> Key topics: tonality vs modality; pitch centricity; quartal harmonies; binary and ternary forms
>
> Suggested text chapters: Clendinning/Marvin, Ch. 34, 39–40; Laitz, Ch. 30; Lambert, Chs. 1, 5, and 7; Clendinning/Marvin, Ch. 34, 39–40; Roig-Francolí, Chs. 1–3; Straus, Ch. 5

The "Prelude" from Walker's *Prelude and Caprice* provides an accessible starting point for a unit on twentieth-century tonality or a twentieth-century analysis course in general, since students will need to draw on their tonal analytical skills in addition to considering newer ideas. After an initial listening, the instructor can begin discussion by considering two open-ended questions. What is the form of the piece? What key or mode is it in? The second question appears simple, as the music begins in an unequivocal B major (Figure 20.1a), with feints toward D♯ minor (iii), first in measure 5, and then more substantially beginning in measure 16 (Figure 20.1b).

Depending on previous experience, students will likely label measure 16 as either the beginning of the digression of a rounded binary form or the B section of a continuous ternary form.[5] Whether digression or independent B section, the return of the original

Teaching Twentieth-Century Stylistic Pluralism 241

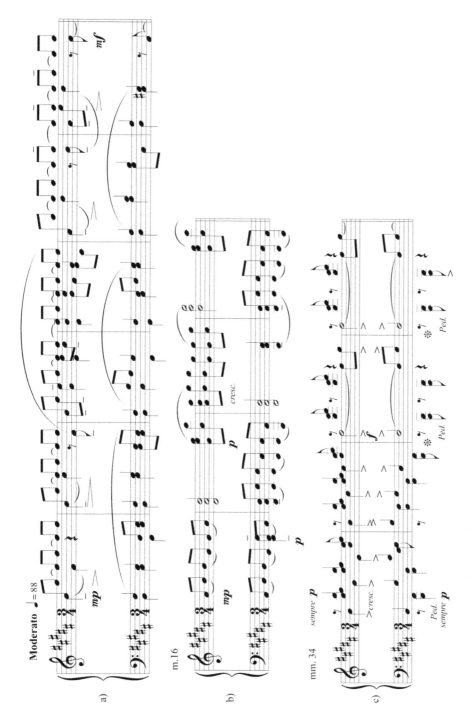

Figure 20.1 "Prelude," from Prelude and Caprice: (a) mm. 1–6; (b) mm. 16–19; (c) mm. 34–37. *Source:* Prelude and Caprice by George Walker © 1975 by Lauren Keiser Music Publishing (ASCAP). Used by permission.

material and tonality in measure 30 is heralded by a strong half-cadence gesture in measures 28–29, thus completing a large-scale arpeggiation of the tonic triad, B–D♯–F♯–(B), which students might recognize as a familiar scheme from their study of common-practice repertoire. Here are the likely interpretive options:

Ternary Interpretation:	A	B		A′
Rounded Binary:	A	dig.	//	A′
Tonal/Modal Center:	B Ionian	D♯ Phrygian	HC: V/B	B Ionian
Measures:	1–15	16–25	26–29	30–44

In fact, the status of the D♯ "minor" music is rather unclear. Only in measure 6 in the tenor do we hear D♯ minor's requisite E♯. Elsewhere, and especially in the digression/B section, Walker presents E♮ emphatically. Thus, the D♯-centered music is a case of the D♯ Phrygian mode. To get a sense of why one semitone can make such a conceptual difference, the instructor should ask the students to sing the moving eighth notes beginning at measure 16, attending to the unusual "upper-leading tone" sensation of the D♯–E–C♯–D♯ figure. Depending on the course context, the instructor might point out that the Ionian/major mode is the inversion of the Phrygian mode, and that Walker seems to play up this relation on the musical surface by reversing the opening descending fourth of the melody (B$_4$–F♯$_4$) upon arriving at D♯ Aeolian/Phrygian in measure 5 (A♯$_4$–D♯$_5$).

Having established that the D♯-centered music projects D♯ Phrygian rather than minor, the instructor might ask if the outer sections are better conceptualized as B Ionian rather than B major. An aspect of that discussion is the degree to which the opening music projects functional tonality. On the one hand, the idiomatic bass line implies common-practice tonality; on the other, Walker generally avoids both the leading tone (as part of a V chord) and 3̂ (as part of a I chord). The absence of these tonal markers suggests conceptualizing the passage as presenting the B Ionian *collection* rather than being in the *key* of B major. The distinction is especially clear in measures 34–37 (Figure 20.1c), where the opening F♯ ostinato is transformed into quartal/quintal harmonies emphasizing B and F♯ and creating a bell-like effect.

Lyric for Strings (Published 1975)

Key topics/concepts: ternary form; motivic development; enharmonic modulation & reinterpretation; music notation

Suggested text chapters: Clendinning/Marvin, Chs. 34 and 40; Laitz, Ch. 30; Lambert, Ch. 5; Roig-Francolí, Chs. 1 and 5; Straus, Chs. 4–5

Lyric for Strings is one of Walker's more popular pieces and can easily be paired with the *Prelude* for either in-class or homework purposes. While on the surface, *Lyric* does not present any issues in terms of tonality/modality – the piece is clearly governed by F♯ major – the harmonic relationship between the outer sections (mm. 1–23 and mm. 59–end) and the contrasting central section (mm. 24–58) provides an opportunity for a more speculative discussion on enharmonic reinterpretation and the role of notation in the common-practice period vs. its role in many twentieth-century styles.

One important distinction that could serve as the basis for such a discussion is the dual role of notation. On one hand, musical notation functions as a code to be interpreted by performers and therefore should be as legible as possible to aid that interpretation. On the other hand, at least in the common-practice period, notation can imply tonal/harmonic function, in which case the relative legibility of a particular spelling is a secondary

Teaching Twentieth-Century Stylistic Pluralism 243

concern. The tonal plan of *Lyric* encapsulates the issue. Figures 20.2a and b map the main tonal areas of the work, along with Roman numeral and formal analyses. As notated, the piece unfolds according to Figure 20.2a. The modulation from I to bbVII is nonsensical. Unfortunately, the sensical reading – reinterpreting E♭ as D♯ – necessitates Figure 20.2b, which has the nasty side effect of disrupting the music's monotonality in order to preserve its harmonic logic.[6]

Of course, the instructor should feel free to delve into the implications of Figure 20.2 as much or as little as the course can accommodate. However, I recommend sharing Figures 20.2a and b with students and discussing the benefits and weaknesses of each reading in terms of aural intuition. One benefit of Figure 20.2b is that it reflects the aural perception that the tonal arrival at measure 59 is new, unusual, or special. One might have a hard time relating the tonality at measure 59 to that of the beginning, despite the thematic return, and the analysis of Figure 20.2b reflects that difficulty. Walker emphasizes this sensation of novelty by composing a new descant above the melody from the opening section. One benefit of Figure 20.2a is that it preserves the parallel between harmonic structure and formal design, where the harmonic relations between the A and B sections are organized by enharmonic thirds. The notated chromatic and enharmonic third relations provide the instructor an excellent opportunity to introduce the suite of triadic transformations that constitute neo-Riemannian theory, discussed in the textbook chapters cited in the preceding text.[7] Figure 20.2c offers one more reading of the large-scale tonal structure of *Lyric*, whereby harmonic motion is governed by the three best-known common-tone preserving operations in pitch-class space: P, L, and R.

In addition to issues of harmony, students should attend to the motivic saturation of *Lyric*, which presents its primary motivic ideas in the first six measures of the piece – a short introduction to the first section proper. The first violins' opening P4 (F♯$_4$–C♯$_4$) is followed by the major lower tetrachord in the second violins and violas (B–A♯–G♯–F♯), then the minor upper tetrachord in the violas (F♯–E–D–C♯). The empty P4 and the two melodic tetrachords

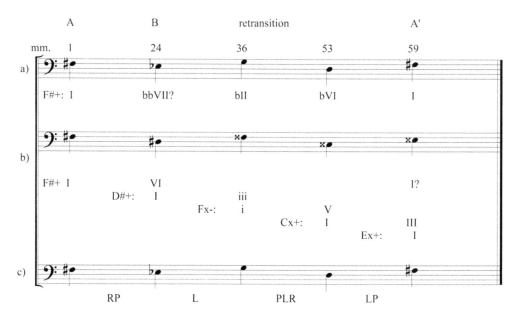

Figure 20.2 Three interpretations of *Lyric*'s harmonic structure.

form the thematic basis of the movement. In measure 7, the main theme, presented in the first violins, recapitulates a variant of the basic materials. The fact that the two tetrachords are intervallic inversions of one another reflects the role of triadic inversion (via the neo-Riemannian transformations) in the piece's large-scale harmonic structure and recalls the similar role of intervallic inversion in the Prelude.

"Caprice" from *Prelude and Caprice* (Published 1975)

"Caprice" from *Prelude and Caprice* is a culmination of some of the topics discussed thus far, particularly modality and motivic intervallic saturation. A jazzy, improvisatory invention, the modal centers of "Caprice" are more challenging to determine than those of the "Prelude" or *Lyric*, with multiple plausible interpretations. Equally important in an analysis of the "Caprice" is the structural role played by interval-class 5 (hereafter ic5) in both melodic and harmonic domains.

Figure 20.3 reproduces measures 1–6 of "Caprice"; annotations are discussed shortly. What is the tonal or modal center of these opening measures? Students might respond with several plausible interpretations, including modes centered on F or D♭. For an aural activity, the instructor might play the right and left hands separately, asking students to evaluate the tonality of the hands individually before considering the whole. In measures 1–2, the left hand offers a modified plagal progression in D♭ major, while the right-hand melody in measures 1–5 outlines F Phrygian, with two non-collectional tones in measure 3.

For a more challenging exercise, students might dictate the melody – or any one of its subsequent variations or recurrences – then harmonize it in different ways in order to realize various latent modal possibilities. Figure 20.4 gives a possible solution to the exercise, presenting realizations of the melody that suggest D♭ major/Ionian (Figure 20.4a), F Phrygian (Figure 20.4b), and C Locrian (Figure 20.4c), respectively. As written, the question of tonal center is only fully answered at the end (mm. 80–95), which prolongs an unambiguous A♭ dominant that ultimately resolves as ♭VII to B♭ (Mixolydian?) in a final cadential flourish.[8]

Putting questions of modality aside, students should notice the preponderance of ic5. Brackets on Figure 20.3 show how "Caprice" emphasizes ic5. Formally, "Caprice" can be analyzed as three increasingly short "passes" through the opening material, with the third pass concluding with a codetta (pass 1 = mm. 1–51; pass 2 = mm. 52–67; pass 3 = mm. 68–95/end). Passes 1 and 3 also present a prominent secondary motivic idea (see mm. 38–40), which, though a transformation of the primary gesture, is still reliant on ic5.

Figure 20.3 "Caprice," mm. 1–6. Brackets label prominent instances of ic5. *Source: Prelude and Caprice* by George Walker © 1975 by Lauren Keiser Music Publishing (ASCAP). Used by permission.

Figure 20.4 Three harmonizations of "Caprice," mm. 1–6: (a) D♭ Ionian; (b) F Phrygian; (c) C Locrian. *Source*: Prelude and Caprice by George Walker © 1975 by Lauren Keiser Music Publishing (ASCAP). Used by permission.

Caprice offers several opportunities for writing assignments. One line of questioning concerns genre. How does the piece fulfill, transform, or subvert the generic expectations of a caprice? How does Walker's "Caprice" compare to other examples of the genre? Students will likely remark on the music's improvisatory affect, resulting in part from the jazzy *Fortspinnung* in the right hand in measures 10ff. Others may note the prevalence of imitative counterpoint and recall the earlier genre of the baroque invention.[9] A second set of questions involves the relationship of the "Prelude" to the "Caprice." Having studied the "Caprice," the "Prelude's" emphasis on ic5 acquires new significance. However, there are also noteworthy differences. The sharp modes of the "Prelude" are answered by the flat modes of the "Caprice." Students might also point to substantial differences in texture and voicing and the contrast between the relatively well-defined tonal centers of the "Prelude" and the more ambiguous modality of "Caprice."

Cello Sonata (Movement i) (1957)

Key Topics/Concepts: interval saturation/cycles; sonata form; pitch centricity
Suggested Text Chapters: Clendinning/Marvin, Chs. 39–40; Laitz, Chs. 30–31; Lambert, Chs. 2,6–7; Roig-Francolí, Chs. 1, 3, and 5; Straus, Chs. 1 and 4

In Chapter 7 of his recent textbook, *Basic Post-Tonal Theory and Analysis*, Philip Lambert classifies post-1900 sonata forms into three categories. The first category includes those compositions that closely follow common-practice procedures; such works might contain two contrasting themes with fifth-related tonal centers, a development, and a recapitulation in "tonic." The second category contains "works that preserve some essential features of sonata form while radically reconceptualizing others." For instance, a piece might contain two contrasting thematic sections but project no fifth-relation, or perhaps dispense with clear-cut boundaries between development and recapitulation. The third category contains works least tied to eighteenth- and nineteenth-century norms, works that "challenge the definition of the form itself" (Lambert 2019, 178).[10] Lambert's categories are intentionally indefinite, and one imagines that sonatas could exist along a spectrum according to their resonance with common-practice strategies. The framework offers a helpful way to explore Walker's approaches to the sonata genre, as his sonata movements occupy various points along Lambert's spectrum.

The first movement of the Sonata for Cello and Piano (1957), *Allegro passionato*, fits squarely in Lambert's first category. The 158-measure movement is much longer than the pieces discussed in the chapter thus far, but Walker's use of some of the hallmarks of common-practice sonata form makes the movement a valuable resource for helping students acclimate to longer analyses. To reinforce the connections, the instructor might first discuss a paradigmatic sonata movement from the late eighteenth century, then introduce the Walker piece.[11] Upon a first listening, many students will likely notice the two contrasting themes in the exposition and the presence of a relatively prototypical recapitulation. A likely formal analysis:[12]

P   Tr.   MC   S   CL   Dev.   P   Tr.   MC   S   CL   Coda
1–13   14–28   29–30   30–40   40–52   53–92   93–105   106–88   119–20   121–30   131–42   143–58

Figure 20.5a reproduces the beginning of the movement's P-zone; Figure 20.5b shows the beginning of the S-space. Students should notice that, from a contour standpoint, the two themes are not especially contrasting: both consist of an ascending leap followed by a stepwise descent. The large-scale structures of the thematic areas are also broadly similar.

In both cases, the cello presents an initial thematic statement accompanied by the piano, which then presents its own thematic statement that eventually dissolves toward the end of the section. The primary points of contrast lie in other musical domains: tempo, texture, and pitch-class center.[13] The rapid ostinato in the piano accompanying the sprawling cello melody contrasts with the cello's comparatively restrained double-stops and the piano's chordal accompaniment in the second theme area. Additionally, the first theme area projects an initial A (Aeolian) tonal center, while the S-zone projects an E pitch (class) center. The characteristic fifth relation between the centers of the P- and S-spaces – a relation that is "resolved" in the recapitulation – is an especially striking similarity between Walker's movement and common-practice sonata procedures and one of the defining traits of Lambert's first category of post-1900 sonata practice.

If the exposition's contrasting theme areas are fairly clear, other formal boundaries are less so – especially the boundary between the end of the secondary theme area and the beginning of the closing zone, and the boundary between the end of the closing zone and beginning of the development. One logical place that students may identify as the boundary between the S-space and closing zone is measure 40 (Figure 20.5c).[14]

When exploring the movement's ambiguous formal seams, instructors may wish to organize a class debate where students are randomly assigned into two groups and asked to provide evidence for one interpretation or another. In the case of measure 40, for example, evidence for interpreting the fermata as the boundary between the secondary theme area and the closing is that the fermata results in a stoppage of musical motion in all parts. Evidence students might present *against* this reading is the fact that the piano introduces what sounds like a new closing theme in measure 39, echoed by the cello in measure 40. In any case, students will need to observe musical parameters beyond pitch and motive in order to develop a convincing formal reading.[15]

The seam between the closing section and development is a bit clearer in comparison. A P-based development begins at the *Più mosso* in measure 60 at the latest. Students will likely find the change in texture at measure 53 suggestive of a new beginning – an

Teaching Twentieth-Century Stylistic Pluralism 247

Figure 20.5 Cello Sonata, first movement: (a) P-space, mm. 1–13, with labeled brackets; (b) S-space, mm. 31–36; (c) junction between S-space and the closing zone, mm. 38–41. *Source*: Sonata for Cello and Piano by George Walker © 1975 by Lauren Keiser Music Publishers (ASCAP). Used by permission.

248 *Owen Belcher*

impression strengthened by the cello's cadenza-like gestures, which, like the music at the *Più mosso*, are strongly related to the movement's P-theme.

Issues of large-scale form aside, the instructor might find measures 1–13 (Figure 20.5a) an instructive passage for either an in-class guided analysis or homework assignment. Some possible leading questions include:

- What is the formal structure of measures 1–13?
- Are there particular pc collections, motives, or intervals at work?
- How does Walker create a sense of closure in measure 13?

One way to interpret measures 1–13 is as a modified sentence phrase type. Under this analysis, a one-measure piano introduction leads to an ascending flourish in the cello that becomes the basic idea of a sentence's presentation phase at the pickup to measure 4. The pickup to measure 6 initiates the altered repetition of the basic idea, leading to the continuation phase at the pickup to measure 9.

Even if the instructor or students prefer to avoid the sentence phraseology, the E♭ at measure 7 and E♮ octaves in measure 8 are important inflection points. These measures – roughly halfway through the excerpt – present the registral climax of the passage and serve as the pivot point from the cello's ascending music in measures 1–8 to the descending music of measures 9–13. The E♭ of measure 7, in particular, projects a strong sense of musical tension: the E♭$_5$ is the first accidental in the piece and anticipates the D♯ (E♭)$_4$ in measure 12. That pitch assumes a "dominant" function, resolving to diatonic harmony in measure 13 ahead of the repetition of the theme in the piano.

Brackets on Figure 20.5a draw attention to the structural role of ic5. Figure 20.6 abstracts Figure 20.5a's ic5 pairs onto a pc-interval cycle. Figure 20.6 makes plain certain observations noted earlier, namely, that the opening passage is centered on pc A, and

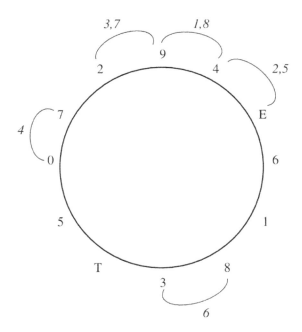

Figure 20.6 A modular representation of a five-cycle. (Numbered brackets refer to the numbered brackets on Figure 20.5a.)

that the E♭ at measure 7 is both a literal high point and a moment of maximum tension in the phrase. Regarding observation 1, the piano introduction establishes A as pc center by articulating the ic5 pairs involving A–E/A and A/D–plus an additional pair (E/B) that serves as a sort of "upper neighbor" pair to the tonic pairs. Under this analysis, the cello's ascending incipit begins in the A-centric "field" established by the piano and moves the pc content clockwise around the cycle, abstractly corresponding to the instrument's literal registral ascent.[16] Regarding observation 2, Figure 20.6 clarifies two special features of the E♭ in measure 7. First, the figure emphasizes the tritone relation between A/E♭ – an interval suggestive of musical distance. Second, unlike the preceding music, E♭ is not accompanied by a partner pc in measure 7 and is thus unable to form an ic5 pair on the figure. The E♭, then, disrupts the process of gradually unfolding ic5 pairs that occurred during measures 1–6. At the end of the excerpt, pc 3 finds its partner, pc 8, and the pair sets up the "resolution" back to the D/A "tonic."

Concerto for Trombone and Orchestra (Piano), Movement iii (Published 1977)

Key Topics: same as those for the Cello Sonata, plus pc-set theory
Suggested Textbook chapters: same as those for Cello Sonata, plus Clendinning/Marvin, Chs. 37–38; Laitz, Chs. 31–32; Lambert, Chs. 2–4; Roig-Francolí, Chs. 3–4; Straus, Chs. 2–3

The finale of Walker's trombone concerto is another example of Lambert's first category of compositions – those which bear strong formal and even tonal resemblance to their common-practice predecessors. However, the finale is not a sonata but a rondo. The formal structure is as follows:

A_1	B_1	A_2	$B_2 \rightarrow C$	A_3	B_3	A_4
1–20	21–44	45–55	56–94	95–104	105–24	125–48

One aspect of Walker's piece that differs from classical paradigms is the central episode, which begins as if it were another iteration of the B episode, before developing into a fughetta based on a new idea. Otherwise, the broad strokes of rondo structure are straightforward. The neoclassical refrains are relatively consonant, rhythmically regular, and firmly centered in F major, while the contrasting episodes are more dissonant, rhythmically unstable, and tonally indeterminate. To an unusual degree, the rondo exemplifies what George Perle (1990, Lecture 3) termed "windows of order" and "disorder," with the orderly refrains perturbed by the disorderly episodes.[17]

While students should explore the myriad ways the episodes contrast with the refrain, they should also consider commonalities. One fruitful entry into a more substantial analysis of the movement is to explore Walker's treatment of thirds. Figure 20.7a excerpts measures 1–8 of the rondo – the trombone's first statement of the refrain's main theme, along with the piano reduction of the orchestral accompaniment. The accompaniment highlights the interval of a third, which also saturates the trombone's melody.

We can contrast this tonal use of thirds with Walker's practice in the episodes. Figure 20.7b reproduces measures 21–32, the opening of episode B, along with annotations. Here, thirds are repurposed as the structural intervals in set class (014) – and, to a lesser extent, (015) – as shown in the annotated example. Note that set theory technology is useful, but optional: the analysis can also be carried out by isolating the motive of "a third and a semitone," whereby the semitone can attach itself above or below to either member of the third.

250 Owen Belcher

Figure 20.7 Concerto for Trombone, third movement: (a) mm. 1–8; (b) beginning of episode B with set classes labeled, mm. 21–32. *Source*: Concerto for Trombone by George Walker © 1977 Lauren Keiser Music Publishers (ASCAP). Used by permission.

Teaching Twentieth-Century Stylistic Pluralism 251

Regardless of the approach the instructor employs, Figure 20.7b can serve as the starting point for an important discussion on analytical methodology and post-tonal music. In my own undergraduate and graduate post-tonal courses, I was frequently flummoxed by two well-known and related issues in set theory analysis. Issue 1 is the fact that relatively little music is as motivically saturated or "worked-out" as, say, the opening of Schoenberg's "Nacht" – one of a handful of touchstone textbook examples purporting to show the explanatory power of set theory. Issue 2 concerns the musical ethics of analytical parsing: the fact that the most analytically "useful" pc sets are often not the most aurally intuitive, and the most aurally intuitive sets are often not the ones we wish they were.

The labels on Figure 20.7b show that, actually, the passage *is* fairly saturated with (014) and (015) set classes. However, the analysis has already conceded that the passage is not reducible to a single germinal trichord and its permutations. Furthermore, while transformations and inversions of the motivic set classes abound, they by no means can account for every pc in the excerpt. It is vital that the instructor emphasizes that this state of affairs is to be expected and that *it is okay*. Instead of lamenting the analysis as somehow untidy, students should be encouraged to explore more interesting avenues of inquiry, such as *how* exactly the different set classes interact, the role of particular pitches or pitch classes in long-range voice leading motion, the relationship between the trombone and piano, etc.

As pertains to issue 2 noted previously, the instructor and students will notice that some of the analytical groupings on Figure 20.7b make more musical sense than others. The instructor should ask the students *why* that might be. Students should explain the reasoning behind their parsing choices and be asked to interrogate the choices of others. For instance, are the asterisked trichords analytically meaningful? The answer is up for debate. Some students might argue that no, the asterisked groupings are not meaningful, because they do not sound at the same time, but ask the listener to aurally "divide" a simultaneity. Other students might argue that yes, the asterisked groupings are meaningful because, although the individual trichords would be difficult to parse aurally, the analysis demonstrates the aural prevalence of interval classes 1, 3, and 4 – that is, that these intervals are "in the air," even if their discrete manifestations are buried within the texture. Figure 20.8 offers a revised analysis of the bass line that students may find more intuitive. Here, motivic trichords are "composed out" through transposition at T_1/T_E and T_4/T_8 – the operative intervals of the trichords themselves. Figure 20.8 should be compared with the asterisked groupings in Figure 20.7b in terms of their respective analytical power and parsing clarity.

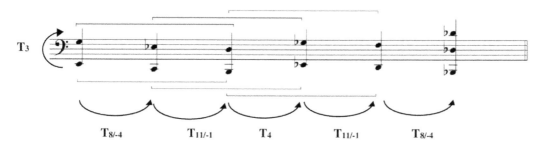

Figure 20.8 Transpositional relationships in the piano left hand, mm. 24–31.

Cello Sonata, Movement ii

Figure 20.9 raises similar questions. The example excerpts measures 1–13 from the second movement of the cello sonata. Annotations show the initial prevalence of set class (015), particularly in the cello.[18] However, by the climax of the phrase (m. 13), (015) plays little role. Instead, the end of the excerpt seems concerned with the set (036) – particularly {T,1,4} – and transpositions that compose out that set's characteristic pc int 3.

Such a state of affairs is only a "problem" if passages like the opening of Schoenberg's "Nacht" are understood to be the ideal. From a different perspective, analyses like the one presented in Figure 20.9 raise interpretive questions that supersaturated phrases like the opening of "Nacht" cannot. For instance, students could be asked about the performance implications of the shift away from (015)-based pc configurations toward (036)-based pc configurations – configurations that eventually even begin to imply a tonal center. Is the shift gradual? Do these two motivic set classes continue to play a role in the movement beyond the opening phrase? These discussion questions can be accompanied by performance and composition activities. Advanced undergraduates and graduate students could be tasked with singing and playing the excerpt on the piano. All students could be assigned a composition assignment in which they compose an eight-measure phrase for solo instrument and piano that, like the Walker passage, transitions from one dominant set class to another. These student exercises could then serve as singing or dictation examples, etc.

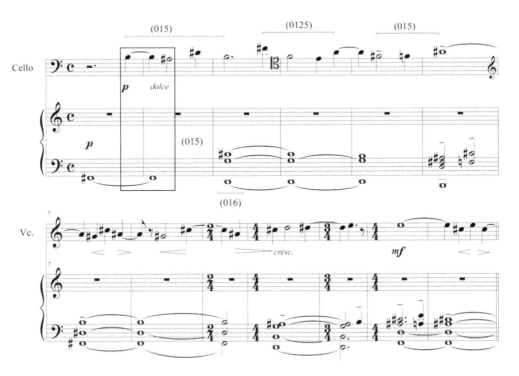

Figure 20.9 Cello Sonata, second movement, mm. 1–13, with labeled set classes. *Source*: Sonata for Cello and Piano by George Walker © 1975 by Lauren Keiser Music Publishers (ASCAP). Used by permission.

Conclusion

The preceding chapter proposes an adaptable agenda for incorporating the music of George Walker into courses devoted to twentieth-century music and analysis. While the inclusion of Walker's music in the classroom is certainly the main goal of the chapter, another important aim has been to outline the types of analytical questions and methods instructors, and students can utilize to interrogate Walker's music. In his recent chapter, "Ten Tips for Teaching Post-Tonal Theory," Joseph Straus succinctly summarizes these twin goals. Straus's tip #2 is to "expand the repertoire" – a suggestion at the heart of this volume (Straus 2018, 80–81). Straus's tip #5, "analyze the music (within limits)," suggests the manner by which one should go about analysis. Central to his pedagogical approach is his injunction to "[m]ake it clear that analysis is not a search for the 'right answer,' but rather an open-minded exploration of ways of making sense of what we hear as we enter the world of the piece and describe our experiences there" (Straus 2018, 82). If, as Straus argues and my own experience supports, students are generally unfamiliar with what many theorists would consider to be the "canonical" works and techniques of post-tonal composition – and are thus ill-equipped to make sense or describe their musical experiences – it is likely that Walker's music and the significant life he led will be even less known to most students. I hope that this chapter begins to redress that unfamiliarity and does so in a way that invites students to build upon concepts and music with which they are familiar.

Notes

1. For example, see Steven G. Laitz (2015), Philip Lambert (2019), Miguel-Roig Francolí (2007), and Joseph N. Straus (2016). Though it should be noted that all these texts make a concerted effort to include a variety of approaches, these texts still privilege practices historically viewed as technically "innovative" by a large degree. Recent efforts at inclusion are made explicit through a comparison of the third (2004) and fourth (2016) editions of Straus. Michael Buchler (2017) proposes a more radical curricular revision.
2. For representative examples of recent approaches, see Amy Fleming and Aaron Grant (2020), David Geary and Robert Komaniecki (2017), Jena Root (2010), and Matthew Santa (2009).
3. Referenced textbooks include Laitz (2015), Lambert (2019), and Straus (2016).
4. See "George Walker," *New Grove Online*.
5. Regardless of the interpretation, students should be able to relate the music at m. 16 to the inner voices in m. 8ff, themselves derived from the opening F♯5 ostinato. Therefore, the putative B-section isn't especially independent.
6. Advanced undergraduate or graduate students interested in pursuing these matters further might start with Daniel Harrison (2002).
7. In fact, it is the conflict between harmonic logic and monotonality in Schubert's D. 960/i that motivates Richard Cohn's monograph on the topic. See Richard Cohn (2012).
8. Therefore, neither of our opening analyses turns out to be "correct"! However, it is quite likely that some students may indeed hear a B♭ mode at the beginning.
9. A larger assignment for the interested or advanced student could involve reading the analysis of Bach's C major invention in the opening chapter of Laurence Dreyfus (1996), and using Dreyfus's suite of motivic transformations to analyze "Caprice."
10. In this third category, Lambert includes works such as Pierre Boulez's *Second Piano Sonata* and Berg's *Wozzeck*, Act 2, scene 1. See Lambert (2019, 178).
11. Lambert opens his text with a similar exercise, focusing on "musical units" in Mozart and Webern.
12. This chapter employs the sonata theory terminology as developed by James Hepokoski and Warren Darcy (2006). This terminology is commonly found in undergraduate textbooks such as Laitz (2015).
13. Because they are harder to discuss systematically, musical domains such as texture are often given short shrift in the headlong rush to calculate prime forms and tone rows, though recent

textbooks and research have begun to highlight the importance of analytical approaches based on musical parameters other than pitch (class).
14. In this movement, there is really no EEC or ESC to speak of. The fermatas, however, do suggest some sort of formal articulation.
15. Note that the material from m. 40ff recurs near the end of the recapitulation, ahead of a short coda. Therefore, it *does* serve a closing function, and students should eventually decide on a possible formal boundary, even if that boundary is ambiguous or perhaps even several measures long.
16. The instructor should emphasize here the interpretive danger of overreliance on such correspondences.
17. The instructor is encouraged to assign excerpts from Perle's text. See the Supplemental Materials website for suggestions.
18. To avoid set theory terminology, the (015) set can be recast as "a perfect fourth plus a semitone," even though this conception is actually more flexible, since it allows for (016) as well. The (036) set class can be discussed as a diminished triad.

Works Cited

Alegant, Brian. 2018. "Teaching Post-Tonal Aural Skills." In *The Norton Guide to Teaching Music Theory*, edited by Rachel Lumsden and Jeffrey Swinkin, 147–60. W.W. Norton & Company.

Baker, David N., Lida M. Belt, Herman C. Hudson, eds. 1978. *The Black Composer Speaks*. Scarecrow Press.

Buchler, Michael. 2017. "A Case Against Teaching Set Classes to Undergraduates." *Engaging Students: Essays in Music Pedagogy* 5. http://flipcamp.org/engagingstudents5/essays/buchler.html

Clendinning, Jane Piper, and Elizabeth West Marvin. 2021. *The Musician's Guide to Theory and Analysis*, 4th edition. W.W. Norton & Company.

Cohn, Richard. 2012. *Audacious Euphony: Chromaticism and the Consonant Triad's Second Nature*. Oxford University Press.

Coker, Wilson. 1981–1982. "'The Black Composer Speaks': An Implied Aesthetic." *Black Music Research Journal* 2: 94–105.

Dreyfus, Laurence. 1996. *Bach and the Patterns of Invention*. Harvard University Press.

Fleming, Amy, and Aaron Grant. 2020. "The Rest is Noise: A Historically Integrated Approach to Post-Tonal Pedagogy." *Journal of Music Theory Pedagogy* 34. https://jmtp.appstate.edu/rest-noise-historically-integrated-approach-post-tonal-pedagogy

Geary, David, and Robert Komaniecki. 2017. "Post-Tonal Solmization for Post-Tonal Aural Skills: Implementing Ordered Pitch-Class Intervals." *Journal of Music Theory Pedagogy* 31. https://jmtp.appstate.edu/post-tonal-solmization-post-tonal-aural-skills-implementing-ordered-pitch-class-intervals

Harrison, Daniel. 2002. "Nonconformist Notions of Nineteenth-Century Enharmonicism." *Music Analysis* 21/2: 115–60.

Hepokoski, James and Warren Darcy. 2006. *Elements of Sonata Theory: Norms, Types, and Deformations in the Late-Eighteenth-Century Sonata*. Oxford University Press.

Jones III, Everett N. 2005. "Intervallic Coherence in Four Piano Sonatas by George Walker: An Analysis." DMA Thesis. University of Cincinnati.

Laitz, Steven G. 2015. *The Complete Musician*, 4th edition. Oxford University Press.

Lambert, Philip. 2019. *Basic Post-Tonal Theory and Analysis*. Oxford University Press.

Lumsden, Rachel. 2018. "Enriching Classroom Discussions: Some Strategies from Feminist Pedagogy." In *The Norton Guide to Teaching Music Theory*, edited by Rachel Lumsden and Jeffrey Swinkin, 313–30. W.W. Norton & Company.

Perle, George. 1990. *The Listening Composer*. University of California Press.

Rogers, Lynne. 2018. "Incorporating Writing into Music Theory Courses." In *The Norton Guide to Teaching Music Theory*, edited by Rachel Lumsden and Jeffrey Swinkin, 299–312. W.W. Norton & Company.

Roig-Francolí, Miguel A. 2007. *Understanding Post-Tonal Music*. McGraw-Hill.

Root, Jena. 2010. "Stravinsky's 'Spring Rounds:' A Primer for a Twentieth-Century Musical Aesthetic." *Journal of Music Theory Pedagogy* 24. https://jmtp.appstate.edu/stravinskys-spring-rounds%C2%9D-primer-twentieth-century-musical-aesthetic

Santa, Matthew. 2009. "Teaching Non-Functional Tonality – A Part-Writing Approach." *Journal of Music Theory Pedagogy* 23. https://jmtp.appstate.edu/teaching-non-functional-tonality-part-writing-approach

Sims, Maxine D. 1976. "An Analysis and Comparison of Piano Sonatas by George Walker and Howard Swanson." *The Black Perspective in Music* 4/1: 70–81.

Straus, Joseph N. 2016. *Introduction to Post-Tonal Theory*, 4th edition. W.W. Norton & Company.

———. 2018. "Ten Tips for Teaching Post-Tonal Theory." In *The Norton Guide to Teaching Music Theory*, edited by Rachel Lumsden and Jeffrey Swinkin, 79–87. W.W. Norton & Company.

Terry, Mickey Thomas, Ingrid Monson, and George Walker. 2000. "An Interview with George Walker." *The Musical Quarterly* 84/3: 372–88.

21 Teaching Julia Perry's *Homunculus C.F.*

Kendra Preston Leonard

Composer Julia Perry (1924–1979) is often mentioned in discussions of Black American musicians active in the middle of the twentieth century, but because of the relative lack of access to her music, her works are rarely performed, much less taught in the classroom.[1] Her 1960 work *Homunculus C.F.* for percussion and harp, however, has been published and anthologized and is thus available for study and performance (Briscoe 2004). The piece is an example of serial minimalism, a compositional approach in which Perry uses repetition and slight variation of limited pitch-class sets to create works that presage the more well-known minimalist techniques of Philip Glass and others. Perry uses serial minimalism frequently from the late 1950s on, and many of her works represent early American minimalism. At the same time, *Homunculus C.F.* is also structured by developing variation, another technique Perry uses frequently. She begins each section in the work with what Gretchen Horlacher, in her work on Stravinsky, calls "building blocks," or "immediate and persistent rhythmic motivic repetition" (1992). Here I offer an analysis of *Homunculus C.F.* in the context of these and other frameworks and provide information and prompts for teaching the work in the theory classroom.

Perry's earliest works reflect her upbringing in the Baptist Church and an adherence to diatonic harmony (Giles 2022). Many of these pieces are classicized arrangements of spirituals and gospel songs that, while tonal, use short motives and pedal points or drones and/or repeated pitches in the accompaniment, foretelling her later compositional techniques. After beginning study with Luigi Dallapiccola in 1951, Perry adopted increasingly complex rhythmic writing with emphases on triplet figurations and traditional serial techniques. As Meg Wilhoite has noted, Perry's 1951 *Stabat Mater* uses symmetrical serial rows that are frequently treated in one of several ways: they can be repeated in their original (P0) forms, they can be transposed by just one to three semitones, or they can hinge on central pitches around which other pitches in the row move, as in the first movement of the work. Wilhoite also notes that Perry uses texture to communicate the formal design of individual movements; Perry's later works, including *Homunculus C.F.*, are further examples of this. The *Stabat Mater* also shows Perry's use of drones beneath limited pitch-class sets, foreshadowing her extensive use of serialist minimalism in her later works (Wilhoite 2021). Other pieces Perry composed in the 1950s exhibit similar techniques: her 1953 opera *The Cask of Amontillado*, based on the Edgar Allan Poe story, is marked by intricate rhythmic writing full of syncopation and small pitch-class cells in the vocal lines, and her 1959 *Pastoral* for flute and string sextet exhibits the same use of P0 forms and close transpositions as the *Sabat Mater* and the same complexity of rhythm, imitation, and syncopation as *Cask*.

While we often associate minimalism with White male composers based on the East Coast of the United States, it is worth noting that Perry was 10 years older than, and composing in a minimalist style well before, composers usually associated with the origins of minimalism. Steve Reich, Terry Riley, and La Monte Young were all born in 1935, and

DOI: 10.4324/9781003204053-27

Philip Glass was born in 1937. *Homunculus C.F.* was composed 4 years before Terry Riley's *In C*, and 15 years before Glass's *Einstein on the Beach*. Although Perry's contribution to the genre has been neglected, we can nonetheless apply the tools and analyses of those composers' works and processes to the study of Perry's music, alongside those of serialism, developing variation, and repeated motivic materials. In his research on Young's music, for instance, Jeremy Grimshaw describes the composer's serialist-moving-toward-minimalist techniques, such as "extreme durational parameters" and "contiguous pitch groups," in which pairs of pitches function as "pivot dyads" that make relationships between pitches audible and clarify the connections between variations in rows. These three descriptors are useful for analyzing much of Perry's music (Grimshaw 2004, 42–46).

Homonculus C. F. is scored for four timpani, large and small suspended cymbals, two medium cymbals, snare drum, bass drum, small and large woodblocks, xylophone, celesta, piano, vibraphone, and harp. The work has its origins in Perry's interest in Goethe's *Faust*. In her notes on the piece, Perry writes that she was inspired by both her father's medical offices and Faust's alchemical laboratory, in which his apprentice tries to bring life to a being he calls a *homunculus* – "little man" in Latin. She continues:

> Having selected percussion instruments for my formulae, then maneuvering and distilling them by means of the Chord of the Fifteenth (C. F.), this musical test tube baby was brought to life. The chord of the fifteenth was created from a succession of superimposed thirds:

E	G♯	B	D♯	F♯	A♯	C♯	E♯
1	3	5	7	9	11	13	15

> It is the kettledrum that establishes E as the fundamental tone of the chordal structure in the subsequent duet with harp. The xylophone pivots in the transmutation of the material.
>
> (Perry n.d.)

What Perry describes as the chord of the fifteenth – an augmented fifteenth or two major-major seventh chords stacked together – is also a (0123578T) set, and although she describes it as "pantonal," her usage of it is not tonal in nature (Ammer 2001, 179). Most frequently, she uses small subsets of the chord in non-strict serial applications, and as Mildred Green has noted, she often uses a D♮ instead of a D♯ (1975, 236). The D♮ is usually used in preparation for raising it to a D♯, albeit not in the context of traditional voice leading.

As in her *Sabat Mater*, Perry uses timbral and textural differences to indicate the structure, which is constructed in four sections. Section A (mm. 1–40) uses unpitched percussion, and section B (mm. 41–94) brings in timpani, celesta, vibraphone, and harp. In section C (mm. 95–105), Perry changes the texture from the dialogic writing of section B to an initially more sustained and sparser sound, and then to one in which the harp's blocks of sound drown out almost all else. Section D (mm. 106–80) is full of imitation and small melodic building blocks, in which Perry stacks paired pitches – often equal temperament homophones – and calls for every instrument to express the chord of the fifteenth – the complete pitch-class set – in an extended statement.

In addition to its serialist and minimalist foundations, *Homunculus C.F.* can be read as a work structured by developing variation. *Homunculus C.F.*'s sections all grow from the repeated original rhythmic statements on the first section, with Perry slowly adding in

258 *Kendra Preston Leonard*

pitches from the chord of the fifteenth. Perry's elaborations on the rhythms of the piece and on her presentation of pitches are neither tonal nor strict in their seriality, as they are full of repetition and fragmentation, but they are transformations that propel the piece forward nonetheless, creating overall coherence and continuity. *Homunculus C.F.* is an ideal piece for teaching Schoenberg's writing on developing variation and its application to tonal and atonal music. Instructors teaching the whole piece can ask students to trace elements of variation through the entire work, charting Perry's use of the technique and determining instances in which variations on the original elements spur new variations themselves, and how variations produce or are used as new foundational materials.

Section A (mm. 1–40)

The A section (mm. 1–40) uses unpitched percussion only. It begins with an eight-measure staccato rhythm stated by the snare drum and imitated by the woodblocks. This rhythm is then used as a building block, like a talea in medieval isorhythmic works (Figure 21.1a). This block – let's call it Block α (alpha) – is repeated; modified through fragmentation, augmentation, and diminution; and transferred between instruments in a way that creates complex divisions of the beat and syncopations between instruments. This section is useful for teaching students to identify repeated motivic materials and subsets of those materials and for introducing students to Perry's method of creating an entire section from a single rhythm, plus sounds with long durations. One might also emphasize Perry's calls for instruments to be played with both traditional beaters and mechanics and more unusual ones and how these changes create a wide range of timbres throughout section A.

Block α, which begins in the snare drum in measure 1 and is imitated by woodblocks starting in measure 2, is accompanied starting in measure 9 by a three-eighth-note dotted

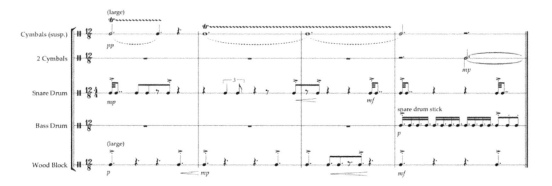

Figure 21.1 Section A: (a) Block α, mm. 1–8; (b) section A, mm. 30–33.

quarter figure – Block β (beta) – in the bass drum, a motive that comes from the subdivision of the meter's primary beat. From measures 9 to 15, Block β occurs on the downbeat of every other measure. In measure 16, where snare rests and woodblocks rest on beat 2, Perry begins to vary the motive, separating the eighths away from the dotted quarter and then bringing them back again. In measure 20, the bass drum is not on the downbeat but instead hints at a rhythmic pattern that begins in measure 33 as Block γ (gamma) that subdivides beats with sixteenth notes. A new variation begins in the snare drum, while the cymbals, heard for the first time, play long suspended notes that tie across bar lines, blurring the downbeat in what Grimshaw would call "long durational parameters," a trait of minimalism. At all times, Block α remains present in its original form.

Yet another rhythmic variant is introduced in measure 21: a thirty-second, double-dotted eighth figure in the snare drum, which transitions here alone from $\frac{12}{8}$ to $\frac{4}{4}$. This element is mixed with elements from Block α, which further complicates the rhythms of section A by including triplets that span portions of two beats. Perry also calls for the large suspended cymbal to be played with a xylophone stick in a trill leading up to the final measures of the section starting at measure 33, where, after several minutes with the dynamics in shades of piano, Perry finally asks for mezzo-forte. In measure 33, the bass drum begins a pattern of dotted sixteenths across the triple-divided quarter notes – Block γ – that leads to section B with one last rise to mezzo-forte (Figure 21.1b).

Students can diagram this section by labeling and following Blocks α, β, and γ from instrument to instrument and identifying how Blocks β and γ are developmental variations of Block α. Questions might include:

- Where do iterations of Block α overlap?
- How do we hear Block α between different voices?
- How does Block α function as a serial line?
- When Block β enters in measure 9, how does it interact with Block α?
- What is the composite rhythm of all the lines together?
- What is the overall pattern?
- How do the triplets in $\frac{4}{4}$ vary from the triple subdivision of the dotted quarter?
- Why might Perry have transposed Block α into $\frac{4}{4}$?
- How does the triple-against-duple rhythmic dissonance create tension in the section?
- How is this section serial? How is it minimalist? How are these approaches connected in this section?

Section B (mm. 41–94)

In section B, Perry introduces the timpani, celesta, and harp and moves quickly through a number of meter changes, continuing to use syncopation, and placing duple meters against triple meters. While section A focused on rhythmic patterns and syncopation, section B presents changing timbres and textures while using a restricted portion of the chord of the fifteenth, expressed initially as D♯/E♭, F♯, G♯/A♭, or pitch-class set (025). Perry later adds E (m. 61) and B (m. 81) to the set, making it (01358). Although Perry writes that she conceived of the pitches as part of a tonal chord, she uses enharmonic spellings for the pitches that do not suggest tonal voice leading or diatonic writing. She does not vary the pitch-class set in any way from its P0 form, instead using it as a limited cell, a common approach in minimalist composition. Rhythmically, Perry continues to use subsets of Block α from section A, again moving them between different instruments.

At the beginning of the B section, Perry establishes two motives. The first is a repeating pattern of pitch-class set (025) (D♯–F♯–G♯): a single staccato quarter note followed by five slurred quarter notes in a melodic low–high–low contour alternation in the timpani. This melodic motive, Block δ (delta), which is a pitched variation on Block α, has different pitches replacing alternating timbres. It pivots around a D♯ and is quasi-palindromic in several instances. The second is the rhythmic motive of dotted sixteenths and regular eighths in the bass drum, a slight variation on Block γ. From measures 41–59, the timpani establish and repeat this block, and when the harp enters in measure 61, Perry fragments and augments it as she assigns the timpani low Es, the foundational pitch for the chord of the fifteenth. She elongates these Es, making them dotted quarters, and gives the harp a similarly sustained line that is a rough augmentation of pitches in the timpani's line, sometimes spelled enharmonically. (See Figure 21.2a.)

At measure 71, the harp performs enharmonic pitches as dyads, while the bass line oscillates around G♯/A♭. Perry preserves the melodic pattern of Block δ in the timpani but begins to speed up the duration of pitches in the harp as a means of transitioning into the tempo change at measure 81 (Figure 21.2b.) The use of limited pitches, sustained pitches, and repetition in this section firmly places the piece within the realm of minimalism.

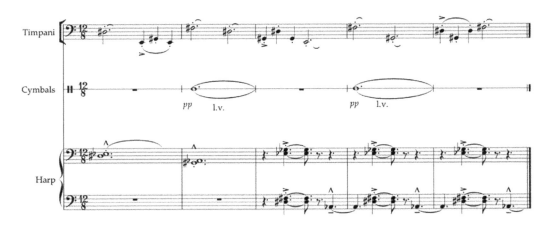

Figure 21.2 Section B: (a) measures 61–4; (b) measures 74–8.

In measure 81, Perry makes a clear tempo change from "Moderato" (dotted quarter = 108) to "Fast" (dotted quarter = 126) and spreads the Block δ melodic pattern heterophonically across the celesta, vibraphone, and harp. She then returns to the original Block δ pattern of quarter notes at measure 89 before transitioning into section C. The last part of the B section (mm. 81) uses (0247) (E–F♯–G♯–B), with measures 89–94 recalling the blocks from the beginning of the section. This material is used in imitation, just as Block α is imitated at the beginning of the piece.

Students can follow the characteristics of serial and minimalist music through the B section and identify Perry's use of pitches from the chord of the fifteenth as limited pitch-class sets.

- Where and how do the statements of the pitch-class set – including statements that are subjected to rhythmic augmentation or diminution – interact with one another?
- Why might Perry have chosen to use enharmonic spellings of some pitches? How does enharmonic spelling affect the analysis or understanding of the piece?
- Where do instances of imitation begin and end?
- How does Perry distribute imitative lines through the various instruments?
- How does Perry develop material through variation in this section?

Section C (mm. 95–105)

At measure 95, the tempo changes to "Moderate," and the harp brings in new textures while maintaining the dotted sixteenths of Block γ. The section begins with fragments from Block α, the original eight-measure talea, and sustained pitches of E–G♯–B–D♯–F♯ (01358) that outline part of the chord of the fifteenth. In using this pitch-class set, pitches are paired in a way that deconstructs the chord and uses F♯ as the axis around which the other pitches oscillate, similar to the way D♯ was used at measure 41. In measures 95–7, Perry brings in most of the pitches of the chord of the fifteenth, starting with G♯ in the celesta and then adding new pitches gradually. In measure 98, Perry interrupts this slow development of the chord with a cluster of pitches in the harp, notated as C♭–D♯–E♭–F♭–G♯–A♭–B (0158), set as a series of dotted sixteenths varied from Block γ. As in other sections, Perry uses a subset of the chord of the fifteenth, now accompanied by sustained notes that draw from it or add to it; occasionally it overlaps with a sustained E♮, shifting the set to (01358) before moving away from it again. In measure 100, Perry alters the cluster by raising F♭ to F♮ and dropping the G♯ to G♭, making it C♭–D♯–E♭–F–G♭–A♭–B (02358). The harp line becomes increasingly insistent, alternating between these two pitch sets, and at measure 101 the harp plays the cluster on every beat. At the same time, Perry continues to vary material from the previous sections in the celesta and the unpitched percussion. The snare and bass drums play variants of Blocks α and β throughout. In Perry's description of the piece, she writes of "distilling" the chord through various instruments, and in this section she comes the closest so far in having a simultaneous statement of the chord of the fifteenth.

Students can analyze the use of pitch through the section. They can look for repeated and varied statements of the sets Perry uses and how she expands and alters the sets throughout. Questions that help with analysis might include:

- How do dyads function in this section?
- How do sustained pitches work as part of the serial and minimalist approaches in this section?
- Where are the points of imitation in this section?

- Where are the instruments in dialogue, and what blocks or elements are used in that dialogue?
- How is the harp part from measure 98–195 derived from earlier materials, both rhythmically and in terms of pitch?
- The unpitched percussion parts in measure 95–8 comprise a short, repetitive block, derived from earlier blocks. What makes its use serial? Where is it synchronized with other instruments, and where does it serve to disrupt the beat?

Section D (mm. 106–70)

In section D, Perry initially returns to a sparser texture that gradually becomes more complex and denser over the course of the section. The xylophone and the vibraphone, to a lesser extent, are the stars of this section. The tempo increases to "Very Fast" (eighth note = 160). Continuing from the previous sections is the mostly staccato articulation of pitched instruments and the low–high–low figuration. The section begins with a new block that is a variation of Block δ – let's call it Block ε (epsilon). (See Figure 21.3a.)

Block ε is repeated several times by the xylophone and is in counterpoint with and syncopated against a similarly new block – Block ζ (zeta) – in the vibraphone, as seen in Figure 21.3b.

These two blocks propel this section forward, as the density grows and Perry brings in additional instruments and pitches. In measure 113, the timpani enter on E, the root of the chord of the fifteenth. The pitches in Blocks ε (E and B) and ζ (D♯ and G♯) are also from the chord of the fifteenth, introduced first in parallel fifths and supported by the harp starting at measure 122. By measure 126, five of the eight pitches of the chord are present, plus a D♮ from outside of the chord. After this elongated statement of the partial chord, the cymbals play a long trill that lasts almost to the end of the section. Perry briefly scales back the instruments from measures 134 and puts the burden of presenting the chord on the vibraphone and harp, while using parts of Block ζ in the xylophone. Again, the chord's pitches slowly build from instrument to instrument, and at measure 150, six of the pitches are present between the harp and the vibraphone, missing only E♯ and A♯, although an A♮ is present, set (013568T). As at measure 126, the statement of the chord of the fifteenth

Figure 21.3 Section D: (a) Block ε, xylophone, mm. 106–11; (b) Block ζ, vibraphone, mm. 106–11.

is sustained through repetition and the trading of pitches between instruments, and at measure 150, the chord is complete except for E♯. Perry then begins to disassemble the set at measure 163. At this point, the harp performs a sustained line of continuously alternating pitches a whole step apart, written as enharmonically spelled dyads (G♯/A♭ and B♮/C♭). This texture takes the piece into its final measures, providing a drone above which other instruments have brief statements of pitches from the chord of the fifteenth.

Beginning in measure 163, the timpani performs a repeated rhythm on E – one last new block drawn from Block α – that appears six times before turning into a long roll in the last three measures. During the last nine measures, Perry gradually builds to the full chord of the fifteenth for the first time. The piano enters for the first time in measure 171, where it plays the bulk of the chord in dotted sixteenths, first substituting D♮ instead of D♯, a replacement Perry has used before; in measure 193, D is raised to a D♯, thus completing the chord in full. From serial and rhythmic perspectives, Perry organizes the chord of the fifteenth so that it is heard in its P0 form. At measure 175, Perry adds in two rhythmic blocks in the snare and bass drums and builds the volume to fortissimo at measure 177. The intensity continues until a sudden stop in measure 180, where the cymbal, snare, and bass drum have dotted eighths on the downbeat, ending the piece.

Have students bracket the blocks used in this section and analyze them in relation to the blocks of the previous sections. How are they related? Ask them to compare Perry's low–high–low patterns in each section so far. What pitches of the set does she select for this treatment, and is there any pattern in her choices? Other analytical questions include:

- Where are the instances of Blocks ε and ζ, and where and how are they varied by inversion, pitch changes, or fragmentation?
- What makes this section minimalist?
- How does Perry use serial rhythms in this section?
- What is Perry doing with meter and rhythm in this section? How does her use of triplets affect how we hear meter and rhythm in this section?
- Identify where Perry uses 4–6 pitches from the chord of the fifteenth. How are they used in serial ways?
- In numerous instances, Perry presents an almost-but-not-quite version of the chord of the fifteenth. Where does she do this, and what effect does it have in hearing or understanding the piece?

Homunculus C.F. is a complex work full of connections and networks of pitch-class subsets, rhythmic phrases, gestures, and textures. It can be analyzed in numerous ways and offers opportunities for exploring specific compositional techniques and approaches, including serialism and minimalism, as a standalone work, as part of Perry's *oeuvre*, as music by a Black American composer, and as a piece from the middle of the twentieth century.

Note

1. For a biography and overview of Perry's music, see Walker-Hill (2007).

Works Cited

Ammer, Christine. 2001. *Unsung: A History of Women in American Music*. Amadeus Press.
Briscoe, James R. 2004. *New Historical Anthology of Music by Women*. Indiana University Press.
Giles, Yvonne. November 5, 2022. "Connect: Stories – The Life & Music of Julia Perry." Lexington Philharmonic, broadcast. https://www.youtube.com/watch?v=lSoZ5Nd_Fec

Green, Mildred Denby. 1975. "A Study of the Lives and Works of Five Black Women Composers in America." Ph.D. diss., University of Oklahoma.

Grimshaw, Jeremy. 2004. "The Tabula (Not so) Rasa: La Monte Young's Serial Works and the Beginnings of Minimalism, 1956–58." *Interval(Le)s* 1/1: 77–120.

Horlacher, Gretchen. 1992. "The Rhythms of Reiteration: Formal Development in Stravinsky's Ostinati." *Music Theory Spectrum* 14/2: 171–87.

Perry, Julia. N.d. "Program Notes: Harrison, *Suite for Percussion*; Perry, *Homunculus C. F.*" CRI. Accessed February 16, 2022. https://hcommons.org/?get_group_doc=1003817/1617030980-CRI-LP-252done-crl252Homunculusprogramnotes.pdf

Walker-Hill, Helen. 2007. *From Spirituals to Symphonies: African-American Women Composers and Their Music*. University of Illinois Press.

Wilhoite, Meg. 2021. "Analysis of Stabat Mater." *Julia Perry Working Group, Humanities Commons* (blog). https://hcommons.org/docs/analysis-of-stabat-mater/

Index

aliyah 202
Angelou, Maya 24
Audacity 196
autotelic gesture 42

Babyface 190, 192–3
BandLab 178–9, 182, 184, 188
Batiste, Jon 50
Beethoven, Ludwig van 9–10, 129
Bell Biv DeVoe 195
Beta Israel 202
Beyoncé 64–7, 156, 181–3, 190
binary form 119, 240; balanced 51; expanded 113, 115; rounded 51, 110, 112, 240, 242; simple 51
Black Lives Matter 171
Blige, Mary J. *197*, 198
blues 8, 23, 67, 124, 164, 203; cadences 47; collection 123; elements and inspiration 72, 123–4, 172; harmony and progression 47, 123; *The Weary Blues* 124–5, 226–7
B.o.B. 191, *192*
Bologne, Joseph 85, 89, 130, 133, 135, 137; String Quartets (op. 1 no. 1) 82, *83*, 130–2, 134; (op. 1 no. 2) **49–50**; (op. 1 no. 4) 45, *46*, **50**, 85; (op. 1 no. 5) 132, 143
Bonds, Margaret 18, 20, 119–23, 237
Boyz II Men 190, 195
breakout chorus 207
bridging 133, 164
Brown, Bobby 195, *197*, 198
Brown, Jr., Uzee 15, *19*
Burleigh, Harry 81, 86, 109, 112–18
Burleigh, Louise Alston 113

Campbell, Tevin 195
Carey, Mariah 190, 195
Chapman, Tracy 50
chord of the fifteenth 257–63
chromatic mediants 58, 89, 92, 115
Ciara 65
closure 28, 33–6, 39, 47–8, **49**, 141; aural identification of 41; cadential 103, 139, 143, 164; scale-degree 47

Coleridge-Taylor, Samuel 60, *62*, 81, 85–9, 91–2, *93*, 130, 139–40
Cook, Will Marion 81
cotillion 110–12; Francis Johnson's *Bingham's Cotillion* 110; Francis Johnson's *Collection of New Cotillions* **49**, 51, 110–12
country music 17, 59
Cruz, Taio 188
cut'n'mix style 208–9

D'Angelo 190
Dawson, William L. 89–90, 113; *see also* New Negro Movement
Dédé, Edmond **49–50**, *50*
Destiny's Child 195
Dett, R. Nathaniel 23, 82, *84*, 85
dictation 72–3, 75–6, 78, 158, 182, 252; harmonic dictation 75–6; melodic dictation 75; rhythmic dictation 74, 196
doo-wop 190
Du Bois, W. E. B. 64, 116

Eastman, Julius 218–20
electronic dance music (EDM) 25, 159, 164
Elliot, Missy 23
emblem 109, 112, 116
empathy 163, 165, 171, 174
Enlightenment era 57
Evans, Faith 197
Ewell, Phillip 40, 59, 93, 99, 217; "White racial frame" 22, 40–1, 72, 81, 129

Flo Rida 182–3
Fortspinnung 245
four-on-the-floor 179–81
funk 178, 190, 203, 205–6

galop 29; Francis Johnson's "Victoria Galop" 28–9, 31–9, 118
Gaye, Marvin 190
Gaynor, Gloria **49**
Gestalt hearing 76
Giddens, Rhiannon 28–30, 32–5, 38–9

gospel 8, 10, 17, 126, 203, 256; artists 48; style 9, 207, 209

Haydn, Joseph 9–10, 129
hip-hop 10, 17, *59*, 65, *164*, 190; in teaching 106, 160
Houston, Whitney 190, 195
Hughes, Langston 119–22, 124–5, 226–7
hypermeter 104, 153, 190–3

Iglesias, Enrique 50
improvisation 8–9; in aural skills pedagogy 72, 74, 76–8; improvisatory characteristic in notated music 111, 124, 244–5; in performance 28–9, 101–3, 166, 171–2
interleaving 164

Jackson, Janet 190, 195–6
Jackson, Michael 151–3, 179, 194
James, Etta 23, 51, 65
jazz 9–10; characteristics 124, 228, 236, 244–5; harmonies 102, 104, 106, **122**; influence 190, 198; jazz-specific unit in music theory pedagogy 99–108; Latin 59; *see also* James, Etta; Rada, Ester; swing
Johnson, Francis "Frank" 28–9, 109–10; *see also* cotillion; *galop*
Johnson, J. Rosamond 81, 85, 89
Joplin, Scott 21, 40, 72–9, 81, 89, *90*, 119

Kahina, Chezira 60
Kater, Kaia 43–7, **49**
Kaytranada 26
Keys, Alicia 193, 195–6
King, Betty Jackson 60, *61*
Kinney, L. Viola 62–4

Latin jazz *see* jazz
Lizzo 179, *180*, *192*, 193

Mahler, Gustav 137
maqam saba 67
Mars, Bruno 191, *192*, 197
massenqo 206–8
Maxwell 195
melodic-harmonic divorce 67
Minaj, Nikki 186, *187*, 193, 195
minimalism 256–7, 259–61, 263
modal mixture 57–60, 76, 104; examples of 60–9, 114, **122**, 132–4, 231; in modulation 82, 85–6, 117; *see also* chromatic mediants
modes 217, 220, 244–45; aeolian 242, 246; dorian 38; hemitonic 205; ionian 242, 244, *245*; locrian 244, *245*; mixolydian 69, 244; phrygian 242, 244, *245*; *see also* pentatonic
modulation 51, 58, 81–2, 91–3, 111, 114, 207; to closely-related keys 82–5; to remote keys 86–90, 117, 242–3; in sonata forms 132–5, 139, 141–2
Monaé, Janelle 24, 163–70, 172–5
Motown 23, 190
Mozart, Wolfgang Amadeus 58, 129

narrative 124, 163, 165, *166*, 171, 203–6; album 163–4; musical 39, 58, 174, 201, 210; sonata 133–5, 137–9, 141–3; story and lyrics 34, 171, 175; tonal 91–3, 166; visual 208
Nashville numbers 192
Nelly 186
Neo-Riemannian analysis 226, 230–1, 243–4
New Edition 190
Newman, Alfred 64
New Negro Movement 113
Ne-Yo 194

pentatonic 21, 112, **122**, 218, 220, 226, 228, 230–1, 236; minor pentatonic 20, 38, 67
period 48, 50, 60, 77, 130, 153, 190; contrasting 35, 48, **50**, 112; double 77; parallel 29, 34–5, **35**, 36, **50**, 60, 151; three-phrase 77
Perry, Julia 7, 256–63
Perry, Zenobia Powell **215**, 218, **218**, *219*
pitch-class set 256–7, *252*, 259, 261–3; analysis *220*, *250*, 251–2; subset 257, 263; theory 215–17, **218**, 219, 224, 239, 249
Price, Florence 10, 138, 226; songs by 124–5, 226–8, *229*, 230–3, *234*, 235–6; symphonies by 86, *88*, 135, *136*; *see also* New Negro Movement
Prince 23
progressive soul *see* soul
promenade concert 28–9
protonotation 41–5, 48
Pro Tools 196
punk 172, 174

Rada, Ester 201–10
ragtime **122**, 123; *see also* Joplin, Scott
R&B 10, 17, 65, 194, 196, 206; contemporary 190, 193, 195, 198
reggae 203
Rihanna 50, 65, *181*, 182, *183*, 190

Schenker, Heinrich 59
Schoenberg, Arnold 59, 215, 219, 240, 251–2, 258
Schubert, Franz 137
Schumann, Robert 58
Seal 193
sectional form 29, 35
sentence 48, 50, **50**, 248; sentential 82, 130, 132–3, 139, 142
serialism xvii, 216–17, 257, 263
shuffle rhythm 194–5
Simone, Nina 23, **50**, 201, 203–6
slavery 28, 59–60, 64, 116–17, 120–1, 204

soul 8, 190, 203; artist (*see* Rada, Ester; Stone, Joss)
sound palette 25–6
spiral curriculum 18, 40, 164, 201, 207, 216
spiritual 18–20, 81, 85, 112–15, 117, 256
srdc (phrase type) 50
Still, William Grant 40, 109, 113, 117; *see also* New Negro Movement
Stone, Joss 195
Swanson, Howard 119, 121, 123
swing 100, 191, 194–6, 198–9

table notation 182–3, 187, 189
talea 258, 261
Technotronix 179
ternary form 110, 111, 113, 123, 240, 242; in sonata forms 135, 137
textural graph 25–6
texture 41, 47–51, 150–1, 154–5, 191, 210; in analysis 110–16, 134, 174, 256–63; chorale 218; contrapuntal 166; in fundamentals class 24–6; homophonic 113, 115–16; layered 165–6; rhythmic 36

Tharpe, Sister Rosetta 48–50
Timberlake, Justin 190
timbre 7–8, 25, 33, 191, 210, 217; in analysis 165–6, 171–5, 207–8, 257–60
TLC 193
tokenism 22, 40, 59, 93, 126

Underground Railroad 171

Vandross, Luther *197*, 198
verse-chorus form 65, 143, 179, 184–8, 192, 207; simple 164–6, 171

Weeknd, The 184, 195
White, Clarence Cameron 84–5
Williams, Henry F. 24
Wonder, Stevie 9, 11, 67, *68*, 190, 195–6
Work, Jr., John W. 18, 20, *21*

Yola 23

Z, Pamela 24

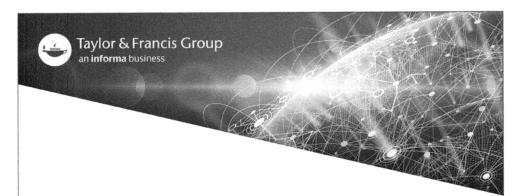

Milton Keynes UK
Ingram Content Group UK Ltd.
UKHW031122031224
451949UK00020B/390